FOR
SURRENDER
IS OUT OF THE QUESTION

FOR US
SURRENDER
IS OUT OF THE QUESTION

A story from Burma's never-ending war

MAC McCLELLAND

SOFT SKULL

Library of Congress Cataloging-in-Publication Data

McClelland, Mac.
  For us surrender is out of the question : a story from Burma's never-ending war / Mac McClelland.
    p. cm.
  Includes bibliographical references and index.
  ISBN 978-1-59376-265-0 (alk. paper)
    1. McClelland, Mac. 2. Women political activists—Burma—Biography. 3. Political activists—Burma—Biography. 4. Americans—Burma—Biography. 5. Burma—History—1948 6. Burma—Politics and government—1988- 7. Ethnic conflict—Burma. 8. Social conflict—Burma. 9. Burma—Social conditions. I. Title. DS530.53.M37A3 2010
    959.105—dc22
                                2009043448

Cover design by Adrian Kinloch
Interior design by Elyse Strongin, Neuwirth & Associates, Inc.

Printed in the United States of America

Soft Skull Press
An Imprint of Counterpoint LLC
2117 Fourth Street
Suite D
Berkeley, CA 94710

www.softskull.com
www.counterpointpress.com

Distributed by Publishers Group West

10 9 8 7 6 5 4 3 2 1

BURMA

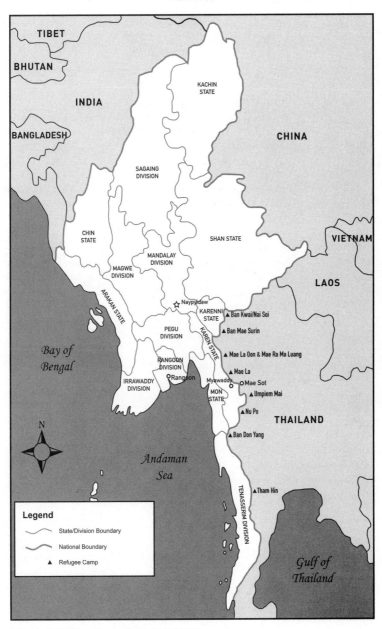

© Map by KHRG [Karen Human Rights Group], 2007

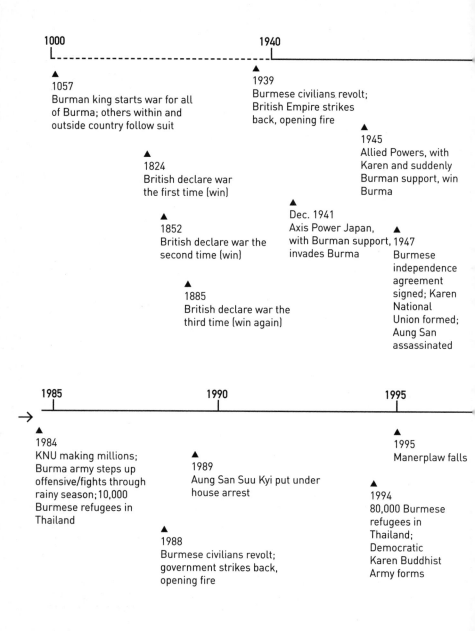

1000   1940

1057
Burman king starts war for all
of Burma; others within and
outside country follow suit

1939
Burmese civilians revolt;
British Empire strikes
back, opening fire

1824
British declare war
the first time (win)

1945
Allied Powers, with
Karen and suddenly
Burman support, win
Burma

1852
British declare war the
second time (win)

Dec. 1941
Axis Power Japan,
with Burman support,
invades Burma

1947
Burmese
independence
agreement
signed; Karen
National
Union formed;
Aung San
assassinated

1885
British declare war the
third time (win again)

1985   1990   1995

1984
KNU making millions;
Burma army steps up
offensive/fights through
rainy season; 10,000
Burmese refugees in
Thailand

1989
Aung San Suu Kyi put under
house arrest

1995
Manerplaw falls

1994
80,000 Burmese
refugees in
Thailand;
Democratic
Karen Buddhist
Army forms

1988
Burmese civilians revolt;
government strikes back,
opening fire

DATES

1950 — 1960 — 1970

1950
After contributing briefly to war effort and eternally to ideology of KNU, Ba U Gyi killed

1960s
Four Cuts begins

1958
Government gives Ne Win temporary power to avoid a coup

Jan. 4, 1948
Independence Day;
UN Convention on the Prevention and Punishment of the Crime of Genocide

1962
Ne Win, having lost election, takes power in a coup

1950s
US, fighting war on communism, supports KMT rebels in Burma

Jan. 31, 1949
Karen National Union declares war on insurgent-besieged Burma

2000 — 2005 — 2010

1997
Huay Kaloke burned down for the first time; 48th anniversary of KNU war; 105,000 Burmese refugees in Thailand; President Clinton mandates Burma sanctions; happy 16th birthday Htan Dah!

2003
Aung San Suu Kyi's convoy attacked; US passes more sanctions

2009
50,000th Burmese refugee leaves Thailand. Camp population still at 160,000.

1998
Thailand accepts Burmese-refugee assistance from UNHCR

2007
Draft resolution on Burma brought before United Nations, vetoed; monks lead massive protest through Burma's streets, violently smacked down

FOR US
SURRENDER
IS OUT OF THE QUESTION

"Do you want a cigarette?" I ask Htan Dah, holding up a pack of Thai-issue Marlboros. We are sitting on opposite sides of a rectangular table, the type I'd call a picnic table, talking over the spread: three bottles of vodka, two cartons of orange juice, plates of sugared citrus slices, nearly empty bottles of beer and bowls of fried pork, sweet corn waffles, pad thai, a chocolate cake. We share the benches with two guys each, and half a dozen others hover. Most of them are listening to Poe K'Ler Htoo, who is working through a light slur to tell his new favorite story. This morning, he sent an email to Htoo Moo, the coworker around whom he's draping his arm, asking if he'd finally finished a report. Htoo Moo somehow accidentally cc-ed the rest of the staff—including the administration of the organization that employs them—when sending back a simple response: Fuck you, Poe K'Ler Htoo.

The men are all in their twenties. Most of them are solid and strong and hunky, tight pecs and asses nearly all around. Their faces shine sweaty because they're drunk, and it's July. A few of them are smoking. One holds a guitar. They laugh when Poe K'Ler Htoo gets to the climax. Some of them received the email or have heard the punch line already and nod, smiling, into the post-anecdote silence, young professionals talking about interoffice inbox blunders, like outgrown frat boys unwinding after another tedious workday. Except that they're stateless. They are all penniless. They speak three or four languages apiece. Two of them had to bribe their way out of Thai police custody, again, yesterday because they're on the wrong side of the border between this country and the land-mine-studded mountains of their own.

Htan Dah's silky chin-length hair slips toward his eyes as he leans forward. My Marlboros picture a baby reaching for the cigarette of the man who holds her, absentmindedly exhaling a cloud of smoke around her face. It's an episode in a series of legally mandated photographic deterrents, scabby hospital patients hooked up to respirators and cancer-rotted mouths and throats, but it doesn't deter Htan Dah. Nor is he deterred by the fact that he doesn't smoke. Tonight, he is flushed with heat and booze and the virility and extreme hilarity of his comrades. Tonight, as always, he is celebrating the fact that he's still living.

He takes a cigarette. "Never say no," he says, and winks at me.

I.

EVEN ON a Saturday, the refugees were up at dawn. The roosters of Mae Sot had been crowing for hours already, the packs of stray and unleashed domestic dogs fighting intermittently throughout the night, the wiry migrants working overtime at the construction lot across the verdant residential street since darkness had begun to fade.

Downtown, the western central Thailand city contains several blocks' worth of congested, though hardly happening, streets lined with stores full of jewelry and bikes and food processors. At its center is a market—flip-flops, live frogs, long green beans—and on the fringes a few guesthouses and bars that cater largely to the community of well-tanned aid workers supporting the city's exiles.

Though Mae Sot is a major receiving hub for people, pirated teak, and other goods that enter the country illegally from Burma, and the population is loaded with smugglers, dealers, documentless immigrants, and slaves, the atmosphere of the border town is serene. Beyond the city center, past factories and karaoke joints, the alternating fields and rice paddies and shack-filled villages and suburban homes and temples and rickety corner stores are all quiet. Out there, just a couple of miles from downtown, the noise is reduced to the occasional outburst of Buddhist bells or motorbikes whizzing by.

Though everyone was awake at the office and staff quarters of Burma Action (BA), it was quiet in there, too.

The employees—twentysomethings all, males, except one—who hadn't yet crawled from their sleeping spaces on the floor and rolled up their cobalt mosquito nets for the day could hear from their beds the light clangings of breakfast preparation: pots being washed in the stainless steel sink, motorbike keys hung on metal hooks after a market trip, knives slid off the stone counter and carried toward the cutting board. Upstairs, they were too far away to smell the steam that escaped the rice cooker in the kitchen. A couple of them had already gotten up and stumbled, still rubbing their eyes, straight into the computer room. Since it was the weekend, their work hours would be healthily interspersed with naps and guitar playing and Ping-Pong. Technically, they didn't have any schedule at all, much less mandated hours on Saturdays; they worked at will, with only occasional deadlines to direct them. Still, some took their places in front of the four computers and turned them on, chatting and stretching in their seats while they waited for the machines to boot up so they could get some work done before breakfast.

Half a dozen employees were there now, and as many more were out on long field assignments. Almost all the organization's work was done by refugees, though a few Thai citizens and Western do-gooders helped with administration at headquarters in Bangkok. Sometimes, the office hosted volunteers sent by charities or aid groups. The pale auxiliaries from Australia or France or the US or UK stayed anywhere from a few weeks to a couple of years. Those times, like today, a staff member took a motorbike to the bus station to wait for a foreigner to off-load. This time, on the first of July, 2006, the bus, my bus, arrived in the late afternoon. I wasn't connected to any organizations—I'd just happened upon BA's website and, interested in the crisis in the Texas-size Southeast Asian country the page was going on about, eventually volunteered via email—so my background was something of a mystery to the staff. No one in the house could pin down its origins, but there was a rumor that I was Norwegian.

I walked up the driveway in the early evening, through the gold-detailed black gate that stood heavy sentry at the road. I'd followed The Guy who came to meet me, whose name wasn't The Guy, but whose actual name I hadn't caught when he'd mumbled it twice in a row and then just shaken his head and laughed when I'd asked him to repeat it one more time, in a three-wheeled tuk-tuk from the station. I watched him, compact and strong looking, buzzed black hair, sharp cheekbones, cinnamon skin, sliding the gate slow and screaming shut behind us as my hired driver puttered away. The house was big but run-down, two stories of worn wood and dirty concrete with a balcony on the left, cement garage on the right. We entered the latter, where The Guy pushed his shiny red motorbike in among a couple of dingier ones. Behind them was a picnic table with benches, and behind that, against the back wall, a single metal range hooked up to a propane tank. We cut around the table, to the left, into the house.

"Kitchen," The Guy said. It had a sink and some dishes; the cooking took place out in the dining room/garage. He took a few steps farther. "Bathroom." He gestured into a cement block through an oversize wooden door. There was a squat toilet, of course, set into the floor, and in lieu of toilet paper a shallow well, serviced by a tap, a little plastic bowl floating on top. There was also, running the length of the left wall, a giant waist-high cement trough filled with water and dead mosquitoes.

"What's that?" I asked.

"Water."

Sure. "For what?"

"A bath."

I looked at it, jet-lagged, hazily noting some of the differences between this bath and my conception of a bath. This wasn't my first time in Southeast Asia, but I'd only ever taken showers. I wondered if I was supposed to hoist myself in there and splash around. I wondered if he wondered what I thought a bath was.

"How does it work?" I asked.

He exhaled hard through his nose, a whispery snort. "Like this," he said, pantomiming filling a bowl with water and dumping it over his head. "Are you hungry?"

Back in the dining room/garage, I sat at the table with a plate of rice and some durable pieces of fried pork. I asked The Guy what was in the soup he offered me.

"I don't know the word in English," he said. "Leaves?"

Close. Twigs, actually. The Guy pulled a stump of wood up to the short, benchless edge of the table, next to me, content to perch there quietly and watch me chew through the sautéed woody stems.

"So, where are you from?" I asked.

"Me?"

Silence. He wasn't asking rhetorically.

I nodded.

"I am kuh-REN. Everybody here, we are all kuh-REN."

Oh, man. It was starting to come together now.

When I'd landed in Bangkok, a BA employee had picked me up at the airport to make sure that I found the bus station and the right eight-hour bus north. She was tiny and Thai and heavily accented, and repeatedly told me during our cab ride that everyone I was about to be working with was Korean. It seemed sort of weird that a bunch of Koreans would move to Thailand together to work for peace in Burma, but I thought that was nice, I guessed, and even wrote in my journal, relievedly, inexplicably, "Koreans tend to have <u>excellent</u> English skills."

When I'd arrived at the Mae Sot bus station, the clearly Southeast Asian The Guy had asked if I was his new volunteer.

"Yes," I'd said. "*You're* not *Korean.*"

I'd done my homework before I left the States. I had read about the Karen. Unrelatedly, I even had a brilliant National Geographic–

style coffee-table book with pictures of women adorned with stacks of gold rings, members of the few remaining long-neck Karen tribes of not-so-distant relation. But I'd only seen the word written down, and had assumed, incorrectly, that it sounded like the name of my parents' blond divorced friend. I didn't know how it was pronounced any more than most Westerners would've been certain how to say "Darfur" ten years ago.

IMAGINE, FOR a moment, that Texas had managed to secede from the union, and that you live there, in the sovereign Republic of Texas. Imagine that shortly after independence, a cadre of old, paranoid, greedy men who believed in a superior military caste took over your newly autonomous nation in a coup. Your beloved president, who had big dreams of prosperity and Texan unity, whom you believed in, was shot several times in the chest, and now the army runs your country. It has direct or indirect control over all the businesses. It spends .3 percent of GDP on health care, using your oil and natural gas money to buy more weapons, which Russia, Pakistan, and North Korea have been happy to provide, and the agricultural sector has nearly collapsed. Free press is illegal. So are gatherings of more than five people. A trial, much less legal representation, in the case of your arrest is not guaranteed. In the event of your interrogation, be prepared to endure tactics of the awful and the totally queer: crouch like you're riding a motorbike, for hours, be hung from the ceiling and spun around, and around, and around, burned with cigarettes, beaten with a rubber rod, put in a ditch with a dead body for six days, locked in a room with wild, sharp-beaked birds, made to stand to your neck in a cesspool full of maggots that climb into your nose and ears and mouth. But if you do manage to stay out of prison, where most of your activists and dissidents have been rotting for decades, you are broke and starving, and you're trying to personally teach your children to read, assuming they've survived to be children, since there's a 30 percent chance that they'll be devastatingly malnourished under the age of five and a 10 percent chance they'll die before they reach that birthday. What's more, you and your fifty million countrymen are trapped inside your 268,000-square-mile Orwellian nightmare with some 350,000 soldiers who are on active duty, not reservists, not just enlisted and awaiting a tour, but actually armed and deployed all the time. They can snatch people—maybe your kid—off the street and make them join the army. They can walk into your neighborhood and grab you as you're going out to buy eggs and make you work construction on a new government building or road, long, hard hours under the grueling sun for days or weeks without pay, during which you'll have to scavenge for food, since you don't have any money, lest you work yourself to death. You'll do all this at gunpoint, and any break will be rewarded with pistol whipping; it's possible, and entirely permissible, that you'll be killed for malingering, or getting smart, whether you're an old lady or a priest or what, at forced work, walking down the street, wherever. Your life in the Republic of Texas sounds like a dystopia a screenwriter made up. Your life is roughly equivalent to a modern-day Burmese person's.

Now imagine that you belong to a distinct group, Dallasites, or something, that never wanted to be part of the Republic in the first place, that wanted to either remain part of the United States, which had treated you well, or, failing that, become your own free state within the Republic, since you already had your own infrastructure, and social structure, and community leaders and culture all in place. Some Dallasites have, wisely or unwisely, taken up their rifles to battle the government, and in retaliation for this armed rebellion, whole squads of the huge army have, for decades, been dedicated to terrorizing your city. You and your fellow Dallasites are regularly conscripted into slavery, walking in front of the army to set off land mines that they and your own insurgents have planted, carrying hundred-pound loads of weaponry and supplies under severe beatings until you've lost your use, which is to say you've become permanently injured or died. If you're so enslaved, you might accompany the soldiers as they march into your friends' neighborhoods and set them on fire, watch them shoot at fleeing inhabitants as they run, capturing any stragglers. If you're one of those stragglers, and you're a woman, or a girl older than five, prepare to be raped, most likely gang-raped, and there's easily a one-in-four chance you'll then be killed, possibly by being shot, possibly through your vagina, possibly after having your breasts hacked off. If you're a man, maybe you'll be hung by your wrists and a fire will be built under you and burn you alive. Maybe a soldier will drown you by filling a plastic bag up with water and tying it over your head, or stretch you between two trees and use you as a hammock, or cut off your nose, pull out your eyes, and then stab you in both ears before killing you, or string you up by your shoulders and club you now and again for two weeks, or heat up slivers of bamboo and push them into your urethra, or tie a tight rope between your dick and your neck for a while before setting your genitals on fire, or whatever else hateful, armed men and underage boys might imagine when they have orders to torment, and nothing else to do. You can't call the police, which are also run by the armed forces. And though you've been sure for decades that the United States can't possibly let this continue, it's invested in your country's oil and will not under any circumstances cross China, which is your country's staunch UN and economic ally, so you really need to accept that America is decidedly not coming to save you. Nobody is. Now your life is pretty equivalent to a modern-day Burmese Karen's.

THOUGH THEY'D been speculating about the new volunteer all the way into this early evening, no one created any fuss when I turned the corner from the kitchen into the large living room. Four pairs of dark eyes looked from a small TV screen up to me. I smiled, but no one said anything. The Guy, leaning against the wall with his arms folded, didn't make any introductions, so I approached the only other girl in the room, who was standing in the back, and asked her name.

She looked nervous, but after sucking in a breath she uttered three syllables, completely unfamiliar Sino-Tibetan sounds fast in a row, and I didn't understand. I towered over her tiny frame. When I leaned in closer and asked her to repeat her name, she backed away while she did. I still didn't get it well enough to say it back to her, but told her my name in return. She just nodded.

I sat on the marble floor among the legs of the white plastic chairs the guys were sitting in, quiet in the surrounding rise and fall of their soft tonal syllables, deep, bubbling, like slow oil over stones. The TV blared Thai. As it grew dark, mosquitoes sauntered in through the screenless open windows. In season on the mosquito-transmitting menu at the Thai-Burma border: malaria, dengue fever, Japanese encephalitis. My breeding and upbringing left me with no natural resistance to the two latter, and I'd opted against taking the sickening drugs for the former. Not wanting to further alienate myself by being the white girl who ran upstairs to hide under a mosquito net at dusk, I watched the guys laughing and talking, like a partygoer who didn't know anyone where everyone was having too good a time to care. They were fit, bare calves and feet splayed in front of their chairs, their smooth faces smiling easily. I pulled my air mattress out of my bag and started blowing it up. I incurred some mosquito bites. I shifted my sit bones on the shiny tile. I stood up.

"I'm going to bed," I told The Guy.

He nodded, and looked at me for a second. It was seven-thirty. "Are you okay?" he asked. I'd just taken twenty-seven hours of planes and automobiles and felt exhausted and alone. He wasn't sure if I was going to lose it, but clearly I looked like I might.

I said that I was fine. He knew I was lying, but what could he do? I'm like a baby I get so incapacitated and pessimistic when I'm sleepy. I wasn't sure if I was going to lose it, either. But I'd glanced the phrases "Forced marriage" and "Human trafficking" on a piece of copy paper taped to the scuffed flat paint covering the wall behind the computers in the adjacent room, so even though I didn't know what that was about, I suspected that in this crowd, the circumstances didn't warrant a breakdown.

The wooden steps that wound from the living room ended upstairs at the front of the house. To my right was a big open room, its floorboards littered with straw sleeping mats. Straight from the steps, across a short landing, was a bedroom, my room, wide but shallow, more wood floors and walls, containing the door to the balcony. I dropped my air mattress in the back right corner, under the big blue mosquito net, and lay down.

Maybe I'd thought it was going to become clearer upon my arrival, but I realized I had no idea who these people were, or what they did here, or even what I was going to do here. I appeared to have my work, whatever it was, cut out for me, since The Guy seemed to be among the few who spoke English. My digestive system had its work cut out for it, too, since these guys apparently ate sticks.

A 1911 census reported that the Karen lived in Burma "peacefully, quietly, unobtrusively . . . avoiding all contact with the tribes they passed . . . preferring the hardship and obstacles of hills, jungles and uninhabited regions to the dangers of conflict with fellow beings." Every missionary, explorer, and ambassador who ever encountered the ethnic minority that had for centuries farmed the mountains along the Thai border commented on their docility. And, lying there, feeling left out because I couldn't participate in a language I didn't understand, listening to my housemates laugh and holler downstairs, the Karen seemed nice to me, too. I couldn't have guessed then, drifting to sleep to the sound of their amiable chatter, that every last one of them was a terrorist.

HTAN DAH dropped a pile of thinly sliced onions and whole garlic cloves into a wok of hot soybean oil shortly after dawn. He'd been up in the middle of the night, waiting alone in the living room for one of the World Cup matches, most of which aired at seriously inconvenient hours in Thailand. I'd been up, too, and had seen him in the chair he'd placed a few inches in front of the little TV when I'd gotten up to go to the bathroom. "Don't you ever sleep?" I'd asked him, but he didn't respond, or if he did, I didn't hear it over the broadcast.

His coworkers had inadvertently slept through the match. Most of them were still sleeping now. I climbed out from under my mosquito net and walked softly out of my room and past a few of them sprawled on the floor of the big open one. When my feet hit the cool tiles at the bottom of the steps, I turned toward the sound and smell of searing allium.

Htan Dah stood at the gas range, which spat oil at his baggy long-sleeved shirt. It was the same thing he'd been wearing the day before, when he had strode into the living room as I tried to figure out how to blow up my air mattress, sitting on the floor with the limp plastic splayed over my knees, surrounded by guys not speaking to me. When I'd looked up into his wide, round face framed with chin-length black hair, he'd given me an amused smile and asked, "Can I help you?"

I sat down at the picnic table in the dining room/garage, a couple of feet from where he was cooking, and we exchanged hellos. He was a little chubby, I thought, watching him in his loose clothes. He picked up and tilted the wok, concentrating harder than he needed to on the swirling herbs. Htan Dah was worried about me. As the office manager of Burma Action for the past two years, he'd heard the nighttime weeping of plenty of self-pitying philanthropists, who tended to arrive tired and instantly homesick. The last girl, a Canadian with a lot of luggage, had started sobbing almost as soon as he'd picked her up from the bus station, and couldn't be calmed even by the hours she spent taking calls from her boyfriend back home. She'd cried for days.

Indeed, I'd had a very sad moment last night when, after my air mattress deflated shortly after I lay down on it and my angles pressed hard into the wood floor, and I realized that the ants patrolling the grounds were trekking right through my hair, I'd actually hoped for the worst, hoped that I had contracted malaria or Japanese encephalitis from the mosquito bites raging hot and itchy on my legs so I had a legitimate excuse to bail back to the States. That way, I wouldn't have to be mad at myself for being too chickenshit to hack it through loneliness and less-than-ideal bathing arrangements. I'd even considered taking the bus back to Bangkok and calling my airline, betting myself that there was room on a flight out. If there wasn't, I reasoned, I could just hang out on Khao San Road and read books. I hated Khao San Road, with its hennaed European backpackers and incessant techno and beer specials, but at least it was familiar. I'd realized then that I might start crying. But I was determined not to. Instead, I saved the tearing up for when Htan Dah put another bowl of stick soup in front of me now and asked, "How long are you staying?"

"Six weeks," I said, my throat tight.

He was too shocked to notice. "Six weeks!" he hollered. "Why not four months? Or six months?"

"Six weeks is a long time to go out of the country in America," I said. "Besides, I was in Thailand for a month two years ago."

"How many times have you been here?"

"Twice."

"Wow," he said. Then, more softly, "You have traveled a lot. That's nice."

He had no idea, even. "Have you traveled?"

"No, I cannot."

"Why not?"

"Because! I am Karen!"

"So what?"

"So, I cannot go anywhere." He dumped chunks of raw, pink meat into the oil, which sputtered furiously. "If I go outside, I can be arrested."

"Really?"

"Yes! I am refugee!"

Htan Dah's exclamations suggested that none of this should have been news to me—though I soon realized that this was also just how he talked. But all I really knew was that I was working for an organization that promoted democracy in Burma. The books I'd read about its evil dictatorship hadn't said much about refugees, or mentioned that most of the Burmese refugees in Thailand were Karen, and BA hadn't told me that my housemates were from Burma, or were refugees. I'd only just figured out that no one here was Korean.

"I'm sorry," I said. "Why would you be arrested because you're a refugee?"

"Because(!), I don't have Thai ID. I am not Thai citizen, so, I cannot go outside refugee camp."

"Really?"

"Yes! I can be fined, maybe three thousand baht." That was nearly a hundred dollars' worth of Thai currency, in a country where the average annual income was about three thousand bucks. "I can go to jail, or maybe, be deported . . ." We looked at each other, and he nodded in my silence, emphasizing his point with a sharp dip of his chin. "You have a lot of experience. You have been to a lot of places."

"Did you live in a refugee camp before?"

"Yes. Before I came to BA."

"How long have you lived here?"

"In Thailand?" Htan Dah asked. "I was born in Thailand."

A BA staffer with a slight frame and sweet face had sat down on my side of the picnic table, but as far from me as possible on the bench. I'd looked at him several times while talking to Htan Dah, trying to include him in the conversation, but he'd so far produced just a fixed, nervous smile. "How long have you lived here?" I asked him directly.

"Me?"

"Yes, you."

"Maybe . . . six . . . years," he said.

I asked him his name but, as usual, didn't grasp it the first time. I asked him again.

Ta Mla wrote the romanized version on a piece of paper and said it again. His name was pronounced just like it's spelled. I asked him

to spell everyone else's, which were also transliterated mostly pho-
netically, but that the beginning *h*s were silent and something additional was off about the spelling of "Htan Dah," the pronunciation
of which I still hadn't quite caught. Ta Mla seemed to know as many
English words as Htan Dah did, but couldn't call them up as quickly,
and his pronunciation was often difficult to understand. We repeated
ourselves a lot while we traded names and birth dates. He was born
in 1979, which made him a year older than I was. And Htan Dah was
a year younger still.

"Will you go . . . to . . . market? Today?" Ta Mla asked.

"I hope so," I said. I hadn't brought a towel, and The Guy had
promised last night to take me to buy one that afternoon, so I could
bathe. "You guys don't have a hot shower, do you?" I asked. Ta Mla
looked at me blankly. I turned to Htan Dah, who wore a scowl that
meant he didn't understand the words I'd just used.

"What?" he asked.

Of course, most everyone in the developing world doesn't take
hot showers. But they are by no means unheard of in Thai cities, and
I'd seen a tiny, on-demand water heater on the bathroom wall. "You
guys have a water heater in the shower. Does it work?" I explained
what I was talking about, but neither of them had ever known what
that thing was for. It didn't work, it turned out, and everyone here
used the cold-water trough for bathing anyway, and if they hadn't
showered here, and they'd lived in refugee camps before. . . .

"Have you ever taken a hot shower?" I asked Htan Dah.

He frowned and shook his head briskly.

"Do you know what I'm talking about?"

He nodded. "I have heard of it," he said. His face suggested he
was lying.

I turned to Ta Mla, who was watching us with severely creased
eyebrows. "Have *you* ever taken a hot shower?" I asked him.

He hesitated. "Hot?"

"Yeah, hot. Like, you take a shower, but the water is warm."

He hesitated again. "Hot shower?" he asked.

"Yeah. In America, we take showers with hot water. Have you heard of that?"

He looked between Htan Dah and me, still making that face. Finally, he shook his head. "No, I do not know it."*

"Oh, man, you guys should take a hot shower sometime," I said. "It's great. We could heat up water in the teakettle and fill up a bucket or something."

Htan Dah immediately said that he would like to try. But Ta Mla considered for a moment, just to imagine the novel repugnance of it. "I think cold is better," he said.

Having finished cooking and seen that someone was keeping me company, Htan Dah excused himself and left me at the table with Ta Mla. We sat in silence for a bit, smiling often at each other.

"What do you do?" he asked finally.

"I'm a teacher."

"Oah? A teacher! That is . . . very . . . wonderful."

"Yes, I like it."

"In Norway?"

"No."

IT WAS sweltering in Bangkok. During the dry season, it's hot up in Mae Sot, too, dry air crawling across the continent toward the sea. But in the summer, when wet air blows in off the water, a cool wind rushes through the mist shrouding the tree-covered hills, softening the temperature up west beyond the central plains. Often, it rains for days, hard, persistent downpours from leaden skies, or light showers tinkling in sunlight. Today the air came warm and calm through the windows above a wide wooden bench in my room. I was falling asleep with a book when Htan Dah appeared in the doorway.

---

* Later, when Htan Dah and I were watching a pirated Angelina Jolie DVD, I pointed to the steam filling the screen as she stood sexily under a showerhead. "Look," I said, "hot shower," and his mouth dropped open with sudden comprehension.

"I think you are hungry," he said.

He was right. I'd chewed through only a few pieces of the hard fried pork nuggets he'd made for breakfast and hadn't finished my rice, which I'd wetted down with salty stick soup. Htan Dah explained that The Guy, whose name turned out to be The Blay, was busy today. "I can take you to market," he said. "Maybe you want to buy some food."

I sat up. "Okay. And a towel?"

"Okay. Yes, after. I think it will be okay if you go with me."

I couldn't see any reason to think otherwise; he seemed as capable of running an errand as The Blay. "Okay. . . ."

However brave I was on plane, boat, or foot, when it came to motorbikes I was a pragmatist—which is to say alarmist. Reportedly, dozens of people died in Thai motorcycle accidents every day, and hundreds more were injured, many of them permanently, horribly, disfiguringly, I imagined. I panicked quietly in the driveway while Htan Dah backed his bike out of the dining room/garage. He stopped next to me and looked up expectantly. He didn't offer me a helmet.

Passengers in Asia don't hold on to their drivers as do girlfriends in American music videos and '80s movies, so I gripped the seat under my ass as Htan Dah pulled out onto our street, slow and sure. Most of the houses were behind gates and greenery, though the structures varied from more two-story spreads to one-room stilted huts, most of those made at least partially of tattered wood. We drove on the four-lane boulevard that led to the freeway, past a water buffalo grazing in the grassy median, then turned down an alley before reaching the narrow, busy *sois*, or streets, of downtown. People and stalls with banana roti, whole grilled chicken, grilled chicken parts on a stick packed the fronts of the stores. Among them was the big bright Hong Long Minimart, in front of which we parked tight in a long row of other motorbikes.

Htan Dah kept his head down, lost his grins and volume as we walked through the store, as if we were in church. "What are you looking for?" he practically whispered.

"I don't know."

I didn't. Though the Hong Long had the look of a shimmering American supermarket, I knew there was no wheat bread or peanut butter. We walked past shelves of shampoo and whitening cream, canisters full of socks, novelty-ice-cream freezers, shining displays of cosmetics. Htan Dah shuffled close behind me as I wandered around orderly, well-lit aisles stocked with cheap candy and ramen and shrimp-flavored peas. When I yelled "Look! Yogurt!" he gave me a stiff smile. I looked around to see if everyone else was being quiet. They weren't.

I spent a small fortune—nearly $20, half a week's stay in a guest-house—on what staples I could find: containers of dairy, cashews, the store's single package of cheese, which was orange and processed. I was hungry, or my upwardly mobile Western version of it, and when we stepped out onto the sidewalk and the sun hit my face with the spoils hanging from my fingers in plastic bags, I was triumphant. "Ta-da!" I sang. My companion looked at me, his face expectant and then vaguely confused. He had turned automatically when I'd trilled the self-satisfied interjection.

"Oh my god! That's your name, isn't it?" I asked. "Do you know that phrase? It means 'Look what I did!' or 'Hooray!'" But Htan Dah's smile was still pained, and he nodded just barely perceptibly, though I was blathering excitedly, though everything he said in the house seemed to be punctuated with exclamation points. His movements became tense, his steps halted and cautious as we made our way to the motorbike.

"Didn't you notice the police(!)?" he asked when we got home.

No. I hadn't registered the officer while we were leaving the store. I had noticed Htan Dah's discomfort and, earlier that morning, that he'd peered out the dining room/garage door repeatedly while we'd been eating breakfast. He'd ultimately gotten up and closed it, block-ing out much of the light and the view of anyone who might be walk-ing by. Htan Dah was registered with the United Nations High Commissioner for Refugees. It said "refugee" right next to his picture on his UNHCR papers. Which is why he'd identified himself that way when I asked him if he'd traveled. He would continue to remind me, a little impatiently, as a substitute for a negative when I'd ask him if he'd ever been to the movies, or driven a car: "I am refugee."

But he wasn't, actually. Thailand never signed the 1951 UN Convention Relating to the Status of Refugees, and wasn't bound by the international treaty to recognize and protect them. Though the country formally accepted UNHCR assistance with Burmese refugees in 1998, the agency didn't have the authority to grant them refugee status there. Thailand refers to the 157,000 Burmese refugees in nine camps within its borders as "displaced persons fleeing fighting"—indeed, the No. 1 answer camp dwellers give when asked the reason for having left Burma is "running away from soldiers." They are not protected under any laws. Outside the confined sanctuary of the refugee camps, the undocumented nonnationals are, as in most countries, violating immigration statutes.

Enter one of the world's most notoriously corrupt police forces, whose members generate a whole other income by robbing refugees. Those who are caught doing anything outside camp—working, shopping, walking—can be arrested and jailed, fined, deported. The UNHCR has acknowledged that rounded-up refugees have, despite carrying official UNHCR paperwork, been sent back to Burma. Everybody knows, though, that every scuffle with a Thai police officer can be ended with a bribe. Those who can't afford bribes or, less likely, are picked up by an honest Thai cop, pay too: In the mid-'90s three refugees who were arrested while collecting bamboo outside their camp were sentenced to three years in prison.

So everyone who lived in the house did so illegally. Every one of them had been arrested at least once, and when Htan Dah said that he could be arrested if he went outside, he didn't mean that he maybe could possibly be arrested, hypothetically. He meant that if he went outside, his being arrested was entirely, any day, likely—unless he was accompanied by a white person, in front of whom the cop, who looked at our faces and then walked right past, wouldn't want to do something so unsavory as to blackmail an indigent war victim.

I had misunderstood Htan Dah before we left. He'd said, "I think it will be okay if *you* go with me," not "I think it will be okay if you go with *me*." He'd meant not that I would be okay, but that he would. It was ironic that a young woman of European descent was his antidote, since his country's last 120 years of international and civil war and humanitarian crises partially started with one.

II.

PEACE HAS never been Burma's strong suit.

Well before the first century BCE, a people called the Pyu settled in what is now north and central Burma, in the great river-veined plains that give way to vast tracts of forested hills. The Pyu were so devoted to love and Buddhism, legend has it, that they wouldn't even wear silk for fear of imposing on the worms that excreted it. Archeological evidence shows that they set up lovely cities, with irrigation systems, and prayed, and made inscriptions in stone—and warred with each other for power. And then they got sacked.

Though the Pyu's religion ultimately survived as Burma's primary, they were absorbed into other migrating and conquering cultures. One was the Mranma, typically transliterated as Myanma, colloquially pronounced Bama, also called Burman, now commonly called Burmese.* Today, they are Burma's dominant group, in all meanings

---

* In addition to describing the Burman ethnicity and attendant language, "Burmese" also refers generally to people from Burma, including members of other ethnic groups. Although my BA housemates would never refer to themselves as "Burmese," despite its technically being their nationality, for consistency and simplicity I'll use "Burmese" to mean nationality and "Burman" to specify ethnicity. As for the name of the country, though the military junta switched it to the more formal "Myanmar" in 1989, the junta sucks, and activists and pro-democracy advocates therefore refuse to recognize its right to do so.

of the word. But back then, they were just one ethnocultural group intermarrying and -mingling with other ethnocultural groups in their kingdom, which was in the north of the country. There was also the Mon kingdom in the south, and princely Shan in the northeast, and elsewhere Chin, and Kachin, and Arakanese. And among yet many others, there was another group, who some historians have posited were actually Burma's original settlers. Nobody quite knows where they came from; likely, it was from the north. But whenever, and from wherever, the Karen got to Burma, many settled in the hills running the border with what is now Thailand. They came to call the land Kaw Thoo Lei: land of—depending on the interpretation— white flowers, or no blemishes, or no evil. For centuries, they lived, as French explorer Henri Mouhot commented in the mid–nineteenth century, "on almost inaccessible heights . . . for the sake of their independence." Though remote, those inaccessible heights are fertile, covered in mixed deciduous forest: hardwoods, ferns, bushes, bamboo, a lush flush of green over the mountains, which they quietly farmed.

Since Htan Dah grew up in a refugee camp, he'd never lived on that land, but it was what he struggled to regain as an employee of BA. If he inhabited a peaceful Kaw Thoo Lei, currently labeled on a Burmese map as the misleadingly autonomous-sounding Karen State, his life would look much like that of the area's original settlers. He would live in a hut he'd built, with the help of his neighbors, out of bamboo and thatch. He'd fetch water for drinking and cooking and cleaning from a stream or river running near the village, in which he could also catch fish. He'd collect eggs from his chickens and maybe there'd be pigs living under his elevated house, and after a rice-based breakfast he'd spend some of the day cultivating more rice and vegetables in a nearby field before returning to his home, which would rest in the shade of coconut palms and papaya, in a village of twenty or a hundred households. At the end of the day, fires would be lit all around to prepare rice with produce and meat, probably caught, possibly turtle, snake, fish, lizard, monkey, boar. Once in a great while, and even less often these days, given their dwindling numbers, someone might kill a tiger. And as daylight and the smell of cook smoke dissolved, frangipani would perfume the crisp, tree-filtered air while Htan Dah visited with other villagers over rice wine, gossiping over the sounds of settling livestock and screeching creatures coming out to take over the night. A general outline of his year could be sketched by the Karen names for the thirteen months of the lunar calendar: *tha lay*, searching; *tay ku*, cutting; *thwee kaw*, drying and burning; *lah kli*, seed; *de nya*, lilies; *lah kü*, month of the farm; *lah nwee*, seventh month; *lah ho*, eighth month; *lah köo*, many lizards; *si muh*, little sun; *si sah*, little starlight; *lah naw*, oilseed; *lah plu*, spirits of the dead. To ensure the feeding of his family, he would work hard and often, together with other men and women of his village, independent, irenic, all set about with acacia trees.

Or as British Major John James Snodgrass would put it in the early nineteenth century:

> The houses of these strange people are of the most miserable description—mere pigeon houses perched in the air on poles, with a notched stick, as the sole means of egress and ingress to the dwelling; they are, however, well adapted for protecting their inmates from the ravages of the periodical deluge, and the still more destructive inroads of prowling tigers, in which the woods abound. The Carians, although the quietest, and most harmless people in the world are nevertheless of the strongest and most robust frame. . . . The women generally bear the marks of premature old age, probably from a too liberal share of the hard work falling to them, which, in more civilized countries, devolves wholly upon the male inhabitants.*

---

* It's all relative. Living in the jungle isn't all glamorous, for sure: It's far from impossible that a Karen State–dwelling Htan Dah would be illiterate, and malaria-ridden, and could be bitten by a Chinese ferret-badger or Javan mongoose or something, in which case his village doctor would make a poultice out of all kinds of crazy shit, including, quite possibly, actual shit, which may or may not result in a serious infection, from which he may or may not die.

These tribes' lifestyle had long been disparaged by the Burmans, too. "Karen" was, to them, a classification for illiterate, swidden-farming, animist (read: non-Buddhist) lowlifes—not a particularly respected culture, not when some of the other cultures were building a magnificent civilization.

Even back in the time of the Pyu, Burma was an important trade route, nestled, as it is, between south-central China and easternmost India, on the Bay of Bengal and Andaman Sea, the western edge of the Southeast Asian peninsula. By the sixteenth century, it was a center of world commerce, with towns modern, rich, and popu-lous, where you could get anything: painted cloth from Masulipatam, Bornean camphor, Sumatran pepper, Chinese porcelain and cotton and sandalwood, wools and velvets and scarlets from Europe. Rich in trade, metals, and gems—and with flatlands of Mesopotamian fecundity—Burma was valuable indeed. Westerners passing through, whether Italian, Portuguese, or English, were uniformly impressed. "The accounts [of] all these travelers," commented a writer later reviewing their reports, "even when every deduction has been made for glamour and its consequent exaggeration, prove that this empire, established on the delta of the Irawadi, was in the sixteenth century possessed of a might, a wealth, a splendour and an importance which have never since been approached in these regions."

But what Burma also boasted in abundance was war. In 1057, one Burman king had kicked off a fight for dominance of the whole coun-try, from which point on the Burmans and Mon and Shan engaged in constant and mighty battle. And though the fights were largely for property and plenty, they certainly weren't free from ethnic issues. One eighteenth-century Burman king, Alaungpaya, recruited forces to take the country back from the Mon with a partly us-versus-Mon platform, then sent his opponents the gift of a thousand bodiless Mon heads. And where there was war and ethnic chauvinism, there was brutal Karen oppression. Being backward and backwoods and con-sidered little better than dogs, they were subject to slave raids and the heavy taxation of whoever was winning—usually the Burmans. And, Karen lore has it, Alaungpaya's troops destroyed their villages when passing through en route to eastern military campaigns, just for fun.

So when the British came into Burma swinging in 1824, the Karen had little trouble picking sides. Alaungpaya's son was waging a policy of wild expansionism that his conquer-happy father had instituted, and he'd finally extended his territory right up to the edge of British India. Britain had some military might and hostility to spare now that it had dispensed with Napoleon. The civilizations had failed to achieve adequate diplomatic ties; the time had come for them to clash. When Burmese armies encroached into a British protectorate, the soldiers of the English East India Company went to war. And not everyone they encountered in what was technically enemy territory was hostile. Major Snodgrass, whatever his feelings about the Karen standard of living, was quite a bit more gracious in describing their character, writing again in his awesomely titled *Narrative of the Burmese War, Detailing the Operations of Major-General Sir Archibald Campbell's Army, from Its Landing at Rangoon in May 1824, to the Conclusion of a Treaty of Peace at Yandaboo, in February 1826*:

> These people appeared heartily glad to see us, and cheerfully assisted in repairing the roads; they also brought ducks, fowls, and other articles for sale, for which they found a ready and most profitable market. They willingly undertook to carry letters and communications from one corps of the army to another; and no instance occurred of their having deceived or disappointed their employers. They seemed most anxious for the expulsion of Maha Silwah, from Mophee, (only five miles distant,) and gave much useful information regarding his strength and situation. . . . [The next day] The column marched in order of attack upon Mophee, and arrived in front of the old fort about eight o'clock in the morning: the advance guard immediately pushed forward to the work, and the enemy was seen rushing into the

jungle in the greatest dismay and confusion. Our approach seemed to have been wholly unknown and unexpected; we found their dinners cooking, and every thing bore the appearance of a hasty flight. It certainly reflected no small honour on the good faith of our Carian friends, that our movements, known to so many, should have been so inviolably kept secret.

But however well things were going with the Karen, not so much for the war with the rest of Burma, which was, by one historian's estimate, the longest and most expensive in British India, costing it 15,000 soldiers. The Burmese fought like hell. Even after Burma's king realized his forces were far outmatched by Western firepower, even after the destruction of his entire navy and army and officer corps, he threw an army of conscripted, barely armed peasants at the British, the only men Burma had left, before finally giving up— after two years—some territory and a lot of reparations. The Burmese were hardly itching for another go-around less than thirty years later, when the British, looking for a fight and more territory, invaded again in 1852. Again, the British engaged the resisting Burmese and won, much more easily this time, and annexed the southern province of Pegu, dividing the country into sovereign Upper Burma and Lower Burma of the British Empire.

In addition to the battle, that Second Anglo-Burmese War sparked two other ugly fights. Party to the European victory were the Karen, who had once more acted as guides for the invaders. The British stormed Shwedagon Pagoda, the ancient 300-foot-tall golden stupa that enshrines eight of the Lord Gautama Buddha's hairs, the most sacred site in a devoutly Buddhist country; the Burmans destroyed the crops of nearby lowland Karen, murdered children in rice mortars, and burned villages for miles around.

The other nasty scene was unfolding in the ruling palace of what was left of Burma, where a war between loyalists and revolutionaries ended when Mindon Min overthrew his half-brother king and assumed the crown. That coup begat more violence: After Mindon Min's death one of his sons ascended the throne by executing many of the other heirs. So it was that the Royal Thibaw Min, King of the Umbrella-Bearing Chiefs, the Arbiter of Existence, the Great Lord of Righteousness, was consecrated Burma's final monarch amid the (depending on whom you ask) strangling or clubbing or elephant-trampling to death of princesses and princes in big pretty red velvet sacks, dozens of royal family members slaughtered. It was just a regular old reign-securing measure, but it made a mean splash in newspapers in England,* which was looking for an excuse to depose the sovereign leader and take over the rest of the lucrative Southeast Asian kingdom it already largely controlled.

Such an excuse, the story goes, finally presented itself in the form of that aforementioned young woman of European descent: Mattie Calogreedy, a half-Greek, half-Burmese palace maid who was having an affair with a French engineer of the Burmese king's. When Pierre (seriously) went home to Paris and returned with a French wife in tow, a scorned Calogreedy slept with a Burmese administrator in exchange for an incriminating secret document, which she handed over to the British, which contained proof of their worst nightmare: an alliance between the Burmese and the French(!). The *Times* of London called for war. The French, who'd tried to take India and were well on their way to establishing French Indochina, neither confirmed that they had Burma's back nor denied that they were up to something. The Burmese, conveniently, fined a Scottish trading company for failure to pay royalties. The British demanded, among other things, that Burma submit the matter to an arbiter and, oh, relinquish its sovereignty in the manner of Afghanistan before it. Thibaw, the last king of Burma, the Arbiter of Existence, prepared for combat. He couldn't win, and he knew it, but the Burmese were

---

* Also making a splash in publications like the *Pall Mall Gazette*: Burma's Kengtung had as many tigers as people!

going to die fighting before they'd live without trying to maintain rule over what was rightfully theirs.

Having prevailed in the Third Anglo-Burmese War in just a few weeks, the British deposed Thibaw and shipped him and his wife off to exile. It was 1885. The Western victors didn't realize it at the time, of course, but their battles on that field were just beginning—as were those between the Burmans and the Karen.

III.

"SO," THE Blay said, smiling at me in a way that was more cocky than friendly, the way I soon realized was just the way he smiled. It was my second morning at BA. He'd asked me to a meeting after breakfast, and he, Htan Dah, and a couple of other guys sat across from me in the living room, in the white plastic chairs. Htan Dah was holding a notebook and ready pen, which for some reason made me nervous. "You are English teacher."

"Yes. . . ." It was true that I taught college composition, and that in America such courses are generally classified as "English." I suspected, though, that this was a cultural nuance that didn't translate. I hadn't explained it in my introductory email to BA that said, "Hello there. I've been interested in volunteering on the Thai-Burma border for some time. I am an English instructor at the University of New Orleans. Do you need volunteers?" because I'd assumed that if they did need volunteers, a longer dialogue about my possible contributions would ensue. Instead, all that followed was a message saying

We welcome to be the volunteer with BA.

We would like you to teach English writing skills such as memo, letter and *statement writing to our staff and/or share your skills of computer, for example Microsoft offices program, or helping staff for translating document to English.*

For accommodation, if you stay and live with our staff (the staff share bedroom together), you can learn their lifestyle, learn more on Burma issues and have experiences. If you are flexible about food you can eat with us (traditional food).

And then one more asking what time someone should meet me at the airport. And apparently even that limited job description, written by someone in Bangkok, hadn't made it to Mae Sot before my arrival.

"I'm sorry," The Blay was apologizing. "I thought before you were strategic planner."

"I don't even know what that is," I said, though it did explain why The Blay had, over stick soup my first night, told me he had some objectives or something for me to look over, to which I'd responded, though I'd had no idea what he was talking about, "Okay." Ta Mla must have cleared up the confusion, relaying what he'd learned at breakfast yesterday about my profession. His vocabulary seemed so limited that I hadn't tried clarifying the difference between an English teacher and an *English* teacher to him, either.

So here was The Blay asking me if I could organize and teach two classes, one in basics to beginning students, like Ta Mla, who barely spoke English, and one in article/essay/memo/letter writing to advanced students, like The Blay, who spoke it pretty well. The advanced class would run from ten in the morning to noon, and the beginners' from one to three, every day. The Blay was either not daunted by or not comprehending my explanation that I had approximately no qualifications for teaching English as a second language, particularly to students whose language I didn't speak. I had two days to prepare.

"I need to be at professional level," The Blay said. He moved to the table against the front wall of the room, where his laptop was set up, and clicked on something that launched "Say You, Say Me" on loop, adjourning the conversation. As the rest of the group dispersed, Htan Dah ushered me into the adjoining narrow, cramped computer room, where three of the desks were occupied. He gestured at the lone available one and told me I was free to use it for my classwork.

I sat down at the computer with a notebook and pen. Originally a Midwesterner and constitutionally a nerd, I was instantly energized by being handed an assignment that was potentially too big and too far outside my abilities to complete. And I'd been feeling much better. I'd been negotiating the squat toilet without incident. Also, the night before, I'd walked into the bathroom with my towel, shut the giant wooden door behind me, and stripped off my clothes. I'd stood next to the high trough holding a plastic bowl of icy water and taken just a few breaths before dumping the contents down my neck and chest. My body went rigid and my heart into hard beats with the shock of it, and it took a lot of goes before the wet became more refreshing than traumatizing, but I was clean. We'd had more from that bottomless pot of stick soup, but I was snacking on yogurt and nuts, so my stomach wasn't so achingly empty. At night, the darkness in my room was so complete that I felt warmly, tightly wrapped in it, and I fell asleep listening to the lizards chirping on the ceiling, one of which had crapped on me. Now, my morale high, I started searching the Internet for do-it-yourself ESL courses while the same soothing Lionel Richie song played over and over in the background.

After several hours, I took my notebook back into the living room and sat down to do some brainstorming on my lesson plan. Near me, in a chair in front of the TV, sat an unfamiliar face bearing a wicked scar. His hair was cut military close, and he was lean but well cut, like most of the other guys.

"Very beautiful," he said after a while, and I looked up to see him nodding at Christina Aguilera dancing around the screen in bursting silver lamé.

I smiled and agreed.

"Where do you come from?"

"The United States," I said. "Do you live here?"

"No. In camp." Christina Aguilera went through three costume changes in her music video before he asked, "Do your parents have divorce?"

"Are my parents divorced?" I started laughing. "Yes, actually, they are. Most people's parents are divorced in the United States."

He nodded steadily. Yes, he'd heard of this. "You are very lucky!" he said with his eye on the TV. I wasn't sure what to say to that. "You have democracy! You want divorce, you get. You want go, you leave. How did you get here?"

"I flew here. On a plane."

More nodding. "How much it costs?"

"One thousand three hundred sixty-six dollars," I said. "That's . . ." I did some math in the top margin of my notebook, above TIPS FOR WRITING A MEMO. "Fifty-four thousand six hundred forty baht."

"Fifty . . ." He narrowed his eyes.

"Fifty-four thousand six hundred forty. Here." I turned my paper toward him and pointed at the number.

His face didn't unfurl, and he just shook his head, then shrugged before saying, "A lot."

"How much money do you make?" I asked Htan Dah at dinner. For the past three meals, he had come to get me from my room when he was done cooking, and then he and Ta Mla had sat at the table with me. The others trickled in or came and went while I ate.

"Five hundred baht per month." About $13. Ta Mla was smashing fish paste and rice into neat little cones between his vertical thumb and four fingers before scooping it up to his face. Htan Dah shoveled a huge spoonful of rice into his mouth. I had a spoon, too, which he always set out for me. Tonight, he'd also set a plate piled with finger-thick, footlong branches topped with comely green leaves in front of my place.

"What is this?" I asked.

Htan Dah and Ta Mla both scowled at the little woodpile as if they'd never seen it before, though they'd each just put an end of one of the limbs between their teeth and then quickly chomp-chomp-chomped it into smaller pieces before swallowing. "I don't know(!)," Htan Dah said. Each word was a note higher than the last, a singsong in ascending tones. His exclamations, I realized, made him sound like Yogi Bear. He laughed and shook his head. "You want to try?"

"No, I'm good."

"What about fish paste?" he asked, nodding at the ever-present bowl of sedimentary oil on the table. His eyes sparkled fiercely. "You don't like fish paste?" That morning, when he saw me turn my head to escape the smell as Ta Mla splashed the sauce onto his plate, he'd opted to describe how thoroughly you had to let the fish rot before you mixed it with chilies and oil while I tried to eat.

"Shut up," I said.

The Blay walked in singing. "Say it together. . . ."

"What is this?" I asked him, pointing at the branches.

"Morning glory?" he guessed. He laughed. "No. I don't know." Another unfamiliar face joined him in the dining room/garage, and together, they left.

"How many people live here?" I asked Htan Dah.

"Maybe . . . ten."

I'd seen a lot more dudes than that milling around the house. Many of them were dudes in Che Guevara T-shirts. "Who lives here? You, Ta Mla, The Blay, Htoo Moo"—he of a silent *h* and the constant smiling and the never talking to me and the stupefyingly round and hard-looking ass—"Ta Eh Thaw. . . ." That latter was the girl, whose name I knew now that Ta Mla had written it down for me. "Who else?"

"Gaw Sayyy," Htan Dah began, drawing out the final syllables of the names, "Eh Soooe, Georgieee, Eh Kawww*. . . . They are inside. In Burma."

"Doing what?"

"Doing interviewww, taking videooo, taking picturrre. . . . They go to the village, and they tell about what is going on in Burma, and about how to unite for democracy. Also, they ask, 'Have you seen Burma army? Have they raped you, or shot you, or burned your village?'" This explained the "Human Rights Vocabulary" transla- tion cheat sheet I'd seen my first night. I'd gotten a better look at it that afternoon while organizing my class, studying the fifteen most used phrases. One side listed words in Karen script, a train of circular characters, loops that extended lines or swirls above and below the baseline. The other side was in English: 1.) Killings 2.) Disappear- ances 3.) Torture/inhumane treatments 4.) Forced labor 5.) Use of child soldiers 6.) Forced relocation 7.) Confiscation/destruction of property 8.) Rape 9.) Other sexual violence 10.) Forced prostitu- tion 11.) Forced marriage 12.) Arbitrary/illegal arrest/detention 13.) Human trafficking 14.) Obstruction of freedom of movement 15.) Obstruction of freedom/expression/assembly.

"Then what?"

"Then they enter information into Martus."

"Into . . . what?"

"Human rights violation database."

"Then what happens to the information?"

"We can share, with other HRD."

"With other . . ."

"Human rights documenter."

---

* Okay, this guy's name isn't really Eh Kaw. This is where I tell you that a few of the names from now on have been changed for the safety of those individuals who are still refugees and could be deregistered or deported for having gallavanted, however gallantly, outside camp in Thailand. So this is a good time to confess, too, that Burma Action is not called Burma Action. The organization asked me not to tell you what it's really called, either, since it illegally houses a bunch of illegals, whom it employs to do illegal activities in two countries.

"So you guys collect it all . . ."

Htan Dah stared at me.

"And then what? Then it just sits there?"

Htan Dah shrugged.

"How do the guys get to the villages?"

"They walk."

That explained Htoo Moo's ass. "How long are they gone?"

"Depends. Maybe three months."

"Do they just hide around the jungle that whole time?"

"Yes(!)," Htan Dah said. "If they are caught, they could die."

This, though probably obvious, caught me off guard. Htan Dah and I watched each other for a moment.

"Do you ever do that?"

"No. I am office manager."

"Do you?" I asked Ta Mla.

"*Yes*," he said, nodding gravely. "I am . . . human rights . . . documenter."

Well, somebody had to document it—stealthily. One activist who gave an interview to a PBS *Frontline* reporter served seven years in prison. Another was sentenced to twenty-five years for giving an interview that was critical of the regime to the BBC in 1997. Of the 173 nations in the Reporters Without Borders Press Freedom Index 2008, Burma ranked 170th, behind Iran and China and Cuba and every other country except the "unchanging hells" of Turkmenistan, North Korea, and Eritrea. Burma is third in having the most journalists in jail. If one exile newspaper's tagline, which quotes Napoleon,* is right that one newspaper *is* worth a thousand bayonets,† and the employees of BA were fighting one of the largest armies on the planet by keeping villagers abreast of relevant world news and trying to col-

---

* Incorrectly.

† "Four hostile newspapers," he actually said, "are more to be feared than a thousand bayonets."

lect the villagers' struggles to disseminate to the rest of the world, they did indeed need a solid grasp of English.

WHEN I'D told The Blay that I had no qualifications to teach English as a second language, I'd meant, really, that I had one, sort of: five years of high school and college French.

"Okay, you guys, today we're going to conjugate some verbs," I told my afternoon class, the beginners. BA apparently had another office in Mae Sot, and most of my students apparently lived there. So, after one more full day of frantic Internet searching for a month and a half of lesson plans, Htoo Moo had, with neither a word nor a helmet and with a maniac's speed, driven me to Office Two on the back of his motorbike. The beginner's class contained Ta Mla, Ta Eh Thaw, and five people I'd never met. One of them was a middle-aged woman smooth of face and voice whose first question was how long I was staying and whose second was how they were supposed to have enough time to improve their English in six weeks. I'd only been in Mae Sot for four days, but even I was savvy enough not to use the "Six weeks is a really long time!" defense again with someone who'd probably lived in a refugee camp for twenty years. Instead, I just shook my head, my mouth open, apology creasing my forehead.

My morning class, the advanced students, had been easier, since their comprehension was higher and I hadn't had to painstakingly guide them through the very basic conversational interviews with each other and verb forms I hadn't thought about since second grade. Like the beginners, they all had brand-new notebooks with creatures and chaotic shapes in gaudy colors on the front and multiplication tables on the back. They were made for five-year-olds, possibly Japanese ones, but they'd been bought special for the occasion. As I settled myself on the blue tile floor, against one edge of the white-washed drywall, the morning students pulled up a bench and a couple of chairs or sat on the floor with me. Having gone to graduate school for writing, I had, unsurprisingly, decided to run the class as a work-shop. After I regaled them with my tips on memo writing ("Most important: connect your purpose with the needs and interests of the reader"), for which they all leaned forward eagerly, we set up a sched-ule for them to bring in short essays describing a typical day in camp. The Blay, for all his insistence that I bring him up to professional level, hadn't shown, but we'd assigned due dates for four students I'd just met, as well as Htan Dah and Ta Mla.

"Ta Mla!" I said after the afternoon class ended. It was two-thirty; I'd only managed to fill an hour and a half of each two-hour session, and I was exhausted. "You're in both of my classes!"

"Yes," he said, following me out of the room into the humid sun-shine. "I . . . want . . . to learn. *Very* much." His voice, like his fea-tures, was soft and serious. In our three hours of class together that day, I'd realized that he was taking in quite a bit more of what I said than his English-speaking abilities might've suggested. I just had to ask him enough questions and be patient enough to let him fully answer. He offered to give me a ride back to our office/house. Though I was relieved that he drove way slower than Htoo Moo did, he also seemed much less steady.

First thing the next morning, Ta Mla was sitting in the living room, facing the computer room when I strolled out of it after sending an obligatory email update back home. I'd also taped up a piece of paper saying that if I was hit by a motorbike/killed by a diseased mosquito/trampled by elephants, call my father, with his contact information.

"Are you finished?" Ta Mla asked.

"Yes." He didn't appear to be doing anything. "Were you waiting for me?"

"Yes. I . . . wait. For you."

"You didn't have to."

"Yes. I wait for you. I have . . . no . . . friends . . . at the moment."
It did seem awfully quiet. Though it smelled like Htan Dah had been

cooking, it didn't sound like anyone was in the house. "Have you eaten . . . your . . . breakfast?"

"No, I haven't. Do you want to eat with me?" We walked toward the dining room/garage. "How long have you been in Thailand?"

Ta Mla told me, while he gathered his tidy fingerfuls of rice, that he'd left Burma in 1999, when he was twenty, because he wanted to go to school. He was born in a small village, just sixteen houses, that had a teacher only for kindergarten; to attend middle school, he had to move into a dorm a five-hour walk away. When he finished, he worked as a security guard in the village where he was born. Once, when he was fourteen and away from home, Burma army planes flew overhead before anyone could run away, strafing and dropping bombs. His father was hit in the thigh and ankle, but he recovered. Ta Mla's job after that was to look out, warning everyone when government soldiers were coming so they could grab their babies and some rice and disappear into the jungle, which is about as much security as a village guard can provide. Though serving as an early warning system is a pretty risky job—sentries are killed if they're spotted—Ta Mla managed to avoid detection, and for three years he worked and lived with his family. But he wanted to continue his studies. And considering the country's abysmal infrastructure and economy, the best place to go to school in Burma was in Thailand.

Ta Mla had already been settled in Ban Salah refugee camp, near the Salween River, for a year when the Burma army attacked his village again. The villagers had been warned and dashed into hiding, though a few straggled behind a bit to feed their hungry chickens—who knew how long they were going to be displaced this time? But the soldiers made it to the village before all the villagers had made it out, and they opened fire, injuring six and killing two. One of the dead was Ta Mla's uncle. The other was his father.

Ta Mla was twenty-one. He could have gone home to the village where his family was murdered, but army offensives were becoming so frequent and disruptive that he'd probably be unable to cultivate enough food for himself, and even if he could, it would likely be stolen or burned by government soldiers. He couldn't get a job in Burma, because he wasn't qualified to do anything and they were few. He couldn't continue his education in Burma, even if the government didn't regularly shut the universities down, because he didn't have any money, just like he didn't have any identification papers, or money to bribe his way into some. He could, of course, have resigned himself to sitting in a six-foot square of hut floor area—the space each camp refugee is allotted per international humanitarian recommendations—literally all day, forbidden to leave camp or work, waiting for his monthly or semimonthly rations like a paycheck, maybe get married and have some babies so they could do nothing, too. Given his options, and his anger over his father's death, well, that would be when taking up arms as an insurgent became the clear path.

IV.

THE BRITISH takeover of Burma, one historian has pointed out, was
basically the Iraq War of the 1800s. Strategists had assumed it would
be cheap, fast, and easy, the colonialists sweeping in and simply
installing a new government. Instead, the occupiers found themselves overwhelmed, besieged on all sides by insurgencies. By the
end of 1886, the year after the third and final war, the British had
forty thousand troops stationed in their new territory, more than
three times the number they'd deployed for the invasion, more than
was required to occupy all of Egypt, a country one and a half times
Burma's size. Hundreds of Empire troops were killed in uprisings in
which thousands of Burmese guerrillas died. As a method of battling them, British soldiers and even civilians destroyed the natives'
access to key resources—food, shelter, personnel—by burning down
villages. It was a brutal and high-casualty tactic. "We simply wiped
out the village and shot everyone we saw," wrote Sir James George
Scott, an intrepid administrator who, in addition to killing Burmese,
introduced them to football. "Burned all their crops and houses."

Another method of maintaining control was again employing
the trusty Karen. You'll remember that some Burmans considered
the minority subhuman—take the Rangoon viceroy, who in 1851
told an American missionary that any literate Karen he encountered

would be shot—but the British thought they were just lovely, model workers whether as nannies or army men. And some were Christian, too, since the missionaries had been having luck up there in the hills where they lived. Vast numbers of Karen were enlisted as soldiers and military police, and they helped put down popular revolts. During World War I, three of the sixteen Burma Rifles companies were Karen. The British selected them and other hill tribes to form most of Burma's army, a slap in the face to the warmongering, long-powerful almighty Burmans, about whom many British felt the same way bigoted Burmans felt about the mountain minorities. On top of these insults, these tribes were, unlike the Burmans, left largely to their own devices by the royal administration, which, as a matter of written policy, did not "oppress them or suffer them in any way to be oppressed." Under the British, ethnicity became primarily, exaggeratedly important. Under the British, the Karen, long considered inferior slave labor, acquired autonomy, a growing ethnic nationalist identity—and armed authority.

Predictably, this didn't do a lot to quell tensions in a polyethnic country with a millennium-long history of racism-tinged war. At the turn of the twentieth century, the Karen were no longer divided against the majority Burmans by only language, culture, religion, and tradition, but now also by treatment under—and loyalty to— His Majesty Edward VII, King of the United Kingdom and the British Dominions and Emperor of India. Further fueling a nationalistic Burman fire were the quarter of a million Indians who began pouring in yearly and working successfully in government and business ventures; the British far favored them, too, over Burma's native majority. The 1930s brought a series of riots in which hundreds of Indians were massacred. When the Burmans turned their discontent on the British, they were massacred in turn; when several thousand students, civilians, and monks demonstrated in Mandalay in 1939, government troops opened fire. Fourteen were killed.

The infuriated and humiliated Burmans agreed that they had no

choice but to fight for independence. And a crew of nationalist leaders called the Thirty Comrades were under the mistaken impression
that the Japanese were the ones to help them get it.

IN DECEMBER 1941, a few days after the bombing of Pearl Harbor, the
Imperial Japanese Army marched into Burma, with the Japanese-
trained Burma Independence Army close behind them, picking up
random recruits along the way.

Unfortunately for the Karen, these untrained soldiers-come-lately
tended to be recently released criminals or general scumbags. They
looted and profiteered unimpeded. Some units burned down a Karen
orphanage and Catholic mission and slaughtered Karen civilians.
They raped Karen women as they happened upon them. Even the
war-crime-propagating Japanese thought the BIA was out of control and demobilized it, deploying in its place a new "Burmese" army
loaded with Japanese soldiers.

By the spring of 1942, the invaders had vanquished the British in
Burma, deposing the last unified government the country has ever
seen. But the Japanese were soon taking heavy losses in the war,
where British forces were conducting a tremendous counterattack in
Burma assisted by Indians, Gurkhas, Chinese, Africans, Americans,
and, of course, minority peoples of Burma. Like Major Snodgrass
before them, the British and American forces in the Burma theater
during World War II found the Karen invaluable allies.* They laid
mines. They assisted airstrikes. They stashed Allied troops and supplies dropped into Burma by parachute. They showed the British,
who were struggling to use tanks and trucks in the jungle, how to use
elephants. They fought fiercely. In their capacity as protectors of the

---

* And not just the Karen; several ethnic groups joined the Allied side. The British recruited and armed an entire fighting force of Kachin, for example, under whose direction some
Allies adopted the practice of lacing the roadside with hardened, pointed, shit-smeared
bamboo spikes and covering them with vegetation so that the Japanese would be impaled
and, if they lived, infected when they dove for cover at the sound of gunfire.

Allied troops hiding in their villages, they were tortured and killed for refusing to surrender their comrades. So many Karen were tortured to death by the Japanese for their unwillingness to disclose the whereabouts of embedded secret serviceman Major Hugh Seagrim that the Brit finally gave himself up to certain execution, dressed in traditional Karen costume, heavy, embroidered homespun. "The Karen," said Field Marshal William Slim, author of *Defeat into Victory: Battling Japan in Burma and India, 1942-1945*, "are no fair-weather friends."

Not that the Karen had a lot of options beyond violent devotion to the Allied cause. It was unthinkable what would happen if the victors were the Burman-allied Japanese, who'd taken to pressing Karen and other natives into forced labor. Their only chance at autonomy was a British-brokered and -enforced Burma deal. The war between the Karen and the Burmans was then, as it had long been and is to some extent today, a war between Anglophiles and Anglophobes. The Karen told the British that they were happy to help—so long as the Europeans returned the favor after the war. British commanders and senior officers swore that the Karen would be rewarded with independence. One British civil serviceman had written in his appropriately titled *The Loyal Karens of Burma* that in the earlier days of British occupation, the Karen were "the staunchest and bravest defenders of British rule" and that without their "loyalty and courage . . . the Queen's government would, in all probability—for a time, at least—have ceased to exist." In this world war, too, the British, by all accounts, could not have won Burma without the assistance of the minorities. Allied Karen killed at least 12,500 Japanese troops in Burma in just the last months of the war.*

---

* It's kind of weird that Burma has largely been forgotten in the popular World War II narrative, given its strategic importance and the staggering casualties there. The theater was Japan's greatest Pacific War defeat: Three out of five of the three hundred thousand soldiers who entered it never went home. More Japanese died there than in the bombing of Hiroshima, even factoring in the radiation-exposure casualties of the following several months.

In early 1945, another—most unexpected—group joined the British offensive against Japan: the Burmans. The Japanese were not going to win, and had made it clear that they had no intention of relinquishing power even if they did. The Burmans had bet on the wrong horse, and they knew it. Led by Aung San, a prominent member of the Thirty Comrades and the Burmese minister for war under the Japanese, the nationalists switched sides just months before the Japanese surrendered, just in time to demand British independence as their reward.

Postwar, the British on the ground laid out a nice, sensible plan for rebuilding Burma. The country was in ruins, everything from its economy to its roads to its rice paddies. The governor aimed to slowly prepare the nation for self-government under overarching British rule—after the necessary reconstructions. Moderation, though, was not an option for Aung San. No would-be Burmese leader could survive a call for *eventual* independence. Anyone with hopes of ever being in charge had no choice but to demand independence right now. Politicians 5,500 miles away were on board with that, anyway; the Labour Party had won Britain's election and was dropping colonialism like hot to the floor. Some Conservatives wanted to stick around and oversee Burma's transition to independence, but England had way bigger problems—like Gandhi, and rebuilding London—and the Empire was being hastily dismantled. Now Britain didn't even *want* to do anything but comply with Aung San's demands.

But the nationalists weren't the only ones making demands. For the Karen—being traitors to their country and all—total and permanent annexation to British India may have been the best possible scenario. Short of becoming British subjects, they needed their old allies to make their autonomy a nonnegotiable condition of an independent Burma, as they'd been promised. A Karen group of representatives went to England to cash in on that pledge. By that time, though, His Majesty's Government didn't in fact have the means to make good on it. The British weren't going to risk Aung San's inciting a nationwide revolt over negotiations about hill tribes that likely lacked the political and military clout to maintain independent states anyhow. The prime minister received the Karen delegates, couldn't offer them what they came for, and sent them on a tour of a local soap factory. The minorities had been sold out. Literally: In lieu of liberty, they were given some money.

"All loyalties have been discarded and rebuffed; all faithful service has been forgotten and brushed aside," wailed Winston Churchill. "We stand on the threshold of another scene of misery and ruin." He condemned his opponents in Parliament, that the abandonment "should ever haunt the consciences of the principal actors in this tragedy." Whatever. Churchill wasn't in charge anymore. The agreement his successor signed with Aung San promised ultraquick independence and included a provision expressing hopes that the hill peoples would cooperate with unification.

At least Aung San was unification's best chance. He knew the Karen were both armed and suspicious, and he seemed genuinely, if a little unpopularly, interested in a union of autonomous nation-states. He proffered peace with the Karen after the Burma Independence Army massacres. He expressed his desire to appease the minorities in numerous speeches, publicly insisting that "Burma should consist of specified autonomous states . . . with adequate safeguards for minorities." He insisted that the hill tribes be part of the independence process. He held a conference where the Shan, Kachin, and Chin agreed that they'd give the Burmese government their cooperation and get autonomy.

The Karen didn't even go to the conference. One of their most prominent leaders, Ba U Gyi, hadn't *wanted* a fight; born to wealthy Karen landowners at the turn of the twentieth century, he was a university-educated lawyer who'd practiced in London, a gentleman, handsome, with a kind face, soft-looking beard, and handlebar mustache. He'd advocated nonviolently for Karen autonomy, joining Aung San's pre-independence Cabinet, helping organize the Karen delegation to England, filing resolutions with the British government. But his minority voice had been drowned out in Aung San's Executive Council, London had brushed off his delegation, and his resolutions had been ignored. So instead of attending Aung San's conference, the Karen held their own, where they formed the Karen National Union. They also boycotted the national elections. The British would save them, they were sure, or the Americans, or both. It was 1947. If Pakistan could be independent, they could, too. And they'd been too terrorized by the Burmans for too many centuries to submit to their authority.

In the end, agreements made or not made didn't matter much, because the brand-new Union of Burma was soon to fall under spectacularly evil and incompetent military authority. In July 1947, Aung San, the father of the republic, and the peaceful union and minorities' only hope, was assassinated—along with a Karen leader, a Shan chief, and an important Muslim figure, among others—by political rivals in a shower of bullets at a meeting of his interim government. On January 4, 1948, at 4:20 AM, the exact moment Burmese astrologers had deemed auspicious, Burma became independent. On the pole in Fytche Square, Rangoon, the British flag was exchanged for the Union of Burma's as British officials and their misty-eyed wives stood by. The new and first president was Shan. But the surviving council member who became prime minister announced that he was 100 percent in opposition to the idea of autonomous ethnic states, Karen and otherwise.

What happened next was a shit show. Independent Burma had been created by military men. The country was flush with weapons. And the upcoming generation of a country with its own legacy of war had spent its formative years watching Japanese, Chinese, British, Indian, and American soldiers throw down on its soil in the fight of the century. In March, the Communist Party of Burma revolted. The People's Volunteer Organization, a collection of militias, followed. Six battalions of Karen and Kachin fighters held the country together under Lieutenant General Smith Dun, a Karen supposedly named after the protagonist in *Mr. Smith Goes to Washington*. He was commander in chief of the army—which was in mutiny. Still loyal soldiers at first, even to a government that wouldn't grant them independence, the ethnic units rescued towns from Communist Party control. Some Karen in the military police, also in mutiny, captured another town. They gave it back, and a commission was established to settle the rift between Karen and Burmans. The prime minister wanted the minority to participate in the government through the parliament. The Karen said they'd never get their fair share. No one would compromise. By the summer, Karen and Burmans were killing each other. The newly formed Karen National Union started aggressively arming fighters, aided by some old British special forces soldiers, who smuggled weapons to them. For decades, the Karen had been putting down violent uprisings. Now, amid the deepest internal chaos the country had seen yet, they were going to mount one.

IN THE late summer of 1948, Karen police stopped helping the government keep the peace and started attacking government stations after Burmese paramilitary police assaulted one of the headquarters of the Karenni, an ethnic cousin to the Karen. On Christmas Eve, Burmese soldiers killed dozens of Karen in church and hundreds of others in surrounding villages, and weeks later a Karen village was attacked by Burmese military police, who killed 150 civilians. The armed wing of the Karen National Union stormed the Burmese treasury. Led by Major General Ne Win, a Burmese army battalion burned down an American Baptist mission school for Karen. On January 30, Karen settlements in Rangoon were shelled with machine guns and mortars.

On January 31, 1949, Karen and Burmese fighters battled in the streets just outside Rangoon. Karen forces set up a siege from the suburb of Insein and came within four miles of the capital. The country had been independent for barely a year, and several other insurgent groups were already at war with the government. Now the KNU was officially at war, too. Karen Lieutenant General (Mr.) Smith (Goes to Washington) Dun was replaced with Ne Win as commander in chief of the Burma army, while Karen villagers were mobbed. The three Karen battalions that made up a third of the Burma army revolted, turning their British training and leftover British weapons on the government. They took Mandalay with the help of Kachin soldiers. They took Toungoo and Henzada. They might have taken the capital—and the government—if they'd really gone for it. They didn't, though, not hard or fast enough.

Hundreds were killed in the siege from Insein, which lasted 112 days. It was a disorganized smattering of battles. Rangoon movie theaters still ran several shows a day, civilians could pay a couple of rupees to take a tour bus to the front line and shoot at Karen fighters, and neither the Karen nor the Burmese won any decisive victories. Instead, they began a lifetime of war, the same war that led Ta Mla to enlist as a KNU soldier in 2000, that brought Ta Mla and me together in the Mae Sot house, a war older than the both of us combined. "Ba U Gyi was no terrorist," the former British governor of Burma had told the *Times* of London back in those beginning days. "I, for one, cannot picture him enjoying the miseries and hardships of a rebellion. There must have been some deep impelling reason for his continued resistance."

However complicated the history and politics of it, though, and whether or not the Karen were erstwhile allies and all-around stand-up guys, United States law put my country and my new roommate on opposing sides of the fight. Burma's government, after all, was internationally recognized, a member of the United Nations. And that landed the Karen National Union, which was waging an insurgency against that government, squarely inside the United States Department of State's designation of third-tier terrorists.

There are lists, of course, of groups that are specifically designated as terrorist organizations. The KNU wasn't on them. But the USA PATRIOT Act of 2001 added another, very inclusive dimension of terrorism, the third tier, to the lawbooks, classifying as terrorist "an organization that is a group of two or more individuals, whether organized or not, which engages in" any terrorist activity. Which includes, per clause (iii) of section 1182 of Title 8 of the US Code, even "the use of any . . . explosive, firearm, or other weapon or dangerous device (other than for mere personal monetary gain*), with intent to endanger, directly or indirectly, the safety of one or more individuals or to cause substantial damage to property." Which certainly includes the KNU.

The title of section 1182 of Title 8 is "Inadmissible aliens." Also banned from the United States at the time, besides Ta Mla: Htan Dah. Though he'd never been a soldier himself, his dad was in the KNU, and spouses and children of any person who has engaged in terrorist activity are specifically barred from the States in the PATRIOT Act,[†] too, terrorists by association. And even if his dad hadn't been in the KNU, Htan Dah still couldn't have immigrated to America, having engaged in so much terrorist activity himself.

Under US immigration law, one has "engaged in terrorist activity" if one "commits an act that the actor knows, or reasonably should know, affords material support" to someone doing something terroristy or in a terrorist organization—like Htan Dah's dad, and Ta Mla, and a hundred other people Htan Dah knows. "Support" includes activities as specific and potentially dangerous as providing weapons or explosives, as well as vaguer and less insidious exertions, such as providing "service" and shelter and "intangible" property. Htan Dan had assisted, tangibly and intangibly, I guess, with food or motorbike rides or moral support, plenty of KNU soldiers in his

---

* ?!

† The PATRIOT Act made it illegal, additionally, to even try or verifiably *want* to provide material support to a terrorist organization. Thus were two Iraqi Kurds living in upstate New York convicted for *conspiring* to provide material support. "If a terrorist came to Albany," the US attorney leading the prosecution said, "my opinion is that these guys would have assisted 100 percent." The men were sentenced to fifteen years apiece.

life, so the possibility of his entry into America was out. And even if Htan Dah hadn't given his support generously and willingly—which he had—there's no amount of support too minimal to be considered material support, and there are no exceptions even for people who've provided said support under duress. (For example, a Sri Lankan fisherman who fled to the States after being kidnapped by the Tamil Tigers in 2004 was instantly detained upon his arrival for having provided the group material support—money for his own ransom.) To win exemption from the automatic inadmissibility of providing material support requires proving with "clear and convincing evidence" that, whether you provided the support willingly or at gunpoint or what, you had no way of knowing that the people you helped, or who were making you help them, were terrorists.

With all those laws in place, and with The Blay's and Htoo Moo's and Htan Dah's dads all in the KNU, and BA sometimes collaborating with the guerrilla organization, not one of my coworkers was legally allowed into my country. And two laws passed after the original 1990 material-support law—one in 1994 and another in 1996, after the first World Trade Center and Oklahoma City bombings, respectively—*criminalize* material support, so that if Htan Dah, much less Ta Mla, had found his way to America, he could have been immediately jailed.

So, among the other possibilities not open to Ta Mla after his father's death, in addition to safely growing enough food to feed himself, getting a job, going to college, traveling legally outside his home country, traveling without threat of harm or death inside his home country, or living anywhere but in an active war zone or a refugee camp: applying for asylum in the United States.

When Ta Mla enlisted, he knew he'd be in boot camp for a year: six months of theory, six months of practical. For three weeks, he waited at a KNU headquarters in Burma for the rest of the recruits to be collected. The guerrillas needed to get to Shan State, to the north, for training. But since they have a far more cordial relationship with the Thais than the Burmese, they were loaded into vans and driven east over the border, back into Thailand, so they could do the bulk of their traveling there before recrossing. More cordial, but, as we know, not *that* cordial: Thai police officers stopped the enlistees and wouldn't let them through. The class went back to Karen State to start training, but Ta Mla had by then had time to reconsider his decision. He wasn't looking for a physical fight, and he wanted to finally get a high school education, which he could obtain in camp. After several weeks, he went back to Thailand, leaving the other new soldiers to their preparations for war.

V.

FOR TERRORISTS, even from the nebulous third tier, these guys had really, really boring meetings. Every Friday morning, all the staff got together at Office One to discuss the progress they'd made on their projects, any prospective projects, ideal future improvements, standard organizational housekeeping. Htan Dah had asked when I'd woken up if I wanted to attend, as the meeting took place early enough for me to still make it to my ten o'clock class. I'd agreed, groggily; though I was going to bed by nine, I was having trouble dragging myself out from under my mosquito net every day. The shotgun stress of putting together and performing four quality hours of broken-English class a day was wearing on me. That, and the lack of protein in my diet. While I ate about every three hours in the States, my housemates observed only breakfast and dinner, and I hadn't eaten any meat since I'd arrived nearly a week ago. I hardly ever ate meat back home, and when I did I had the luxury of being picky about it. Here, I almost exclusively ate rice. Here, I'd recently come upon Htan Dah in the kitchen, holding a piece of pork so gamy I could smell it from the doorway. He was standing in a big red puddle, and when I'd asked him if it was blood, he'd looked down at his flip-flops, submerged to his feet. "Yes," he'd said, and narrowed his eyes at my fatuity. "From the pork."

When the meeting started, I sat on the edge of the hushed living room filled with twenty or so guys and a couple of girls, all cross-legged and grave-faced on the floor. The Blay introduced me in English, though I'd met most everyone by now. He then announced that Htan Dah was formally responsible for me, so if I needed any-thing, that was whom I should ask, at which point Htan Dah gave me a nervous eyebrow raise, smile, and thumbs-up. Staffers said their piece in a monotonous Karen drone. Occasionally the group laughed quietly, all together, the contained, inauthentic laughter of the con-ference room. There were many periods of silence in which throats were cleared. One of the guys had offered to translate for me at the beginning of the meeting, but he wrote only eight of the nine hun-dred sentences spoken on a dry-erase board at the front of the room. His bullet points were hardly enough to retain my attention, so I occupied myself by reading a profile of a ladyboy movie star in the *Bangkok Post*.

Afterward, we settled down to breakfast, and I eyed the revolu-tionary pictured on Htan Dah's chest; he was, apparently, the one whose turn it was to wear a Che shirt that day.

"Isn't the idea to document the human rights violations in Burma, and walk all over the countryside preaching to the villagers about democracy, so you can fight the government peacefully?"

"Yes(!)."

"What's with you guys and the Che shirts?"

"Because! He is revolutionary. We want also to be revolutionaries. He is good role model for us."

"But you know that that revolution was violent."

"Yes(!). I know it. But I would like to know more about Che, about his life. About . . . his struggle."

Htoo Moo walked out of the bathroom and into the dining room/ garage, wet and half naked. The past couple of days, he'd seemed to stop toweling off and getting dressed for a while after his showers. It was possible he'd just become more comfortable with my presence, but I had a suspicion that he'd caught me marveling at his butt. He stood now at the end of the table in nothing but a pair of little shorts, his hair dripping and pecs glistening. I paused, ready for a break or a new participant in the conversation, but he just propped one leg up on the bench where I was sitting and started picking up chunks of fried pork and popping them into his mouth.

I turned my attention back to Htan Dah. "Why don't you wear Gandhi shirts?"

"They didn't have any Gandhi shirts. Also, because Che is attractive." He smiled at me radiantly. "I like his style."

At dinner, after class, I told Htan Dah that I'd emailed home and asked someone to send a biography of Che Guevara to the BA post office box. He was excited. He seemed equally excited about the mention of my having friends I could contact in the United States.

"Do you have picture?" he asked. "Of your friend?"

I knew better than to travel anywhere, let alone remote destinations, without pictures of my friends and family, but here I was, photoless. I apologized, regretting my lazy packing, until I remembered that I could in fact show Htan Dah nearly everyone I knew. "Let's go to the computer room," I said.

Thus were several Karen refugee activists of Mae Sot, Thailand, bestowed with one of democracy's greatest gifts: that of wasting exorbitant amounts of time on social networking websites. I logged in to MySpace, explaining to Htan Dah that it was a website where people could make pages about themselves that friends and strangers could look at. I clicked through some of my pals' profiles, talking about who they were, or where they were or what they were doing in the pictures. Htoo Moo, who was working diligently at the next computer, glanced over as nonchalantly and infrequently as possible. Htan Dah said very little. Once, he asked me to clarify the gender of the girl I was pointing to on the screen. "Are you sure?" he asked. "She looks like a boy." I laughed and told him that she was a lesbian, my ex-girlfriend, actually, which seemed to clear it up for him. Other than that, he mostly just stared at the monitor in stunned silence, for so long that it actually started to weird me out.

"What do you think?" I asked him when I'd finished the tour.

"Wow," he said quietly.

"So, those are my friends," I said. He made no move to get up or take his eyes off the web page.

I asked him if he wanted to see how the website worked. I showed him the browse feature, dropping down the long list of countries whose citizens we could gawk at. "How about Myanmar?" he asked, spying the country in the options.

I was surprised it was there, and even more surprised that our first search turned up some three thousand profiles. The junta has some pretty awesome restrictions on owning electronics, especially computers. In 1996, Leo Nichols, honorary consul for Norway and Denmark and friend of Burmese activists, violated the Computer Science Development Law and was sentenced to three years' hard labor for the illegal possession of fax machines* (a sentence he never served: When he was taken into custody, he was denied medicine and tortured, and died). There are Internet cafés, but they get raided, like meth labs, cops rushing in and yelling at everyone to take their hands off the keyboards and then inspecting what's up on the screens; the café workers are required to automatically capture customers' screenshots every five minutes and submit their web histories, along with corresponding home addresses and phone numbers, to the state for scrutiny. The Committee to Protect Journalists ranks Burma the No.

---

* Some other specifications of the law: Section 31: Whoever imports or keeps in possession or utilizes any type of computer . . . without the prior sanction of the Ministry of Communications, Posts and Telegraphs shall, on conviction be punished with imprisonment for a term which may extend from a minimum of 7 years to a maximum of 15 years and may also be liable to a fine. Section 32: Whoever sets up a computer network or connects a link inside the computer network, without the prior sanction of the Ministry of Communications, Posts and Telegraphs shall, on conviction be punished with imprisonment for a term which may extend from a minimum of 7 years to a maximum of 15 years and may also be liable to a fine.

1 worst country in the world to be a blogger, ahead of China and Egypt and Iran—prison sentences for them have been at least as high as twenty years. Humanitarian geeks in India and Germany, though, worked full time to keep Burma's citizens in illegal international Internet access with proxy servers that update when the government figures out how to block them. From the looks of it, they were doing their job.

On MySpace, ink-haired Burmese teenagers and twentysomethings stared at us from the angles of people who've taken their own pictures: the chin-down-sexy-eyes-up shot, the haughty chin up/eyes half-closed, the profile with eyes askance. Their faces were surrounded by HTML-coded sparkles, animated hearts and stars, slaughtered English colloquialisms. Htan Dah looked at the profiles, pausing long and hard at each picture that came up.

"I don't know them," he said finally.

This conclusion struck me as pretty foregone, since he'd never lived in Burma. "Did you think you would?"

He looked at me, realizing his mistake. "I don't know," he said softly.

I felt bad. Guilty. Embarrassed, actually. There had been a time when I'd called myself a refugee, just the summer before. Though I hailed originally and most recently from Ohio, I'd lived in New Orleans when Hurricane Katrina hit. There'd been a big to-do in the media about whether we New Orleanians displaced around the country should be called refugees, and I'd ardently defended the word's use. Nay, I'd *insisted* on it. I'd brought nothing on my evacuation from the Gulf Coast but an extra pair of underwear, a toothbrush, a serape, and a deck of cards, and when the levees had broken, I'd been broken down for days, for lack of a job and an income and certainty. Calling myself a refugee had made my plight sound as heavy and traumatic as it had felt, even after I'd moved back to the city four months after the storm and then, just weeks ago, unable to take the stress, back out again. Here's what I *had* had, though, I realized, sitting next to Htan Dah: Citizenship. Domestic peace. The right to work, own property, travel, vote, believe in the possibility of future opportunities. Refugee, my ass.

We made Htan Dah his own profile, and finally, he'd had enough MySpace for one night. He left the computer room, and I checked my email. But five minutes later he reappeared. "I want to practice," he said, and logged in, staying up long past the time Htoo Moo had quit work for the night, after I'd gone to bed.

BREAKFAST THE next day was business as usual, with my asking Htan Dah how he was doing and his saying "I am great! I am living!" with glittering eyes and teeth. When I sat down to dinner that night, though, he and Ta Mla and Htoo Moo spent a fair amount of time watching me and muttering to each other in Karen.

"Something on your mind, tiger?" I asked Htan Dah.

"We are talking about your girlfriend," he said.

Yeah, I'd thought that conversation had ended a little too easily. "All right. You can talk about it with me."

"Do you ever have boyfriend?"

"Yes. I've had boyfriends and girlfriends."

This produced a moment of confused silence, which I filled with a lame description of the sexuality continuum, along with an explanation of the somewhat loose sexual mores of modern American gals like myself. Htan Dah responded by telling me that they had heard of gay people, since a visitor to the house had informed them of their existence—last year.

"Last year!" I hollered.

"Yes!" he yelled back. "In Karen culture, we do not have."

"What do you mean you 'do not have'? You guys read the newspaper. You have the Internet."

"But in a village, Karen village, we do not have," Htan Dah said.

"There's never been a gay person in a Karen village in the history of Karen society?" All three men shook their heads. "Come on."

"If there was a gay person, they would leave," Htan Dah said. "It is not our culture."

"Let's just say there was a gay person," I said. "Couldn't they stay in the village?"

"No," Htan Dah said. "I would not allow gay people in my village."

"Are you kidding me!?"

Htan Dah held my gaze, though his seemed more uncertain the longer it went on.

"Are you going to make *me* leave?"

"No! For you, in your culture, it is okay," he said. "You are not Karen. But in our culture, it does not belong." Htoo Moo and Ta Mla were nodding, and I scowled at them.

"You're a refugee," I said. "And it sucks. It's ruining your life. But you would force another villager to become a refugee because they were gay?"

Nobody said no. I turned on Htan Dah; I was maddest at him, and he was probably the only one who could follow my fast, heated English. "If there was peace in Burma and you lived in a village and there was a gay Karen person," I asked again, "you would want to make that person another Karen refugee by making them leave?"

That, or my anger, shut him up. "I am interested in your ideas," he said, evenly, after a minute. "I think it is important to keep an open mind."

I shut up, too, and focused on eating rice for a few awkward moments.

"So," I said eventually. "Do you guys have sex?"

Htoo Moo and Ta Mla shook their heads while Htan Dah said, "Sometimes."

"Ever?" I asked Htoo Moo.

"No," he said.

"Why not?"

"Because, I am not married."

"What about you?" I asked Htan Dah.

"Yes," he said, nodding hard once. "I am married."

"You're *married?*"

Htan Dah laughed. "Yes! I am married."

"I didn't know that. Where is your wife?"

"She is in camp. With my kid."

"You have a *kid?*" They were all laughing at me now, because I was raising my voice. "I can't believe I didn't know that." Other things I didn't know: that everyone currently in the house save Htan Dah and The Blay, who were married, apparently, was a virgin. This extended even to kissing. Their society was way removed, literally and figuratively, from the Asian cultures in which prostitution is a mainstay. And these guys hailed from the parts that had long been converted to Christianity, which had brought premarital-sex-forbidding to the traditionally less conservative animist tribes. Htan Dah asserted, obtaining the agreement of the other guys, that if an unwed couple was caught fooling around, a village chief might force them into marriage on the spot. Htoo Moo volunteered that he wasn't actively looking for a girlfriend and that he wouldn't know what do with her even if he found one.

We'd long since finished our meals. Though I was, as always, ready to lie down by nightfall, Htan Dah told me I had to accompany the three of them into the computer room and show them MySpace again.

"Not for me," he said. "For Ta Mla."

Of course.

The rainy-season air was sticky. Ta Mla and Htan Dah and I crowded around a computer and played on the Internet, our cheeks flushed with satiety and humidity and new camaraderie. After I got up to pee, the sweaty Htan Dah stripped to the waist, so that when I got back, he was all sculpted arms and torso.

I'd assumed that the bulk underneath his baggy clothes, beneath his wide, round face, was soft. Just before I'd left for the bathroom,

I'd even tried to use as delicate a translation as possible when referring to a chubby girl on the computer screen. I shouldn't have been so surprised by Htan Dah's abs, since he'd told me earlier that sometimes, when the guys were bored, they exercised compulsively, doing marathon push-ups like prisoners or something. But his toplessness and his shape caught me so off guard that "Look at you, sexy!" fell out of my mouth. And that caught him off guard, and he laughed.

Htoo Moo, meanwhile, continued working at a nearby computer, even though it was late, and a weekend. The communication gates between us had evidently opened, though, so he interjected burning questions about American life as they came to him.

"Do you eat rice in America?"

"Yes."

"Really?"

"Yes. Usually I eat brown rice."

"Brown rice?"

"It's rice with the hull still on it. Do you know what I'm talking about?"

"No. I don't believe that."

"Htoo Moo, I swear, it's rice, and it's grown in the same way, but it's brown, because it's still hulled."

"Have you ever eat tiger?"

"*Eaten* tiger. No."

"Have you ever eat . . . monkey?

"'Have you ever *eaten* monkey,' you mean. No."

"Are there black lady in America?"

"*Ladies.* Yes. . . ."

"Are they tall?"

"It depends. What the hell do you mean?"

"What language do they speak?" Htan Dah chimed in.

"English."

"Really?"

I gaped at him, disbelieving, but before I could formulate a response, Htoo Moo said, "In America, you have cream to grow hair." He ran his hand over his baby-smooth jawline.

"Yeah. I think that's true. I think it's generally for people who are bald, though."

"Do you have that?"

"Hair-growing cream?"

"Yes."

"Yeah, totally."

Htoo Moo and Htan Dah's eyes widened at the prospect of a beard. "Really?"

"Oh, yeah. I use it on my ass."

The sarcasm seemed to translate; as disappointed as they must have been, the two laughed for minutes.

We made Ta Mla a MySpace profile, and he and Htan Dah started giving the other guys in the house tutorials in Karen as they wandered into the computer room. My work was done here. When I finally tried to leave, it was hours past my usual bedtime.

"You cannot go to your bed," Htan Dah said. "The Blay called and said he will have a very important meeting with you when he return."

It was ten-thirty. I looked at Htan Dah skeptically.

"Yes," Htoo Moo piped up. "He will be back soon. He said, 'Do not let her go to sleep. I have very important matter to discuss with her.'" As I made my way through the living room, I could hear them calling after me that The Blay was going to be very disappointed.

The other day, when I'd asked my students what they did for fun, I'd had to explain the concept of "fun" for about five minutes before anyone could answer me, and then the answers were "Nothing," "Nothing," "Watch TV," and three "Talk"s. If college kids with all the freedoms in the world were pumped about social networking, these peers of theirs, who were effectively under house arrest with no games and few books, were fucking elated. And they managed fine at it without me. Still another profile had been created by the time

I finished brushing my teeth, and when I went upstairs, every computer screen was lit, the guys gathered around and talking to each other quietly about what they'd found, looking at pictures of girls and boys Japanese and Brazilian, and scrolling through the faces of Burma, a window into a world they considered home but where some had never been and most would probably never be a part of.

VI.

"EVERY GUN that is made, every warship launched, every rocket fired signifies, in the final sense, a theft from those who hunger and are not fed, those who are cold and are not clothed," President Dwight Eisenhower famously said in his speech "The Chance for Peace." "This world in arms is not spending money alone. It is spending the sweat of its laborers, the genius of its scientists, the hopes of its children. . . . This is not a way of life at all, in any true sense. Under the cloud of threatening war, it is humanity hanging from a cross of iron." True story. By 1950, Burma was in progressively rougher shape. Where there'd been world war, there was now deeply divisive and ceaseless civil war that had brought anarchy and rebels and bandits and a total collapse of infrastructure. And things really didn't improve when the Truman and Eisenhower administrations flooded the country with weapons, driving the government to build the military machine that commands Burma to this day.

Under the chaotic circumstances after independence, Burma was vulnerable to the worst sort of people who might be interested in it: commies. "Communist control of Burma would be a great strategic advantage to both the Chinese Communists and the USSR," the CIA warned. "It would drive a wedge between India-Pakistan and Southeast Asia, facilitate Communist penetration into Indochina and the other countries of South and Southeast Asia, and in a psychological sense give impetus to the claim that Communism in Asia is an irresistible force." Preach on, State Department:

> British and American officials generally agree that the situation in Burma is deteriorating at an alarming rate, that Burma is the 'soft spot' of Southeast Asia and that because the Government and people of Burma are apathetic to the Communist threat and highly suspicious of British and American motives, it is difficult to find any way in which we can render assistance.

"Assistance" is sort of an interesting way of putting it, but in any case, some of Chiang Kai-shek's Chinese Nationalist army, the Kuomintang (KMT), had retreated into northeast Burma after their whupping by the Communist Party of China. The KMT had set up house on Shan lands, where it was enlisting warriors, organizing an army, building a resistance to Mao Tse-tung's government.

Ideological proxy war! The KMT started receiving arms, organizing, and funding from the United States of America, in the CIA's very first secret war. China had been lost to communism, and Burma was not about to be let go the same way. The US built a surrogate occupying force that ultimately comprised some 15,000 soldiers, with the aim of deliberately breaking the country into "racial and geographic units" that could be used as bases to attack China, which would also draw Chinese soldiers away from their (other) front with the States, the Korean War. But even after the Korean armistice, CIA support to the KMT continued. The Burmese government was convinced that the United States was provoking China to invade Burma, or at least trying to get Burma significantly threatened by the prospect of invasion that it would align itself with the US for protection. (*The New York Times* also reported that that was the general idea in a special report on the CIA many years later.)

Rangoon asked Washington to halt the incursion. Washington

denied, denied, denied. When Burmese soldiers killed three white guys fighting alongside the KMT, on whose bodies they said they found notebooks and diaries containing New York and DC home addresses, the US Embassy in Bangkok claimed they were Germans; Thai police concurred—two French Foreign Legion defectors and a random bandit, they said. Either way, even the United States ambassador to Rangoon was lied to about his country's involvement.* Indeed, the US was so innocent and friendly that it was kicking the Burmese government tens of millions of dollars in military aid, to help defend against threats like, I don't know, a rebel Chinese army that somehow found itself armed to the teeth with American weaponry.

Rangoon wasn't exactly fooled. It had been having enough trouble establishing peace in its democratic republic. Now, thanks to its sovereignty's being flagrantly violated by the United States, it was sweating a Chinese invasion and sparring with yet another insurgency. The Thais joined the fray, too, providing crucial support to the KMT. And also fighting alongside the KMT were the forsaken but still-trusty Karen.† Clearly, Burma's US–assisted military needed cohesion and ultimate priority in order to fight the US–backed KMT, and it began aggressively expanding under the (justifiably) paranoid General Ne Win, he of the Karen Baptist school burning of 1947. A military-run government entity opened a bunch of businesses and bought up many other existing ones, including a bank, until it held the lion's share of Burmese commerce. Civilians in government posts were replaced with soldiers. The Burmese prime minister had been doing the best he could, but the stressed government was racked with rifts that couldn't be mended, and the military was starting to take charge.

---

* When he eventually found out what was really going on, he resigned. It wasn't until more than a decade later that the Americans actually admitted to the Burmese government what they'd done.

† They weren't really wild about the Reds either: The leader of the Communist Party of Burma had called revered Karen leader Ba U Gyi a "lackey of imperialism," as communists are wont to do.

In 1958 the Burmese army, now bigger and badder and more in control, surrounded the government seat. To avoid a coup, the prime minister handed over power to Ne Win to run a caretaker government until the next elections. The War Office was running the country now. There were no royals, no colonials—there was no government that could or would even bother trying to keep the country from militarization at a time like this. The KMT ended up selling and sharing their military equipment with other insurgents. There were a fuckload of guns in Burma. A lot of them were ours.

Burma was so vulnerable that it needed to team up with those willing and able and close enough to help the government take back its country: commies. In 1961, after years of KMT occupation of Burmese land near China's border, twenty thousand People's Liberation Army soldiers came after them. Together, the PLA and the ferocious Burmese army routed the KMT at last. But that one war ended was hardly the only war going, of course.* The Shan had formed an army, in response to the Burma army's continually coming through their territory to fight the KMT. The Allies's old mighty fighting Kachin founded an armed resistance as well. And as for our protagonists, the Karen had been pushed way back away to higher border ground by the new and improved Burmese military. And now their Chinese allies had lost. They'd even suffered the death of Ba U Gyi, who had been gunned down by a Burma army unit. But whatever their setbacks, they weren't any more inclined to stop fighting than they'd ever been. Before he was killed, Ba U Gyi had laid out the four principles of the Karen revolution, principles that had become religion and law:

---

* Nor was that the end of the KMT's role in history. Throughout their tenure in Burma, they'd been dragooning villagers as workers in a burgeoning opium trade, and after their defeat, plenty of KMT stayed behind to build a hulking narcostate, some of them joining forces with Zhang Qifu, better known as Khun Sa, a.k.a. the world-famous Opium King.

1. For us surrender is out of the question.
2. Recognition of Karen State must be completed.
3. We shall retain our arms.
4. We shall decide our own political destiny.

If the Karen insurgents were going to have to wage their war from the literal and figurative periphery of the country, so be it.

Ne Win wasn't giving up, either. The period of his caretaker military government over, he'd had to cede power back to the prime minister when the people of Burma voted for him overwhelmingly in the next election. But the general thought he was the better man for the job, and nobody could stop his army from taking it. Given the recent events, the soldiers had more arms and a better excuse than ever. Besides, everybody else was doing it: Burma was literally surrounded by military dictatorships in Thailand and Pakistan, which bordered it to the west at the time.

Like the artistic young Hitler before him, Ne Win hadn't dreamt as a child of destroying millions of lives with gruesomely misguided evil. No, he wanted to be a doctor. Unfortunately for Burma, and for history, and for Htan Dah, he failed his second-year exams. So he started a coal business, but he couldn't get a foothold in an industry dominated by all those damned Indian immigrants. It's not like he was satisfied just working his job at the post office. Even when he became a military man, being a rank-and-file soldier wasn't enough, and then neither was having worked his way up to commander in chief. Shortly after the prime minister was restored to his elected office, Ne Win arrested him and dozens of other ministers and chiefs. Ne Win, warmonger, paranoid, xenophobic, racist control freak, declared himself president of Burma.

In the 1950s, Burma had hundreds of newspapers and magazines that were free to print what they pleased. Within a month after the coup, Ne Win had dismantled the free press, instituting the crippling censorship practices in place ever since. The prime minister had recently held a Nationalities Seminar to settle unrest between the increasingly armed ethnic groups and the government, but Ne Win halted the reconciliation process. He ended state scholarships that sent students to study abroad. He fired the experienced bureaucrats. Foreigners—be they aid workers, advisers, teachers, tourists—were declared verboten, as were horse racing and beauty pageants and nightclubs and Western dancing. Later, he threw several hundred thousand Indians out of Burma. Suddenly only one single crappy plane flew in and out of the country, and only to Bangkok. The military dispensed with the constitution and seized businesses in every sector, from oil to print, while loading government positions with soldiers. There was no civilian government anymore, and hardly any civilian industry. Soldiers controlled much of the economy, running it with a system of kickbacks and bribes in which every individual stood to gain as much as he was willing to exploit from others. Within five months, industrial production was down 40 percent. All major businesses were nationalized under the ruinous Burmese Way to Socialism. The only beer in the country was made by the People's Brewery and Distillery. Ultimately, Ne Win's Burma Socialist Programme Party became the only political party allowed. Burma, and any remote hope it had of overcoming ethnic tension and political aggression and total weapon saturation to become a thriving independent nation of any sort—let alone a democracy—effectively died in 1962.

In 1966, President Lyndon Johnson invited Ne Win to the United States for an official visit. Really, Johnson just wanted to make friends. America had invaded Ne Win's country when Ne Win was in charge of the army, and then Mamie Eisenhower had gone and talked shit on Ne Win's wife within her earshot when the couple had last visited. A Red scare was a good reason to intervene in a sovereign nation's affairs, but a military dictatorship enacting murderous human rights and economic policies, not so much. An independent socialist military regime was better than a Russian or Chinese communist satellite. Lunch was had. Golf was played (though Ne Win wore a metal helmet, just in case). As long as Burma was going to stay neutral, Washington was going to stay out of its business, regardless of the horrors it was about to start visiting upon its people.

VII.

HTOO MOO, unsurprisingly, did a lot of squats. The night following the MySpace-a-thon, he walked into the dining room/garage, where he stood at the end of the picnic table stretching his arms out in front of him and clasping his hands. "Have you exercise today?" he asked me, his feet planted shoulder-width apart, his knees bent as he started repeatedly dropping his ass toward the floor.

Htan Dah and I were sitting at the table with 7-Eleven spoils. Hungry and in search of supplemental calories after dinner, I'd persuaded him to come with me to the convenience store I'd discovered just a couple of blocks away, on the way toward Office Two, to buy chocolate-flavored whole milk. His swig of the little bottle I'd bought him had elicited a face of shock and confusion, followed by this verdict: "It's sweet!"

"I have, actually," I answered Htoo Moo. "I did yoga in my room this morning."

"What?"

"Yoga," I repeated. "It has a lot of stretching, and breathing, and strength building. From India. . . ."

"Oh, yes, yes, I have heard." Htoo Moo shook his head.

"It's exercise!" I said. "It can be really hard, and you can become really strong—" Htoo Moo dramatically reached his arm over his head, then his other arm out to his side, like a ballerina, then bent over with a sassy flourish. "That's not what yoga is like!" I said, and he laughed.

"If you do not exercise, you will not be strong."

"I am strong."

"I do not think so. I think you will get fat."

"I'm not going to get fat!"

"I think so."

I leveled my gaze at him and spoke slowly. "Do you want to wrestle?"

He didn't. But an hour later he did want to go for a walk to get snacks for the World Cup match later that night. He, Ta Mla, and I brought armloads of fruit back from the big roadside stall around the corner, dumping them on the picnic table. We stood around and peeled rambutan, fruit like a tiny Koosh ball, digging our fingers into tough red skin covered in wild bendy spines. The white flesh beneath tasted much like lychee, its cousin, like lightly perfumed gelatin.

"I thought this was for the game tonight," I said as we tore through the supply. "Shouldn't we be saving this?"

"We want to eat it now, we eat it now," Htoo Moo said. "It doesn't matter." And he was right, since every man in the house was about to accidentally oversleep the middle-of-the-night match anyway. Not a single alarm existed in the BA household. The guys always told me that if they just told themselves to wake up at a certain time, they would—famous last words in every culture.

"Here," Htoo Moo said, foisting half a kilo of pineapple on me. I declined, already full of pineapple and rambutan and chocolate milk. "You don't eat enough rice. You need to eat that, so you will get strong."

"I am strong."

"I don't think so."

We continued to argue about my fitness, until I finally raised my voice and my shirt, exposing my abs. "I am strong!" I yelled. "I'm solid! Do you want to punch me in the stomach? Come on. You and

me," which is a fighting colloquialism that's ridiculous to say to anyone, much less a remote Southeast Asian hill-tribe coworker peace-
activist refugee whose hands have touched neither woman nor white
person in any capacity, much less a punching one, ever in his life.

Htoo Moo laughed like a lunatic, steadying himself with one hand
on the table as he actually doubled over. He declined, and dropped
it. But when I said, minutes later, that I didn't think I was going to
shower, he insisted that I should.

"What do you care?" I asked. "Why don't you lay off me? It's chilly
outside, and the water in that trough is freezing."

"If you take cold shower," he asked, pausing to smile patronizingly
at me, "will you die—or not die?"

TWENTY-EIGHT-year-old Htoo Moo was, like Ta Mla, a human rights
documenter. A couple of times a year, he shouldered a bag carrying
whatever he wasn't wearing of nine shirts, three pairs of pants, two
pairs of shorts, four pairs of underwear, and two pairs of socks, plus a
tape recorder, six tapes, a notebook, three pens, a digital camera, a
battery charger, a kilo of sugar, cold, sinus, and stomach medicines, a
bottle of water, and 150 bucks' worth of Thai currency and trekked
clandestinely into Burma.

His most recent trip had started with a six-hour drive by BA-
arranged car, five hours in a longtail boat watching the banks of the
Salween River and a darkening sky, and two days of walking over
mountains and jungle trade paths subsisting on just sugar and found
water until he reached a village. Even by Karen standards, this settlement was pretty remote; a fish-paste purchase was a day's walk away.
At night, he slept outside on the ground, and during the day he stood
thigh-deep in a river, trying—though he couldn't get the hang of the
procedure, however effortless the villagers made it look—to help net
fish, chatting up villagers about abuses by the State Peace and Development Council. That's what the government of Burma calls itself,
which would be funny were it not tragically otherwise.

After a month, Htoo Moo walked two days to KNU headquarters to interview the prisoners-turned-porters seeking refuge there. The Burmese military has long used villagers for labor, including portering, but the past decade had seen an increase in offensives against armed opposition groups, and more offensives meant more work to be done. Consequently, there'd also been an increase in the military's filling its slavery needs with convicts.

Burma's biggest and most infamous lockup, Insein (pronounced "insane," built by the British for the crime-infested territory), is notorious, but the conditions in its other forty-three prisons are just as heinous. Detainees—who are not uncommonly arrested and sentenced without charge or trial—are generally not allowed reading or writing materials and share an overflowing bowl for a toilet with maybe eight other men crammed into their cells. With provisions for neither hot nor cold, any weather extreme is torturous, plus there's the constant threat of overt torture, should the authorities want to extort money or information. Many inmates see sky for but five minutes a day, when they are emptying their shit buckets. The few who receive medical attention risk deadly infection from used needles. Work is uncompensated and forced: weaving straw mats, making incense, plowing paddies like oxen, cleaning prison grounds. There's no soap and little medicine, except maybe on the day the International Committee of the Red Cross came to visit, which it started doing in 1999. Escaped prisoners whom human rights documenters like Htoo Moo and Ta Mla found and interviewed told how short-lived those perks were:

> They never gave us any vegetables or meat. Sometimes the ICRC would come to visit, but prison authorities told us that if we had anything to report to the ICRC we should first tell them. So when the ICRC actually came we were not allowed to say anything. When the ICRC visited, the prison authorities prepared good food for us. But when they left, they took all the food away again. The ICRC was

told that the prisoners get this food every day. But we never really received it. The ICRC left things such as cups and soap for prisoners. But we never got to use these things. The food they served when the ICRC came was curries and bean dishes, every other day we just got rice and bad fish paste. The ICRC also brought us soap, toothpaste, dishes and cutlery but the prison authorities took all this away once the ICRC had left.

And:

ICRC also brought us medicine. But we never received it. . . . We could not share our ideas or feelings with the ICRC. If we did, the SPDC [State Peace and Development Council] would put us in dark jail and they would torture us as well. We could not express any feelings, we could only tell what they order us to.

Indeed, prison authorities did bug an interview that was supposed to be confidential between a prisoner and a UN envoy in 2003. But even those Red Cross brief and insubstantial reprieves were fleeting. The organization was thrown out of the country after 2005.

Still. Whatever the hardships of being a Burmese prisoner, portering is a worse fate. Those who can afford it pay bribes to stay in prison—if the alternative is donning the dark blue porter's dress and being driven in crowded trucks to the front line.

A brutal and dangerous enslavement, portering has been feared long and wide. In *Heart of Darkness*, Marlow, whose diary entries in the book mirror the journals and experiences of Conrad's time in the Congo, describes deserted villages of natives fleeing from porter duty for the ivory trade, from which they knew they were unlikely to return alive. In Burma, porters follow soldiers, carrying woven bamboo baskets on their backs. Survivors swear the loads weigh up to a hundred pounds. Htoo Moo had pictures of the lesions the straps left in their shoulders, giant, disgusting open wounds, raw, pink holes infested with flies and maggots, as if pieces of their bodies were already dead. Porters receive little food, rest, or water and endure repeated beatings with fists and kicks and bamboo. Soldiers motivate porters who've fallen down from weakness by stepping on their necks or striking them with the butt of their rifles, and prisoners who still fail to get up are shot or left to die. When necessary, porters do double duty as minesweepers, either walking ahead of the soldiers to detonate the explosives or attempting to dig them out of the ground with their bare hands. Offenses by the SPDC—which, though the name of the government, is also what people call the army, since the government and the army are the same thing (though the army actually has its own name: Tatmadaw)—can be partially charted by the trail of porters' corpses left in their wake. By the time human rights organizations come in to investigate, sometimes all that's left to be photographed is piles of bones in navy uniforms. Though soldiers tell the porters that they'll be killed if they're captured by the KNU, some stack the odds of escaping against those of surviving their portering stint and decide to take that chance.

On his last trip, Htoo Moo had met the most recent batch of porters the KNU had intercepted; they were working at headquarters, farming and keeping house for a month or two while the soldiers questioned them for SPDC intelligence before sending them home. For a few days, Htoo Moo recorded long, heavy interviews with the twenty-eight escapees, mostly Burmans, who talked about nearly being killed by soldiers, and he even interviewed deserted Burmese soldiers, who talked about doing the killing of the porters:

> We had permission to shoot any porter that tried to flee because they didn't want the KNU to get any information about the Burmese army. I personally experienced three porters being killed by Burmese soldiers. One porter couldn't bear the burden of his pack anymore so he asked to go home but they forced him to keep going and after we had climbed another mountain he tried to flee and a soldier just shot

and killed him. Another porter actually confronted a soldier and said, "We are one; we come from the same country, is it fair to treat us like this?" The lance corporal, his name was Kyaw Oo, said to him, "Are you confronting me?" And then he shot him dead. With the last porter, in the night one of the guards fell asleep and the porter tried to flee. But there was another guard who was awake who saw him and shot him dead.

Did you use prison porters or villagers?

They were all villagers, captured and forced to become porters. But at the Kaw Moo Rah base they used prison porters. When we were on patrol we used villagers as porters.

That soldier had ended up a prisoner-porter himself, having been convicted of desertion and conscripted into portering for his former fellow military men. One of the reasons he'd run away from the army was that he'd never wanted to be a soldier in the first place; he had been arrested at a bus stop and pressed into service when he was twelve. But he felt he certainly couldn't serve after witnessing the atrocities his army inflicted on its countrymen. Some of the other escaped porters were so horrified by having witnessed SPDC abuses of ethnic villagers and even fellow Burmans that they joined the KNU. All were happy to get their stories on record with Htoo Moo.

The path out of headquarters was tricky—it was laden with land mines, and diverged at one point, where the right turn led to a rural community and the wrong one to an SPDC camp—so two KNU soldiers accompanied Htoo Moo on the walk, from dawn well into nighttime, to the next small village. They entered it to find that some sort of plague had landed on all ten houses, and most of the people there were dying. One house contained a dead boy whose father, the only family member left, was too sick to bury him. The villagers encouraged Htoo Moo to look, to bear witness, and he did.

He visited the ill and took pictures but left after a few days, because there was nothing else to be done.

By the time he'd walked two days to another village, documented the story of a boy who'd been shot with his father and brother by SPDC soldiers while cultivating rice; by the time he'd looked at the fresh bullet holes in the boy's shoulder and ass, and at the bloody track another round had grazed into the side of his head; by the time the boy had explained how he'd sent other villagers back to the field to get his brother and father as soon as he'd staggered home but it was too late, they were already dead; by the time Htoo Moo had taken pictures of the boy's wounds, which had been treated with only boiled water and cotton dressing, he was ready for a rest.

"The SPDC is coming," the chief told him.

You've never heard of Four Cuts, but it's a Tatmadaw strategy that every Karen child knows very well: cutting off the enemy's sources of food, finance, intelligence, and recruits (and, some say, their heads). Unfortunately for villagers, these sources of support include the villagers themselves, in addition to their rice, livestock, and able-bodied sons. Does this sound familiar? The military government that seized control in 1962 had learned the lessons of Western subjugation amply; some Burma army officers had even gone to London to study British warfare. Like the great colonialist power before them, Burmese soldiers in the '60s—the Karen war still raging—started walking into defenseless villages with guns blazing and burning them down, issuing orders to Karen villagers, who were potential insurgents, that they could be shot if they kept more food on their farm than was needed for one person, or traveled at night, or traveled out of their village at all, or ran from Burma army troops that were shooting at them, or didn't. Unfortunately for Htoo Moo, the Four Cuts campaign was, even decades later, alive and well.

The Burmese military had assumed, correctly, that the village where he was staying, which was in an area under KNU control, was home to some KNU members and sympathizers. A scout had spotted assailing soldiers, and it was time to go. So this is the drill: You have to flee, carrying everything you can, big heavy loads, as much rice as you can stand on your back in giant baskets, any clothes or anything else you want to own for maybe the rest of your life, your baby. Htoo Moo helped the villagers hide rice, salt, fish paste, and some extra sets of clothing among the surrounding trees before they all took off together in the early evening. Htoo Moo followed the eighty villagers along a path he hadn't noticed hidden beneath tall grass. Figuring a six-hour walk put them far enough out of harm's way, they stopped at midnight and Htoo Moo slept, finally, on the forest floor.

The next morning, he woke up to find people quickly gathering the food and family they'd brought. A scout had arrived with news of the SPDC's offensive; everyone needed to leave. Htoo Moo had slept through breakfast, and there wasn't time to make more. While people were getting ready, he sat on the ground and counted. Neighboring villages had evidently joined the flight; there were two hundred heads in the makeshift camp. They had with them one KNU soldier. Not wanting to further strain the villagers' supplies, he stalked an enormous rat he'd spied lumbering around and killed it with one strike of bamboo. When Htoo Moo smiled, pleased with his efficiency, an old man next to him laughed. "Before you woke up," he said, "I tried to kill that. I think it was already tired."

The villagers fled from seven in the morning until noon. Some of the shoeless children lost flesh and bled as their feet pounded the ground, and some of those cried silently as they ran. Htoo Moo carried his bag on his back, the dead rat in one hand, his digital camera in the other, occasionally snapping pictures of the exodus. When they stopped, he dug his fingers into the rat's skin and ripped it off. He tore the meat into pieces and went in on lunch with another man, who provided a pot containing some chilies and salt. Five minutes over a fire later, seared jungle rat was served.

Htoo Moo could finally relax: His belly was full of warm meat, and he lay back on the cool jungle bed beneath the canopy of an abundant tree. He closed his eyes as sleep started to descend upon him, and then the sound of gunshots.

Gunshots. He clutched his bag and got to his feet as the villagers started hustling. Nobody screamed. The boy with the bullet holes Htoo Moo had photographed had been carried by village men in a hammock this far, but now he jumped up and started running, new blood rushing from the wound in his ass. Htoo Moo took off, ahead of even the village chief, reaching a flat-out run, crashing shoulder-first through tall croppings of bamboo in his path, before realizing that he had no idea where he was or where he should be going. He stopped, turned around a couple of times, and considered ditching his camera. What if the SPDC caught him? What if they had him in captivity and saw that he'd been taking pictures of gun-shot farmers, prisoner-porters with skin disease, cigarette burns, knife wounds, raw and infected shoulders that bore the permanent scars of carrying, over mountains, for days or weeks at a time? He'd keep the camera for the moment, he decided. But sometimes fleeing groups ran head-on into other military divisions, and the villagers in the back had the best chance of being ambushed or taking stray gunfire from the pursuing ones. Though he felt like a coward, he fell back into the middle of the throng. Indeed, by the time they stopped at nightfall, news had spread through the crowd that one man in the rear had been shot dead.

Htoo Moo lay down but couldn't sleep. He listened to the men next to him talking. Of the two hundred people, they four had guns. They counted their ammunition and determined that they had four or five rounds apiece. One admitted that he had only three bullets left. "No problem," another told him. "You will just aim very well."

After three days of squatting and swatting bugs in the jungle, Htoo Moo told the chief that he wanted to leave. Sometimes, villagers hide out for weeks because they don't know if it's safe to go back yet. Sometimes, it never is. Sometimes, those who've had to leave behind sick or elderly or shot who couldn't run have to sneak back to bury their bodies quickly, looking over their shoulders—assuming the bodies haven't already been disposed of, burned along with the rest of the village. Htoo Moo didn't know how long this displacement was going to last, but he needed to get back to work. A hunter was making his way back toward the border, and Htoo Moo could follow him away from the escaping villagers.

"I will take you myself," the chief said. "I am ready." He was in no hurry now. He'd heard news over the radio that the soldiers had stopped at the village and weren't pursuing them. He didn't have to run, and he didn't have anywhere to go: The SPDC had killed the pigs and the chickens, then burned the village to the ground.

In the face of the oncoming attack, the KNU had set up scores of new land mines, and the old way in was no longer a safe way out. Htoo Moo and the chief trudged through the jungle for three days back to KNU headquarters, where they shook hands and parted. Soon after Htoo Moo and yet another guide started off from base, the parasites that had entered his body through mosquito spit and been multiplying in his liver burst through the cells that hosted them and flooded Htoo Moo's bloodstream. He trekked, though more slowly, through his fever, stopping when the retching brought him to his knees. "Don't rest there!" his guide screamed when he moved toward a smooth patch of soil just to the side of the path. He'd nearly knelt on a land mine. It took another two days to reach the riverbank, where he bought antimalarial tablets with his last few baht and boarded the boat toward what had, by default, become home.

"I WILL take you to Office Two for school today," Htan Dah said Monday morning. We were both, as usual, up at dawn. I'd admitted to him that Htoo Moo's driving terrified me, and I was pretty excited to hear that. I was also excited about the stack of neatly sorted and stapled papers I was carrying out of the computer room, a twelve-page workbook of English exercises for my beginner students I'd labored over all weekend, having got a better sense of their skill level the week before.

"Look what I did!" I said, holding the pages out proudly. "All this!"

"Wow," he said, fingering them unenthusiastically. "That is . . . not so much."

I swung the papers at him, hitting him in the arm. "This was really hard. This took a lot of work."

He just laughed at me. "This morning, I have interview. But I will be back in time for breakfast before we go."

The previous night, when I'd sat down next to Htan Dah in the living room as he watched Thai soaps—because, he insisted, they helped him learn the language—he'd told me that he'd been selected to interview for a journalism-school program at the University of Chiang Mai. It was a free, eight-month, highly intensive and selective course aimed at training reporters and editors from ethnic communities. I'd shot some standard interview questions at him, for practice, and promised him that they were going to ask why he should be picked.

They did indeed, he told me when he got back. He could hardly contain his awe of my powers of prediction.

As we ate breakfast, we made plans. I'd promised to take him into a city someday and to the movies, to which he'd never been, and he'd said he would take me to his camp, several hours' drive southeast, to see pictures of his wedding. This was another reason he was keen on driving me to school: Though any motorbike trip was possibly dangerous for an undocumented runaway refugee, throwing a foreigner into the mix opened up the potential for even long drives. "No one bother me," Htan Dah had said, "if I am with very beautiful white girl."

Our meandering conversations and schemes helped occupy Htan Dah while he kept me company during breakfast and dinner. He'd continued to sit diligently at the table with me, though he always finished eating before I did, with his lightning-fast shoveling and chewing. That morning, as I ground every last bit of rice into oblivion between my molars, he finally called me on it. As much as he enjoyed our chats, I was sure, his job as office manager, handling the books, the money, the cooking, hardly left him time for two-hour brunches.

"You are so slow," he said, watching me chew. "Why don't you eat fast?"

"Why should I?" I asked. "I'm not in a hurry."

"But what if you are under attack, or have to run away?"

"Htan Dah, I'm from Ohio."

"Yes, but I am refugee(!). We are taught to eat fast."

Be that as it may, we were in peacetime Thailand, so this attack seemed like an incredibly hypothetical scenario, even though Htan Dah had mentioned something about refugee camps' getting burned down on the very first day of class. But in all the times in my life I'd envisioned what it was like to live in a refugee camp, which had been approximately zero times, a camp being under attack and burned down wouldn't have entered the picture. Since I'd been unable to imagine it, and since I'd gotten the sense that Htan Dah, with his copious exclamations, had a flair for the dramatic, I'd kind of dismissed it.

So boy, did I feel like an asshole when he turned in an essay with this intro for workshop on Tuesday:

> Having been fallen a sleep at midnight, my parents, sister, aunt and I heard the children's screaming and the voice of the shelling mortars simultaneously came about, and suddenly jumped through the ladder from the top to the bottom of the house to get away from the attacking troops' ammunitions without grabbing any facility.

THE KAREN resistance had begun well armed—British occupation and World War II may have been fleeting, but weapons last a really long time—and though they had lost their chance at the capital, in the decades following independence, the KNU built the largest, richest, and most threatening insurrection in town. The rebels commanded the passages to Thailand, taxing the teak and other smugglings flowing through the porous border. By the '80s, the KNU claimed its annual income from border taxes and trade was in the tens of millions a year US, plenty to buy more guns and ammunition. Despite Four Cuts, huge pieces of what had always been Karen land in the area that even the government called Karen State were under KNU control, which infuriated the regime. Also, there was that whole bad-blood-from-being-on-opposite-sides-of-international-wars-for-more-than-a-century thing. And so in '84 the Burma army, which had historically instigated only dry-season assaults, started fighting right through the rainy season.

Which brings us to a wee Htan Dah living in Thailand with his mother. For years, small groups of Karen had stayed in the neighboring country during offensives, running from Four Cuts but returning home when the fighting subsided. This time, the Tatmadaw was intent on cutting off the KNU's black-market tradings and funding, and gaining control of the border area. It didn't retreat when the monsoons came. Now that the refugees were in as much danger as combatants were year-round, it wasn't safe for them to go home. In 1984, ten thousand refugees, including Htan Dah's family, had set up more permanent camp on the Thai side of the Moei River. And the civil war roiled on. In fact, though it was nearly forty years old, it was escalating, and no one—not the government, not the rebels, not the villagers—predicted peace anytime soon. By 1994, the fugitives totaled eighty thousand.

For a while, the asylum seekers in Thailand were safe. Though they worked as illegal and terribly underpaid and underappreciated immigrants, if they could find work at all, at least whole battalions of Burmese soldiers were less likely to march into a sovereign country to attack them. But what the Burma army could do was arm and otherwise supply and aid a different Karen group to do so, if only a breakaway Karen group would form and start attacking other Karen. Which, sadly, is what happened.

According to Karen villagers, Burmese soldiers had for years been spreading discontent with the KNU among other Karen inside Burma. KNU leadership was largely Christian, and Karen villagers were largely Buddhist or animist, and the Burma army claimed that, as such, the Karen revolution would benefit only Christians. Further, if the KNU won, they would at least marginalize and possibly kill Buddhists. And it was true that, though they didn't torture them, the KNU sometimes used villagers as porters. And it was true that the rebels often depended on the villagers' food sources, and that the government had enacted Four Cuts in retaliation for KNU attacks and to stanch the group's viability.

A monk started turning people within the KNU itself, and some of the KNU's practices made that pretty easy. Several of its leaders were using the money the organization was still earning from border taxes and selling teak to build great big houses. Rumor had it that sympathetic overseas donors were sending chocolates and cigarettes, but the guys at the top were eating and smoking them all. A Christian commander didn't allow some Buddhist soldiers to leave their posts to pray, and in swooped a monk of discontent. He preached to the Buddhist KNU soldiers that they shouldn't fight alongside the KNU because they killed Burmese, who were Buddhist. He preached that he could get them weapons, and food, and indeed he could, since he was buddies with the junta.

Eventually, in 1994, several hundred soldiers defected. They called themselves the Democratic Karen Buddhist Army, or DKBA. They didn't behave much like democrats or Buddhists, and they had a thing for killing Karen civilians. But they were most certainly an army. They passed out flyers telling the refugees in Thailand, many of whom were KNU sympathizers or soldiers or ex-soldiers or families of soldiers, to return home. Their warnings unheeded, they started attacking.

The huts at Huay Kaloke were cloaked in thick, warm Thai darkness when soldiers moved in on the seven thousand refugees living in Htan Dah's settlement in January 1997. Residents generally went to bed early; there was no electricity, and flammable materials cost money that nobody had. Htan Dah's mother wanted to provide her kids with the opportunity to study at night if they needed to, and sometimes hired herself out as daily labor, plowing fields for about a dollar a day. That was less than half of what the legal Thai workers alongside her made, but she needed to buy candles—she wasn't wild about her kids using homemade lamps, which were essentially tin cans filled with gas and set on fire—and nails, since that scavenged-bamboo-and-thatch hut wasn't going to hold itself together. The small encampment had become overpopulated, so that there wasn't even enough space to play soccer, and Htan Dah barely ever left it. But a Christian organization had donated some books, and NGOs were running a full school system now, and Htan Dah had exams the next day. He had stayed up past sundown, studying by candlelight, and had been asleep for hours by the time the sound of gunshots reached his family's shelter. Some children somewhere screamed as he leaped off the floor along with his parents, sister, brother, and aunt. Though a short ladder provided access to the hut, they jumped through the front door, over it, and onto the ground. They ran, backs and knees bent, low to the dirt, for the surrounding woods as troops set fire to the camp. The bamboo and thatch huts went up like tinder, burning hot and fast. The members of Htan Dah's family kept their mouths shut so they wouldn't catch the attention of the troops, moving quickly and quietly among the chaos. Htan Dah kept his head down, so that he hardly registered the other people running alongside them, not even noticing that some of them were in their underwear. "Please, God," he prayed. "Oh my God. Save me. Save my life," over and over again. "Please, God. Oh my God." It was a few days before his sixteenth birthday. He prayed and ran until he reached the forest, where, like everyone else, he stopped, turned around, and stood silently watching the camp—bedrooms, books, photos, shoes, a shirt woven by a grandmother—burn to the ground.

The next morning, the refugees returned to the smoldering plot. What had been a tightly packed village hours before now reminded Htan Dah of deserts he'd seen in pictures, only made of charcoal instead of sand. His family, like many others, had taken nothing when they fled. Thai authorities decided not to move the refugees from Huay Kaloke despite its clearly dangerous location just inside an unsecured border, so the residents made beds in the ash. They began slowly rebuilding, though they were afraid to continue living there. None had illusions that the Thai security posted at the front gate was there to protect them. To be sure, the refugees had long ago noted that the function of the guards was not so much keeping danger out as keeping the refugees in, collecting bribes from those who wanted to leave the camp to work or collect firewood or make a trip to the market. The assailing troops met no resistance on their way into Huay Kaloke that night. And no one stopped them less than fourteen months later when they drove vehicles full of soldiers in again.

"How do you know the Thai soldiers just let them drive right in through the front gate?" I interrupted Htan Dah as he was telling me this story in more detail later, on the reading bench in my room. That an army would allow a raiding foreign army unfettered access to seven thousand sleeping civilians—twice—was frankly a little far-fetched. The atrocities of the Karen crisis are so incredibly outlandish and untold that they often seemed to me, then, literally not credible. Even with my refugee pal, my partner in online-social-networking crime right in front of my face, I thought this story sounded a little conspiratorial and fantastic, maybe hearsay, the exaggerated gossip of victims trying to piece events together after the fact. I knew better than to find this nonintervention of people trying to kill their own people hard to believe. A lot of people in Thailand, of course, feel about Burma the way most of the world feels about, say, the entire continent of Africa. Still, I suggested, "Maybe the soldiers were trying to protect the gate, but the soldiers just went around or something."

Htan Dah had told this story before, and to several foreigners, but

never to one rude enough to suggest that he was a liar. He cocked his
head and paused. "Because," he said, crinkling his eyebrows, taken
aback because I distrusted him, and because his life had been such
that he didn't find this series of happenings hard to believe at all.
"There is only one road. The only way into the camp is through the
front gate(!)."

Everything he said was, of course, true. For a second time, Htan Dah
was awakened in the middle of the night to gunfire and shouting; for
a second time, he flew from his house with his family and the clothes
he was wearing and ran and prayed until he reached the safety of the
surrounding trees. He was again lucky enough not to run into any soldiers, who would possibly have been drunk or on speed and have asked
him if he was Buddhist or Christian. (Like the other Christians the
Buddhist soldiers encountered, he would have lied.) But this time, the
soldiers set up mortars and shelled the camp, too, while setting fire to
it. This time, a pregnant woman and mother of two was shot dead and
two girls from Htan Dah's school who'd hid near their burning house
suffered burns that later killed them. This time a seven-year-old died
of shrapnel wounds and dozens were injured, and nearly the whole
damn thing was burned down all over again.

"We accept that we were inactive," Thailand's National Security
Council secretary-general conceded. Not inactive enough. Shortly
after the first attack on Huay Kaloke, human rights workers reported
that the Thai army had forced a group of Karen males who were
seeking reprieve from the bands of murdering, torturing government
soldiers in their village back across the Burmese border. Later that
night, Thai forces loaded about six hundred Karen and Burmese
women and children onto trucks and sent them to a Thai province,
and then, a few days later, back to Burma. That same week, Thai
border soldiers turned around about a hundred men running from an
offensive, urging them to go back and fight for their villages. Three
thousand refugees were sent home from Kanchanaburi, where they
were seeking asylum, and nine hundred newly arrived women and

children were forced to walk back to their villages from which they'd just fled.*

When the UN, EU, and US heard allegations that the Thai army was sending fleeing civilians back into a war zone, they asked it to desist. The commander in chief lied outright to the press, claiming that the refugees *wanted* to go back. Bullshitting though it may have been, the army consented. For a while. In the meantime, new refugees were being denied entrance to Thailand. The refugees, as well as democracy activists inside Burma, humanitarian organizations, and the international community, asked Thailand to allow the UNHCR into the camps to provide assistance, but back then the country said it had the situation under control. Already sanctuary to evacuees from Vietnam et al. by the time the Karen rolled in, the Royal Thai Government was hardly in a hurry to recognize that it was the only option for yet another desperate population. Nor would Thai officials want to deal with the prickly Burmese junta for complicating (read: acknowledging) the dire humanitarian crisis it was causing with official international involvement. The UN had confirmed that "violations appear to be committed consistently and on a wide scale by the soldiers of the [Burma] Army against innocent villagers (particularly those belonging to the ethnic minorities) in the form of summary or extrajudicial executions and arbitrary killings which occur in the contexts of forced labour, rape, forced relocation and confiscation of property." But the commander in chief of the Thai army was at it

---

* Thailand may not have signed the UN refugee convention, but it *did* sign the Convention on the Rights of the Child, which states, "In accordance with their obligations under international humanitarian law to protect the civilian population in armed conflicts, States Parties shall take all feasible measures to ensure protection and care of children who are affected by an armed conflict," giving special protection to children who either have or are seeking refugee status and taking "all feasible measures to ensure that persons who have not attained the age of fifteen years do not take a direct part in hostilities." Additionally, the 1948 Universal Declaration of Human Rights, to which all UN members are bound, states, "Everyone has the right to seek and to enjoy in other countries asylum from persecution."

again. Karen refugees were victims of fighting inside Burma, he told
the *Bangkok Post*, not victims of warfare, which, the semantically
aware might argue, is basically the same thing. Whatever they were,
by the end of 1997, the UNHCR reported that there were more than
105,000 of them in Thailand, with the disclaimer that they could
have been grossly undercounted. It estimated, also, that it was helping only some 2,100 of them. But whatever else it might be fair to
call Thailand, it was not "inactive": Authorities were, for example,
forbidding all those victims of fighting from cutting bamboo to build
crude shelter. An NGO had to start supplying them materials.

Ultimately, after the second attack on Huay Kaloke, Thailand
accepted the UNHCR's help. It also announced that it would close
the camp, which the Karen had established more than a decade earlier, and move the residents to other camps farther from the border. Htan Dah's family set up a temporary shelter made of sticks and
a raincoat, under which they lived while they were waiting to be
shipped elsewhere.

The trucks didn't arrive for almost a year and a half. When they
did, Htan Dah tried hard not to get sick as he was driven for two
hours along narrow, winding roads to Umpiem Mai, where he and
his family, together with relocated refugees from some of the other
destroyed camps—Mae La, and Sho Klo, and Maw Ker, and Don
Pakiang, Ta Per Poo, Kama Lay Kho, Mae Ta Waw, Kler Kho, and
Mae Ra Ma Luang were attacked and burned, too—joined the growing number of inhabitants there and set up house again, this time
where the population in exile eventually became twenty thousand
strong, where Htan Dah eventually grew up and got married and had
a baby of his own, where the cold, wet winds cut through the shacks
stacked high in the hills of central Thailand, far away enough from
the attackers.

FINALLY, AFTER a week and a half in the house, I was starting to feel
secure in my routine and surroundings. I had been sleeping long,

restful, clotheless nights in my own room, going downstairs mornings, to chat with Htan Dah while he cooked, or after he finished and came to fetch me, saying, "Now you can eat, because you are always hungry," teaching class four hours a day with an hour break in between at Office Two, and coming home to Htan Dah waiting in the dining room/garage amid parked motorbikes and rice and oily piles of fried green beans, which he'd been making just for me. But when I came home the night after Htan Dah had turned in his Huay Kaloke story, not only was he not in the dining room/garage, but a dozen people I'd never seen before, including another white person, were.

I found my friend in the computer room, where I walked up behind him and ran my hand down the back of his head. "What's going on?" I asked him.

"HRD," he said. "They have come back from inside. Also, we have new volunteer. She is from Israel, I think."

Moments later, I ran into said Israeli as I walked through the living room. "Hi, I'm Abby," she said. In perfect East Coast American English.

"It's nice to meet you," I said, shaking her hand. "Where are you from?"

"New York."

I didn't know how long she'd been there in the house teeming with chattering Karen dudes, but she sure looked happy to see me. She asked me how long I was staying, and where I was from, before she got to what she really wanted to know.

"Do all these people really share one bathroom?"

"Yeah."

"Really? Do you really just fill the bowl up in that trough and like, throw it on yourself for a shower?"

I, of course, replied with another nonchalant "Yeah," as if I'd been filling up bowls of freezing water full of dead mosquitoes and throwing them at my naked body my whole life. When she asked me if I drank the same water the guys did, I responded similarly. And truly, I *had* been drinking from the two giant plastic tubs beneath the simple clay filters into which the tap water was poured. As of exactly eight hours ago. The Blay had offered me the nonbottled business on my first night, saying that "maybe nothing would happen" to me, but as that was an enormous maybe in Thailand, where you could contract not just vomiting and diarrhea but also hepatitis and typhoid from the water, I'd somewhat huffily refused. I'd been drinking and brush-ing my teeth with bottled water until that very morning, when it was explained to me that previous volunteers had partaken of the big tubs with no trouble.* Though I'd been doing it only half a day, I told Abby that it was fine, expertly filling my new role as the person who had been there longer and was, therefore, cooler.

"Well, you seem like you have it under control," she said, finding my display of assimilation utterly assuring.

"Yeah, you'll be fine. What do you do?"

"I'm a strategic planner."

Ah, so that was the source of The Blay's confusion.

"I was set up as a volunteer here through the American Jewish World Service."

And that was the source of Htan Dah's.

"Oh my god, Htan Dah," I muttered as I turned away from her to walk back into the computer room. When I got to the desk he

---

* The filters are effective indeed, though very low tech: 87 percent clay, 13 percent rice husk, pressed and fired and painted with colloidal silver. Though they cost less than ten bucks to make, water that has passed through them is safe enough for even my pampered North American gut. Perfected, based on a pre–Columbian American design in the '80s and distributed internationally by US–based Potters for Peace beginning in the '90s, the filters have eliminated diarrhea in test households in Thai refugee camps and been spread worldwide through UNICEF, Doctors Without Borders, and the International Organiza-tion for Migration to curb the death toll of the four thousand people a day killed by diarrhea from unsanitary water. The NGO Burmese Youth Project had given BA these two filters for free, before its initiative to mass-produce them for refugee camps was shut down for lack of funding.

was sitting at, I bent down low into his face. "That volunteer is not Israeli!" I whisper-yelled.

"Really?"

"Yes!" I hissed. "She's an American! Did you think she was Israeli because she's Jewish?"

Though a lot of remote hill-tribe people have probably never heard of Judaism, and would fail to associate the word "Jewish" with Israel, or maybe with anything, some Karen have learned it in their indoctrinations into Christendom. In 1812, Massachusetts Baptist Adoniram Judson set sail on the very first ship of American missionaries to go overseas. When he landed in Rangoon, he had high hopes of making converts of Burma's deeply Buddhist natives. It took him six years to get just one. The fellow was baptized on a June day, in a pond watched over by a giant Buddha. When Judson finally gave up on the Burmans and walked into a Karen village, however, he hit the missionary jackpot.

To hear a Christian tell it, the Karen, who were mostly animist and some Buddhist, had an ancient legend about a god called Y'wa, who had created woman from the rib of man. Also, the couple lived in a paradise of fruit trees until they cursed themselves by eating from the one that had been forbidden. Also, you could probably guess which kind of reptile talked them into doing so. And it got better: Karen mythology told of a younger white brother who would deliver the race when he came from overseas. Bearing a book of truth.

But then to hear a historian with a doctorate in Oriental studies tell it, the idea that those ideas got there before a Christian planted them is nonsense, and the Karen wholly and happily embraced Christianity because it was a way of attaining literacy and higher (advanced/Western) civilization while sticking it to the underestimating Buddhist Burmans.

Either way, the conditions were ideal for Judson. So many Karen converted so enthusiastically that the Karen village became the hottest missionary spot on the globe.* So much energy—and fund-raising—was being devoted to the Burmese minority that when the trend started to fade, a 1907 report announced "a very marked decline in the cult of the Karen."

Pros: The missionaries built schools. And churches. And a semi-nary. They devised a written language for one that had been only oral, into which they translated the Bible and for which they cre-ated dictionaries and a grammar book, converting many rice-farming Karen heathens into educated and potentially capable professional Christians—which was part of what made them so appealing to the colonialists.

Cons: The American missionaries were complicit in the Brit-ish smear campaign against Burmese (read: Buddhist) character that helped justify later wars, writing well-publicized tracts about how without the white man (and his god), the whole country was evil ("almost to a man dishonest, rapacious, prone to robbery, and to robbery ending in blood"), beset by evil ("ever since the English governed the country the tigers do not seem so ferocious as they were when the Burmans governed it"), and full of little brown pagan babies destined to "go down to the tomb without God and without hope." Famed supermissionary Judson even explicitly endorsed the second war as "the best, if not the only means of eventually intro-ducing the humanizing influences of the Christian religion." The prevalence of Christianity in the Western ruling government and infrastructure like churches, schools, and hospitals undermined the benevolent influence and long-established importance and author-ity of a crucial institution—the Buddhist monkhood—in a country where the social structure was already being upended. It was also a source of ultimately violent division between Karen and Burmans,

---

* It was the cause of some sectarian territorialism. As one Boston pastor wrote, emphasis his, "*This field belongs appropriately to the American Baptist churches.*"

who started burning down churches and reportedly crucifying con-verts, as well as between Karen and Karen—as anyone who lived at Huay Kaloke could well attest.

So the seminal overseas American mission of one Baptist left quite the legacy: By the time Judson died, in 1850, there were seventy-four Christian churches attended by eight thousand converts in Burma. Today, estimates of the occurrence of Christianity among the Karen in Burma range from 20 to a whopping 40 percent. And today, as in Judson's day, there are still many Christians involved in Karen aid and education efforts, albeit with the setting largely changed to refugee camps—where 60 percent of Karen are Christian. Some of these aiding and educating Christians still believe, as some mission-aries two centuries before them claimed, that the similarities in the Bible and Karen lore were inspired by God and predated Christian-ity itself. Others, who found that idea too good to believe, even for believers, have speculated that the Karen must have run into the Nestorians, mid-migration, somewhere around the eighth century, and others that an Italian missionary had made it all the way out to Karen territory and spread the story of the white brother-savior in the mid–1700s—which would explain why a British diplomat who went into Karen territory in 1795 caused something of a stir when excited villagers mistook him for their messiah.* And still others couldn't help making the leap that the Karen are one of the lost tribes of Israel. Most of my housemates had been to camp, and so been aided and educated by Christians, some very conservative: It was why the unmarried ones were avid virgins, and why, the guys told me, they'd heard of birth control only in their last year of high school, when one visiting Irish instructor spilled the beans. It was also why Eh Soe said to Abby over dinner,

"You know, I might be Jewish, too."

---

* A Muslim also visited a Karen village in 1816 and gave them a book he said contained writings about the true God, but he didn't stay long, and he wasn't so much a white guy.

Eh Soe, pronounced like the ExxonMobil fueling omnipresence Esso, was one of the newly arrived guys, just back from several months in Burma. He was short, even shorter than the other guys—who were mostly a couple of inches shorter than my five feet, nine inches[*]— with a little potbelly and black hair that stuck up perfectly on end from all over his head. He talked fast and gesticulated liberally and spit red juice from the betel nut that stained his teeth and thick lips. He was very agitated because he'd been in the jungle so long that his Yahoo email account had been deactivated for inactivity. He was also very agitating to me.

There's no privacy in a village, much less in a packed refugee camp, or a Karen hut. But though dudes wandered in and out of my room at will, they assumed they shouldn't wander in too much when the white girl was actually in there, and certainly never at night. I'd been somewhat selfishly using their discriminatory politeness to my advantage. This was a safe house and place of employment, after all, but after my screaming-cold after-dinner showers I stretched out in the privacy of my own space, nude under the sheets, reading books and writing notes in the silence, listening to the call of the tokay lizard in the ceiling come like clockwork, every night, once a night, calling out a midpitched and perfectly articulated "uh . . . oh," and then waiting a couple beats before another "uh . . . oh," and then another one of those again before, with longing and decreasing determination, "oh . . . oh . . . oh," while I listened below him, beaming, luxuriating in the calm and euphony and fresh cleanliness.

Eh Soe was either unaware of or completely indifferent to the etiquette the guys and I had established, and when I got out of the shower that night I found him on my reading bench. He'd set up

---

[*] I asked Htan Dah once how tall he was, and he responded, "Who knows?" The practical answer was that he was a little bit shorter than I. But I said reflexively, stupidly, "You should know how tall you are." For what? So he could get on a roller coaster? Get a driver's license? Tell a doctor at an annual checkup?

camp with a big blue mosquito net, a cell phone, and a pack of che-roots, and was smoking one of the long, thin, supercheap cigars.

"Oh, Eh Soe," I said with insincere apology, as if I were explaining to a customer service representative that there'd been some kind of mistake. "I sleep in here."

"Okay," he said.

"So . . ." I stood in the doorway, and he didn't make a move. "I'm about to go to bed."

"Okay," he said, and continued chatting on his cell phone and smoking, while I begrudgingly put my dirty clothes back on and got into bed, tossing exasperatedly around as he kept me up for hours.

Abby, on the other hand, was not about to put up with such sys-temic disregard for personal space and such an absurd bathroom-to-users ratio, and announced that she was moving out, into the vacant little house next door, and would come over just to work and eat.

It *was* pretty hectic in there. Eh Soe was one of several guys who were back. One of the coordinators from Bangkok had come up to Mae Sot for several days of meetings, as had the guy who recruited bright young future refugee activists from the camps, who'd brought with him the newest crew of recruits, who had collectively been arrested en route and spent five days in Thai jail before paying thirty-five thousand baht—a staggering $900, a huge blow to BA's budget—to get out. (When I asked one of them how jail was, he said just, "Boring and dirty.") Some international human rights documenta-tion organization that was going to train staff had arrived, plus Abby, plus Htan Dah's wife and baby, who were taking a reprieve from the hard rain in camp, where, Htan Dah liked to tell me, the monsoon-season climate and insufficient shelter "kills kids."

One upshot of the flurry of activity was that Htan Dah had less time to cook. The second morning of the new order, he bought a pumpkin and asked me if I could do something with it, plus potatoes. Did I know how to make potatoes? "For my kid," he said. "I want him to eat potatoes, so he can grow up strong like American." Really, the problem was that when Htan Dah stuck some rice in his son's mouth, he immediately spit it back out.

"You're in a lot of trouble," I said, "if that kid doesn't like rice."

He laughed, but then said, forlornly, "Yeah."

That night, after class, I got busy in the dining room/garage, chopping onions and garlic and chilies for a pumpkin curry simmered in coconut milk. The Blay and Eh Soe and Htoo Moo all found my doing culinary labor hilarious, and made fun of me as they passed through. "Ooooh, *you're* cooking?" then laughing, that sort of thing. That frazzled me, combined with the fact that it was hot as balls outside and hotter still next to the gas range, and the guys were all getting hungry and I was making food for the whole group, food I was afraid they might hate. Though I'd seen my father do up fried potatoes a thousand times, I'd never actually done it myself, and Daddy hadn't been using a soybean-oil base and a wok. "Yes, I'm making dinner," I barked at Htoo Moo. "And if you don't like it, you're fucked."

The diners waiting at the table watching me laughed at this. "No," Htan Dah said, his son in his lap, his eyes on fire. "We don't fuck. We eat."

The guy who was bored in prison said the potatoes smelled burned. One of my students from Office Two said the curry tasted like Thai food, which it was. I asked him if he liked Thai food. "Some. Not all," he said, then got up and walked away from the table, leaving his mostly full plate behind. Most of the other guys said the curry was too sweet (by which I believed them to mean that it didn't contain fish paste), but Htan Dah and Abby and I ate ourselves sick. Htan Dah even asked me if I would make it again sometime, and I kept asking him if he wanted me to make it exactly the same, because I wanted him to keep telling me he really liked it, and he kept saying "Yes," and I was happy, "because," as I wrote in my notes, "I am Queen Dork."

"What do you normally eat here?" Abby asked me. I told her that the guys ate only twice a day but that wasn't enough for me, so I'd

been supplementing my Karen rations with dairy from 7-Eleven.
After dinner, we went to pick up yogurt, and she tried to get a better lay of the land. Were you supposed to say Burma or Myanmar?
(Burma.*) How was I managing to sleep on the floor? (I wasn't. The
air mattress I'd brought was the best fifteen bucks I ever spent.) So,
what was going on in Burma? (That was kind of a long and intense
story. I'd email her the synopsis I'd emailed my family and friends.)
Okay, she'd look it up on Wikipedia. What was I doing here? (Who
could say? Truly, I'd just come across a program for teaching in refugee camps on the Thai-Burma border a couple of years ago when I
was dicking around on the Internet and hadn't shaken the urge to
get involved—and get informed about something that sounded like
a pretty big deal but, for some reason, nobody seemed to have heard
of. So here I was.)

I bought ten yogurts, and stuck them in the refrigerator when
we got back to the house. Besides ants and an old melted popsicle,
they were the only items in there; my roommates, who weren't used
to having refrigerators or electricity, didn't keep leftovers around.
There certainly wasn't Tupperware in the house. But then, in just a
few days, it was just ants and melted popsicle again. The yogurts had
been eaten.

Abby told me that I should write my name on my food. There was
no ownership in the house; if someone bought a bike, other people
rode it. If someone bought food, people ate it. Marking my name
on my goods seemed way too douchey. Bitching about my loss to a
roomful of broke exiles, though, I was totally okay with.

A few hours after hearing me do so, Htan Dah walked me over to

---

* It was a small but consistent form of resistance, reminding yourself and anyone who
heard you that the government that changed the name is illegitimate, and sometimes giving you an excuse to explain the existence of that illegitimate government when someone
asked why you called it Burma instead of Myanmar. The United Nations and *The New York
Times* may have adopted the name change, but *The Washington Post* and even the United
States government had not. Most important, our housemates—and the organization we
were working for—called it Burma, and if that was their call, that was the call for us.

the refrigerator. He opened it and, with a big smile, showed me what he'd bought: yogurt. Corn yogurt, with kernels of corn and also a few fat red beans in it. It was pretty good, if a little unsettling, though I mocked it to Abby at dinner that night when Htan Dah was talking to someone else in Karen, using English I thought was too fast for him to understand.

"You don't like corn yogurt?" he asked, looking right at me when I looked up.

I swore that I did, that corn yogurt was my favorite yogurt, and had to start buying it to prove it, and to unburden my wretched conscience.

With two divas now dining at the house, Htan Dah started straying from his basically pork-and-green-bean-only market acquisitions and bringing home crazy ingredients: Cauliflower. Tofu (which he chose poorly, as the sopping bag of it smelled like so much ass that, however it broke our hearts, we had to throw it away). Tomatoes. Onion-filled omelets now made an appearance at every breakfast. Abby and I resolved to do some bridging of the cultural culinary gaps ourselves and make dessert as a lunchtime treat. At the end of the week, on Abby's third day, we bought five apples, two pineapples, a cantaloupe, a watermelon, and five bars of shitty chocolate, the only kind of chocolate in Mae Sot (which still cost $4). It wasn't like we could bake an apple pie in a wok, so fondue it was.

"We made lunch!" I said to Htan Dah, retrieving him from the computer room after we melted the chocolate over the range and set sliced-fruit-brimming bowls on the table.

"Who?" he asked. "You and the Jew?"

"Htan Dah." I shook my head curtly and lowered my voice. "I already told you that you can't call a person 'the Jew.'"

"Why not?"

"We've talked about this!"

We had.

"She is not a Jew?"

"She is a Jew! But you can't call her that."

"Why not?"

"I don't know! It's rude! It sounds racist or something! You just don't do that in our culture." He refrained from conceding that anything I was saying made sense. "Anyways, you know her name!"

Most of the guys had never had chocolate, which I'd anticipated based on Htan Dah's reaction to the chocolate milk. But it went over way better than the pumpkin curry. "Very good," Eh Soe said, stuffing a piece of watermelon dripping with juice and melted candy into his mouth. He nodded at the spread. "Once a week."

Ta Mla exploded in, effulgent, positively glowing, from outside. He rattled off an excited story in rapid-fire Karen before translating very slowly for Abby and me. He'd run to the gas station, where he'd turned around and found himself face-to-face with a cop. "Come with me," the officer said. Ta Mla panicked but followed him, since he didn't have any choice. When they arrived at the cop's truck, he asked Ta Mla to help him load some wood into it. After he did, the cop said "Thank you," hopped in his vehicle, and drove away. Ta Mla had thought it was all over, right there, that he was getting arrested, again, on a bright Friday morning before lunchtime on the first rainless, sunshiny day in weeks. Close call. I'd never seen him happier. Still, he unconsciously clutched his gut while he talked. Abby and I winced; imagine the horror of a Thai cop coming up to you in a Thailand you weren't supposed to be in and speaking to you in Thai that you barely understood. Ta Mla didn't have the English to describe this feeling adequately, though he tried.

"The police," he said, pausing lengthily to choose his words, "is . . . suck."

Abby's eyebrows went up as she gave a somewhat confused laugh, then looked at me.

I shook my head. "I've been trying to teach them that it's a verb."

In class, we were plugging away at practical grammar. My afternoon beginner class seemed frustrated, at the scope of the work I was doing in the amount of time I was attempting to do it, and at their inability to communicate with me on the level they wanted to. My being there speaking English in front of them every day just exacerbated their desire to master the language, and my trying to communicate with them made me frustrated that I didn't speak Karen. But we were still making progress. Some of my morning sessions went swimmingly, continuing with workshops and writing exercises and covering verb tenses and number agreement that I often felt they comprehended, and the successes made them happy and upbeat and say "Thank you" afterward. In both classes, I got giant smiles whenever I said "Good!" like I meant it, which I did. My students were hard workers, attentive, incredibly eager, and their English skills, which they were getting more comfortable showing me, were at least as excellent as I imagine many Koreans' must be. Htan Dah said something to me about present continuous tense, which, had I not looked it up practically the day before, I couldn't have named to save my life. When, once, as I wrote a sentence on the dry-erase board, he said, "That's passive voice," I started laughing so hard that I had to put my marker down. "I love the shit that you know, baby," I said, and if I could whistle, I would have.

Burma boasts one of the poorest education systems, monetarily—and dare I say *the* poorest, philosophically—in the world. A lot of its schooling amounts to an attempt at systematic brainwashing, and even that is underfunded, with education getting about 1 percent of GDP by even the sunnier estimates. The Burmese government reports that the nation's adult literacy rate is more than 90 percent, which a lot of people think is a lie, and which seriously contradicts the government's own estimate that less than 20 percent of its citizenry could read, reported in its 1986 application for Least Developed Country status in a bid to get special international support. The high figure seems further unlikely since only half of Burmese children are enrolled in secondary school.

That's way more of the population than receives education in, say,

Afghanistan, but "education" in this case is something of a misnomer. Memoirist Pascal Khoo Thwe reported that when he enrolled in class in England after escaping Burma, he was weirded out by the exercise of expressing an opinion, for which he had no model or practice. Instruction in the schools is so inadequate that tens of thousands of students subscribed to magazines with names like *Educator* and *Goal* that contained grade-specific educational supplements—until 2008, when many of the publications were banned by the Ministry of Education via the Press Scrutiny and Registration Board. Parents who want their children to go to high school may have to pay in cash and labor, which many don't have the means to provide. Teachers are so underpaid as to fall into the general population of desperate and starving, which makes them susceptible to Burma's widespread culture of graft. To pay their bills, some wring bribes from their students by teaching only some of their lessons during the school day and the rest during expensive tutoring sessions after hours, or selling them overpriced goods they feel obligated to buy, or exam answers, or good grades on exams. One of my students, Wah Doh, a tiny twentysomething kid with energy entirely out of proportion to his size, started high school in a big city in Burma but moved to a refugee camp over the border when he couldn't afford to pay his teacher for the next grade level.

And that's in Burma proper. Karen villagers endure so many attacks and so much running and instability that they generally don't even have enough food, much less school supplies or money to buy them. As we've established, the best place to get an education in Burma is in Thailand, where a force of Karen leaders and eager beavers and European and American nationals and local Thai workers and authorities and scruffy white bachelor's-degree-holding volunteers and Christians and Jesuits and Japanese bust their asses to ensure the education of displaced Karen like Htan Dah—which is why he could articulate more grammatical rules than I could. Though it was all pretty slapdash at first, the NGOs have had a long time to get their incredibly complicated act together.

In 1996, the Committee for Coordination of Services to Displaced People in Thailand, the network umbrella of NGOs providing said services, conducted a survey to determine the educational needs of refugees from Burma on the Thai border. A year later, the Karen Education Project was launched. Today, school services are administered to the Karen refugee camps through a remarkably coordinated international NGO patchwork of immense scale and efficiency. The camps' more than sixty schools and one thousand classrooms provide nursery, primary, secondary, and post-secondary instruction in which students are taught four languages (English, Karen, Burmese, Thai) and a standard range of subjects (math, science, health, social sciences, geography). There are courses outside of school, too: vocational skills from blacksmithing to baking to goat raising, crafts such as soapmaking, literacy programs, HIV awareness. Most schools offer two periods of art classes, including sewing and music and drawing, per week, which is more than my elementary school outside Cleveland had. World Education, based in Boston, offers money and materials and training for special ed and operates schools for deaf and blind students. More than half a dozen different organizations hold training for teachers in curriculum mapping, classroom management, general teaching skills, and more than a dozen other subjects. The Shanti Volunteer Association from Japan operates a library program. Handicap International works on mine-risk education and social inclusion, in addition to holding workshops on how to produce and use prosthetic devices.

Or as Ta Mla put it in his workshop essay, "Learning in Refugee Camp":

In the camp, there are many different kinds of learning to learn. For example, agriculture, leadership management and teacher preparation course as so on. Therefore, if you want to join any courses you can chose, it is the student's choice but you have to site entrance exam. The students who fail the entrance exam, they do not allow to attend even they really want to join in.

Through doing exercise, we can work together with our friends if we are not sure as well as we can ask teachers to explain. We can do separately if we feel that is no problem in it. If any students feel unhappy, we can inform teachers in order that to do something on us for preparing medicine. We are studying in school on Monday to Friday in every week. Every weekend, we have a holiday to relax ourselves and hand out with our friends as well. School started in the morning at 9:00 to 12:00 every day. In the lunchtime, we have time for an hour. In the evening at 1:00, we started again and the school is over at 3:00 in an evening. . . . In the evening at 6:00 to 9:00, we have to attend night study. We usually go to bed at 12:00 in every night and we feel very happy at school.

Together, these organizations serve some forty thousand students. That makes this education program bigger than at least 98 percent of school districts in the United States. Enrollment is near 100 percent, and the dropout rate as low as 3 percent. And they pull it all off in bamboo-and-leaf structures with no electricity. Thailand doesn't allow refugees from Burma to erect permanent buildings on its soil. Karen refugee "schools" registered the highest proportion (100 percent) of temporary classrooms of all UNHCR–surveyed refugee education programs, including Iraq's. Some of these Karen students are packed more than fifty to their classrooms, which are divided by bamboo screens. In an intensive 2005 education survey, the biggest student concern by far was that classrooms were too crowded and noisy. This, not surprisingly, was the same overwhelming complaint of the teachers, in addition to their salary being too low (a little more than $10 a month).

Yes, they do it all on an annual budget of $7 million. If you're wondering who puts up that cash, the answer, incidentally, is that you do—12 percent of it, anyway. The United States Agency for International Development is on the case, and the bulk of the rest is kicked in by "other" (charity, church, private) donors and the

Netherlands. But the programs are increasingly underfunded, with a shortfall of more than half a million dollars in 2008. Plus, they use the curriculum of the Karen Education Department, which is, naturally, unaccredited, which grants graduating students a certificate that is completely worthless outside of their refugee camp. Not that they have a lot of places to take it anyway. Two online courses are available through Australian universities for a lucky few students: Seventeen graduated from them in 2006. But then what? World Education trains some high school graduates to become teachers for the new classes. There's a post-secondary Further Studies Programme, a Leadership Management Course, and an English Immersion Programme, but there are very limited openings. For the most part, even those with schooling and skills have nothing to do. Wah Doh had gone through several years of both FSP and EIP, but he was as illegal and unemployed and prospectless as ever. Some education workers in the camps have become, in addition to their many other duties, lobbyists trying to cajole the Thai government into letting refugees leave the camps for Thai university. Godspeed to them.

Coming from such a drastically different and faraway culture, I built on this educational foundation with inadvertent lessons in the random and semi-useless. I mentioned that as a teenager I'd had braces, but nobody knew what I was talking about, and when I explained what they were, everybody thought I was crazy. "Most Americans aren't born with perfectly straight teeth. Haven't you ever noticed that Americans you see in pictures usually have straight teeth?" They hadn't, but I guess you wouldn't, if no one had ever told you that you should care. When I told them that the orthodontic device cost a few thousand US dollars and that millions of Americans got them, they were speechless. Then one of them finally asked, "Why?" When one of my students saw my credit card, she asked me what it was. Abby, too, had encountered this information gap when she ran out of money on her Thai cell phone. She pressed The Blay, through his repeated

*No*s, as to whether it was possible to add minutes over the Internet. He finally conceded, "Yes, you can do it on the Internet"—adding, by way of explaining why that wasn't possible, "but you need 'credit card.'" I passed my plastic around for show-and-tell, trying to describe how it worked, which some people sort of understood, but most people didn't. When I wore my glasses to class, I brought along my contacts in their case and opened it for exhibition. After I described how I put them in, one of my students asked if he could try. (Absolutely not.) One day, at my afternoon class's urging, I took down a list of things they wanted me to take videos of and send to them once I got back home, things they'd heard of but never seen. This is what it says in the margin of my school notes from that day:

-clubs
-strippers
-city/skyscrapers

And though he wasn't one of my students, Htoo Moo, too, found me endlessly enlightening.

"Why do you think I have dark skin and you have white skin, and I have eyes like this and your eyes are like that?" he asked me one day as we took a break on a grassy knoll. We'd gone for a bike ride, so I wouldn't get fat.

"Evolution and migration, I guess."

He shook his head. "That is stupid."

"What? It's not stupid. Do you know what I'm talking about?"

"Yes, I have heard. I don't believe that."

"Really? I think most people believe that."

"Crazy people."

"So you believe that God made you look Asian or something?"

He shrugged. "Also, you have all this." He reached over and tugged on my arm hair. "So much of this. Why do you have all this?"

"It's really not that much."

"Yes, I think so."

"That's only because you're freakishly hairless."

It was hot outside, but not oppressively, another lovely and non-raining day. It was a perfect day for Frisbee, one of which I'd carried nearly ten thousand miles across land and sea only to have Htoo Moo scoff at me when I'd asked him to play earlier.

"Come on," I said, trying again now. "Can't we please play Frisbee? It's exercise! It can be really hard if you play it right."

"That is a game," he said, which was what he'd said earlier.

"It's a sport!" I said, which was what I'd said earlier.

"Maybe for a girl. Or children."

Frustrating as that answer was, it was at least less heartbreaking than Htan Dah's. "How can I play a game sometimes when there is a war?" he asked me back at the house.

He was, understandably, having a stressful day. The guys needed to make time for class because they needed to speak English to spread information to and from BA trips into Burma, but they also needed to keep BA running to be able to make those trips. That week, the week Abby and the guys from inside and the international human rights documentation organization trainers and the staff coordinators and the new staffers arrived, everyone was bogged down with conferencing and report making. One day, morning classes were canceled for meetings. Another day, Ta Mla and Htan Dah were absent, and then someone else was. At the beginning of another morning class, Wah Doh used his new letter-writing skills to compose me a note:

To,

Teacher

I feel a little bit sick. So, please let me to take a rest for oneday.

Sincerely,

Wah Doh

But then, finally, after a full week of meetings and two full weeks of teaching, everyone felt comfortable with me and had more time and turned in their homework and together we pressed grammatically onward—coordinating conjunctions, and conjunctive adverbs, and "We use articles before singular nouns, you guys, seriously, in English, every time"—starting off the next week with revitalized attendance, including several new beginner students who'd just returned to live in Office Two from a trip inside. Except then, one morning, though he'd left Office One on a motorbike immediately behind Htan Dah and me, Ta Mla didn't show up for class.

VIII.

HISTORICALLY SPEAKING, Thais kind of hate the Burmese. In the sixteenth century, one of Burma's fierce conquering kings, Bayinnaung, vanquished kingdoms from India to Laos, gaining still more territories when regions preemptively surrendered at the very prospect of his attack. When he asked his next-door neighbor Siam for a white elephant, that sacred animal of Buddhist reverence, it refused. Bayinnaung's army invaded and took four, plus the king, along with thousands of other captives, and sacked the capital, Ayutthaya. Then the crown prince of Siam slew the crown prince of Burma on elephantback in battle. Then, in the eighteenth century, Burma's King Alaungpaya launched his own invasion of Ayutthaya, grand city of temples and art and palaces covered in gold, and demanded submission as the emperor of the universe. When Siam refused, Alaungpaya took Chiang Mai and all of what is now northern Thailand, and re-sacked Ayutthaya, burning the whole magnificent thing to the ground.

To this day, a lot of Thais are still pretty mad about that, and the relationship between the two countries has continued to smolder. Every Thai student learns that the jerky Burmese committed atrocities against them and their capital. Burmese military officials have been overheard at embassies making fun of the Thais for being whiny bitches. Newspaper clippings document scuffles that still go down on the border: "Thai and Burmese troops have clashed twice in the past two years"; "Four Thai rangers were reported to have confronted 100 Burmese soldiers on the border near Phu Nam Rawn after the troops intruded into Thailand. . . . After tense negotiations the intruders stepped back into Burmese territory with the excuse that they 'did not see the Thai flag' which fluttered on a tall tree."

And so, historically, the Thais have found common cause with the KNU, which happened to have an army positioned between them and their former war enemy. They had some common ideology, too. Though factions of communist leanings and alliances within the KNU developed and caused rifts in the early days, the organization ended up even more staunchly anti-communist than it had been during its alliance with the KMT. (Super-Christian, as well, with a Seventh Day Adventist president at its helm, strictly barring drugs and adultery and even booze.) These Karen may have been rebels, but they were no pinkos. Eventually they were wearing shirts that said "Karen Freedom Fighter: Anti-Drug, Anti-BSPP [Burma Socialist Programme Party], Anti-Burmese Communist . . . KAW THOO LEI—Never Accept Communism." It was a pretty smart thing to put on a shirt. Who wouldn't help these drug-eschewing, communist-hating Jesus-lovers?

Well, not the United States and all its arms and soldiers and democracy, which is probably what the KNU was going for. But Thailand did! In the '60s, the country was terrified that the tide of communism might wash right over it. It was fighting a commie uprising within its own borders; China was supporting communists in Burma, some of whom were making worrisome alliances with the ethnic Shan armies on the northern border; the Karen had fought alongside the Thai- and US-backed KMT, had been a solid buffer against the Burmese for the British, and controlled plenty of teak to be plundered; and the Thais never really liked the Burmese anyway. So they sold the Karen arms and provided them sanctuary on Thai soil.

But nothing paves over old hatreds like money. As Thailand developed politically and economically, it made friends with Burma on paper, cutting a trade agreement in 1990. And though the two countries have had a few mild modern military skirmishes, a full-on Burmese declaration of war on Thailand isn't much of a threat anymore. But as a vestige of the good old Red Scare days, Thailand was, as I soon realized, still KNU-friendly.* The Burmese exile paper *The Irrawaddy* mentioned a "KNU colonel"† who was arrested in Thailand for transporting illegal migrants and firearms—which sounds pretty serious—but almost immediately released. A report in the Thai newspaper *The Nation* told of an accusation by the Burmese government that the Thais were giving leftover ammunition to the Karen guerrillas after joint US–Thai Cobra Gold military exercises. When my housemates' arrests led to jail, they often called the KNU, which sent someone who could negotiate a cheaper bribe to get them out. When they made car trips inside Thailand, they were accompanied by KNU soldiers, in whose company they could more likely pass through Thai checkpoints.

Without KNU soldiers, my coworkers, who didn't even have citizenship papers from Burma, much less documents saying they could hang around Thailand, traveled at great risk. The UN issued cards to some refugees that allowed them to travel in certain places, but the system for dispensing them was erratic, dependent on the camp where you were registered and when you'd got there. Htan Dah's wife, for example, had a pink card and could travel back and forth from camp to Mae Sot. But neither Htan Dah nor Htoo Moo nor Ta Mla had cards, and so technically they could travel nowhere without the possibility of arrest.

The Blay was the only one who could go wherever the hell he wanted, because he had the best card of all: a Thai citizen ID. One of my students had told me that these were available for eighty thousand baht—more than $2,000. I thought this a hefty price for some paperwork at

---

* Which is to say KNLA-friendly. Though technically the KNU is the political wing and the KNLA is the armed wing of the KNU, KNU leaders are commanders in the KNLA and have guns, and KNLA soldiers are in the KNU, so "KNU" is used colloquially to refer both to the political wing and the army.

† See?

the embassy or whatever, but of course it turned out to be an entirely black-market affair. Htan Dah explained to Abby and me over dinner one night that refugees could pay a series of huge bribes to Thai cops, who'd then do some paperwork and photo fudging that would allow the refugee to take on a legal Thai identity—of a dead Thai person.

When the Karen settled on the Thai-Burma border, they settled on both sides of it. Had the British drawn their border a little differently, all those Karen may have ended up Thai Karen. Which probably would have been fine with the Karen and the Thais, who got along relatively well. "As regards those populations that are dependent on the King of Siam," wrote a French archeologist appointed to the area at the turn of the twentieth century, "there is a hierarchy with the Siamese at the top of the social ladder and the Kariengs at the bottom. They all live quite content with their lot, moving in their proper spheres with some degree of independence." In the late 1800s, Thai Karen were granted citizenship by King Chulalongkorn. The ruler was fond of the race—and of writing poetry.

> So tranquilly they plant their rice,
> birds in paradise, the dense woods.
> Glad bodies entice; minds at ease,
> they scorn worldly progress.

He also wrote one about how Karen girls were hot but stinky.*
But some Karen settlers ended up as Burma's Karen, and some of those are now refugees, with citizenship in no country. If Htan Dah

---

* "Girls, girls; these Karen are lovely,
hair bunned with pins comely, so fair,
decked with pins richly, at great cost.
Their faces talced, they're so, so demure.

"Frisky dances; the girls' glad steps whirr.
But, if you approach, bad odour—
robed in homespun smocks."

had eighty thousand baht—more than thirteen years' worth of his wages—he could start calling around to people who knew people who could put him in touch with a Thai Karen village headman who knew a family who had a son that had been born within a few years of Htan Dah and had died. Over a period of many weeks, he told us, he could travel to the village, meeting the family, and to local Thai police precincts and administrative offices, hemorrhaging money to every person who helped him in the arduous process of assuming the citizenship of the dead guy.

At this point, Abby and I piped up that people paid a lot of money for fake IDs in the United States, too.

"Why do you buy fake ID in the United States?" Htan Dah asked.

"To buy beer," we said, and Htan Dah kind of looked at us like we were idiots, which, at the moment, we were.

The Blay came from a big, relatively well-to-do family that had pooled serious resources to buy their son the safety of a dead man's life in Thailand. All Htan Dah had was a KNU card that identified him as a member of the organization, to use as a bargaining tool with Thai cops. It never got him out of paying bribes, but it had so far kept him away from prison or deportation. It did have the downside that if he ever wanted to resettle to the United States through the United Nations, it proved him an actual card-carrying member of a terrorist organization. But Htan Dah wasn't planning on resettling anyway, because he thought it amounted to abandoning his "duty" to his people. He was born on January 31, 1981, the thirty-second anniversary of the day the Karen rebels declared war, earning him the "Htan," or "resist, against," in his name. On his application to become an employee of BA, under the question of how long he thought he'd work for the organization, he'd written, "As long as it takes." Deciding to get the KNU card was no contest.

The day that our morning class had been canceled for meetings, Htan Dah had driven me to the post office to mail some postcards. Inside, as I got in line, he retreated to a corner, then came over and whispered to me that he wasn't legal there, as though I'd forgotten, so maybe I should try another, faster line, then retreated again, came back and whispered that maybe I should just stay in the line I was in so as not to draw attention to us, gave a little nervous laugh, then walked tightly back to his corner. When I finished and turned around to give him the tilted "Let's go" nod, the smile that broke open exhibited more relief than I'd ever seen on anyone's face.

A couple of days after Ta Mla's near arrest at the gas station, Ta Mla drove around town having his picture taken and taking it to the right people to get his KNU card. It was the closest thing to even a modicum of protection he could obtain, but still, it wasn't enough.

IX.

Wed, 19 Jul 2006 07:49:47 -0700 (PDT)
To: HelloFromThailand list
Subject: Fuck the police

Yesterday, one of my students was forty-five minutes late for class. He'd gotten a ride to the other office, where we hold the sessions, from another BA worker. Mu Na suggested we start anyway, and Htan Dah said, "Yeah, maybe they got arrested," which I laughed at, because I thought he was joking. Not so much. It's about two miles from the office in which we live to the one in which I teach, but Ta Mla and That Khaing were stopped by the police and detained on the way there. They showed up eventually, as the cops had just wanted to be paid off. They kept That Khaing and told Ta Mla to go get them what they asked for; he returned with a bottle of 100 Pipers whiskey, which he bought with money pooled from the rest of the staff, and they both were released.

So they walked into class, which we hold on the tile floor of the main room of the office/house, and they told their story. They left one minute behind Htan Dah and me, so I was surprised they'd had trouble. "We passed a checkpoint," Htan Dah said. "Didn't you see it?" No, dude. I *wouldn't notice a Thai police checkpoint unless it sat on my face, as it is of absolutely no consequence to me. Htan Dah hadn't panicked as we'd driven by because he'd assumed, correctly, that he wouldn't be stopped if he was wrapped in white girl. We all talked about how cops sucked and the situation sucked and not being legal sucked for a few minutes, and then all the students just looked at me. I said something too quickly and quietly for them to understand about how I felt stupid now, because it seems ridiculous to tell Wah Doh that the sentence he wrote contains a verb tense inconsistency when Ta Mla and That Khaing are sitting in the corner trying not to throw up because ten minutes ago, they thought they were going to jail.*

The other day I found out that for $2,500, the refugees can get citizenship papers. As I mentioned in a previous email, these guys only make $13 a month, so they could obviously never afford it without a lot of outside help (before considering the logistics of it, I asked in response to this information, like a total jackass, "So, are you trying to save up?").

So basically, I've decided to buy Htan Dah (whose name, by the way, means "resist," as in injustice) his papers. He's really smart, and dedicated, and while a lot of these guys are applying for resettlement with the UN and trying to leave the country forever and forget about Burma, he's not leaving until either democracy is established or he dies. He has a chance to go to a journalism school in Chiang Mai on a scholarship from some do-gooder American organization, where he'd take intensive English courses, and learn about, well, journalism, and I think he could really make a difference in this struggle, and in this organization, between his intelligence and his abilities and his charisma. But he can't go to Chiang Mai, because he's illegal, and if he's caught on the bus he could be jailed, or deported, and his refugee status cripples him in so many ways with the work he's trying to do (besides in, like, trying to go buy eggs). Anyways, he's my friend, who keeps me company and makes me nasty-Thai-chicken-less meals, and if any of my friends back home told me that two grand would save his or her life, I would, of course, find a way to get a hold of it. I've got an apartmentful of furniture that cost about that much, and I guess I feel like a person is worth more than a couch set and a bookshelf.

I've heard a dirty rumor that these emails get forwarded to people who forward them to people who forward them to people, and my goal is to get at least fifteen of those people to pledge to send me checks for $100 (I've got three promises already). I hope others will make up the difference with smaller donations of $50, or $20, or even $10, and if that fails, I'm going to strip down to my skivvies, hold a bikini car wash at the end of the street, and earn the money one soapy motorbike at a time. If you're not moved by the plight of the refugees, maybe you'll consider patronizing your faithful friend or blogstress. Or just try to keep her from doing anything in her underwear on a Thai street corner (Grandma). So don't be shy; email me and let me know how badly you want to financially support my mildly insane vision (or just say hi; I don't really leave the offices, since they can't really leave the offices, so email has become sort of absurdly exciting).

TWO DAYS before Ta Mla and That Khaing,* who'd newly arrived from inside, got arrested, Htan Dah had finally said yes when I asked him if he wanted help cooking breakfast. He'd given me a cutting board and several small heads of garlic, and I'd dutifully begun peeling the fibrous skins.

"I miss you, Htan Dah," I'd said, my eyes on my sticky fingers. "We haven't spent so much time together lately."

His head had been dipped low, his hair hanging in sheets above the heavy marble mortar in which he was pounding chilies with a

---

* Like Htan Dah's, That Khaing's is a less-simply-transliterated name: The pronunciation is fast and sounds like the "Tha" in "Thatcher" plus "Khai" (rhymes with "lie").

matching pestle. He'd looked up and stilled his hand for a moment, the front, shortest layers of his hair landing on his cheekbones. "Yes," he'd said. "Why not?"

"Because you're very busy. You have your work, and your wife, and your kid. You just haven't had so much free time."

He'd continued looking at me, then gone back to pounding. "Yes," he'd said. "I miss you, too."

The morning after the arrest, we were chopping and slicing and smashing at the table when the rest of the house got up and started bustling around. It was agreed that they should all drive the most out-of-the-way back way to wherever they were going. Each incident with the law renewed the fear of the Thai in them for a little bit, though it wasn't like it was anybody's first time or anything. It wasn't even Ta Mla's first time.

Previously, he'd been arrested along with a friend, a girl, who'd started sobbing when the cops said Ta Mla could go but she couldn't. He hadn't been about to pay his way off with a woman, so they'd charged him ten bucks for each of them when he'd refused to leave without her.

"How many times have you been arrested?" I asked Eh Soe when he came into the dining room/garage.

My relationship with Eh Soe had improved somewhat. Every morning, I crawled out from under my mosquito net shortly after dawn and walked past him on my way out the door. Every morning, I went straight downstairs and started helping Htan Dah cook rather than just watching him. And every morning, Eh Soe walked into the dining room/garage an hour or so later and punched me in the arm. When I'd asked Htan Dah what was up with the guys hitting me all the time—Htoo Moo had also taken to slapping me if I was standing near him, or at the very least pulling my arm hair—he'd smiled paternally and said it was because they loved me.

Indeed, Eh Soe and I had started getting along by treating each other like nine-year-old siblings. I had colored and hung an anti-smoking sign above my reading bench, which had become his bed. He had lain underneath it and continued to smoke. He had repeatedly told me to shut up while I yelled at him to go smoke and talk on the phone somewhere else while I was trying to sleep, but then told me after he hung up that I wasn't staying long enough, and should stick around for a year. He'd told me I wasn't his boss, and I'd told him that he could stand to be a better roommate. He thought that was hilarious, and reason to mock me, and had taken to saying "Okay, my roooommaaaate" and "Yes, my roooommaaaate" before completely disregarding whatever courtesy I was asking of him. So even though I kind of wanted to kick Eh Soe in the dick, we were communicative, sometimes chatting from our separate beds at night, like at a sleepover.

"Two times," he said, answering my question. "In two years with BA." He smiled. "Once a year. Once, I paid five hundred baht. I show my ID"—Eh Soe had a student ID from Burma, a real one, since his aunt had put him through some school there—"and say, I'm Burmese! I'm Burmese student!" At this point, he started laughing hard, which made Htan Dah and Htoo Moo, who'd sat down as we prepared to fry up breakfast, do the same. "But he knew I was refugee, and so I said, Okay, I will give you two hundred fifty baht. But he said, No, no, it's not enough. So I had to pay him much more."

"Why don't you ask Htoo Moo how many times he has been arrested?" Htan Dah asked me.

"Okay," I said. "Htoo Moo, how many times have you been arrested?"

"Six times," he said, which set the other guys giggling again. Htoo Moo got arrested the most and let go the least. Usually, he spent a day or four in jail, then was offered freedom for cash. Once, he was leaving a refugee camp on a bus and the police got on and asked him for ID. I don't have one, he said. I am a student. He had seen in movies that students were respected. Where do you study, they asked. In a monastery, he said. What's the name of it? I don't know.

He was taken off the bus and to a jail, where he spent one day and one night. Then they transferred him to another jail, just this side of the Thai border, with men and women in one room. Girls were crying. The cops punched one of the prisoners in the stomach and back of the neck until he spit up blood, then said they'd let people go for three hundred baht. Htoo Moo had only eighty. But ten people bought their way out and left. In a while, the cops came back and said, Okay, two hundred baht. Five or six more prisoners left. The cops came back and said, Okay, one hundred baht. A few more captives straggled out. When the cops announced that ten people needed to go clean the garden, Htoo Moo volunteered, and even after it was clean, he still swept at the ground like a madman, like the work would never be done, because inside, people were getting beat up. In the end, the cops drove the broke hangers-on, eleven of them, over the border and dropped them off in Burma—though luckily, not directly at an SPDC holding center. So Htoo Moo and the others walked along the river for a while, pooled their cash to hire a boat, and got dropped back off on the Thai side. But they were lost. Htoo Moo asked his companions if they knew the way; nobody did, so they walked until midnight, when they heard monks chanting and followed the sound. The monks fed them rice, told them they got people like them every day, and showed Htoo Moo the way to his brother's village, nearby. An older gentleman asked the monks if he could stay with them forever. Another guy said that he had twin babies and a wife and no bus fare, so Htoo Moo gave him twenty of his remaining forty baht and set off for his brother's. But sometimes when he got arrested, he just had to pay five hundred baht or so, and he preferred those times.

"Why do you get arrested so much?" I asked. "Is it because when you're on your motorbike you're always looking over your shoulder? Because you always do that, and it makes you look really suspicious."

"Also," Htan Dah laughed, "he looks Burmese." Htoo Moo's smile lit his dark, oval face. "As for me, maybe I can pass for Thai."

"Really?" I asked.

He shrugged. "I think my face looks a little bit Chinese."

Still, Htan Dah had been arrested three times in the last two years. Once, he paid five hundred baht. Once, he and the three guys he was with, two of whom didn't have KNU cards, paid two thousand baht each. Once, he was just sent back to camp. (That time, he'd been caught by a member of the Thai army—a less crooked organization, according to the refugees, than the Thai police.) Worst, a few months ago, he'd been driving down our street when a neighbor pulled out of her driveway without looking and hit him with her car. She convinced him that it was his fault because he hadn't gotten out of the way. Regardless of how untrue that was, she gave him the option of being turned in to authorities as an illegal or paying her $250. Lucky for Htan Dah, BA covered the bribe, which was two years' worth of his earnings.

"Yesterday," Htan Dah said, "I see the police on our way to Office Two. We didn't get arrested because I was praying."

"Oh yeah?" I asked. "You don't think that could have anything to do with the fact that you were with me?"

Htan Dah laughed and nodded. "Maybe if I go with Ta Mla, I would already be in jail." That hypothetical made him laugh even harder. "That Khaing is lucky Ta Mla came back with whiskey," he choked out. "If Ta Mla disappear, That Khaing is screwed by the cops."

When we hopped on his motorbike on the way to class that morning, he went the same cop-laden way as ever. "If I get stopped," he'd said before he left, buckling his helmet, "you have to protect me."

I got a ride back from Office Two from a different student, who, like most everyone else, drove tensely even along the alternate route. At the house, Htan Dah was nowhere to be found. What's more, his assertion that if he didn't cook nobody would turned out to be true.

There still wasn't any dinner at seven, and still no Htan Dah, who usually started cooking around four. I hoped he was just busy, and since I didn't see any groceries to cook with, I sat down at the table with a bowl of rice. The Blay started frying some thin, crispy wafers made of beans and rice powder. "Poor dinner," he said, laughing.

That's where I was when Htan Dah finally came home. Though he was safe, and though he was, as always, perfectly cheerful, there was horror behind his smile. Finding his American houseguest eating a bowl of plain white rice was like seeing your visiting mother-in-law relegated to eating the ketchup packets out of your fridge.

The next morning, Ta Mla passed cops again on his way to class, but they were already busy with two other people. He sped up anyway. At the break between classes, I followed Wah Doh, the wired, wiry kid who had written the sick note, into the little Office Two computer room to help him with his HRD translation, as I often did. Today, he also wanted to show me a word he saw all the time so I could explain its meaning to him: *marginalized*. (He grasped the concept pretty quickly.) Once, he'd asked me the name of the thing that people used to bind other people's feet against their will. I told him I didn't think we had a word for that in English. (I was wrong. The noun he was looking for was *fetters*, the verb being *to fetter*, but it's a very old word and one that is, for good reason, not currently supercommon. When Htoo Moo asked me later for the word for systematically slicing open the skin on someone's forearm, I told him I didn't think we had a word for that, either.) In return for my English help, Wah Doh blathered at me in Karen for a couple of minutes, as he liked to do, gesturing wildly and unhelpfully, with the idea that this was a way of instructing me in the language.

I didn't even try to follow him this time. When I'd come downstairs to cook with Htan Dah before breakfast, he was gone. Eh Soe had served Abby and me a pile of raw green beans he pulled from somewhere, so I hadn't eaten anything substantial since the morning before. I was considering going to the only Italian restaurant in town later to pick up a ton of takeout, maybe introduce the guys to pasta.* But for now, I was hungry, which I handled about as well as I did being tired, so I found Wah Doh's immersion session annoying at best. When he finished, I just stared at him.

"Do you know what I said to you?" he asked.

"I know you know I don't."

"I said, 'If you eat too many eggs, you will get fat.'"

Back in the classroom, the afternoon session was awfully empty. I wandered into the other room, which held the little TV, and a dozen sleeping refugees at night. Mu Na, the only girl in the advanced class, was standing in the middle of the floor, swatting the ass of the guy who'd bent over to pick something up next to her.

"Good butt," she said, laughing, when she saw me looking at her. "Good butt for slapping."

Indeed. "Where are my students?"

Only Ta Mla, Eh Na, and Collin came to my beginner class that day; everyone else was busy. The four of us sat in chairs—a rare departure from my having my legs folded under me on the floor at the front of a crowded classroom. Eh Na didn't even work for BA, but had joined the household and the class when he'd recently escaped from inside. His face was remarkably wide, and he bore the pink scars of bites and cuts from doing jungle labor at gunpoint. He was as quiet as he was dark-skinned, serious cocoa, not the softer brown of his colleagues. Collin was a chatty fortysomething with twinkly eyes and a bowl cut. He meant to use the paltry attendance to get more gabbing than work done.

"May I ask what is your religion?" he said.

"I don't have a religion," I told him. "I was raised Catholic, but I don't believe in God anymore."

He gave a tight nod, registering that. "You are . . . atheist?"

---

* I wasn't the first white person with this idea. And the volunteer who'd carried through had just been frustrated when the guys had insisted on eating their pizza and spaghetti over rice.

"Yes."

"If you are atheist, what do you do when you are in trouble?"

This made me laugh, not because it didn't make sense for him to ask me that, but because it did, perfectly, sadly. "I guess I try to find a solution."

He nodded again. Then, "You don't pray?"

"No."

"Never?"

"Ever."

"What if your trouble has no solution?"*

"I'm from Ohio, Collin." My shoulders dropped with pity. "I know it's difficult for you to imagine what I mean, but I really don't have the same kind of trouble as your trouble."

After I got home, I told Abby I'd join her to buy souvenirs for her boyfriend. We walked into town, though I was limping slightly. The squat toilet had finally bested me, as they seemed to on every trip; they can be treacherous when they're wet, and they are, of course, always wet, since after every use water is thrown into and all over them. I'd been careless stepping off ours, one foot at a time in the squat position, letting my balance slip as my first foot hit the ground, smashing my other foot into the ceramic toilet platform, crushing it underneath my body weight. Though I'd avoided plunging my foot into a urine-filled toilet bowl, my big toe was seriously suffering, and I shuffled painfully along the highway in my flip-flops in the late afternoon heat.

The most interesting thing that had happened to Abby that day, she said, was that Eh Soe had walked up to her and asked, "What is the word when a man and a woman sleep in bed together before they are married when it is not polite?" When she'd asked him if he meant "premarital sex," he'd confirmed that he had, and asked her to write *premarital* on his hand. (He knew how to spell "sex," he'd told her.)

---

* In a survey of the Burmese refugees in camps on the Thai-Burma border, the percentage of respondents with "no religion" was zero.

I wasn't sure, I mused, what the most interesting thing that had happened to me recently was. Ta Mla had told me he was looking for two things: a wife and a way to get out of Thailand. As for the former, he wasn't particular: "I will marry white, Thai, Karen; as for me, it doesn't matter." Regarding the latter, I fielded questions about how people get married in the United States and then scandalized him into speechlessness and hard blush by saying that if he were so inclined, you know, he really didn't have to get married to have sex, if he didn't want to.

But then again, the more interesting conversation may have been with Htan Dah, who had told me that That Khaing had chest hair, and then made That Khaing lift up his Che shirt and show it to me, and then asked me if I was familiar with this sort of thing, chest hair.

When Abby and I got back to the house with some of the ubiquitous yellow shirts that commemorated the Thai king's yearlong sixtieth-anniversary celebration, making the populace one nation under color coordination, Htan Dah was in the dining room/garage with fried green beans and fried eggs with onions. He looked like he'd been waiting.

"Just for you," he said, smiling at me and gesturing at the food. And indeed it was; none of my housemates sat down to dinner with me.

"I am sorry about the poor food," The Blay said, passing through.

I objected to his apology, pointing happily at Htan Dah's eggs and beans.

We made more of the same for breakfast the next morning. It was Friday. So soon enough, the BA employees who lived in Office Two started arriving in pairs on motorbikes and filing in through the dining room/garage door. I wasn't particularly interested in the weekly all-staff meeting, since I knew by now that about five phrases would be translated for me during the whole hour-long affair. When I'd finished eating, I went upstairs to reclaim my old reading bench and rest before class.

"What are you doing?" Htoo Moo asked, popping into the room. He was wearing his pleated navy-blue Dickies with a loose black tank top. The sunlight coming in through the open balcony door shone off his cleavage.

"I'm resting," I said without moving.

"Why? What did you do today?"

"I'm going to teach English today. I taught English all day yesterday."

"Oh, wow," he said. "Was that heavy?"

"Shut up, Htoo Moo," I said as he started giggling. "Have you ever taught English before? It is actually really hard." The more I defended myself, the harder he laughed. "You have to make a lesson plan, and be ready to be flexible given your students' needs. Plus it takes a lot of energy to engage your students, especially when there's a language barrier." The harder he laughed, the louder I yelled, which just exacerbated the former. I forced myself to stop talking, and just lay there shaking my head and clenching my teeth until he walked away, laughing all the way down the stairs.

I was in the same spot when Eh Soe walked in after the meeting ended.

"What are you doing?" he asked. He talked faster than anyone in the house, maybe just because he could, because his English was better. It made him sound fussy. That, and the fact that if Htan Dah's intonation was like Yogi Bear's, Eh Soe's wasn't entirely unlike Snagglepuss's.

"Nothing, Eh Soe. I'm resting. How was your meeting?"

He sat down on the end of the bench, pushing my legs out of the way with his ass. "Fine. Why didn't you come? We talked about you."

I sat up. "You guys were talking about me?"

"Yes."

"What did you say?"

"Just, is it useful to have English classes, should we have English instructors in the future . . . like that."

"Well what did they say?"

"They were just discussing if it is a good use of time when we are very busy, and our English teachers come only for a short time, is it long enough to learn anything or make a difference."

My mouth went dry. "So what did they decide? Do they think it's helpful for me to be here?"

"They were just discussing."

"I mean, you can't expect miracles in a month, and it certainly can't hurt for my students to be taking classes, or even just having English speakers around. Plus I paid for my own trip, and I buy some of my own food, so it's not like it isn't cost-effective. You should have come and got me when they started talking about teaching so I could have participated in the conversation!"

Eh Soe shrugged. He repeated, more firmly, "They were just discussing."

By the time I returned home from class that day, I'd sunk to the full depth of a morale crisis. Due to busy schedules, the enrollment of my early, advanced class had suddenly dropped from seven to three. It also seemed to me, however delusional, that my students/coworkers/housemates—and, I'd thought, friends—weren't being as friendly. They had decided, I had decided, that I was useless. So I nearly cried thankful tears when Htan Dah walked up to me after I got back to Office One and said, "Can you help me with something?"

It took me about five seconds to find the organizational map of the United Nations on the Internet.

"Wow!" Htan Dah said. "Thank you!"

By the time I'd finished showing him some tips for effective Googling, I felt much better.

"It's getting late," I said. "Do you have a lot more work to do today?"

He shrugged. "Are you hungry?"

"Always."

He thought for a moment. "What should we cook?"

"What do we have?"

"Nothing."

"Okay . . ."

"Eh Soe can take you to the market. Do you want to go?"

Eh Soe never went to the market, but I thought it was nice of him to give Htan Dah a break from grocery shopping. "Okay." I'd never gone anywhere with Eh Soe before. I was about to realize that I should have kept it that way.

I'd gotten a lot better about being on the motorbikes. One recent day, I'd noticed when Htan Dah and I were almost all the way to our destination that I'd forgotten to spend the ride picturing skulls crushed against the pavement like so much fruit. He was trustworthy, stable, careful, and the panic that had before made me hard and tense throughout—with my small, soft, precious head exposed to the wind and the sun—had suddenly turned to something warm and liquid like tea.

Eh Soe, however, careened carelessly around corners, too fast in traffic, turning his head back to talk to me, terrifying me by taking his eyes off the road. He tipped his face almost far enough around to make eye contact with me when he told me that any groceries that were about to be bought for the office/house, I had to pay for. There was no more money in the food budget, he said, not looking at the oncoming traffic and sharp impending bend.

The house food budget was forty-five hundred baht, or a little more than a hundred bucks, a month. With all the extra people around and hungry visitors coming through, there wasn't anything Htan Dah could do to make the budget stretch that far, not that he'd really tried—we want to eat it now, we eat it now, budget be damned. And so the market funds had dissipated completely two days ago, a whole twelve days shy of the next check from the organization. If I wanted to eat anything for the next ten days, Eh Soe advised, I had to buy it, and I couldn't very well eat in front of everybody else, so I should buy food for them, too.

"Do you really think that's fair?" I asked.

"Of course," he said, steering with one hand and gesturing gratuitously with the other. "If I have no money, and you have a lot of money, you should buy the food." Once we parked, he started grabbing big bagfuls of stuff, and when I started to protest that that was kind of a lot, he reminded me that there were, like, seventeen people to feed. And here I'd thought Eh Soe was just being sweet in offering me a ride.

When we got back, Htan Dah was in the dining room/garage talking to Abby. He met my gaze, but not so easily as usual.

"Did you make Eh Soe take me to the market to tell me we ran out of money for food?" I demanded. "You should have just told me, Htan Dah."

"I'm sorry," he said. "I didn't want to bother you."

"So how did you guys buy this?" Abby asked, looking at the packed plastic bags Eh Soe and I had dumped on the table.

"I bought it," I said.

Abby was appalled, and more so when I explained that I was going to buy food for so many people for such a long time. She argued with Eh Soe that they were taking advantage of me because I was white and nonindigent, and he argued that if you could afford to buy food, you should, period. She said that just wasn't the way it worked, and as far as Abby's and my life were concerned, she was absolutely right; I had some disposable income, and when I was in the United States, I spent zero percent of it buying food for hungry people, refugee or otherwise. But we weren't in the United States, and that policy wasn't exactly defendable, and anyway, I found out that Htan Dah had taken out a personal loan from a friend to buy the beans and eggs he'd made me the night before. Dinner and breakfast, through the next two weekends, was on me.

"What would you guys do if someone didn't come up with the money to buy more food?" I asked Htan Dah.

"We eat rice. And salt." His use of present tense was not an ESL error; they ran out of food money almost every single month. At that point, they just lived off whatever was left of their staples, which were delivered courtesy of the Thailand Burma Border Consortium. In 1975, the Committee for the Coordination of Services to Displaced Persons in Thailand was formed in response to the refugees coming in from Vietnam. For years, it administered assistance to the incoming Indochinese population. When Karen refugees started arriving in 1984, the Royal Thai Government asked the organization to supply basic food and medical supplies. By 1994 so many Burmese refugees were setting up camp in so many locations—and the original refugees weren't going anywhere, and were multiplying—that the Thai Ministry of Interior requested that sanitation and educational services be implemented as well. By 1997, the organization had its energies and abilities completely expended by Burmese refugees, whom it began serving nearly exclusively. Additionally, several members of the CCSDPT formed another group dedicated to providing them aid.

This was the Thailand Burma Border Consortium (TBBC). Every month, the NGO drove a truck up to BA and unloaded these refugees' rations: thirteen bags of rice, fifty kilos each; one bag of dried yellow beans, forty kilos; two tins of fish paste, sixteen kilos each; forty bottles of cooking oil (which always, always ran out); a five-pound bag of chilies; and fourteen kilos of salt. BA then distributed some of this to Office Two, to another office farther up the border, to the Karen Student Network Group, and to villages in Burma via the HRDs.

TBBC also provides monthly rations to every household in every camp, keeping the refugees fed for 58¢ a day.* Since its beginning, there's been a name change to broaden the organization's appeal to donors—it used to be called the Consortium of Christian Agencies. Now most of its funds are institutional, but it was originally funded entirely by churches and other Christian charities. In 1990, its fund-raising goal was about $1 million. In 1996, the budget was $8 million. Today, it spends $35 million a year, and has collected hundreds of millions in its history of keeping Burma's refugees from starving.

To celebrate not eating just rice and salt, I gave Eh Soe another ten bucks and sent him to pick up a case of twelve 22-ounce bottles of Chang beer and some change. He came back with fourteen and none. It was Friday night, after all. Any Karen women in the house instantly disappeared; Eh Soe said it was common for women to let men get drunk without bothering them or bothering to listen to them act like fools. I found Htan Dah's wife and the female staffer, Ta Eh Thaw, in the family room and tried to talk them into joining us for a drink with much idiotic pantomiming, since the former didn't speak English, but they declined.

We sat at the picnic table pouring strong cheap beer over fat round ice cubes that someone had procured, repeatedly clinking our small glasses and coffee cups together at my insistence. We tore into the market spoils with abandon, the guys firing up the wok and spit-ting fish bones on the table and flicking cheroot ash and hocking loogies onto the floor and badgering me with rounds of questions that started with the usual "If I go to America" (will people be nice

---

* The minimum standard of calorie consumption set by the UNHCR and World Food Bank is twenty-one hundred per day. The rations provided by the TBBC provide twenty-one hundred and two. As an adult in camp, in one month you're given to eat exactly 15 kilograms of rice, 250 grams of fortified flour, 750 grams of fish paste, 330 grams of salt, 1 kilogram of mung beans, a liter of cooking oil, 40 grams of dried chilies, and 125 grams of sugar. Unless you're pregnant—in which case you get a little extra produce and eggs—or a severely malnourished child—in which case you also get milk powder.

to me even though I'm Asian, can I marry your sister, etc.). Generally, Htan Dah's kid was terrified of white people—he at least looked worried or at worst started howling whenever Abby or I approached, even though Htan Dah said soothing things to him like "Do you want to go to your auntie?" when I was nearby. (He said it in Karen, but when I'd pressed him to translate for me, he broke down and did, embarrassed.) But that night Htan Dah got the 17-month-old adorably drunk, and he became thrilled to meet us.

Abby and I, of course, were completely freaking out about the hammered infant. "Htan Dah," I said, wincing at the child's blissfully glazed eyes, "that baby is *drunk*."

"Yes," Htan Dah said. He raised his eyebrows innocently and pointed to a bowl on the table. "But also he has rice(!)." However we screeched and admonished them, the guys all insisted that at a year and a half, that kid was wayyy past the reasonable Karen drinking age.

Eh Soe became very serious and started waxing philosophic about his positions on gay rights (he wasn't sure), discrimination (he was against it, possibly even re the gays), freedom (for), premarital sex (for, though he hadn't yet had it with the girlfriend he was interminably chatting on the phone with), and the most popular guy in the house (him). By the end of the night, he was just plain wasted, and beseeched me to send an email home that the staff had run out of underpants and could someone please bring us some on an airplane. (I did.) We arm wrestled. (He lost.) Htoo Moo asked me if I had any lady friends I could hook him up with, and when I asked him in return if *kaw la wah*—white people—were okay, he said, "Yes. Very yes." He was sitting next to Ta Mla, who held two of Htoo Moo's fingers, his middle and index, in the way that is common platonic male affection in their culture and many others but that Htoo Moo seemed to be aware was not common in mine and therefore endured uncomfortably. The Blay asked me if I liked this place, then, after I answered in the affirmative, stopped talking to me, which was about as much interaction as I ever had with him.

Htan Dah's cheeks got a little pink, but he refrained from getting obliterated, certainly way less drunk than his kid. He told me how his mother had taught him to cook. While he'd watched her, she'd told him that he would one day have to cook for himself, because he couldn't assume that his wife could or would or should do it for him. He wished he farmed his own food, concerned that a lot of the produce sold in the markets was grown with chemicals. He was interested in working in a restaurant for one year, just for fun, just to learn to cook new things, and better, but didn't think he'd ever get the chance.

"Would you do it if you got a Thai ID?" I asked.

"No," he said softly. His exclamations had faded with the daylight and his sobriety. "It's only for myself, not for my duty to my people. It's not for the cause. Not for the war."

The room never became as loud as a normal party, just as the house was never as noisy as a normal office during the day. There was no radio. The TV in the living room was turned down low. Sometimes a novelty cell phone ring went off.* On Saturdays, the guys played quiet Ping-Pong. Tonight, however much we drank, it never got so boisterous that someone upstairs couldn't have easily taken a nap. When I laughed particularly hard at something Eh Soe said, Htan Dah actually shushed me, because to be illegal someplace was to be illegal all the time, in the house or out, drunk or sober, he always had to be on the lookout.

We ran out of beer at eleven-thirty. The guys were chatting softly, intermittently, wound down and subdued. Eh Soe was keeping his sweaty face only far enough off the table that he could get a cheroot in and out of it. Ta Mla and Htan Dah had disappeared, the latter leaving a glassful of Chang behind. I stumbled into the computer

---

* Ta Eh Thaw's was a cheap, jangly incarnation of "Another Saturday Night." Eh Soe's was "Jingle Bells." "Nice ringtone, dude," I said the first time I heard it. He, missing my sarcasm, had smiled eagerly and lifted his eyebrows and asked, "Do you like it?" "No." I felt bad later when he changed it.

room, where I found them, HRD interviews and Excel spreadsheets on the monitors in front of them, respectively.

"Are you guys *working?*" I asked.

They nodded.

I didn't really know what to say, so I said, "But, Htan Dah. You still have *beer* left."

He waved his hand at me. "It is nothing." I followed him as he walked back into the dining room/garage, took the glass down in one swallow, and went back to work.

I stood there watching them for a bit, immobilized with drunk and awe. I fancied myself a pretty hard-core worker, "But it's nearly midnight!" They ignored me. "You guys are drunk!"

Htan Dah looked up at me, but didn't say anything.

"And we're celebrating!"

"Yes, we can celebrate," he said finally, turning back to his computer. "But consider IDP."

"Okay," I said, turning to head back to the remaining revelers, though if there was anything in the world I most certainly did not want to consider when I was trying to have a good time, it was IDP.

DURING ONE of our talks in our room, Eh Soe got pretty worked up about internally displaced persons, or IDPs. His job with BA was community organizing; he'd trained for two months to learn how to empower villagers. He was dispatched into Burma for weeks or months at a time to ask villagers how they could have meetings and solve their own problems, never being didactic or demanding but encouraging them to lead and survive, holding critical-thinking and confidence-building and creative-brainstorming workshops, not saying that Westerners know definitively that democracy is a good system or where diarrhea comes from—these guys weren't about to impose another kind of dictatorship onto anybody—but urging villagers to discuss whether the former could work and the latter could possibly be caused by bad water rather than bad karma. Community organizers going to Karen communities, however, tend to work in the remote, mountainous locations where they're concentrated, not flat, luxuriant lowlands like where Eh Soe came from.

His first trip was in October 2005. He couldn't sleep. He was hungry. His legs ached violently from climbing mountains. He was tired. Though he was only in Burma for a month and was supposedly avoiding offensive areas, he had to flee from the SPDC. When he was laid out with a fever for four or five days, he had no access to medicine, just some herbs someone had found him. Complaining to me about it, he admitted that he still fared better than his coworker, who didn't shake his fever for three weeks.

"It was very terrible,"* he said, laughing at how very terrible it was. "He almost died that time."

But as bad as that had been, Eh Soe's most recent trip, the one from which he'd just returned, had focused on IDPs, whose habitat was even worse than mountainous villages in that it was usually mountainous but also lacked even the meager amenities of villages. This is a UN definition of IDP:

> Internally displaced persons are persons or groups of persons who have been forced or obliged to flee or to leave their homes or places of habitual residence, in particular as a result of or in order to avoid the effects of armed conflict, situations of generalized violence, violations of human rights or natural or human-made disasters, and who have not crossed an internationally recognized State border.

For four years straight, Burma made the Internal Displacement Monitoring Centre's list of the world's worst displacement situations, right along with, recently, Iraq and Sudan and the Democratic Republic of the Congo and other conflict-ridden nations people

---

* Eh Soe admitted also that his job was at least better than Htoo Moo's, because, he said, laughing again, "If you go into a village with a camera, the SPDC will kill you."

have actually heard of. Eastern Burma alone—that is, the part of town that's home to our minority protagonists—is packed with well more than half a million IDPs, more than twice as many as the whole great internationally war-torn landscape of Afghanistan.

This is how their situation is described in an advocacy-group newsletter:

> As a consequence of the poor living conditions that IDPs are forced into, illnesses are frequent and malnutrition is rife. The threats of military attack, food insecurity, and illness and injury are the primary obstacles to the IDPs' survival.

They have, as the IDMC points out, no income, a disrupted social organization, and "profound psychological distress," and are documentless, worldly-possession-less, hiding, and/or under attack.

This was Eh Soe's take: "I don't understand how people live in the jungle. People think IDPs don't have skills, they are poor and stupid and sitting around, but they survive there." He shook his head. "I won't go back there again."

"Really?" I asked. He'd already told me that he went back to his own village during the summers, rough and risky traveling, because he missed his mom. I couldn't believe he'd flat-out refuse to go to the IDP settlements he was assigned to for work.

"Okay. Well, later, probably. But it is not easy to live in the jungle." He waved his hand dismissively. "Forget about living in the jungle. Oh my god." He shook his head again, harder, faster, increasingly flustered as he thought about it. "Oh my *god*. That is *not* a practical place to live."

Being probably one of the more treacherous tracts of geography the world has to offer, Burma's jungle is indeed not a practical place to live. Back in the day, it was one of the country's best defenses. The very ill-fated eighteenth-century Manchu invaders could have told the soon-coming British what awaited them when they stepped off their ships there: dysentery, cholera, malaria. It wasn't any less hard on the powers that swept in 120 years later for World War II. Scores of Allied troops had to be evacuated for disease and exhaustion. Soldiers died of typhus. One detachment in the Japanese 54th Transport Corps lost several men to tigers.* There's a tree whose sap causes the body to erupt in horribly painful boils that can kill you. The survival guides issued by the United States Army Air Forces Office of Flying Safety, Safety Education Division maintained that in the event of an emergency landing, an able-bodied man could survive for *weeks* in the jungle—if he always moved calmly and slowly, used his parachute as a sturdy tent, stayed dry in the crushing humidity by changing his clothes often, drank water only if it had been boiled for three minutes or treated with iodine or Halazone tablets, used his signal pistol to scare off tigers or "angry" elephants, didn't sleep directly on the ground, had mosquito netting and preventative malaria medication, and was never, ever barefoot.†

This is where hundreds of thousands of unarmed and unequipped civilians and babies try to survive in the rugged and disease-ridden terrain through shelterless heavy rains and also, now, the ground is covered in land mines. Wah Doh was one of these survivors. Burma army troops came into his village when he was thirteen; he and his family fled, and weren't able to go back for sustained fighting in the area. For six months, they lived in a cave with, by his estimation, four or five hundred other people. There was little space. There was no school. Wah Doh cried a lot at the sound of gunfire, though the adults sang to calm the kids, to calm themselves, to occupy their empty time. Since the little bit of rice they'd carried out of their vil-

---

* They even fell prey to one that killed two soldiers inside a week. After the first man died, his comrades set a trap and waited in a stalking platform in a tree for the man-eater, which did show up, but only to eat one of the hunting soldiers' heads right there in the little tree house they'd built.

† The pilots were also advised to avoid Burma natives because they are unfriendly and "superstitious and suspicious," but if forced to interact with them, try to win them over with string tricks like cat's cradle rather than threatening them with "terrorist methods."

lage was all they had to last, Wah Doh's family daily ate rice soup: water with a few grains of rice in it.

At BA, I was always the tallest person in the room, but next to Wah Doh, I was a giantess. His telling me this story during one of our between-class translation sessions made me wonder if his teenage diet was why this full-grown male just a few years my junior no way weighed more than ninety pounds.

"Were you bored?" I asked.

He looked at me a little impatiently. "What was 'bored'?" he asked. After they left the cave, his family had to stay on the outskirts of a village for an additional year and a half, until they were sure it was safe to return to their own.

So consider, as Htan Dah suggested, IDP. As urgent and vast as his crisis was, if you were one of them, your crisis would be much, much direr. The Burma army has come into your village and burned it down, along with your crops. The government has ordered you to move to one of the hundreds of concentration camps it sets up for ethnic scum like you. This camp is really just a big empty field on which you can forage for food and sheltering supplies anytime you are not being used as a slave for portering, building and/or maintaining army camps, and other "public infrastructure projects." It's not like there's sanitation or medicine there, and you could very well be worked or tortured or shot to death, so you run away, into the jungle. Let's hope you were able to bring some rice! Ideally, you have hidden some, as did the village Htoo Moo ran away with, among the trees. If not, you can go back to your village under the cover of night and try to salvage some from your old reserves, which the assailing troops scattered all over the ground and burned. Or maybe your village hasn't been attacked or burned down, but you've just miraculously survived being used as a human land-mine detector and are afraid of being conscripted for that duty again, or you've just realized you're pregnant and don't want to risk being raped into a miscarriage, so you still run away into the jungle. Since you don't have a house, or a kitchen, or a pot anymore, you can soak rice in green bamboo stalks for half an hour, then roast the bamboo over a fire until it's cooked. Or you can soak the rice in your *longyi*—Burmese sarong—for an hour, bury it a foot under the ground, then build a fire on top, which will steam the rice in about fifteen minutes, and which is really handy when you don't know how long it will be before you have to start running again. When the rice gets low, you'll eat rice porridge, and soon, when things get really desperate, rice soup. This, again, is all assuming you've got access to that rice. Or fire. Or, for that matter, water. And that it's nighttime, since cook smoke can be seen by government troops during the day, so it'll give away your hiding place. You'll probably have to scavenge, looking for bamboo shoots, mushrooms, trying to eat bark, but it really stresses you out, since you know a lot of people step on land mines this way; so many are laid, "in stark contrast to the complete rejection of mine use that we see elsewhere in the world," says the International Campaign to Ban Landmines, that they cause one in twenty-five deaths in eastern Burma. But maybe in your hunt you'll find a piece of plastic, which would be pretty neat, because then you could live under it, which will be especially helpful if it's the season when it rains for several months solid. Keep your eyes and ears peeled for advancing troops. Hope there's not a measles outbreak. If you can muster the energy, try to help give the kids some sense of normality, holding school in the dirt. Some of the kids are pretty unfocused, many of them suffering from acute malnutrition, and you don't have any supplies, but the activity helps distract you from what happened with your toddler, who, as an IDP in eastern Burma, had a more than one-in-five chance of dying before his fifth birthday, and did. If your surviving child gets sick, you've sworn to carry her to the nearest welcoming hospital. It's in Thailand, just through hostile, enemy-controlled jungle, over a mountain range and a river that rushes from its headwaters in Tibet toward the Andaman Sea, and past a corps of shady Thai border police. Watch out for land mines. And soldiers. And tigers.

So you're fending entirely for yourself in the middle of the open

Burma jungle, kind of like a shot-down Air Force pilot but without the handbook or hope of rescue. Unlike in the case of Htan Dah and his fellow refugees, and unlike what they do for even those other internally displaced populations in places like Iraq or Sudan, none of the major international aid players, UN or Doctors Without Borders or International Committee of the Red Cross or Mercy Corps or otherwise, has official responsibility for you. It's possible you'll get ideological fortification from a community organizer like Eh Soe now and then, but that hardly meets your essential needs. There is a crew called the Back Pack Health Worker Team, eighty-some groups of two to five Burmese, mostly Karen, each that trek around Burma with up to forty-pound bamboo baskets strapped to their backs packed with donated supplies picked up in Thailand, delivering babies, handing out minimal meds, doing land-mine-related amputations with whatever it takes, wire saws and hacksaws and knives. They target 170,000 displaced people with their 294. Seven have been killed. One has been arrested and remains in prison. The Karen Department of Health and Welfare also sends some medics out with supplies. Hope that they'll come to an area near you. Otherwise, your best chance by far of getting any relief is from the army of a roving Pasadena-seminary-ordained American ex-Special Forces soldier named Dave.

LET'S BACK up for a second. Karen State was not always, even in recent history, one of the worst places you could live. It has been the staging area of a deeply divisive ethnic and political war for many decades, yes. But remember that in 1984, when Htan Dah was a toddler living in Thailand, he was one of ten thousand refugees from Burma there. Out of several million Karen—estimates vary from three to six; Burma hasn't had a decent census since 1931—that's not so bad, relatively speaking. It wasn't until ten years later that the number was eighty thousand, and a decade after that that the number doubled, plus nearly another hundred thousand outside

Thailand and at least half a million more in the Burmese jungle. Part of the difference was the fall of Manerplaw.

Though the junta didn't recognize Karen State as autonomous, during the long time that the KNU had a lot of eastern Burma under its control—and a lot of the Karen under its protection—it functioned as if it were, as well as it could in a war. The Karen National Union had divided Kaw Thoo Lei into districts and townships and tracts, and it held elections for positions on committees. It harvested and sold teak and taxed the border, and in the '70s, it built Manerplaw, an elaborate headquarters with a parade ground and departments like finance and education and transport and health and welfare. There were doctors and engineers and rubber stamps with official insignia. There's a flag, a wide horizontal stripe each of red, white, and blue, red sunrise against blue sky in the upper left box, where the US's stars go, superimposed with the golden drum of their ancestors. There were economic stimulus programs that implemented basket-weaving training. For twenty years, Manerplaw thrived, the last democratic stronghold in the country. The Burma army had tried to take it repeatedly, of course, but had always failed. Until the DKBA formed, forged an alliance with the regime, and gave up all the KNU inside information you could please.

One warm winter night in 1995, the Karen at Manerplaw gathered what they could carry and set the whole headquarters ablaze, fleeing by the light of the flames as the Burma army closed in. It was only a matter of time before the Burma army's capture of that long-contended and crucial post led to its takeover of another key stronghold, Kaw Moo Rah, which was shelled so hard that it lit up the sky and shook the houses of Mae Sot. It's hard to know how many thousands of soldiers the KNU had at the time; some say five, and some say fifteen. Whatever the number, a sizable portion discontinued their service then, disillusioned, and where the resistance had once controlled huge areas of Karen State, it now had only a few disconnected pieces of land. It was open season on Karen civilians.

The Burma army started destroying thousands of villages and trying to force their inhabitants into several dozen concentration camps (though without so much the "camp" part, really, since there was no infrastructure or shelter). In response, tens of thousands of desperate Karen threw themselves into the arms of unmitigated jungle or across the border into Thailand.

Enter Dave. Dave grew up in Thailand, the son of American missionaries of some repute, his father a gruff and understated preacher, his mother an ex-showgirl who says she was second in line to play Julie Andrews's part in *The Sound of Music*. She smiles when she explains that she thought her husband was brash when they first met but was soon so won over by his passion for Christ that she quit her promising career and moved with him to Thailand. She'll sing for you, if you go over to their Chiang Mai house for pancakes, and she'll tell you about how they gave their son a found bear cub for a playmate, and how it was the cutest thing when Dave would wrestle the bear, and how everyone was sad to have to get rid of the bear after it got a little rough with Dave's young sister.

When he grew up, Dave went to Texas A&M and became a Special Forces soldier, doing anti-narcotics in South America, working with special forces in Thailand. He met a girl, who thought he was a little brash, but he wooed her into a mountain-climbing date, and beyond. They got married, he quit the service, and he joined Fuller Seminary in California, ultimately deciding that he, too, should become a missionary.

He was in Thailand doing God's work when the big post-Manerplaw offensives were displacing people like crazy. When he went to the border with a backpack full of supplies, he ran into a KNU medic-soldier who was also eager to help. That day in 1997, with the KNU in full retreat and refugees and IDPs swarming the borderlands, the two men treated as many wounded as they could, picking up a guy who'd stepped on a land mine and taking him to a hospital to have his leg amputated, back and forth over the border, rushing into Burma to help the injured as if the whole country were a house on fire. The Free Burma Rangers was born.

The first Free Burma Rangers team consisted of two medics, a nurse, and a soldier—Dave founded the organization in collaboration with key KNU personnel—along with a videographer, photographer, reporter, and pastor sent to the jungle for a three-week relief mission. Since then, 110 teams have conducted more than 350 missions that have treated some 360,000 people. And they're all dispatched with medicine and video cameras and at least one gun from a base that Dave has built right in Karen State, right in the middle of enemy territory.

"The purpose of the training is to train, equip, and inspire you to serve your people and help them get freedom," he explains to his new recruits, ethnic guys from Burma, sometimes peppered—or salted, I guess—with a few white Christians, during the six-week training on base. Dave is buff and sinewy and fair. He is a charismatic brightness in the vast green jungle camp. "We call ourselves the Free Burma Rangers because we want everyone in Burma to be free. A ranger is one who can go alone, or go in pairs. No matter what the obstacles, he will always try. If a ranger has a weapon, he can fight. If he has no weapon, he can still do something to help. No one can stop the Free Burma Rangers from serving and loving other people. And no one can stop you from serving your people."

Training involves war-game-like drills, with burning buildings and unconscious villagers and enemies attacking from the wings. The rangers complete intense physical obstacle courses, plus training in swimming and lifesaving, backpack flotation, using maps and compasses, operations order, building rope bridges, rappelling, land-mine removal, video camera use, CPR, first aid, syringe and IV use, human rights interviewing, counseling, crack surgery and dentistry.

So this is where Dave lives, along with his wife and two little towheaded girls and a boy, running his own kind of insurgency from the middle of the jungle in the middle of this war.* The whole thing operates on a budget of about $1 million a year, and the whole budget, like all of the money that fed Karen refugees for years, like some of the money that still educates and feeds them now, comes from individual donations and church groups, via Internet donations and checks. Additionally, PO boxes in Thailand receive contributions of supplies: toys and vitamins and toothpaste, all sealed into little plastic bags with postcards full of Bible verses.

But Dave tells his recruits that they can all work together even if they're not Christian, because they're all God's children, and God is bigger than everything. Training includes liberal amounts of praying. Before the missions, team members confess their sins to one another. During the missions, they pray over their patients, and hand out Bibles where few other books exist. They pray that God will keep them safe and give them signs so that they can avoid conflict with or capture by the Burma army. Dave says there's no other explanation for his being alive today. Once, when he was being pursued by more than a thousand Burma army troops, he says, the only way to survive was to hunker down and pray for safety. It worked. The teams press on whether fighting is heavy or not, whether or not Dave's baby girls are with them. Prayer has, according to the Free Burma Rangers, made Burma army soldiers get lost in pursuit or mis-steer their boats, has helped teams find

---

* Dave's wife, having found the Karen to be incredibly generous regardless of their situation, wouldn't have it any other way. "The gifts they gave were of themselves," she explained in an interview. "Their time, energy, and love. In my experience in the West it is easier to go to the store and buy a trinket as a gift. For this reason I have chosen to raise my children in this war. The influence of these people is something I have never experienced anywhere else." Sometimes the girls go on the missions, but the lifestyle isn't all rough: Dave has implemented the use of pack animals, and subsequently kept the girls in ponies. Also, they got to learn to swim the fun way. You can see Dave chucking the youngest daughter into a raging river by the seat of her underpants in a video the family made to submit to the "Postcards From You" segment of PBS's *Arthur* cartoon.

their way when they're lost and alone in the middle of completely encompassing land-mine-filled jungle. They've got a list of miracles longer than the Salween River.

And like any decent paramilitary force, they've got uniforms, too. I saw one of the specially printed T-shirts—soft jersey knit, in nice army olive, with FREE BURMA RANGERS in a white insignia over the left breast—hanging to dry in Office Two on one of my first days teaching. I didn't know what FBR was, or how much cred it had, when I laid eyes on the shirt, but I told Collin I'd do anything to get my hands on one. What with the flattering color and emblemed front and motto—"Love each other. Unite and work for freedom, justice, and peace. Forgive and don't hate each other. Pray with faith, act with courage. Never surrender."—printed in Karen on the back, I just thought it was a really nice shirt.

"Nice shirt," Htan Dah said the first time I wore the one Collin had quickly gifted to me. Every coworker I saw that day said the same thing. I was the pinnacle of refugee activist fashion. I didn't realize until Lah Lah Htoo showed me one of FBR's videos that the reason people were impressed with my outfit was that the rangers were highly respected as total fucking badasses.

Lah Lah Htoo wasn't one of my students but served a function in Office Two similar to Htan Dah's in Office One. Like Eh Soe's, his black hair stood up enthusiastically from his head, only Lah Lah Htoo's shock was taller. An artistic type with a penchant for drawing and singing, he was alone among the guys in that he wore chokers. Or as Eh Soe put it, "Lah Lah Htoo can't play football. He is very good at painting." When he spotted (and complimented!) my shirt while I was on break between classes one day, he invited me into the little Office Two computer room and loaded up a DVD. Some of the BA guys had been on missions with FBR. The two groups shared information; via villagers' and their own observations, they did collective reconnaissance on the Burma army so they could prepare the civilians they encountered—and be prepared themselves, an early warning system for the guys running around in the field. And since the ragtag little groups of Karen, mostly young, mostly men but some women, working for these two NGOs are nearly the last defense against the massacre in Burma's hills' going completely undocumented, they also shared footage. But where BA made heartbreaking videos with villagers running and babies crying, FBR made soul-crushing videos with adults weeping openly and villagers bleeding a lot.

The video Lah Lah Htoo loaded starts with war footage, guys shooting guns in tall jungle bush and loud rocket fire, and a village burning down and screaming women running for their lives, before moving briefly to photo stills: a picture of villagers standing over a group of dead bodies, a picture of a beaten woman with her shirt torn open, dead on the forest floor, a picture of murdered children on the ground, lying all lined up in a row. Then the camera centers on the face of a seventeen-year-old boy with lifeless, unfocused eyes, rolling his head on the ground, moaning, while a hand pets his cheek, a *longyi* held up below his neck so he can't see what's going on with the rest of his body, which is that a few men hold on to his completely exposed lower leg bone, a bloody white stick still hung with a few slick and glistening black-purple sinews, protruding from a bloody knee, a land-mine wound swarmed by flies. Then he's in a thin hammock, with a man in cheap plastic flip-flops at each end of the bamboo pole from which it swings, and another walking alongside holding an IV drip dangling from another piece of wood, being carried through the mountainous terrain. For four days. Which is how long it takes the team to get him to a clinic on the border, where a proper amputation can be done.

By now, instantly, I'd twisted my face into a permanent wince, and it didn't get any easier to watch. A husband and wife sit next to each other on the ground while he explains that their two sons and daughter were taken by Burma army troops that stormed into their village. Local Karen leaders negotiated the return of the two boys, but they haven't seen the girl since. "We want her back," the woman says, smiling sadly, before dropping her face to her knees, covering it with her pink sweater, and starting to sob. When she calms down a little, the man says, "My wife and I are like dead people." There are people getting ready to run from an attack, like they did at the village Htoo Moo visited, little girls running around talking fast directions to each other while they throw shit in baskets and sacks they can carry strapped to their foreheads. A man on his back breathing hard and fast and shallow as Free Burma Ranger medics jab their fingers and instruments into the bloody stump below his knee where his calf and foot were before he stepped on a land mine. Skulls and bones on the ground and a ranger telling how he brought a bunch of children's presents donated by kids overseas only to find that there are no children in this village anymore. Rangers tearing out infected teeth with pliers. Rangers stitching up a gaping, blood-spurting hole in someone's foot. Rangers cleaning the gory, festering wound on a little kid's leg as the child stands still, calm, pantsless. Rangers delivering a baby in the darkness by the green glow of the camera's night mode, in open jungle air, on the jungle floor. The partially decomposed decapitated head of an old man on the ground, which the rangers bury when they find it. A shot of a Burma army compound, the camera zooming in shakily on the faces of the boys with rifles, the hiding cameramen whispering breathlessly to each other. Shots from an FBR team that came under attack when they went back to a village of some recent IDPs to see if they could recover any food; the camera jostles violently as they run along, set to the sound of gunfire cracking and thundering through the trees. An FBR team rushing to the scene of a new attack and meeting two fleeing villagers, young guys who tell them they were taking a smoke break with four other friends when the explosions and bullets started coming. They're not sure if the guys who were running with them survived, since there was so much shooting. By way of illustration, one of the guys points to a bullet hole in the side of his loose jacket. A man rocking the tiniest sleeping baby and complaining about the Burma army because his wife died during childbirth in the jungle while they were running.

He worries that he has no idea how to take care of this child without her. Tears streaming hard and quiet down the face of a woman mindlessly fingering her jacket zipper with one hand, standing among the ashes of her old village, in which her husband was killed. A toddler barely grown enough to stand picking his way through the jungle as his village flees, carefully parting the brush with his chubby little fingers and stepping through with his bare, scratched legs and feet. Three more stills: a dead villager facedown on the ground. A dead villager faceup on the ground. A five-year-old with a bullet in his leg. Video of yet another land-mine casualty, medics holding a bleeding, seething, sinew-dripping, mangled hunk of something vaguely human looking, recognizable as a foot only because it comes at the end of an ankle. An FBR team leaves a group of IDPs and the IDPs call out please don't leave us, please come back. A man keeps hiding his face it's so contorted with sorrow as he says, sobbing convulsively, "I don't understand why they killed my children. They didn't even know their right hand from their left hand," while the woman next to him weeps silently and gnashes her teeth. The video ends with a quote from Galatians on the screen: Let us not grow weary while doing good. In due season we shall reap if we don't lose heart.

Currently, FBR is running some forty full-time teams on month-long missions in Burma throughout the year, treating about 2,000 people in each, trekking hundreds of miles. They find malaria, AIDS, gastric disease, dysentery, colds, diarrhea, severe vitamin deficiency and malnutrition, worms, anemia, skin disease, skin infections, respiratory infections. When the Burma army massacred villagers in Htee Law Bleh in 2002, rangers were there to treat people who didn't die from their gunshot wounds and photograph a pile of dead children. Sometimes the team members get shot at. Sometimes they fall fatally ill or are captured and tortured. Just like Htan Dah always reminded me about the BA field workers, if FBR personnel are caught, or get a disease, or step on a land mine, they can be killed. Sometimes, they are: six of them in the organization's first ten years.

"What do you think?" Lah Lah Htoo asked me when the video was over.

I thought I might like to close myself in the bathroom so I could punch myself in the chest, just a little, to try to release some of the tightness and weight there, let my face into my hands and press hard.

"Good video?" he asked, because I was taking so long to answer.

"Yeah, it's a good video."

He nodded and waited politely for me to continue, but I just sat quietly, awkwardly, before simply nodding back at him.

"Do you want to see picture?" he asked.

Not really. I knew what types of violent and devastating pictures these guys had on their hard drives, and the strain of watching the video had taken the wind out of any morbid curiosity sails I might otherwise have been flying. But I didn't want to be rude, or a pussy. "Sure."

Lah Lah Htoo browsed through some files on his computer before finding what he was looking for and giving his mouse a hard double-click. An image filled the screen. My mouth dropped open.

Lah Lah Htoo, who'd seen the FBR video a thousand times, had instantly and completely switched gears, evidently, at the end of our screening. He smiled proudly now as I gaped at a picture of him and The Blay and That Khaing. It looked as if their likenesses had been cut from separate photos and pasted on a black background. They were, for some reason, dressed for a rap-video parody. There were bare chests. There were necklaces. There were black knit skullcaps and low-slung pants. The three affected tough-guy postures, crossed arms.

"What do you think?" he asked.

"This is the gayest thing I've ever seen."

Lah Lah Htoo stopped smiling. "Not gay! Gangster."

"Mmmm. . . ." I looked back to the picture. The Blay was scowling vigorously, with a pouty-lip thing going on. "No, it's pretty gay."

"Not gay!"

"Okay, whatever."

We sat in silence again as he beamed at the screen.

"So . . . what do you guys do with the videos you make?"

"We send them. To human rights organizations, UN, news."

"Do they ever use them?"

Lah Lah Htoo shrugged.

"I can't believe I never heard of any of this before I got here," I said. "Seriously, my friends are really smart. Nobody I know has ever heard of this."

"So," he said, nodding emphatically, "you will tell everybody in America."

It was easy for even my really smart friends to be ignorant of this war, the world's longest-running war, such an active war; it didn't get a lot of media play. "I don't think there's enough news in the Karen war itself," a *New York Times Magazine* editor told me once. He was certainly right. As juicy as the real-time footage was, the situation is, as even FBR's Dave once put it, "not a car wreck. It's a slow, creeping cancer," a conflict that'd started sixty years ago, which is actually the opposite of news. Every year, when the United States Department of State slams Burma in its "Country Reports on Human Rights Practices," saying that the government rapes and tortures and kills people and indiscriminately and indefinitely and illegally detains people and blah-blah-blah, the media ignore it.

Except the Burmese media, which report how the Burmese government is flabbergasted by these absolutely flabbergasting charges. Take this press release from the Permanent Mission of the Union of Myanmar to the United Nations Office and Other International Organizations, in Geneva. It's a re-release of the press release whereby Burma's Ministry of Foreign Affairs rejects 2008's State Department report. It's titled, aptly, "Ministry of Foreign Affairs of Myanmar rejects US State Department's human rights report." It explains how the US has, due to its dire need of fact-checkers, made Burma sad, and how, further, Burma is rubber and the US is glue:

The United States Department of State released on 25th February 2009 its 2008 Country Report on Human Rights Practices of over 190 countries, including Myanmar. As in the past, the report repeated its unfounded and unsubstantiated allegations of human rights violations in Myanmar.

It is saddening to find that the report contained the usual sweeping accusations of human rights abuses in Myanmar without verification of the validity and accuracy of the information and reliability of its sources. Instead of making false allegations at other nations regarding human rights matters, the United States should concentrate on uplifting its own human rights records.

Myanmar has long been a victim of a systematic disinformation campaign launched by anti-government elements, generously funded by their foreign supporters. The rootless allegations of human rights violations which invariably emanated from anti-government elements have found their way into the reports of the U.S. State Department. Thus, there is a need to verify all information before it is judged fit for inclusion in official reports.

Verify this: Even if you haven't had the pleasure of opening a Martus database of human rights violations and being assaulted by the headlines of the hundreds of reports being collected there by independent documenters and nonprofits—A WOMAN GANG-RAPED AND STABBED TO DEATH IN MURNG-SU; GUIDE BEATEN TO DEATH BY SPDC TROOPS; A WOMAN CUT TO DEATH IN THE THROAT, IN KUN-HING; VILLAGERS ROBBED, ARRESTED, TORTURED AND KILLED IN NAM-ZARNG; A HANDICAPPED WOMAN GANG-RAPED, CAUSING DEATH, IN LAI-KHA— it's possible you may have actually seen some of the FBR footage I watched with Lah Lah Htoo. PBS's *Frontline* did an episode called "Burma: State of Fear" in 2006 that followed the "mainly Christian medics who bring aid to villagers being targeted by the Burmese government" and even borrowed some of their film. *Rambo*, the 2008 one, which deals with the plight of the Karen, which the movie's white lead actors also think is pronounced like the name of my parents' blond divorced friend, opens with some BA footage and FBR footage that's as disgusting as the outlandishly gory effects in the rest of the film. And even if you've missed all those, and your media aren't reporting the story, you don't have to take Lah Lah Htoo's word, or my word, or the State Department's word that the regime is violating international law and human decency to an astounding degree every day. FBR has a website. And a Wikipedia entry. You can just google the organization's name. The guys have it all on tape, filmed in bloody, handheld real time. You can verify that shit on YouTube.

X.

IT WASN'T like the Karen were the only people suffering severely in Burma. After Ne Win got back from golfing with US diplomats in Hawaii, he subjected the whole population to increasingly crushing oppression. His junta was like a rightfully insecure boyfriend; it knew it wasn't good enough, and so knew only how to be paranoid and controlling. The policies of isolationism enacted within months of the coup prevailed for decades. The government was (not surprisingly) intensely nationalist protectionist, Western- and ethnic-insurgent-hating, with a capability for militarism that matched its vast legacy of it. The only sanctioned literature included such classics as *Cruel and Vicious Repression of Myanmar Peoples by Imperialists and Fascists and the True Story about the Plunder of the Royal Jewels*, published by the media group of the Committee for Propaganda and Agitation to Intensify Patriotism. There was no TV until 1980. Under the Burmese Way to Socialism, farmers were forced to sell grain on the cheap to the government, which in turn sold it to export or the black market. Unless they wanted to buy their rice back off the black market for ten times what they'd sold it for, the farmers got to eat whatever crap was left over. A disincentivized agrarian class turned what had been, before World War II, the world's largest exporter of rice into a net importer.* Meanwhile, Ne Win had gotten those plundered royal jewels he'd been so concerned about back from England's Victoria and Albert Museum. Though they were supposedly held in Rangoon's National Museum, the rumor was that the ones on display were fake, the real ones taken by Ne Win, so he could prance around his house in them, I guess.

In the mid-'80s, the economic policies of Ne Win, who was no economist, became even more crippling. One day, the government suddenly demonetized bills of ten, fifty, and one hundred kyat, the Burmese currency, rendering most of people's cash savings—even the cash in their pockets—instantly worthless. The seventy-five-year-old Ne Win replaced them with seventy-five-kyat and thirty-five-kyat notes. Within just a couple of years, both those just-introduced bills were demonetized and replaced with denominations of forty-five and ninety: numbers whose digits added up to and were divisible by superstitious Ne Win's lucky number nine.†

Up to 80 percent of the country's currency was completely useless. Those who'd managed to wring any more savings out of the dismal economy since the previous demonetization lost them again. This alone would seem to be enough to put an end to the population's civility. Then, a few months later, some students got into a tea-shop brawl with locals—including a high-ranking official's son. When the

---

* "Burma is a country that has never known, and can never know, famine," posited colonial administrator James George Scott, "except as a direct result of civil war and misrule."

† "Superstitious" is not a pejorative in Burma; it is, true to the Air Force survival guide's assertion, a way of life. Even in the early centuries, prosperous cities featured twelve gates, one for each sign of the zodiac. Said Scott on the Burmese's preoccupation with astrology and luck, "Tuesday and Saturday are bad days to do anything. If you commence an extensive work on either of these days, you will soon die. . . . Beyond this, men born on certain days are exposed to dangers in particular months. Children born on Wednesday or Friday ought to be very careful what they do in the months of May, September, and January. The best thing is for them to do nothing, and in Burma they act on the precept with great zeal."

locals were not held accountable for beating the shit out of the kids, students were ready to demonstrate. When several students were killed during those demonstrations, people rioted.

The British, remember, had dealt with their protesters fifty years earlier by opening fire.* Ah, precedent. In March 1988, a few days after the tea-shop incident, unarmed protesters in Rangoon took to the streets. They were shot at. Boys and girls alike were clubbed to death. Students were chased into a nearby lake, where many drowned. Several dozen student activists died of suffocation in a police van. The government shut down all the universities. As the weeks passed, the hot, broke, and restive Burmese became increasingly angry. The price of food went up prohibitively. In June, thousands of people poured into the streets around the country. The radio reported that students were being killed, but the demands for a revolution continued.

In late July 1988, Ne Win did something astounding. In a televised speech, he lamented the lack of trust in the government and said that, clearly, elections would have to be held. Burma hadn't had elections in three decades, and last time they'd led to Ne Win's coup. He called for a multiparty government, which was surprising, since at the time Burma had a one-party system made up of only his Burma Socialist Programme Party, and he was the one who'd made all the other political parties illegal. Though it seemed like good news at first, it wasn't, exactly.

> Although I said I would retire from politics, we will have to main-
> tain control to prevent the country from falling apart, from disar-
> ray, till the future organizations can take full control. In continuing

---

* To their credit, the colonialists didn't always handle Burmese rabble-rousing so igno-
miniously. Students launched major protests, for example, in response to the Rangoon
University Act of 1920, which made higher education less available to the masses. At
times throughout the early 1900s, citizens were able to peacefully organize, rally, and protest. It's a right they haven't had since, for nearly a hundred years.

to maintain control, I want the entire nation, the people, to know that if in the future there are mob disturbances, if the army shoots, it hits—there is no firing into the air to scare.

But wait. There was more. He later appointed as his successor Sein Lwin, the one who'd ordered the attacks on the protesters in the first place—the guy people called The Butcher. It was like a really extreme version of George W. Bush resigning at some point in his presidency and telling rioting American liberals to calm down, everything's cool, because Dick Cheney would be in charge now.

This was not what the people were gunning for, which was the resignation of the whole horrible government. At the astrologically auspicious moment of eight past eight in the morning on August 8, 1988, Rangoon dockworkers went on strike. Tens of thousands of Burmese throughout the country marched, hollering for democracy, crowding the streets of every major city, without interference from the regime. All day, people cheered and gave speeches. Then, around midnight, the military/government, which had no interest in giving up power as the people demanded, cut the electricity, drove in tanks and trucks, and opened fire, shooting, as promised, to hit.

For five days, the death toll climbed as neither soldiers nor increasingly incensed civilians stood down. When a group of doctors and nurses at Rangoon General Hospital called for the army to stop shooting people, it shot at them. Rumors circulated that the army was tossing bodies of the wounded into the incinerators along with the dead. On August 13, in an apparent bid to restore order, the army withdrew and Sein Lwin resigned. But the people were fired up.

"It is hard to describe the thrill people felt in finding their voices for the first time, in being able to speak out," Pascal Khoo Thwe wrote in his memoir. And it's hard to understand for anyone raised with free speech and institutional encouragement to think and argue for herself. Infrastructure was at a standstill as workers walked out of their jobs punch-drunk and giddy with their new liberties: the freedom to get together and talk about whatever they wanted. In late August, a massive crowd that had gathered on a slope of the Shwedagon Pagoda was addressed by a slight but steady woman. She was Aung San Suu Kyi, the daughter of Aung San, and many thousands—tens of thousands, hundreds of thousands, they say!—of people listened to her call for a democratic government, though she'd never been involved in politics. "I could not, as my father's daughter, remain indifferent to all that was going on. This national crisis could, in fact, be called the second struggle for independence."

The protests didn't end until six weeks had passed. Survivors and state radio reported hundreds killed. Doctors in Rangoon claimed wildly that three thousand unarmed civilians had been murdered on August 8 alone. The government was "overthrown" in a coup, which was generally believed to have been staged by a behind-the-scenes Ne Win. It got a new, heartwarming name: the State Law and Order Restoration Council. (It adopted its current name, the much friendlier-sounding State Peace and Development Council, in 1997.*) The new government announced that it would hold elections, but nothing changed. Though 234 parties registered, their campaigning was rigorously restricted. They could choose their insignia only from a preapproved list, which included tennis rackets and beach balls. Hundreds of political activists were in jail. Aung San Suu Kyi was locked under house arrest. Still, when the elections finally took place, in May 1990, two-thirds of those eligible to vote did. The National

---

* The same year that the name changed, a couple of Burmese companies known to be strongly connected to, if not straight-up part of, the junta hired Washington PR and lobbying firms, causing speculation that the switch was the work of American image-makeover ingenuity. When I asked a senior vice president of one of the firms, Jefferson Waterman International, he insisted that though JWI published newsletters about how Burma is totally swell and contracted to set up meetings with US government figures, his firm's consultants "don't change names. We wouldn't tell a government to change their name." (In case you're wondering, the adverb that would best describe how this information was asserted to me is "angrily.")

League for Democracy, Aung San Suu Kyi's party, won 60 percent of that vote, and the majority of the seats in parliament. The people had called the government's election bluff by voting against it.

"Don't gamble with the Burmans," warned the *Handbook of Burma and Northeastern India* put out by the US Army Air Forces Tactical Center in 1944—"they're poor losers." Indeed, like a rebuffed petulant child, the regime simply refused to give up its property, declared the elections invalid, and locked itself in power, which it retains to this day. In the meantime, it has cracked down harder than ever on its citizenry. There's the Printers and Publishers Registration Law, which requires that all printed material—magazine, hand-lettered flyer, whatever—pass the inspection of the Press Scrutiny and Registration Division of the Ministry of Information before publication. Verboten is the distribution, in any medium, of any information that is unfriendly to the state, the state ideology, members of state government, the state of state government, the state socialism program, the state of the economy, or the state of the union (plus Internet porn). BBC and Voice of America radio broadcasts have been jammed. CNN has been blacked out. Universities have been shut down regularly, for long periods of time; when open, students might be forced to do their classes at satellite locations to keep them from congregating on main campuses. Aung San Suu Kyi has largely been kept under house arrest, despite having won the Nobel Peace Prize the year after the elections; one of the two times she was let out, a mob of government-backed goons attacked a convoy carrying her through the street and beat some of her supporters and colleagues to death—up to a hundred, they say!—though she escaped; though only to be arrested again; she was still incarcerated when I arrived in Mae Sot. And there has been, of course, an expansion of the military, requisite to keeping the mean peace. There were 200,000 Burma armed forces soldiers before the 1988 uprisings. By 1996, there were twice as many.

The Burma army did need all the troops it could get in the days following the '88 protests; the countrywide rebellion wasn't the only fight in town. The ethnic groups in the eastern hills were still at work on their armed revolution. Thousands of the student demonstrators joined the Karen, fleeing for days, weeks through the jungle to their territory, arriving at encampments with signs saying things like "Welcome to the Karenni Liberated Zone: you will possess our land only over our corpses." The primarily Burman protesters formed the All Burma Students Democratic Front at mighty Manerplaw and became an armed resistance, the Karen rebels teaching the students jungle warfare and fighting alongside them as the army came in hot pursuit, battling face-to-face, old school, the government using unarmed captured civilians as human shields. Between firefights, the authorities spoke to the protesters via state radio, urging them to come home. Like diabolical stepparents in a fairy tale, they baited the students with sweet entreaties over the airwaves: "Come back, children, we still welcome you with open arms. . . ." Those who turned themselves in disappeared. Government aircraft dropped leaflets on the bases, some claiming the exiles would be safe if they just went home, some saying they would be bombed in their hiding spots if they didn't.

The rumor and lifeline of hope among the Burmese hiding in the jungle with the battle-hardened Karen was that Americans were coming with arms and Special Forces soldiers and battleships. When they didn't, the KNU tried nevertheless to seize the day, calling a conference with the sudden, unexpected, and welcome allies, but the seventy student representatives were incapable of constructive dialogue. Pascal Khoo Thwe, who was present, blamed their lack of any model but the regime, which had taught them only to be defensive and uncompromising. The students went back home, or to another country to live in exile, having grown tired of waiting at the border for Western reinforcements to help take Rangoon, leaving the Karen back to fending for and waiting by themselves.

It was just as well that the Burman students gave up: The enormous demonstrations and ensuing murders and unfair fights were barely covered in the United States. Amnesty International released some literature that nobody really read (and that the Burmese state media dismissed as "fabrications" that "emanated from jealousy against establishment of a peaceful and prosperous socialist state"). The United States wasn't going to take any significant action against the regime, and then only some pretty questionable action, for years.

XI.

ABBY AND I agreed that the next person to remind us not to consort with Burmese spies got punched in the face.

I was, like all Americans without a visa, authorized to stay in Thailand for only thirty days. But since Burma was such a short jaunt away, I could do a border run and reenter Thailand with a fresh, thirty-extra-day-allowing stamp. I prevailed on Abby, who didn't need to leave the country, who had responsibly paid for and received her extended tourism visa before she left the States, to go with me anyway. The night before we left, Saturday night, the night after we got drunk on Friday night, we got drunk again, to the sounds of our coworkers badgering us to keep quiet about their whereabouts and ethnicity.

"Do not give any information," The Blay said for the eleventh time while we drank Chang, again, out of coffee cups, again. His had a drawing of a teddy bear and some German words on it. Mine featured a cartoon middle-aged white man in a cape and said SUPER DAD. This time, I asked someone where they'd gotten all these mugs. No one knew. This time, we were sitting on the floor of The Blay's room instead of at the picnic table. He stored a few proper glasses on a shelf in here, he showed us, but there wasn't enough company worth taking them out for. Ta Mla was drinking, but just for the moment; by ten, he was back at work at his computer. Htan Dah's kid had joined us and was already totally blotto, but shared a cup with his dad. Eh Soe had disappeared—not that he'd have been much of a conversationalist anyway. That morning, in response to a simple question, my hungover roommate had answered me with entirely nonsensical English and, when I asked him to repeat himself, tried again, and then again, before quitting and saying, "I have a very terrible headache."

Abby and I mentally inventoried our surroundings. We'd never been behind the door of this long, narrow afterthought off the living room before. It ran the length of the house but for the back corner, which the computer room took up. It was the only room in the house that was occupied by only one person. In addition to solitude, The Blay had, we realized when we were finally invited in for the party, something else no one else did: a mattress. The queen rested on the floor under an enormous pea-green mosquito net and an unsettlingly large pile of stuffed animals. When Abby had walked in and laid eyes on the teddy bears, she'd asked The Blay what the hell. He'd shaken his head and laughed softly. "My wife," he'd said, and Abby had raised her eyebrows at me.

"If anyone ask, you do not know us," he continued now. "Never give this address or phone number."

"The Blay," I said, leaning forward and looking him in the eye. "I'm pretty smart. I know not to tell anyone where to find a bunch of illegal refugees."

He looked down and nodded, like he was satisfied, like he believed that I understood. But then: "There could be spies."

"We know!" Abby and I yelled.

The staff was terrified of spies. With the help of informers, Burma's military/government has instilled a pervasive fear and paranoia in its citizenry—fear and paranoia so ingrained and severe that people also police themselves. Anyone can become a spy, and the government is always recruiting: friends or neighbors or even family members who

tell on people they know because they are coerced into it, or because they need the money, or because the only way to protect their own families is to turn in someone else's. Between soldiers, undercover agents, regular cops, plainclothes cops, and civilian informers, everyone in Burma understands, and has deeply assimilated, that you never know who's safe to talk to. The host of the Burma *Frontline* special, for example, wanted simply to drive past the house of Aung San Suu Kyi. Several cabdrivers turned down the job, because they didn't want to be seen doing it, and the driver who did agree to take him made the crew hide the camera. The Western journalists who do go to Burma write about being torn between getting the people's stories and getting the people in deep shit for being caught talking to them.*
And it's not much easier for the Burmese to communicate with less conspicuous people or even people they *know* they can trust: In the '90s, the government reportedly opened a new spying facility that allows it to tap phones, faxes, and emails around the nation.

The fact that my housemates didn't live in Burma anymore didn't by any means make them immune to intelligence efforts. Even the Thai government had to contend with spies from Burma. At a 1997 National Security Council meeting, a Thai army general speculated that Burma was spending 20 to 30 percent of its military budget on intelligence. Two years later an initiative to issue green cards to qualifying immigrants from Burma was said to be postponed due partly to concerns that Burmese soldiers were disguising themselves as workers to obtain documents to stay in the country. In 2003, the number of Burmese spies slipping in as workers was continuing to increase, to the point that a report to the prime minister recommended involving villagers near the border in security efforts—calling, essentially, for turning Thai civilians into spies to spy on the spies. In December 2008, Thai authorities in Mae Sot arrested ten armed Burmese nationals,

---

* Not that the journalists themselves are necessarily free from the danger. One American magazine columnist who was secretly (he thought) interviewing villagers in 1999 woke up drugged and naked in an alley, beaten and covered in urine and feces.

who admitted they'd been sent by the Burmese military. According to Thai army intelligence, there are two types of spies from Burma in Thailand: those who collect information about the neighboring country, and those who watch people like The Blay.

Other pro-democracy organizations on the Thai side of the border had warned BA of the schemes the latter type used. There was a story that the phones of such an organization rang late one night. "I'm a refugee and I need help," the voice on the line said in Karen. "Please, can you help me? Can you come pick me up?" The sympathetic listener went to meet the caller. He didn't come back. Though it sounded like an urban legend, a refugee's scary story to tell in the dark or around a campfire, it certainly wasn't unheard of for Burmese soldiers to enter other countries and then abscond back across the border with unwilling expatriates in tow. The DKBA was well known for kidnapping refugees in Thailand, and well known to be a pawn of the regime's. Not that the SPDC was above doing the work itself. Burmese soldiers killed one Karen refugee and injured another on Thai soil in 1997, then forced several dozen others back across the border into Burma. In 1999, the Burmese military found two students, leaders of the All Burma Democratic Students Front, who had been living in exile in southern China. The activists were abducted and taken back to intelligence headquarters in their home country. In January 2009, a dissident monk who was hiding in the sanctuary of Thai monks was interviewed by a reporter. "Please don't name the monastery," he pleaded with the writer. "There are Burmese government agents everywhere." A month later, an intercepted 42-page report compiled by the Burmese Southeast Regional Military Command that detailed the activities of the KNU, dissident groups, aid groups, and NGOs on the border further confirmed what the monk and Thailand and everyone else had known for years.

BA included spy awareness as part of new staff training. Just a few nights ago, The Blay had told Sheh Reh, the guy who'd just been to jail and didn't like my burned potatoes, why he should be cautious about answering the phone. "A spy could call the office," The Blay had explained as they were sitting in his room talking before bed. "They will tell you they need your help, but even though you're worried about them, you must be careful."

Sheh Reh had already been wary enough of his new job with BA. He hadn't really wanted it, but had gotten so bored sitting in the same dirty refugee camp for ten years, teaching for six hundred baht, or about $15, per month after he graduated. And he couldn't go home to Burma, because when he lived there, he'd often had to run away with the other three hundred people in his village to avoid being conscripted as a porter. The SPDC had eventually made them leave the village entirely, forced them into a relocation labor camp a four- or five-hour walk away with no sanitation or education, and burned their village down, so he'd recently applied for and undergone BA's five-week village-organizing training. He didn't particularly want to go inside Burma to do that job, either, because it was dangerous, and he was scared, and he knew that if he got caught there he'd be killed.*

And then, the very night that The Blay had warned him about the phone, someone called at 3 AM. Though he was sleeping closest to the phone, Sheh Reh froze. How would he know if it wasn't really a refugee? Would he turn down someone in actual need of help? Would he break, and endanger his friends, his coworkers, his people by answering the call for assistance? The phone rang more than a dozen times before Htoo Moo got up off the floor and crossed the living room into the computer room to answer it. Sheh Reh panicked as he heard his coworker ask "What?" several times. Maybe Htoo Moo wasn't sure whether to believe the caller and was asking him to repeat himself. After a moment, Htoo Moo put down the phone while Sheh Reh involuntarily held his breath and listened. It was, it turned out, a friend of mine who was too excited about having finally negotiated

---

* "But," he added as he was telling me about his reservations, "we must work or it won't change."

her international calling card number, PIN number, and the correct sequence of country code, area code, and phone numbers to check the time difference when the call finally went through. Htoo Moo went upstairs to wake me, and Sheh Reh lay there in the dark heat, surrounded by mosquito netting and a layer of guilt and fear.

But despite the incessant, irritating warnings; despite Abby's having just read an article by a BBC reporter who'd visited Burma only a few weeks earlier and been watched by a guy pretending to endlessly read the same single page of an upside-down week-old newspaper; despite my having recently trudged through an academic treatise on how the government fed, via swarms of informers, its obsession with knowing about every movement and conversation that occurred within its borders, Abby and I were still somehow surprised when we were dropped off at the Burma border, just three miles from our house, on a lucid Sunday morning and had taken but a few steps onto the Friendship Bridge before becoming host to our very own Burmese spy.

In 1997, a bridge spanning the Moei River was opened in the presence of Burmese dancers, Thai spectators, and officials from both countries. The road between Mae Sot and Burma's Myawaddy is a link in the Asian Highway, a ninety-thousand-mile UN dream connecting the continent from the Korean peninsula to Turkey. After years of negotiation, Thailand had talked the reclusive regime into letting the Royal Thai Government build and pay for the 80 million–baht ($2 million) bridge that would, incidentally, allow the junta improved control over Burma's thriving, insurgency-funding black market. And after years of delays—nearly two, as Burma halted construction in a dispute over riverbank sovereignty—the pathway to better cross-border trade* and tourism was complete. And here Abby and I were, nine years and some fourteen hundred feet of concrete later, accepting greetings from a friendly Burmese stranger.

---

* Thailand reportedly earns a billion baht ($28 million) a month from the trade between Myawaddy and Mae Sot.

"Hello!" he said, trotting quickly to get ahead of our long American strides. He took his place just in front of us and turned his body at a ninety-degree angle to ours, walking sideways to facilitate conversation and acknowledge our polite hellos back. "Where are you from?" he asked.

"The United States," Abby said.

"Very good!" he said, nodding. The man was attractive, with small, shiny eyes and shiny white teeth in a thin face. He had a traditional cotton *longyi* tied around his slim waist, but he was wearing expensive-looking black leather slides and a fancy watch. His short black hair was immaculately trimmed, the clean line at the back of his neck exactly parallel to his clean collared shirt. At that point, he could have been any enthusiastic native, I guess, a stunningly put-together and well-dressed plebeian in one of the most poverty-stricken countries in the world who'd just happened to be hanging around the bridge checkpoint when we showed up. We put on our appropriately affable faces. Then he said, "You work with refugees?"

We didn't look at each other and immediately shook our heads.

"We're tourists," I said.

"Really?"

We told some lies about sightseeing and, at the man's prompting, how long we were staying in Thailand. He asked if we were tourists, and we said again that we were.

Our trio approached the other security gateway, at the other end of the bridge, a large edifice with a walkway through the middle and guards hanging around outside. The roof connected the two-story buildings that stood on either side of the bridge's width, all modern-bunker looking and white paint, and the man ushered us into the structure on the right.

Though both slender, Abby and I were bigger than everyone. The wee guards pointed us into two empty chairs and took our passports to someplace we couldn't see while we watched the unhurried movement in the small office. Some of the guards were wearing black velvet flip-flops with their uniforms. One such man brought our passports back and demanded money. Though the fee to get into Burma was 500 baht, and we knew it, the guard charged us 510 each, because he could. And though we glared at him while doing so, we paid it.

When we stepped back into the dazzling sunlight, our man was still there.

"Where do you want to go?" he asked.

"We don't know," I said. "We don't have a plan."

We didn't. We'd come across the border because of my visa and, honestly, the kind of curiosity that makes people ask, when they hear someone has killed himself, how he did it. What would the country from which our housemates had been so violently expelled, in which the people were suffocating and starving, look like? Abby and I wandered down the main road with the man at our side. We passed song-thaews stuffed with dark-toothed men and women and their children. Open-front shops sold food, portraits, and cheap electronics. As in Mae Sot, vagrant dogs ran as freely as squirrels in a New England park, but there were some stray goats for us to take pictures of as well.

"It looks like Thailand," Abby said quietly to me, which made sense, as a decent arm could have thrown something at it from there. She took in the buildings and the road and the people, all of which seemed worn-out and visibly dirty. "But crappier."

The three of us walked farther into town, Abby and I looking around, the man scampering along next to us. "You work with refugees?" he asked, smiling.

We still didn't exchange glances, but were becoming more sour toward our escort by the second.

"We already told you we're tourists," I said, at the same time that Abby said, "No, you already asked us that. We're tourists." He asked again how long we were staying in Thailand and what we were going to see, and we told the same lies.

"What's that?" I asked, pointing across the street to a wide, several-story building. It was white and dingy, and on the front of it hung a large poster picturing the faces of heavily made-up women and tough-looking men.

"Cinema," the man said.

"Oh, really?" I asked while Abby got her camera out. "What's playing?"

"Movie is about fighting," he said, smiling, still, eternally. "War between the government and rebels."

"What rebels?" I asked. "Like, KNU rebels?"

"Yes," he nodded emphatically, and laughed.

"Who wins?"

"The government," the man replied. "The government always win!* Like ahrnuld!"

Abby and I looked at each other to see if either had registered the word he was saying, but we both shook our heads.

"Like what?" Abby asked.

"Like ahrnuld," he repeated, and we didn't understand because his pronunciation was off, or because we weren't expecting a Schwarzenegger reference, or both, so we asked him to say it one more time. "The government of California," he said finally, and we got it. Arnold was, actually, a pretty apt simile: strong, untouchable, takes by force.† He always wins. And so did the SPDC, even in a movie theater in land that was technically part of Karen State.

Once upon a time, this town had indeed been KNU controlled. In 1974, ethnic rebels and the government had, just like in the movie, fought right here, and this very place had been burned out, a fox-

---

* Legally, it has to. Burmese movies can't contain any footage that might make the country look bad. Scenes that depict poverty, for example, are against regulations.

† Rambo would be an appropriate metaphor for the junta, too, so it's the ultimate clash of the titans when he goes up against the Tatmadaw in part IV. (Spoiler alert!) It turns out to be kind of a draw, really, since Rambo saves a couple of abducted missionaries and Karen civilians and cuts a few scores of Burmese soldiers into so many disgusting pieces with a giant machine gun but neither ends the Karen war nor upends the big bad regime. Still, the movie was banned inside Burma, where, naturally, it became an underground hit.

hole-and-barbed-wire-surrounded battlefield. The Karen held their line for days. The government obliterated it with a series of air raids, jet strafing and bombing that blew up an oil depot and sent hundreds of grazing cattle scattering while Thai spectators watched the action from across the river. There was no sign of that battle here now, any more than there was of the battle still going on between the same groups not so far from where we stood. Pascal Khoo Thwe, who lived in both cities and villages in Burma until the late '80s, has written about how the greatest dearth of information about Burma occurs within Burma itself, comparing its citizens to the Germans who said they really didn't realize what the Nazis were up to. Burma's government contends to its people, just like it does in press releases that talk smack on the United States, that stories of burning villages and bullet-riddled ethnic villagers is guerrilla propaganda. It's not just the rest of the world that doesn't know what's going on here. Trips to the cinema start with preshow propaganda featuring news clips about, for example, the country's infrastructural progress and end with guerrilla bad guys being roundly and deservedly defeated. Even Pascal Khoo Thwe had believed it, until he arrived at and personally witnessed the devastation in a village—not twenty miles from where he'd lived most of his life.

Our spy suggested that we visit the nearby Shwe Muay Wan temple. We moved on and turned right off the main road. Though he was moving his short legs rapidly, Abby and I gained some distance.

"Can't we ditch this guy?" she asked.

"I think this is his job," I said.

She sighed. "He's really bothering me. Can't we tell him we want to be alone? Can't we tell him we really don't want company or something?"

"I don't know. I mean, I guess you can try." I didn't want to spend any more time with shady slick, either, but had resigned myself to his presence. "I don't think we're going to be able to avoid being followed."

We three took off our sandals when we got to the temple. We

strolled around the complex, the sky-blue tiles between the gilded stupas hot beneath our bare feet, looking at the giant porcelain-white and gold faces and taking obligatory pictures of big Buddha after big Buddha. The man was quiet. The spare worshippers were quiet. The city seemed quiet in this sacred place, like any sacred place.

Back on the street, the man procured a bicycle rickshaw with a chubby driver and told us to squeeze onto the narrow wooden seat in front. The man perched on the side of the cart as the driver started pedaling us, laboriously, at a walking pace, up the gentle hill to the market.

"Your friends are Karen?" the man asked. Abby and I stared at him blankly. The driver panted hard while bikes and running children passed us on the nearly carless thoroughfare. "I see your motorbike drivers. They are Karen?"

Htan Dah and Htoo Moo had driven Abby and me, respectively, to the bridge. We'd hopped off the bikes and stood talking for a moment before the boys turned around and went home. We realized now that the man had been watching us for a while. We realized now that we were being followed for good reason.

"We don't know," I said. "They saw us walking and just asked us if we needed a ride."

"I think they are Karen. I think you work with them or are friends with them," he said pleasantly.

"I think they're Thai," I said. "They just picked us up on the road."

"No, they are Karen," he said. Big smiles. Everything was okay here.

"How can you tell?"

"I can see by their features."

"Oh, *really?*" I asked. Abby asserted that those guys had sure looked Thai to her, and I that all Asians looked the same to me, the both of us shrugging like we were some kind of morons.

"I think you work with them. I think they are your friends," the man said again. We kept denying it and shaking our heads, and whether he was being insistent or just wasn't very good at using past tense was hard to say.

"Where did you get that?" he asked me. He pointed to the bag, the strap of which was slung across my chest, in my lap. The street crawled by as our driver pedaled. Everyone stared as we passed. My bag was a traditional Karen purse, woven out of rough, colored cotton, the type everyone at the house carried. I had taken this beige and white one out of Eh Soe's closet that morning.

"In Thailand," I said saltily, and the man said that it was a Karen bag, said that I could buy one cheaply in his country but that the Karen make them, started to say something else but neither of our American faces were friendly anymore, so he didn't.

The covered market was crowded. We chose our directions in the maze of narrow walkways randomly, turning tight corners around rice baskets big enough to climb into, piles of quickly overripening fruit, stalls stacked with soaps, shampoos, dresses, shoes. The man followed us and occasionally suggested that we might want to buy some cheap jewelry or toys. We touched the velvet flip-flops, picked up and pretended to study some of the noodle packages printed in alphabets that meant nothing to us, but emerged from the market empty-handed. Outside, women squatted in the muddy side street selling cruddy vegetables and meat off mats on the ground. The man seemed embarrassed by this, and walked us quickly past. He told us, his voice low, that we probably didn't want to purchase any of it, because it was not so nice.

Our trio reboarded the rickshaw and set off for another temple at the man's suggestion, turning off the paved main road and onto another, mucky avenue. Adults and children lined the street, some standing around, some walking places, many who caught our eyes and waved or yelled "Hello!" I shouted greetings back. The man was silent, watching the exchanges, until Abby asked him if she could take this road to Rangoon.

The answer is no. Foreigners visiting Burma aren't allowed to

continue unattended on the road past Myawaddy, though in theory
the Asian Highway connected the cities, could provide a route all
the way to eastern Europe. ("All that is needed is for Myanmar to
get its act together," grumbled one unusually candid travel feature
on Thai Airways's website.) To get to the famous port town from
where she was now, Abby's guidebook recommended hopping a
series of state-run buses and trains and even a boat. The man told
her that no path went straight there, she'd have to go way out of
her way and follow the roads roundabout and anyway, why was she
asking? Did she want to see the capital?

"Didn't they move the capital?" Abby asked.

The answer is yes. Rangoon, on the Andaman Sea side of Burma's
peninsula, used to be the country's commercial and political center. It was home to major schools, industry, extensive infrastructure,
government buildings. But in late 2005, the junta started moving
its ministries a couple hundred miles away into the mountains. The
administration built new offices, apartment blocks, even a replica of
Rangoon's ancient, three-hundred-some-foot-tall landmark Shwedagon Pagoda in what used to be a rural village no one's ever heard
of called Naypyidaw. It wasn't just expensive; it was also incredibly
inconvenient, not only for the locals who were enslaved to build all
the magnificent nonsense but also for the government, whose civil
servants were given two days to pack up their departments and lives
and report to work way up north. The BBC quoted the information
minister as having justified the trouble by saying that the government needed a more central, and therefore more strategic, location.
Al Jazeera reported that he'd given two answers different both from
that one and from each other: that the government was expanding,
and couldn't find adequate space to do so in Rangoon, and that the
regime desired a neater, greener, more gardeny capital. Journalists
and analysts suggested that the government feared a US naval invasion, or the wrath of its own people, some five million of whom lived
in Rangoon. Others said the powers that be wanted to move their

bureaucracy closer to the front lines of their war against the ethnic minorities. Many also pointed that Than Shwe, Burma's current dictator, carried the long-burning torch of Burmese superstition and was likely motivated at least in part by the advice of fortune-tellers.

Regardless of the reason, the move had occurred only several months before our visit; maps certainly hadn't been changed. Our spy laughed at Abby's awareness of it, but didn't sound happy.

"How did you know that?" he asked. The answer, of course, was that she currently worked and ate and partied with a crew of activist refugees. But she scowled at him as if he'd insulted her worldliness when she said, "The news."

The shrine at which we arrived shortly was what a travel guide might euphemistically call "unique." An enormous painted metal crocodile with a rectangular temple atop its wide, green back sat gape-jawed in the middle of a giant fenced-in pond. It looked like an attraction at a subpar amusement park, and Abby and I traded reasonably irreverent remarks about it as we circled around to its backside. The entrance to the temple was there, a bridge to the reptile across the pond, beset by an archway with two big pink posts. The one on the left was painted with blue letters we couldn't read. The one on the right carried the translation: DON'T CLIMB LADY.

Beyond the reptile was another, more conventional structure, into which we gals were allowed; it contained a Buddha backlit by a wheel of flashing disco lights around its head. The wood floor was bare, the walls covered in murals. We and our spy wandered through the spacious, echoing room and out to the balcony at the back of the building.

We could see the tall, narrow stupas of Shwe Muay Wan across town. Just below us a patchwork of trees and small shacks made of cardboard, plastic, planks, corrugated metal, thatch spread across our field of vision, toward the main road. We leaned on the railing and looked over the community, at the tumbledown homes. Abby asked me if I just wanted to go back to Mae Sot. I did. Though we'd not been in Burma but a couple of hours, we were exhausted.

On the way back to the rickshaw, the man suggested under-
taking more sightseeing, but we didn't seem to be listening. He
asked us for perhaps the fifth time if we wanted to go sit down and
eat. Between the heat and the guard we'd been keeping up, we were
spent and ravenous. But we both continued to decline, though we
weren't positive whether we should impose the only kind of sanctions two girls from the Midwest and Northeast could: refusing to
spend money in Burma.

When Rangoon launched its "Visit Myanmar Year" campaign
ten years prior, in 1996, Aung San Suu Kyi requested that visitors
stay out of the country in protest of the junta that hoped to gain
legitimacy and cash through tourism. Those who support the boycott
maintain that funding the government with tourism dollars helps
perpetuate the status quo. What's more, "Visit Myanmar" created
construction projects that were completed by citizens who were torn
from their homes and forced to work without compensation—refur-
bishing Mandalay palace's moat, for example. Visiting Burma as if it's
any other tourist destination, some say, implies that there's nothing
wrong going on there, and using roads built by slaves to see sights
at which they toiled insinuates a similar approval. Some guidebook
companies don't even publish a volume on the country, and those
that do, as well as travel magazines, advise visitors to consider their
vacation decisions very carefully before spending dime one. Abby
had nearly refused to accompany me on my border run because of the
entrance fee she'd had to pay the government.

On the other hand, critics of the boycott argue that travelers
should show up to let people in Burma know that the world hasn't
forgotten them and bear witness to what's going on, be inspired to
learn the history or spread the word. Theoretically, tourists could
also act as a sort of protection for the oppressed if they swarmed and
spread out around the country, as human rights are less likely to be
violated in front of wandering Occidental eyes. Additionally, cutting
off the country means cutting off its economy, and it's the people

who bear the brunt of Burma's financial difficulties. Shopkeepers in cities like Myawaddy depend on customers to keep their businesses alive. Anyway, visitors are unlikely to bring the junta to its financial knees by keeping away money from tourism, which doesn't even rank on the list of the country's valuable industries.

Regardless, our shadow seemed like the kind of guy who'd go to a restaurant run by goons. And we'd developed an intense dislike of him. Maybe he was being paid by the government, or maybe he was just fishing for info so he could trade officials for favor or cash or a break, or maybe we had just become paranoid, too. Either way, we didn't want to be subjected to it anymore. Gloriously, as visitors, we didn't have to be.

"We want to leave," we told him.

We traveled along the main avenue for the last time. "Except for these occasional signs for Internet, this could be fifty years ago, couldn't it?" Abby asked. She remarked again that our surroundings looked kind of like Thailand, but worse.

She was right. Hot, crowded, friendly but sad Myawaddy looked like Thailand might if Thailand experienced twelve times the infant mortality and fifteen times the child mortality—the second-highest child mortality rate in Asia, after Afghanistan's—if the life expectancy were nearly a decade lower, and if its GNI were a fifteenth of what it was despite its having abundant natural resources. It looked like Thailand might if Thailand, which is just a little bit smaller and a little more populous than Burma, spent 40¢ per capita on health care rather than $63, or provided 0 percent of childhood vaccinations instead of 100 percent, or were one of only five countries in the world that forbade Boy Scouts, or were the poorest country on the continent and one of the seven poorest countries in the world but had still managed to double the size of its military troops and buy billions' worth of weapons over two decades despite not being at war with anybody but its own run-down people. Myawaddy looked like similar cities in Thailand might if Thailand had long ago run out of fresh paint and spirit. Or as the fat old officer on the Thai side of the bridge that morning put it while he was checking my passport:

"Where are you going?"

"To Burma."

Tongue-clucking. "You don't want to go there." Frowning. "It's no good."

Or as Doctors Without Borders called it, one of the top ten humanitarian crises in the world. Or as Human Rights Watch called it, the country with the most child soldiers on the planet. Or as the United States State Department called it, one of the world's eight worst violators of religious freedom and one of the world's ten worst human rights violators. Or according to Transparency International, less corrupt than only Somalia (and tied with Iraq for second most corrupt). Or according to *Parade* magazine, home to earth's fourth-worst dictator.*

It's not surprising that this government always wins in movie fights with the Karen National Union, given the one singular title it has won of its own, courtesy of the *Far Eastern Economic Review*: "world's most pleasant and civilised guerrilla group."

When our rickshaw arrived back near the bridge security check-point, Abby and I hopped off and reached into our bags for money. Our spy, who spoke for the non-English-speaking pedaler, pulled an ugly old tourism trick and said that the price was twice what he'd said earlier; that quote had been per rider. We rolled our eyes, but didn't argue for some reason, and shoved more cash at the man.

He followed us as we cleared the Burma checkpoint and started back toward Thailand, chatting. We barely responded, walking briskly to the single white line painted across the middle of the

---

* In 2009, Than Shwe was down one spot from No. 3 the year prior, outranked by Zimbabwe's Mugabe, Sudan's Omar Al-Bashir, and North Korea's Kim Jong-Il. But he still held evil reign over King Abdullah of Saudi Arabia, Hu Jintao of China, Sayyid Ali Khamenei of Iran, Isayas Afewerki of Eritrea, Gurbanguly Berdymuhammedov of Turkmenistan, and the terrorism-funding and torture-loving Muammar al-Qaddafi of Libya.

Friendship Bridge, that which denoted a border he apparently wasn't going to cross again that day. He stopped as soon as we arrived at it.

"Do you want to give me a present?" he asked—you know, maybe some money, a token, since we were good friends and he had spent so much time trying to make our day pleasant and had helped us find a good rickshaw driver and had negotiated such a good price and shown us so many good things.

"Eat me," I muttered as we turned away from him, stepping fast over the middle-of-the-Moei demarcation, ignoring his goodbyes and leaving him talking and watching after us as we walked farther into Thailand and didn't look back, until we'd climbed into the back of a songthaew on the eastern riverbank.

When we arrived home, Htan Dah was waiting on Abby's front porch next door. The deep awning off the little house she was renting was supported by two wood poles sunk into a wide, waist-high block of cement people sometimes sat on to chat. He looked at us expectantly as we walked through the gate. He was wearing a black T-shirt featuring a sweet-faced Karen infant and the message, in English, that we must work so that the next generation doesn't suffer.

"Your country sucks," I said, pulling off and dropping Eh Soe's Karen bag, and I slumped down next to him on the concrete.

I told him about our spy. I told him how Myawaddy was covered in a layer of something, hush and hopelessness and grime, how I actually felt totally overwhelmed by his obstacles to achieving a peaceful and fulfilling life pretty much all the time. He was quiet, mostly, listening to me and watching, soft nods here and there, until I was done talking about Burma, and then we were talking about whatever, in the way that we did, and then one way or another we were talking about gays again, and then before I knew it he was on his feet and we were hollering at each other.

"For Karen people, we cannot allow it!" he was shouting. "For you, it is no problem, but in my culture, it is not so easy to say it is okay about gay people."

"If you're going to call yourself a human rights activist," I yelled, "you have an obligation to stand up for human rights. Are you really gonna look me in the face and tell me you think gay people don't count as human? They don't deserve rights? You want to say they are lesser people like the Burmese government says about the Karen?"

"I understand what you are saying! For me, I know you are right!"

"But because you're Karen and it's your culture it's okay for gay people to be persecuted? It's not just your culture that doesn't tolerate people! It's my culture, too! That's everybody's culture!"

"You are right! It is not so easy, but I know I should stand up for them! If I see people, gay people, are being persecuted, I would stand up for them!"

"Oh, really?"

"Yes! I would stand up for them with my voice!"

Passing housemates walked around our conversation, stopping for a moment to watch and listen on the edges before continuing on their way out of or into the house. Shaky and slightly panting both, Htan Dah and I ultimately joined everyone else. Inside, a couple of Office Two guys had come over and rolled the Ping-Pong table into the middle of the living room floor from its resting place folded up against the wall. They looked up, paddles in hand, when I walked in. One of them was my student, and he looked embarrassed to see me; he wasn't wearing pants. I walked upstairs and into my room and past my bed, to where my towel was hanging in front of the open slatted window. When I turned around, I saw the cat.

The gray stray had been hanging around since long before I had, and though she didn't belong to the house, she was part of it now. The day before, she had started bleeding; there'd been blood on the floor where she'd been sitting. Now, she was in my bed, where I never allowed her, lying on top of the coarse woolen blanket I slept with every night. She'd bled out so far that I could see the pool even without moving her.

Downstairs, after I'd had some of Htan Dah's fried egg curry for dinner, after I'd stepped onto the wet cement floor of the bathroom with my hair tied high, after I'd closed the oversized door and stripped off my dusty, sticky, patriotic yellow polo and loose black khakis and scooped up a bowlful of cold water and held my breath and thrown it at my naked chest, after my heartbeat had calmed some with each successive dousing, gasping at the impact, rinsing each arm, and then leg, and then my face of sweat grease and sunscreen, after I'd wrapped my thin seafoam towel around me and walked back out of the bathroom and toward the steps, I felt cleaner, stronger. I got dressed in my room. Eh Soe was nowhere around, so I sat on the reading bench. Htan Dah came in and joined me.

"The cat bled on my bed," I said.

He frowned. "Yes, me too. And That Khaing's."

"I'm sorry I was yelling before."

"I don't mind(!)," he said. "I try to keep open mind. It is important to be flexible . . . to . . . hear other argument."

"I think the world would probably be a better place if more people were like you."

He shrugged.

"Do you wish that you could go to Burma like Abby and I can?"

"I have been(!). Sometimes, after I was born, my mother went across the border, sometimes in Thailand, sometimes in Burma, depending on the war. But I cannot remember. I was very young."

"Did you ever go when you were older?"

"Yes(!). Last year, me and my friend, we swim across the river. We wore dirty clothes so that we look like villager, not from Mae Sot, in case anybody sees us. When we go inside, we know it is very dangerous. We know we can die at any time. But we go because we must fight so it will be better. We must take back what is ours."

"What was your parents' village like?"

"I do not know," he said, shaking his head. "I have never been to my native village. I would like to visit, but I dare not. If I go to my village, to meet my family, maybe SPDC soldier will come and say, 'Who is this guy?' and my family will have trouble."

Htan Dah's older sister had been back there, a long time ago, when she was ten. She left her immediate family at the border and followed a monk deep into the delta, where Htan Dah's parents, lowland Karen settlers, were from, where she'd lived as a child before everyone had fled the flames of the village in a Four Cuts attack, where her grandparents still lived and needed taking care of. She was arrested for being the child of her father, a KNU soldier—a "revolutionary," as Htan Dah always called him. She was released only after the entreaties and vouchings of a former teacher. In a country where activists' families and even lawyers were sometimes imprisoned, sometimes for nothing more than their proximity, as an activist *and* son of a revolutionary, Htan Dah certainly wasn't going to endanger himself and relatives he'd never even met by dropping in on them.

"So then what did you do when you went to Burma?"

"We walked four hours to a village. We talk about the war, tell the villagers about the government, what they are doing, tell them they should empower themselves, they should learn what is going on in their country, so they can start grassroots."

"What did they say?"

"They say, 'We rely on our leaders to make decisions.' They do not want to talk about the war. They just want to farm, to live in the jungle. Like me too."

"Like . . . what do you mean?"

"I just want to live in the jungle."

"How do you know? What if you live in a village and you don't like it? You've never even lived like that, have you?"

"Yes, but it is how my people live. It is tradition. We need to have land so that we can have culture, have freedom. Everything in the jungle is very simple. You don't have to make decision, or worry about police." He shrugged his mouth, turning the corners down. "Just . . . farming, and raising family, and living."

"You have a lot of city skills though. You're up at dawn reading the newspaper everyday online. You're really good at navigating this town and this work, and you love learning about new things. Like, there's no electricity in a village. You've never even had land before. Do you even know how to grow rice?"

However valid that last point, guilt rushed in the moment it left my mouth. Htan Dah just looked at me.

"I can learn," he said finally, flatly.

"At least you seem to like your job."

"I have to like."

I nodded.

"I have to tell you," he said then, "I am leaving."

"What?"

"I am going to Mae La to do training for new staff. I think maybe I would go end of August." That was after I would already have been gone. "But I have to go next week."

"How long are you going to be gone for?"

"Maybe one week."

"A week? All next week? Aw, Htan Dah, I leave the week after that."

"I know(!). I was hoping the training would not be at that time, but they told me, I must go to Mae La."

I looked at him, a little at a loss, not trying to control the amount of sulking happening on my face. "Htan Dah, that's really sad."

"Yes," he said, nodding.

I shook my head, and my shoulders sunk themselves; the grip that came with bad news I couldn't control wrapped itself around my ribcage and squeezed. "That's really, really sad." We both looked at the floor. "Can I go with you?"

"I don't think so! It is not so easy to get white people in the camp." I'd already been told that visitors weren't allowed anymore. When they had been, Karen refugee camps had become something of a tourism trend, which was embarrassing for everybody. Eh Soe had told me how he remembered seeing them, white people driving by, staring, as he'd sat in the door of his hut. Personally, he hadn't really cared whether they visited or not; with or without them, he'd kind of felt like he was living in a zoo. Sometimes, when he'd noticed them watching him from the windows of their four-wheel drives, he'd waved. "What about your students?"

"Yeah, I have class next week. Maybe I can meet you there for one day or something. Can you get permission to get me in?"

"Yeah, maybe. I can ask the section leader. I can try."

I trudged down the stairs with Htan Dah behind me. When I stopped suddenly on the last step, he nearly plowed into my back. "Oh, no," I said, pointing, and he peered over my shoulder. Big, thick pools of plasma dotted the tile floor. "The cat."

"What should we do?" he asked.

"I don't know." Htan Dah's son came running with hard feet and wide stance when he saw his dad. "You should probably keep your kid away from this blood, though."

"I think maybe her babies are dead inside her. What do you think?" Htan Dah grabbed his son's hands over the boy's head, keeping him from walking further than the length of the toddler's upstretched arms.

"Maybe," I said.

"Where is she?"

We checked the living room and computer room before finding the cat in the dining room/garage in a corner lying still. Htan Dah stood over her, frowning. "I feel so bad for her. I am . . . pity. A lot."

"I don't really think there's anything we can do," I said. "Maybe we should just leave her alone."

Htoo Moo was sitting at the picnic table, watching us silently, the unhappiest I'd ever seen him. When Htan Dah walked back in the house, I sat down on the bench across from him.

"Hey, Htoo Moo." I addressed him in a voice for a hospital visit, soft, consoling. "How's it going?"

"Fine," he said, quietly. He didn't smile at me, though he always smiled at me, and everything else. The last time we'd been sitting here, at these exact same places, he'd been telling everyone how when he was last in Burma, he'd stayed at a village having a funeral and celebrated as if he'd known the deceased, loving the community festivities, dancing and getting tanked on homemade whiskey. The only problem, he'd told us, was this withered old man who'd followed him around with his five marriage-age granddaughters in hopes that Htoo Moo would drunkenly tell one of girls he'd marry her so the grandpa could hold him to it. Which had prompted one of the guys to ask, naturally, if the girls had been ugly. "No, no, I would marry them," Htoo Moo had replied. "But they have hillside land. Growing rice on a hillside is terrible." His housemates had laughed because that was a ridiculous reason to not take a wife, but man did Htoo Moo not want to spend his days standing on an incline to cut down all the vegetation that had grown over a fallow field, tilling a hill, harvesting a bluff. He *knew* that was a ridiculous reason to pass up a kind and beautiful woman, so he'd laughed the hardest, wiping his eyes and chuckling at himself long after his friends had stopped.

"Are you okay?" I asked him now.

"Yes," he said, nodding gently.

We sat for a moment, he looking at the table, I looking at him the way Htan Dah had been looking at the cat.

"What did you do today?"

He'd gone to the border to pick up a girl, a friend of a friend, who had moved to Thailand years ago. She'd gotten away from the war in Burma, and had gotten a job as a servant for a rich woman. But the rich woman had beaten her severely.

I'd actually been reading reports like this off one of the shelves upstairs. There are about two million migrant workers from Burma in

Thailand, three-quarters of them illegal. Like the refugees, they don't
have any legal protection and are subject to police abuse. There was
a jail for them in town, actually, off one of the side streets; it just
looked like a great big dog cage, and was so close to the road that
you could see the facial expressions of the people crammed inside
on your way to the nearby guesthouse. Employer abuse is apparently
rampant, with business owners garnishing wages, locking workers
in their rooms at night, beating them, blackmailing them, fucking
them, whatever. And all that was to say nothing of the trafficking,
the masses of women and children from Burma living as sex slaves in
Thailand. That was a whole nother book of testimonials, which I'd
also taken off the shelf, but was having a hard time reading.

This particular woman from Burma was struggling to keep her
wealthy employer happy enough that she wouldn't beat her, but to
no avail. One day, the rich woman beat her nearly to death, called
a cab, and paid the driver to dump the body. He took the money,
but dumped the near-dead maid at the hospital instead. The doctors
there saved her life. Still, she was illegal, so the authorities shipped
her back to Burma. Now she was running away again, and she and
Htoo Moo's mutual friend had called him and asked him to meet
with her, show her around town.

"She's missing a lot of hair," Htoo Moo said, so quietly that I had to
strain to hear him, pointing to his head, "from surgery." He put his hands
back on the table in front of him. "She has . . . scars." He squinted, his
face cringing. "All down her body." He shook his head. "I feel sad."

"I'm sorry Htoo Moo. I wish I could help you feel better." I tried
to think of what to say next, but just sat there with him for a while.
"Is there anything I can do to help?"

"Do you have any medicine?" he asked.

I winced. "Not for that." I watched him watch his still hands.
"You do sound like you might be a little stuffy though. Here, I'll get
you some allergy medicine. It might also help you sleep."

I went upstairs and got a pill out of my bag. When I brought it back down to him, he was sitting just as I'd left him. I got him a glass of water, and sat with him while he drank it.

He said he was tired.

I was tired, too. The darkness had taken the edge out of the heat, but it was still muggy, and late. I said goodnight. Htoo Moo said he was going to bed, but didn't get up, so I walked back into the kitchen, back toward the stairs, leaving him there alone but for the cat breathing slow and hard and bleeding out in the corner.

XII.

"Burma, and its reclusive and repressive regime, may represent one of the most intractable challenges for the global community."

— US AMBASSADOR TO THE UNITED NATIONS—DESIGNATE
SUSAN RICE, 2009

IN AUGUST 2008, first lady Laura Bush made a visit to Mae La refugee camp. She toured the grounds with a shawl of traditional Karen homespun around her shoulders, fringed, embroidered earth tones over her button-down. She brought one of her daughters, and some press, and a gift, ten thousand insecticide-treated bed nets.

Make no mistake: Though most Americans are startlingly uninformed about the shit going down in Burma, your federal lawmakers and political leaders are aware of and on it. In 1997, President Bill Clinton barred new US investment in the country. In 2003, after Aung San Suu Kyi's convoy was attacked, Congress introduced the Freedom and Democracy Act, banning any item produced in Burma from import into the United States, opposing international loans to the country, and freezing assets of the regime in—and denying its members visas to—the States. In 2005, Condoleezza Rice awarded Burma a special designation as an "outpost of tyranny." Bush 43 gave it shout-outs in several State of the Union addresses ("We will continue to speak out for the cause of freedom in places like Cuba, Belarus, and Burma"). There's a US Senate Women's Caucus on Burma, and a Block Burmese Jade Act, and Bush nominated a White House representative and policy coordinator for Burma, and sanctions get repeatedly extended and occasionally further tightened, and there are congressional hearings in which refugees testify about the horror and experts commend the sanctions and cry for more, more, more. Also blacklisting Burma: Australia, which doesn't allow defense exports out or regime members in and has placed financial sanctions against 463 military men, and the EU, which has stripped Burma of trading privileges and instituted an arms embargo. And your usual host of well-meaning celebrities, doing video spots[*] and benefit CDs and writing sort of weird open letters[†] to no one in particular.

---

[*] JENNIFER ANISTON (to aide, outside a movie-lot trailer, frustrated): I've been waiting in there for over two hours, this is costing us way too much money, please, what does he need? A soy maté latte, what? What, are there chemicals in there he can't breathe? Okay, you got the AC off, what, so then tell me what the problem is.
WOODY HARRELSON (throwing open trailer door): I'm not coming out until Burma is free!
[†] "Nineteen years ago, the Burmese people chose Aung San Suu Kyi to be their next leader. And for most of those 19 years she has been kept under house arrest by the military junta that now runs the country. She is the world's only incarcerated Nobel Peace Prize Laureate. . . .

"We must not stand by as she is silenced once again. Now is the time for the United Nations and the entire international community to speak clearly, and with one voice: Free Aung San Suu Kyi.

"In support, George Clooney, Sec. Madeleine Albright, Wes Anderson, Drew Barrymore, David Beckham, Bono, Matthew Broderick, Sandra Bullock, James Carville, Michael Chabon, Daniel Craig, John Cusack, Matt Damon, Robert De Niro, Dave Eggers, Peter Gabriel, Jake Gyllenhaal, Václav Havel, Helen Hunt, Anjelica Huston, Scarlett Johansson, Nicole Kidman, Ashton Kutcher, Norman Lear, Madonna, Mary Matalin, Sen. John & Cindy McCain, Rose McGowan, Orhan Pamuk, Sarah Jessica Parke [sic], Paulo Sérgio Pinheiro, Brad Pitt, Julia Roberts, Robert Rodriguez, Salman Rushdie, Meg Ryan, Liev Schreiber, George Soros, Steven Spielberg, Meryl Streep, Archbishop Desmond Tutu, Naomi Watts, Prof. Elie Wiesel, Owen Wilson"

The trouble isn't so much a lack of measures as their total ineffectiveness (except maybe the celebrities', which could at least put the country on the map of global consciousness). For example: Malaria had long vexed the residents of border camps like the one the first lady visited, of course. But in the '90s, researchers dispatched hundreds of Karen refugees, including Htoo Moo, on epidemiological surveys. From sunset to sunrise the men worked in four-hour shifts, sitting around, talking, catching mosquitoes that landed on them before they bit with a small vacuum for 100 baht a night, bringing the insects back to the Western doctors alive in time-labeled cups. Thus did the researchers determine that malaria transmission occurs in the camps via the mosquito vector that flies in the early evening—not overnight, when people are in bed. Thus were malaria workers desperately disappointed with Mrs. Bush's present. It was a nice gesture, and the publicity was pretty good, but the money spent on those nets, they said sadly, should've gone to drugs that there are never enough of and that have actually been proved to interrupt malaria transmission in camp.

Similarly, sanction proponents say that it's not the idea of sanctions but our execution of them that's flawed: Though US investors have had to pull their money out of, say, Burma's garment industry, they can still deal in its oil and gas, which is where a lot of the junta's big export money comes from. Unocal/Chevron lobbyists (including one Alan Hoffman) have kept Congress from making the company sell its stake in Burma gas fields. No provision mandating that Chevron divest was included in the Block Burmese Jade Act, which was meant to deprive the government of big income and was spearheaded by Joe Biden (whose former chief of staff was one Alan Hoffman). Efforts to strip Chevron of a sweet tax concession on its business in the country got downgraded to a *suggestion* that the company "consider voluntary divestment over time."

Following the junta's gross abuses in the '88 uprisings, world governments had to show some kind of action. So foreign aid, some $500 million a year, mostly stopped flowing. Soon, the regime was drowning in debt. It could have been the end of an evil era, maybe, had capitalism not swept in and saved the day. To solve its cash crisis, the long-closed Burma opened itself to private businesses and foreign trade. International hotels were built; tourists arrived; nightclubs opened; the Thais bought logging rights. Foreign investments kept the economy running, as they largely keep it running now. So if we'd only fashion better and better-targeted sanctions, advocates say, Burma's economy would collapse and the government might just give up and get packing. But whether or not you believe that sanctions were what finally broke South Africa, you cannot believe that they would have worked in that country if half the world's governments had said "We're not going to give you money for your stuff anymore" while the other half had said, "Awesome. More for us."

China is building a pipeline that will carry energy directly through Burma from one of Burma's western ports, easily accessible from the Indian Ocean and Gulf states—which would avoid the long trip around the Strait of Malacca, through which an estimated 80 percent of China's imported crude passes. Thailand has the rights to 1.7 trillion cubic feet of natural gas in one concession alone. One Indian firm has signed up for 5 trillion cubic feet of gas; Russia's got several firms drilling; a single pipeline operated by France, Thailand, and, yes, Chevron earned the junta more than $1 billion in 2008; South Korean Daewoo plans to make more than $10 billion over twenty-five years from its drilling project in the immense Shwe gas reserves; handling Daewoo's exploratory Burma drilling was US firm Transocean. As a member of the Association of Southeast Asian Nations, Burma is included in the free-trade agreement that eliminates tariffs on thousands of products exchanged with India, which has signed an understanding that it will invest billions of US dollars in two Burmese hydroelectric dams. The EU is discussing a free-trade agreement with ASEAN, as well, though England swears that it will ensure that the deal won't benefit Burma—though it's got oil and gas dealings there, too. In 2008 Burma experienced a 165 percent increase from the year before in the number of Chinese multinational companies involved in mining, oil and gas, and hydropower development. Trade between the two countries was up to $2.6 billion in 2008, from $630 million in 2001. Burma is estimated to be running a $2.5 billion trade surplus, with $5 billion in currency reserves.* Indeed, our pulling our cash out after Burma opened its economy up to foreigners in the '90s just concentrated more money and power in the government/army when its businesses could have begun being controlled by nonevil investors and legitimate concerns.

These are the sorts of unhappy, backfirey results US Burma policy has long tended to achieve. Remember all those Burma-invading KMT troops we secretly supported, in our efforts to thwart Red China, who went on to build drug cartels? Well, then, the Reagan administration's solution to Burma's out-of-control opium production was to give the junta millions of dollars for an opium-eradication program involving US aircraft and 2,4-D—the chemical that makes up half the composition of Agent Orange. The Burmese government sprayed it all over Shan villages. The Shan complained that it killed cattle and people.† Also, it wasn't much of a deterrent for those who were opium farmers, who weren't superinclined to plant *food* instead of drugs on that land, now that it'd been covered in poison. Burma

---

* In 2008, despite the jobless and prospectless migrants flooding back into the country after being laid off in Malaysia and Thailand, Burma's prime minister insisted that the new global recession would have no effect on his homeland. State media echoed the claim, in an article titled "We Remain Unperturbed," that the Burmese would fare far better than the Americans, who "are a people who are extravagant and do not hesitate to buy an elephant if it is available on credit."

† Then–Assistant Secretary of State of the Bureau for International Narcotics Matters (and "Just Say No" architect) Ann Wrobleski thought that raining the chemical—which was under EPA review at the time—all over Burmese hill tribes was the best way to get rid of poppies. Incidentally, you may remember the Washington PR firm Jefferson Waterman International, which had ties with the State Law and Order Restoration Council when it became the State Peace and Development Council in '97. That's where Wrobleski went on to work, first as a lobbyist from '91 to '97, and then as the firm's president.

went on to be named World's No. 1 Opium Producer by the US government in 1991, a distinction it held until it was briefly surpassed by Afghanistan in 1999 and then fully usurped by the country in 2003, after the US had ousted the Taliban.

The United States can better target its sanctions all it wants, but those policies will continue to produce undesirable side effects. Already, they've put tens of thousands of Burmese textile workers out of factory jobs—and, as even the State Department has admitted, into sex work. And they will continue to be useless. Burmese timber still comes into the United States through China, and Burmese gems via the $8 billion of jewelry imports from Thailand. In 2008, more foreign companies had invested in Burma's energy sector than ever. According to the Ministry of National Planning and Development, foreign investment dollars in the country nearly doubled in the first nine months of that year compared with the same period of the previous year, and in 2007, foreign investment in oil and gas was more than triple that of the year before. So, as Chevron has pointed out, if we pull out our remaining investments, someone else—and perhaps someone less conscientious*— will just gladly put their money in. The international community can't even agree to stop giving the regime weapons. Norway has gone so far as to ban investment in one of *China*'s manufacturers because said manufacturer sells military vehicles to Burma. But

---

* The current dam projects, for example, are causing rampant displacement and abuse and environmental destruction. And Daewoo was the subject of a complaint that it condones human rights abuses around one of its gas projects, in violation of the Organisation for Economic Co-operation and Development code it's sworn to. Although, "less conscientious" is still sort of relative: In 1996, with the help of EarthRights International, fifteen villagers from Burma sued Unocal—now part of Chevron—for being party to government soldiers' raping, murdering, torturing, and enslaving civilians, tens of thousands of whom were displaced, during the construction of the gas line. It was the first non-Holocaust international human rights case charging a corporation with complicity in foreign-government brutality that ended in a cash settlement. (Though the actual amount was confidential, it was, according to one of the plaintiffs' lawyers, "more money than these people will ever know what to do with.")

even Germany, along with Singapore and Pakistan and Russia and Ukraine and Serbia, has supplied the junta with military equipment, which workers at a Rangoon port say is offloaded from cargo ships in the middle of the night as in an Indiana Jones movie. North Korea, too, which has missiles and will sell them to anyone with the money to buy, and with whom the Burmese foreign minister recently agreed to resume ties after twenty-five years of a diplomatic kibosh. And China, of course, which is the sole buyer of Daewoo's Shwe gas output and has showered Burma's military with weapons. Burma's resources were those that allowed the founding and thriving of Burmah Oil, which became Burmah Castrol, which was bought by BP in 2000 for some $5 billion. They built Herbert Hoover's silver-mining fortune. We know well enough to know that as long as there's money—and energy—to be made in Burma, there's unlikely to be a cohesive or constructive policy of international financial disengagement.

But even if everyone did collectively agree to simultaneously disinvest, including two of Burma's neighbors—the world's two most populous, energy-desperate countries—which is never going to happen—who says regime change would necessarily follow? There's no guarantee that a government that's worked so hard to isolate itself from prying, hostile foreign eyes—that's had its suspicion that the West isn't good for it repeatedly confirmed with incursions and, later, sanctions—will be sad if the whole world decides to just stay out of its business, considering that it puts up all over the country giant white-on-red billboards that say this:

PEOPLE'S DESIRE

★ Oppose those relying on external elements, acting as stooges, holding negative views.

★ Oppose those trying to jeopardize stability of the State and progress of the nation.

★ Oppose foreign nations interfering in internal affairs of the State.

★ Crush all internal and external destructive elements as the common enemy.

"The Burmese," wrote colonialist James George Scott in 1886, "were little inclined to yield to threats." He would know. Not thirty years prior to the first British invasion, in 1824, with thousands of refugees fleeing into British territory from Burma's expansionist rampage, and with concerns about the worst possible future for Burma—that it would become a part or ally of France—the British sent a series of envoys to the country. The first one was stood up by the king, then made to wait, rudely, for two and a half months for an appointment; the second went home in a huff; and the third mission won exactly zero concessions from the Burmese court, leading the diplomat to conclude that the British might just have to go to war. Ultimately, that time, the British didn't do shit, which was part of the reason the Burmese later pushed their borders right up against them in the first place. Another reason was that by then, the Burmese fancied themselves the all-conquering warlords of the universe. They'd subjugated the Thais, the Chinese, and the Mon, among others, sacking kingdoms abroad even while fighting rival ones at home. In 1768, of the more than ten thousand troops that had invaded Burma from Manchu, one of the largest empires the world has ever seen, just a few made it home alive. The Portuguese had tried their hand at conquering Burma, and lost in 1613. When Kublai Khan himself had demanded tribute in 1271, the Burmese started a war with the Mongols that lasted more than a decade, so King Bagyidaw, Emperor of Emperors, Against Whose Imperial Majesty if Any Shall Be So Foolish as to Imagine Anything, It Shall Be Happy for Them to Die and Be Consumed; the Lord of Great Charity and Help of All Nations; the Lord Esteemed for Happiness; the Lord of All Riches, of Elephants and Horses, and All Good Blessings; the Lord of High-Built Palaces of Gold; the Great and Most Powerful Emperor in This Life, the Soles of Whose Feet Are Gilt and Set upon the Heads of All People, would be damned if he was going to just roll over for England, whether it had an arsenal of native scouts and spies and rocket fire or not. Even King Thibaw, even after his country had been licked by the British twice, refused to accept their terms for avoiding the third war. Rather, in response, he went ahead and made his own declaration of war, and furthermore stipulated that if the British didn't step off, he was going to sail over to England with an army of elephants and annex *them*.*

This time, though, with no relationship or leverage to speak of, we're sure that we're going to give a country—that country—a stern and united "Knock it off," and with nary a significant "or else," and it's just going to come out with its hands up. Like even if the nations of the world abandoned all that trade—which they won't; even we haven't—and pushed Burma into total economic collapse; like even if desperation nudged tensions among paranoid generals and a giant underpaid army to run uncontrollably high, the leaders of Burma would just stop fighting their own people, rather than fight them as well as each other to the last bloodied man standing, the welfare of the populace, always, be damned. As it is, Burma's leaders have let the country devolve into chaos. As it is, for anyone outside the upper echelons of the military/opium/industrial complex, the country is already in total economic collapse; the regime works not so much for as in spite of its people, selling off all its resources as if its civilians weren't starving and in the dark and right there, while the generals stow billions in Singaporean shelter accounts.

---

* "To all town and village *thugyees* [leaders], heads of cavalry, heads of the Daings, shield bearers, heads of jails, heads of gold and silver revenues, mine workers, settlement officers, heads of forests, and to all royal subjects and inhabitants of the royal empire: Those heretics, the English *kalás* [barbarians], having most harshly made demands calculated to bring about the impairment and destruction of our religion, the violation of our national traditions and customs, and the degradation of our race, are making a show and preparation as if about to wage war with our State. They have been replied to in conformity with the usages of great nations, and in words which are just and regular. If, notwithstanding, these heretic *kalás* should come and in any way attempt to molest or disturb the State, his Majesty, who is watchful that the interests of our religion and our State shall not suffer, will himself march forth with his generals, captains, and lieutenants, with large forces of infantry, artillery, elephanterie, and cavalry, by land and by water, and with the might of his army will efface these heretic *kalás* and conquer and annex their country."

Some say we can't lift the sanctions because that's the same as admitting that the regime has won, but it's kind of hard to argue, really, that it hasn't. Already, the military's the last institution standing. No other forms of national government even exist in the country. Master creator of the military machine Ne Win stepped down in 1988, but you wouldn't have noticed it; other tyrants just took his place, and he was rumored to have been running the show regardless. He died in 2002, but his dynasty has lived, his same dictatorial song and dance, for decades, the world's longest-standing military dictatorship. Western powers have only helped entrench the regime and its violence against our former ethnic-minority allies there with covert and overt post-independence war efforts and the same sanctioning that didn't work in Iraq and didn't work in Cuba and certainly isn't working in Burma now.

The solution, instead, lies in the United Nations. The Security Council has plenty of critics, sure, who charge and joke that the body is impotent, unable to play a meaningful role in international crises. Sadly, the Security Council has agreed. The UN itself admitted that its policy during the massacres in Rwanda and Bosnia and Herzegovina was devastatingly fatal. So at the 2005 UN World Summit, it was resolved that if a nation is host to any of four "atrocity crimes"—war crimes, ethnic cleansing, crimes against humanity, genocide—that nation comes under a responsibility to protect, or R2P, and the Security Council has committed to take "timely and decisive" action to protect the nation's people. The principle even overrides national sovereignty.

When in 2007 a draft resolution on Burma was brought before the Security Council, some activists and legal advisers felt that there was a strong case for it to include charges of genocide. The UN 1948 Convention on the Prevention and Punishment of the Crime of Genocide defines *genocide* as an attempt "to destroy, in whole or in part, a national, ethnical, racial, or religious group" with at least one of five methods. One of them the SPDC isn't guilty of: "Forcibly transferring children of the group to another group." But "Imposing measures intended to prevent births within the group"? If you count gang-raping and murdering pregnant women, yes. "Killing members of the group"? Check. "Causing serious bodily or mental harm to members of the group"? Check. "Deliberately inflicting on the group conditions of life calculated to bring about its physical destruction in whole or in part"? Clearly. Since the International Criminal Tribunal for Rwanda, systematic rape has also been recognized as a defining feature of genocide, and in Burma, it's systematic, institutionalized, indoctrinated into soldiers. It is, according to defectors, explicitly ordered, and in the name of diluting ethnic blood: "Your blood must be left in the village." Burmese soldiers also force minority women into marriage with them as a means of enslavement. Australian National University's Strategic and Defence Studies Centre corroborates that there was a special Karen-killing terror squad of the Tatmadaw. They went around beheading and detesticling people. Once, they took a kid who was playing volleyball, cut his head off, and displayed it in the jungle, sticking a cheroot in its mouth, which they probably thought was pretty funny. Villagers knew these guys when they arrived because they started stabbing people instead of just shooting them.

But not everyone agrees that these crimes a genocide make; not one government has officially leveled the charge at Burma, and no tribunals have been called. Some academics, journalists, and even activists argue that these genocidal actions aren't sufficiently genocide-like to count. We can't just be throwing the word around to describe any old horror, since then it loses its potency in describing the very specific horror of atrocities we've all agreed are genocides. Or as my father put it when I tried to impress upon him the seriousness of the situation in Burma, "But how does it compare to Sudan?"

If Sudan is the bar against which we're measuring genocide, okay: The SPDC has destroyed more than three thousand ethnic villages in eastern Burma, comparable to the number that have been destroyed in Darfur. In Darfur, nearly three million people have been displaced. In the jungle of eastern Burma alone, an absolute minimum of half a million live displaced, and millions have fled the country. The mortality rate of children under five, a common measure of conflict epidemiology, in Sudan is 109 per 1,000 live births. In eastern Burma, it's 221. In the Darfur genocide, four hundred thousand civilians have been killed. Unfortunately, no one's come up with a comprehensive, widely agreed-upon tally of Burma's casualties. Some experts estimate that a few thousand minorities have been slain a year, every year, since independence, sixty years ago. So, three hundred thousand? One expert put the number at four hundred thousand—as of 1990. A junta chairman once estimated that the body count of Burma's civil war "would reach as high as millions."

According to the International Criminal Tribunal for Rwanda, genocidaires don't have to act hard and fast; slow and even indirect genocide is genocide nonetheless. Also decided in that tribunal was that prosecutors don't have to provide actual official, written proof of genocidal intent to successfully charge genocide; the intent can be inferred. Like from the ashes of thousands of burned villages. Like from the disallowing of Karen language instruction. Like from the UN special rapporteur for human rights in Burma having admitted in 1998 that the systematic violence and destruction were clearly "the result of policy at the highest level, entailing political and legal responsibility." Like from a group of kids in a refugee camp who were given some art supplies and paper and told to make whatever they wanted and drew pictures of people running from a burning village, a woman with some of her clothes torn off by soldiers who are about to rape her, and civilians being murdered while an infant gets tossed into a rice mortar. Like from any Karen IDPs who've been violently chased from their villages by soldiers who've destroyed all their food and livestock in their wake: If they manage *not* to die, it's really not for their government's lack of trying, since it even attempts to, and sometimes does, stop and kill aid workers trying to bring in relief.

Like from the messages SPDC soldiers write on walls or post on trees of villages they attack: "Soon the Karen will no longer exist. Waiting for the day when you will die."

The Karenni and the Shan suffer similar abuses. Twenty-five thousand Karenni have been exiled to refugee camps in Thailand. More than twice that many are stranded in the jungle on the run, and we know what their odds are like out there. A Thai intelligence officer has found leaflets on the bodies of dead government soldiers that identify the Shan race as the enemy that has to be destroyed. Another intercepted document promises raises to soldiers "who are successful in possessing Shan women" for "the purpose of admixture of blood":

> What our noble and numerous Burman comrades of a great racial lineage must particular adhere to and practise is to take victory by absorption of humanity by humanity. It is only through absorption of racial groups who are not Burman so that the victory of the Burman comrades in the Shan State will be stabilized for a long time.

Any UN resolution that charged genocide—or any other atrocity crime—against a country would bring that country under the responsibility to protect. And a draft resolution that compellingly charges genocide against a country is a draft resolution that's likely to get passed—no nation wants to be the one that vetoes that. But the 2007 Security Council draft resolution to declare Burma a threat to international peace and security didn't contain the word—or the evidence for—*genocide*. Nor *ethnic cleansing*, nor *crimes against humanity*, nor *war crimes*. China and Russia vetoed it.

Now a case to again bring a Burma resolution to the Security Council table is gaining momentum. This time, some advocates say, it's possible they'll fight for the charge of crimes against humanity, because the phrase is both more inclusive of the abominations than genocide and, because it's less politicized, easier to prove—the

United Nations Human Rights Commission didn't adopt an official report acknowledging the Armenian genocide of 1915 until 1985. And there's more backup this time: In 2009, the Harvard University International Human Rights Clinic issued a report by five leading international jurists that identified the situations in Rwanda and Darfur as precedents for Burma. The authors admonished that "the world cannot wait while the military regime continues its atrocities against the people of Burma" and that "there is a *prima facie* case of international criminal law violations occurring that demands UN Security Council action to establish a Commission of Inquiry to investigate these grave breaches further." The next month, more than fifty US congresspeople were signatories to a letter to President Barack Obama urging him to lead the establishment of a Security Council Commission of Inquiry into crimes against humanity in Burma.

Possibly further helpful to this cause is the publication of a report from one of the world's foremost human-rights-law scholars asserting that the junta is perpetrating crimes against humanity targeting the ethnic Rohingya in western Burma's Arakan State, as well. Hundreds of thousands of Rohingya have been driven out of Burma by the military, which argues that that race doesn't belong in its country. "Rohingya are neither Myanmar people nor Myanmar's ethnic group," the Burmese consul general has explained. "You will see in the photos that their complexion is 'dark brown.' The complexion of Myanmar people is fair and soft, good-looking as well"—not, like the Rohingya, "ugly as ogres." Among those who do still live there, 25 percent suffer from acute malnutrition. Forced labor and wrongful imprisonment are rife. The Rohingya aren't recognized as citizens and can't leave their state. A hundred who were caught trying to get to Rangoon to find work in 2008 were arrested and sentenced to six months in prison. Within their state, they can't do anything—walk out of their own village, get married—without permission. A couple hundred thousand squat in Bangladesh, about sixty thousand in squalid camps. Many try to flee to Malaysia. They drown in leaky ships or are arrested when they wash up on the shores of Thailand. The minority made big news recently when the Land of Smiles got caught towing a bunch of them back out to sea. The reason this report could help change the game is that it's meant to draw the attention of world players outside of the West. The Rohingya are discriminated against for being, aside from darkies, another hateful thing: Muslims. The hope is that some of Burma's neighbors, particularly Malaysia and Indonesia, will help make some serious racket once it's out that Muslims are being so fatally oppressed.

"The US government and the international community must do something to assist the people of Burma and stop the brutality," said Representative Joe Pitts (R-Pennsylvania) in a speech to the House in 2003. "Otherwise, we will all be responsible for the successful genocide campaign ethnic cleansing going on by the vicious military of the SPDC." The sanctioning Freedom and Democracy Act, which is US law, notes very simply and clearly, "The SPDC is engaged in ethnic cleansing against minorities within Burma, including the Karen, Karenni, and Shan people, which constitutes a crime against humanity." But even after we settle this quibble over semantics and decide that the living hell of Burma is genocide or crimes against humanity or both or what, relief for the people on the ground there could be a long time coming. Even if the UN draft resolution is brought—and in 2006, a proposal just to talk about one was rejected by China, Russia, and Japan—and then does pass, and does contain some of the magic words, and does bring Burma under the responsibility to protect, then the Security Council will still have to agree on what "timely and decisive" measure is appropriate, whether coercive actions like putting peacekeepers on the ground or establishing criminal tribunals—and the secretary-general is a big advocate of noncoercive measures—then find the resources to do it, then actually do it. Such UN action would be unprecedented, and redeeming.

At the current pace, getting to only the point where the Security Council votes on a resolution, someone involved in the process has estimated, will take two or three years. Which, in the scheme of this war, is not so long. Though in a village where inhabitants have been buried up to their necks and bludgeoned to death with a shovel, it's a fucking eternity.

Currently: US policy only imposes sanctions on a country of breathtakingly impoverished citizens. It does not involve calling for the Security Council to invoke the responsibility to protect, or referring Burma to the International Criminal Court. It does not address Burma's committing the sorts of crimes the international community has sworn to prevent. Burma gets less than a tenth of the aid money Cambodia does; people living with AIDS must wait until someone else with AIDS dies so they can take their place on the very short list of people getting AIDS meds; the relief money coming in comes out to less than $3 a person, while in Sudan, each person gets about $50. American policy involves ignoring our old Karen allies. It involves disregarding the Wa,* though they're flooding

---

* In case you want some background info on this ethnic-group-to-watch—and trust me, you do: The Wa are former headhunters (official open season was March to April) who claim as their ancestors not, like most peoples, gods or majestic sea creatures or rainbows or whatever, but slimy tadpoles and ogres. In colonial times, one European visitor to this mountain-dwelling collection of tribes said that they were so dirty that the only thing that kept them from getting dirtier was that more dirt couldn't stick to how much dirt was already on their bodies. They were naked. They were pretty much the closest existing things on earth to actual bogeymen, and the British were terrified of them and left them largely alone, as the Wa couldn't guarantee they wouldn't kill white people who wandered into their territory, their towheads being quite the catch on the headhunting scene. In the late '60s, they were enlisted by China and the Communist Party of Burma to help wrest a bunch of Burmese territory from our old buddies the KMT. With these fierce warriors on their side, the commies took and held thousands of square miles—all the way until 1989. Now the Wa just have the biggest nonstate army in Burma, which they fund by running probably the biggest drug army in the world, a commander of which is wanted by the US government for druglording. So if you want to collect $2 million from the State Department, find out where Wei Hsueh-kang is.

the world drug market with heroin and meth.* It doesn't involve significant dialogue with the Shan and Mon and Kachin, though they'll be crucial to eventually rebuilding the nation and building a more inclusive national identity in a country with seven major and a dozen subnationalities, where the minorities collectively are not so minor, where a settling of the ethnic-war score precedes even so much as a distant dream of a functioning democracy. The US isn't asking, even nicely, its pal Thailand to—in the long, continuing meantime—grant the displaced Burmese within its borders the right to work and walk around, to make them less subject to the whims of a police force that is, as one DEA agent working in Bangkok put it, "so corrupt it turns my stomach," to recognize and protect them as refugees—people with "a well-founded fear of being persecuted for reasons of race, religion, nationality, membership of a particular social group or political opinion"—even though the US Committee for Refugees and Immigrants ranks Thailand one of the seven worst countries in the world in which to be a refugee. Even Iraq and Afghanistan didn't make that list. Or as Collin put it in his workshop essay:

> There has been a civil war in Burma and it becomes a poorest country in the world. The civilian has been faced with many difficulties and became refugees. Numbers of people have fled to neighboring countries to seek asylum. My family and I fled to Thailand and live in a refugee camp. Thai authorities do not recognize us as legal refugee.

---

* Not to be entirely outdone by Afghanistan, in 2007 Burma cultivated 29 percent more opium than it had the previous year. Since Burma is also one of the world's largest amphetamine producers (which the State Department says could turn the Golden Triangle into the "Ice Triangle") and the second-largest producer in East and Southeast Asia of a key raw material in ecstasy—which, unbeknownst to most people, comes from Southeast Asian trees—the regime was recently honored by the United States as one of only three governments in the world that "'failed demonstrably' to meet its international counternarcotics obligations."

Life in the camp is like bird in the cage. The camp is surrounded by the barb wire and you can not go out of the camp. No freedom, no choice to have high education. There are many refugee camps in Thai Burma border. I live in the Mae La camp with my family. Approximately there are more than 40 thousand people live in here. We receive our supplies from BBC (Burmese Border Consortium). We get our ration twice a month. We get rice, fish paste, chili, salt, yellow bean, cooking oil, charcoal and clothes. We have hospitals, schools in the camp.

It is very difficult to have a job to earn money for the family. Few people have job. Some work in the hospital and some are teachers but these people receive very few allowance. Many of the refugees would like to go out of the camp and look for job for their financial. Thai authorities who control the camp do not allow them. Sometime they become black sheep and leave the camp. Many times Thai police arrest them and charge them. Some were sent back to Burma to the SPDC military campaign.

Day by day too many people live life with no hope. Children go to school up to tenth standard and then finish their study. After they have finished tenth standard they have nothing to do accept hang around with friends. Their free time makes bad habits for them.

Every day people have to live with worried life. We are part of DKBA and SPDC target enemy. They try to destroy our camp. DKBA (Democratic Karen Buddha Army) is different political group who separate their self from Karen National Union. SPDC (State Peace Development Council is Burmese regime. Many times they come and destroy our camp even though we live in other country. They had destroyed many refugee camps and we have to relocate our camp many times. These are part of the life in the camp.

Lives in the camp need more security and freedom as human being. We need to recognize as a real refugee.

But there's no popular call for a different policy, because no one's ever heard of this particular genocide, partly because we're not calling it a genocide. There's no mass movement behind the cause. And what's perhaps most heartbreaking about our unawareness of Burma's people is their hyperawareness of us.

The Karen have a story. It's about how, when man was created, the Karen and the European, like all the other nationalities, were brothers. As the first created, the Karen was the oldest brother, and as last the European was the youngest. The two brothers adored each other, and so traveled together when Buddha sent them to settle in the world after bestowing upon them gifts of rope and knives and knowledge and, to the Karen brother, a betel box and forbiddance from opening it until he reached Burma. But the younger brother wanted to see what was inside, and persisted through all the Karen brother's insisting that they shouldn't look until, finally, they did. It was the Karen's land and literacy, which spilled wide and far from their container. They couldn't get them back in the box, and they couldn't carry them as they were, and were forced to move on without them. "That is why the Karen are the orphans of the world and must live from swiddens cut on mountainsides belonging to other peoples," goes the story. But it doesn't end so hopelessly. "One day, our European brother will return to us and make up for the hardship he has caused us. One day we shall have a land of our own."

And it's not just the Karen. The citizens of Burma have followed recent American presidential races closely,* sure that, given the idealized bullshit the US government spouted in the run-up to the Iraq War, we'll invade and depose their dictator, too. With each impotent visit of the UN envoy, tea leaves are sifted for signs of impending change. Like the minorities who thought we'd honor our promise to protect them after that great war, like the minorities who now believe

---

* Though most papers weren't allowed to run President Barack Obama's inauguration speech. One that was couldn't put it on the front page and had to cut some of it, like this part: "To those who cling to power through corruption and deceit and the silencing of dissent, know that you are on the wrong side of history; but that we will extend a hand if you are willing to unclench your fist."

that FBR's Dave must be CIA sent to redeem them, like the rebels and activists waiting for us to reinforce them in the jungles after the demonstrations of '88, like Eh Soe, who danced in his computer chair when BBC Burmese reported that Bush had pledged some tiny bit of money to the country for AIDS relief, however much I insisted that it didn't mean we were about to take interest and action, like even the junta, which went through that exorbitant expense and trouble to move its capital far inland, the Burmese as a whole simply cannot believe that no one is going to come to their country's rescue. In May 2008, US Navy ships arrived in the waters off Burma's coast, after Cyclone Nargis killed 140,000 people, who were given no warning of the storm's landfall by their government. The ships—which the junta turned away—were full of aid supplies, not invading soldiers and weaponry. Still, excited citizens crowded the phone lines of an embassy in Rangoon.

"You're coming to save us," the callers asked the diplomat who answered the phone, "aren't you?"

XIII.

THE MAE Sot gongs broke the nighttime silence, in darkness still thorough but thin-feeling. I guessed it was 4 AM when the shallow tinning struck, and I listened to the distant shimmer and the dogs that caught it and spread it through the city, the far-off barking and howling coming closer and louder in a wave with the ringing at their backs until it smacked against the house, our street's dogs in a sudden frenzy, and echoed still by the woofing and tolling from the temple where it started. The monks were awake, and I was, too.

Downstairs, Htan Dah and I sat at the table preparing breakfast before daybreak was complete. The hours peeling and slicing acidic onion and garlic twice a day had peeled the skin off the tips of my fingers. Left index and thumb. Right index, thumb, and middle. Pink and raw. I showed Htan Dah, who looked at me skeptically and checked his own intact hands. I laughed at him when he scratched his head, showing me why he kept long nails on his pinkies and thumbs. "Also," he said, then pantomimed cleaning out his ear.

Soon a visiting administrator from BA's Bangkok office joined us, a round Australian with a pale, pretty face, walking through the open dining room/garage door and plopping down at the table on the bench opposite mine in the yellowing light. We said hellos. Though she'd walked from her temporary room in town in the early chill, her face was sleepy, and she watched us groggily as we slowly slid heavy knives through vegetables and into cutting boards.

"I tried to give Sheh Reh a hug," I told Htan Dah. Even though Sheh Reh had criticized my burned potatoes. "He wouldn't let me."

Htan Dah chuckled. "Really?"

"Yeah. He came up to me yesterday and told me he was leaving this morning, at four in the morning or something. So I said, 'Oh, well it was great to meet you. Can I hug you?' And he said, 'That's okay.'" I had learned, quite slowly, that "That's okay" didn't mean what it meant to me, which was "That would actually be great, but don't trouble yourself," but was a euphemism for "Absolutely not," so I'd stepped back from him. "He said, 'Just say, Thank you very much.' He said, 'Our cultures are very different.'"

I wasn't totally shocked by Sheh Reh's rejection, since Htan Dah had already asserted that there was no hugging in Karen culture. Period. ("You don't hug your parents?" I'd pressed. Negative. "Or your girlfriends?" Never. "Ever?" No. When I'd insisted, "But you like, wrap your arms around each other when you make out," he'd looked at me like something radically unexpected had flown out of my mouth, like a cockatiel, maybe.) But though the action didn't exist in their personal lives, my coworkers had seen it in movies, and most of them were amenable to the performance of it if the occasion called, the same as I wai'd, or bowed with prayerful hands, at Thais I interacted with. Htan Dah, for example, had been hugged before. Once in his life. By a Canadian.

Htan Dah seemed more surprised than I was that Sheh Reh hadn't acquiesced to my friendly request. "That is strange," he said, his mouth screwed up as he tried to think of an explanation. "Maybe because he is animist."

The Bangkok administrator turned on him. "What do you mean?" she asked, her blue eyes rounder and more awake now. "What would his being animist have to do with anything?"

Htan Dah shrugged. "I don't know(!). Maybe animists don't like to touch people."

The Australian made a face of great doubt. "Well they have to touch each other at some point, don't they? Since they haven't died off and must make more animists sometimes?"

Htan Dah giggled, embarrassed. Some of his excessive othering of Sheh Reh—after all, Ta Mla was animist, and Htan Dah knew he didn't live in a physical isolation bubble—was due to Sheh Reh's being Karenni, or Red Karen, a subgroup of the Karen ethnicity. The Red Karen had their own language and traditional clothing (you could probably guess the primary color) and ceremonies and state, Karenni State, a small piece of land just north of Karen State. In Thailand, they had their own two refugee camps. They also had various subgroups within their ethnic subgroup—specifically, Sheh Reh's traditionally wore short *longyis* and wrapped their knees in thick black cotton. Even within the White Karen, to which all my housemates belonged, there were several subgroups, Sgaw and Pwo and Pa-o and Padaung. Even within my housemates, two of these groups were represented, which I hadn't even realized until Eh Soe told me. He was, for example, unlike most of the guys, Pwo Karen, which had its own dialect and traditional dress and even script.

According to Karen lore, there's a perfectly good explanation for all this. Long ago lived Toh Meh Pah, a virile man with a magic comb of perpetual youth. One day, when his offspring outnumbered the output of his land, he gathered his family and moved everyone to where the soil would be as fertile as his loins. They were separated when some of the band stopped to boil snail shells until they were soft enough to eat. The determined diners cooked the shells for weeks, giving up and getting going again only after some Chinese came along and made fun of their impossible culinary endeavor. By then, though, the trail of the patriarch had been lost, and the family was separated forever. "Karen people are very confused," Eh

Soe had told me. "Even me. I don't understand my ethnic situation." But he did understand Sgaw Karen, which is what he spoke around the house so that he and his coworkers could understand one another.*

"If it makes you feel any better," I told Htan Dah, "Sheh Reh doesn't actually know that much about animism either. He was telling me how his people consult chicken bones to make decisions and to tell them the truth, and he was saying they put a piece of bamboo through the hole of a chicken bone, and read the bones based on how the wood comes out of the hole, maybe, and then he was like, 'Okay, I don't know how it works.' Eventually he just showed me a PowerPoint presentation."

Htan Dah thought that was pretty funny. "He made Power-Point?"

"Yeah. He made it about his customs so he wouldn't forget them, he said." I raised my voice over Htan Dah's laughter. "It was pretty good!"

My cooking partner was in the same place at the table in the dining room/garage with the same chopping knife in hand when I got back from class, around dinnertime. Only now, the room held the darker, oranger light of the setting sun. And I was drunk.

With the drop of attendance in my morning, advanced class, due to those students' work conflicts, I'd consolidated my efforts into just one afternoon class. The beginners came as always, and any advanced students could attend as their time allowed. Ta Mla had asked me before class that day if I would bring my camera and go up to the lake near Office Two with him when class was over. When it was, and we did, I realized he'd leaked the plans. As we sat on the grassy embankment that gave way to the glinting blue, looking

---

* "I speak Sgaw Karen, Pwo Karen," Eh Soe said to me once, counting the languages on his fingers, "Burmese, English, Thai. . . . How many languages do you speak?" When I said one, plus a little French, he shook his head sadly and said, "Oh, you are very stupid."

at perfect rolling hills that turned into dense forest and mountains beyond the farther shore, six of my students rolled up on bikes and motorbikes. They had backpacks and plastic bags full of Chang cans. They passed around my camera and took pictures of us all, or just two of us, or three of us at a time, against the sun that was shining and the sky that was not raining again and the glittering water, and when the beer was gone and we left to go back home for dinner I tipped my head way back on the back of Ta Mla's motorbike, ours being third in a convoy of motorbikes carrying five refugees and their drunk-ass English teacher with my face to the sun and my hair flying behind me as madly as I grinned at the Thais who were sitting on the porches of their wooden shacks, or standing in small, scrappy fields next to their small, scrappy cows, or hovering knee-deep in rice paddies, until Ta Mla hit a gash between the road's shoulder and the adjacent mud and we both smashed our flip-flopped feet into the asphalt to keep the vehicle from toppling. I showed my bloody toes to Htan Dah.

"What happened?" he asked. "Where have you been?"

I told him.

"I think maybe it is better you go with me," he said.

"You didn't come to class today! I *couldn't* go with you. And you missed our party at the lake."

"I had meeting! I am sorry. But Ta Mla is not so steady on motorbike." He started laughing then, and told me that Ta Mla had just started driving recently, and that once, when he was pulling out of the driveway, he drove straight across the street and straight into the small pond that occupied the vacant lot there. It took several of them to drag the motorbike back out. "I am glad you are not injured," he said. "Also, Eh Soe is looking for you."

I turned around and walked into the house. "Yes! My darling! I am here!" I hollered. I found Eh Soe in the computer room.

"I have been looking everywhere for you," he said. "Can you tell me ten proverbs?"

"What? For what?"

"For my class." Every day, Eh Soe disappeared from five to seven. He was, I'd eventually found out, at his older brother's house, tutoring his twelve- and thirteen-year-olds, along with two to four other kids from the neighborhood. The students attended Thai school, but the English instruction there wasn't up to Eh Soe's standards. He didn't get paid for his teaching service, but it was important to him that these kids were well educated. So for two hours each evening, he sat on the floor with them around a little square table in a little rectangular room.

"You're the one who's into proverbs,"* I said. "What's that shit you said to me the other day? 'We are born in a day, and live in a day, and die in a day, it seems'?"

"Didn't you learn proverbs in your education?" he asked.

Probably. "Hold on. I'll be right back." I ran out the computer room door, through the living room, through the kitchen and the dining room/garage, where Htan Dah asked me where I was going now and I shouted that I'd be right back, and out the open dining room/garage door and across the driveway and into Abby's little concrete yard. She was sitting on her little concrete porch.

"I need ten stupid proverbs that they taught us in school," I said. We were saved from several minutes of wholly impotent brainstorming when we corralled and posed the question to a passing The Blay, who, weirdly, instantly rattled off the sought-after list: Too many cooks spoil the soup. A bird in the hand is better than two in the bush. Many small drops make a mighty ocean. An ounce of prevention is better than a pound of cure. Et cetera.

Eh Soe left for class, and Htan Dah and I cooked, and the Austra-

---

* Also into proverbs: FBR's Dave. As he once told an assembly of ethnic leaders from Burma, "One small dog cannot fight a tiger. But many dogs can do something." He also has a knack for metaphor, once comparing Burma to *The Lord of the Rings*: "Mordor is the SPDC, and guys like us are hobbits. We're just little guys trying to do some good. On the surface it seems like Mordor has all the strength and power and might. But if our fellowship of hobbits stays united, good will defeat evil in the end."

lian administrator brought tall, fat bottles of Chang, and we ate and I got increasingly drunk. Htan Dah updated me on the status of my hugless Karenni friend, Sheh Reh: He'd made it to his new post as new staff at a BA office several hours away. He was safe, although he'd taxed the budget when he paid for the ride twice, once to the guy who was supposed to take him and then again to the guy who did take him when the other guy was late and Sheh Reh, alone, identification-less, panicked and bribed someone else to get him there with a hefty amount of BA funds.

I needed more money for Htan Dah.

It weren't as if I could just stroll up to an ATM and withdraw nearly $2,500 in baht, so I'd been making daily trips to the one where the main, four-lane road dead-ended into a three-way intersection at the mouth to downtown. "Hey, Htoo Moo," I said, descending on him in the computer room as he worked diligently on something. "If you come for a walk with me, I'll buy you some ice cream."

I spent the bulk of the ten-minute stroll explaining to Htoo Moo what the cash machine was and how it worked. When we got there, he watched me put my card in, punch in my PIN, and press a couple of buttons. Though I'd told him in great detail, and repeatedly, what was going to happen, he couldn't fucking believe it when money came out.

We walked to 7-Eleven, where I picked out an ice cream novelty and Htoo Moo a milk, his first. He sipped it very cautiously and pensively, and I limped a little with the foot I still hadn't washed the blood off, as we walked back to the house in the warm dark. However often he'd been arrested, Htoo Moo seemed not to be accompanied by the constant, crushing paranoia that followed most of our coworkers around town, and he sauntered casually along the side of the road. I, however, had by now internalized some of their skittishness, and tried to hustle Htoo Moo along by walking fast and keeping the conversation interesting enough that he'd bother to keep up with me. I looked for the source of every nonanimal sound, tensing every time a passing car slowed or we passed other people walking on the side of the road. I was walking so fast that I was panting.

"In America," I said—and he said "Yes?" expectantly, every time—"police aren't allowed to stop you and make you give them money for no reason."

He smiled wide. "Really?"

"Yeah. And they're not allowed to arrest you if you aren't doing anything illegal."

"I would like to go there," he said softly, shyly. Htoo Moo made no bones about the fact that he was trying to flee Southeast Asia entirely, where nobody wanted him anyway. He was applying for resettlement in the United States, New Zealand, Norway, anywhere. His brother had bailed to England. So had Sheh Reh's cousins. Htoo Moo's parents had died young, of poor health, and he had a sister in Bangkok somewhere but hadn't seen her in ten years, and he'd been on the run himself in Thailand for sixteen now, and one of his camp classmates had called him recently from the UK and told him that being an actual citizen was just the bee's knees. When I'd first learned that Htoo Moo was trying to escape, I'd been somewhat surprised. He'd seemed so gung-ho. "I thought you wanted to work for the future generations of your people," I'd said. To which he'd responded, "Yes. But I'm afraid I will die before we get democracy."

"Well, I hope you *can* go there," I said now, because I didn't know then that he actually *couldn't* go there, on account of having materially supported terrorists. "You need to keep practicing your English. Even after I leave, you need to keep practicing with Htan Dah and Ta Mla. You've gotten much better since I've been here, just from having to practice with me, so you have to keep practicing after I'm gone, so you'll be ready when you move to America."

A car behind us slowed, then pulled over to the shoulder and stopped. Htoo Moo stopped walking and turned around to check it out easy as pie, but I broke out in a quick sweat and grabbed his arm.

"Let's go," I said, tugging on him. I hardly expected anyone to give

me and my almighty blue passport any trouble—though someone
could; I certainly wouldn't be the first American detained in Thailand for consorting with Burmese illegals—but Htoo Moo definitely
wasn't supposed to be out here, and who knew who was in that car?
It was possible my presence would protect him, but from someone
who had taken the time to pull over? And anyway, either way, it was
always possible that it wouldn't.

Htoo Moo ignored me and stayed firm but breezy where he stood,
his face on the car curiously, unconcernedly.

"Htoo Moo, what are you doing?" I asked. "Let's go." But he shook
me off and walked toward the car. One of the doors opened, and fear
raced through my tensed torso. But then Htoo Moo started laughing when the driver stepped out, because it was his friend, and they
gabbed on and on, and I stood there contemplating throwing up ice
cream and beer.

Back at the house, boys and both of the white girls were crowded
around a table covered with mugs and more Chang. Even the cat had
joined the party. She'd stopped bleeding, apparently, and wound her
way around the table legs.

"Eh Soe! You're back!" I yelled, catching sight of my roommate.
He looked up at me, and I looked at my watch. "How long have you
been here?"

"Darling, I am already drunk," he said.

Htoo Moo and I had walked in on another gay-rights conversation, evidently a continuation of the debate that Htan Dah and I had
had on Abby's porch the day before. The Australian administrator
was calmly defending gays' honor, and The Blay was furiously rebut-
ting her. "Those people cannot be leaders. You will never see them
in important position," he was spitting, his voice low, his eyes bright,
terrifying. The Australian was holding her ground, and I hated The
Blay so much then that I didn't even care to back her up. Anyway,
Eh Soe was lecturing Abby about socialism on the other side of the
table, so I sat by them instead.

"You have money in your bag," he told her, rolling the wrist of his extended arm so that his palm ended face up, in her face, with every phrase, "so you buy groceries."

"I'm actually buying the groceries," I reminded him.

"Whatever," he said, rolling his wrist again, faster this time, dismissive. "If I have money, I buy the food. Somebody that had money bought this beer."

"Who did buy this beer?"

Eh Soe shook his head and shrugged. "I don't know."

It must have been a Karen. When the Australian had walked in with the beer earlier, she'd said, as she dropped it on the table, "I brought beer." When The Blay had bought beer two nights ago, he'd said, "There is beer."

"This beer is for everyone," Eh Soe said. "Htan Dah's motorbike is for everyone."

"How *did* Htan Dah buy that motorbike?" I asked.

"He borrowed money from people. And they give it to him because they had some."

"Our culture isn't as community minded as yours," Abby said. "If I wanted something big, I would save up money to buy it myself."

"When I was at the lake today," I said, "you know Saw Kaw? He told me I should leave my camera at Office Two. He said that if I left it, many people could use it, but if I took it back to America with me, only one person would be using it."

"Did you give it to him?" Eh Soe asked.

"No."

"You should."

"I probably won't. Commie."

By the time all the beer and fight were gone, it was past my bedtime. I drew a picture of happy stick people for Htan Dah, who hadn't looked very happy when I'd found him in the other room, before brushing my teeth, spitting foamy toothpaste onto the floor of the bathroom. I stripped down and doused myself in cold water, washing everything down the drain hole in the corner. Upstairs, lying down, my head was dull and swimmy. My bus back to Bangkok was leaving two weeks from tomorrow. Htan Dah was leaving a week from today. I hadn't had enough time yet, and didn't have enough time left, and had been staving off the sad panic of a clock running down with my very busy day, but now, with boozy exhaustion enveloping me in the cool silence under my mosquito net and twenty-five thousand baht in my bag, I let it in.

THE NEXT morning, Htoo Moo looked rough. It was Tuesday. My goals for the day were to have a stunningly successful class and to relieve my rapidly diminishing checking account of another fifteen thousand baht. "Eh Soe was talking in his sleep," Htoo Moo said, groggy, slumping down at the table.

Personally, I'd slept pretty well, since Eh Soe hadn't been around to keep me up. He told us, laughing, when he joined us for breakfast that he'd drunkenly picked a phone fight with his girlfriend last night because she didn't invite him to her birthday party. I'd heard Eh Soe's relationship drama before, without even realizing it: He was talking so low and soft one night that I asked him later if he'd been having phone sex or something. Actually, his girlfriend was sick, and he'd made her cry by teasing her about it, and his sexy-sounding talk was just his talking her down. Last night, apparently, he told her that she cared only about her friends and that he didn't want to talk to her anymore. She hung up on him. He tried to call her back, but she'd turned off her phone. After that, he must have passed out in the living room, where Htoo Moo slept, and kept his end of the fight going in his sleep.

"We are okay now," he said, laughing still. "I called her and said that I am sorry to her. I am also very sorry that I can't buy presents for her. She said that"—and here he raised his pitch a little—"it's okay; it doesn't matter." He dismissed the whole event with a wave of his hand. "Love takes care of everything."

I crumpled my eyebrows. "It really doesn't."

"Okay, not the rent. But indirectly."

I scoffed. Htoo Moo, who'd been listening quietly, shook his head and rubbed his eyes.

By the time I got back from class, the two of them were back at the table and way back under the influence of cheap Thai beer. The bottles were gone, but the boys' faces were as pink as the tablecloth affixed to the wood. Htoo Moo's eyes were glassy, and my roommate's were nearly shut.

"Jesus, Eh Soe," I said. "How drunk are you?"

"Not drunk. Darling, I have not had any beer."

"Really? Because it smells like beer even from where I'm standing." I started walking toward him, and he jumped up from his spot at the picnic table and bolted into the house. I gave chase, skirting the table and following him through the door as he ran into the living room, yelling, "I'm not drunk!" We ran a couple of circles around before he turned back out into the dining room/garage and I stopped, laughing, near Gaw Say.

Gaw Say was sweet and slim and not in possession of a huge English vocabulary. I wasn't sure what he did, and he didn't take my class, and he'd arrived at the house from inside or camp or wherever he'd been quite a while after I had, but I liked him, and we chatted, limitedly, from time to time. He had been standing idly in the middle of the living room when we'd come running in. He still was.

"What are you doing?" I asked him.

He thought for a second. "Nothing to do!" he said. He fingered the Ping-Pong table against the wall as he passed it, on his way into the computer room to go back to work.

WEDNESDAY MORNING, Htan Dah's kid joined us in the dining room/ garage. He stood on the bench where I sat, teetering next to me, his eyes and mouth wide open as he took in my forearms. However I moved them, to pick up a knife, or cut through some long green

beans—on a slant, because Htan Dah thought they looked fancier
that way—his stare followed. Finally, he reached out and grabbed the
fine blond hairs with his plump little fingers.

"I saw you guys curled up and passed out on the floor yesterday,"
I told Htan Dah. "You guys are so cute." He smiled shyly. His kid
pointed in his general direction and said, *da, da, da*. "Where does he
go all day while you're working?"

"With his mom. They go to visit with friends in Mae Sot, or some
family. Just, hanging around."

Abby joined us from next door, freshly cold-showered, her hair
damp. "Good morning," she said, sitting down at the table. "How's
it going?"

"Fabulous," I said, while Htan Dah said, "Great! Living!"

She turned her attention to the baby. "And how are *you?*" she
asked in a high pitch, in the way that people do. The kid didn't start
crying. "Wow, Htan Dah!" Abby said. "Your baby is hanging out with
white people!"

"And he's sober," I said.

"Yes," Htan Dah said. "He is becoming adjusted to you." He smiled
proudly.

"Hey," Abby said, eyeing the Free Burma Rangers logo on my
chest. "That's a nice shirt. Where did you get that?"

After class, I took advantage of an open spot in the computer
room to email home the progress I was making on depleting my savings and reiterate that everyone should send me money. Or at least
I tried to. Three-quarters of the way through the composition, the
power went out.

"God . . . dammit," I said.

Htoo Moo, working near me, turned his head. "Why did that happen?" he asked.

I sighed, and because I was frustrated, and because that wasn't
the first time I'd lost work that way there, and because one of my
students hadn't shown up to class earlier—because, we thought, he'd

been arrested, so we sat there waiting and worrying for thirty minutes even though it turned out he'd just broken the chain on his bike—I said, "Because Thailand sucks."

Htoo Moo laughed. Htan Dah, who was also working in the room, did, too, but chimed in, "Yes, but you cannot compare with Burma."*

"Yes, I know, Burma is much worse!" I said. "Can't you guys quit with your cool perspective for five fucking minutes?" Neither of them understood what I'd said then, I was sure, but my getting frustrated and swearing was always funny, so they chuckled, which was further frustrating. "It doesn't change the fact that this is a pain in my ass."

"Compare with IDP," Htan Dah said.

"You can't compare anything with that!" I shouted. I pushed my chair away from my desk, getting up to leave the room full of useless electronics.

Upstairs, I plopped down next to Eh Soe on the reading bench in our room. "What are you doing?" I asked him.

"Nothing, at this moment."

I opened a notebook and pen. "Let me ask you a thousand questions."

"Why?"

"Because, I ask everybody lots of questions."

"Why?"

"I don't know. Because I'm curious. Because you're *sooo* fascinating."

"Okay."

"How long have you been in Thailand?"

---

* This is particularly true as far as electricity is concerned, as Burmese say their country is the blackout capital of the region. Even in Rangoon, residents often get only a few hours of electricity a day. Outside the old capital, some cities don't receive any state electricity at all, but buy it from private companies for reportedly more than ten times government prices, and still only for a few hours a day. The only place in the country that receives reliable round-the-clock power is the crazy new deserted capital in the middle of nowhere, which even boasts a zoo, and with a climate-controlled penguin habitat.

LIKE TA Mla and Wah Doh, Eh Soe came to Thailand to go to school. His primary-school attendance was difficult, though not because his village wasn't big enough to provide that level of education, and not because he had to bribe his teachers excessively, but for a different kind of trouble: forced labor.

In 1955, the government of the Union of Burma ratified the Forced Labour Convention of the International Labour Organization, the UN agency charged with promoting labor rights. And since 1964, the ILO has been sending requests to Burma that it please quit using its citizens for unpaid internationally illegal forced labor. In February 2009, the ILO and the Burmese government extended their supplementary understanding, "which provides a mechanism for Myanmar Citizens to lodge complaints of forced labour through the ILO Liaison Officer in Yangon [Rangoon]" and "ensures freedom from harassment and retribution for complainants and other persons who support the operation of the complaints mechanism." A month later, an internal ILO paper reported that the agency was very concerned about the harassment of complainants, and that one of the persons who supported the operation of the complaints mechanism had only just been released from prison. Overall, it pointed out, though the government had signed an agreement with the ILO years ago to eliminate forced labor, government-forced labor was still rampant in the country.

The Burmese government, naturally, says that it does no such thing, that people in Burma work on infrastructural projects for no money because they *want* to, they *love* to and they love their country, and it's a selfless Burmese tradition that we self-interested Westerners just can't understand. But Htoo Moo has documented it, of course, risking his life running around Burma like a crazy person interviewing escaped, very unwilling, prisoner-porters. In 1999, two people were arrested for having taped forced labor. They're still in prison. In 2002, the Karen Human Rights Group published a volume of SPDC written orders for forced labor, which KHRG had collected over the course of about a year; the book was 187 pages long. The aforementioned PBS *Frontline* video shows footage of hundreds of people working under Burmese soldiers' watch. "Grandmother, how much are you paid for each load of stones?" the cameraman asks an old woman. She fixes him with a long, cold look, then says, "I don't know anything about that."

I hadn't realized that Eh Soe had been subjected to servitude. The only person at BA who'd said anything to me had been Eh Na, my student who didn't work but lived at Office Two and was covered in scars. He'd told me about it between teaching sessions one day, while we sat on the cool blue tiles of the room we used for class, his brown eyes framed by the chin-length pieces of hair perpetually escaping his short ponytail. He'd come to Thailand pretty recently from a big Karen village, Aung Soe Moe, where his family farm had rice, nuts, and vegetables. He went to school and worked his field, and in the cool rainy-season nights everyone warmed up around rice wine and other villagers' company. And every day, Burma army soldiers came and took two, or five, or twenty villagers as short-term slaves.

When Eh Na was eighteen, for example, he encountered some troops on his way to his family's farmland. "Come with us," they said, and at gunpoint gave him a load of ammunition to carry, an unbearably heavy basket to strap to his shoulders. For four hours, he trudged through the jungle with them in his flip-flops, his skin slick with sweat, his back and neck searing, his steps heavy and stiff with the weight. He concentrated on avoiding land mines and fantasized about having a glass of water. He knew better than to think he'd be paid for his contribution, but he had been holding out hope for some food or something to drink before the soldiers turned him around for his four-hour trek back. Not so much.

In the last three years before he fled to Thailand, Eh Na estimated he had to do "only" ten forced labor stints. When he was twenty, he passed some Burmese soldiers on his way to visit a relative in a nearby village. "Carry this sick person," they said, raising their weapons, and he walked holding up one end of a stretcher for five long hours, which would have been bad enough even if the invalid hadn't been fat. Once, he and nine other villagers were forced to haul rice, beans, and wine for an entire day, which meant they had to walk back home in the middle of the night. Once, he was part of a crew that cleaned and built a fence around an army compound. Once, he was part of a crew that cleaned and built a fence around an army compound that was infested with flesh-eating jungle ants. On both occasions, the villagers had to find their own water and food, and on one, had to contribute their own tools and construction materials to the project they were being forced to work on. Once, Eh Na helped build a road by hand, crouching, sweltering, crushing rocks with tiny tools and laying them in the ground. The demands for forced labor were so consistent that some of the three hundred households in Eh Na's village had designated family members to do it, ones who were sturdy enough to survive it (unlike diabetic grandfathers) and whose work someone else could cover in their absence (unlike breast-feeding mothers). But it wasn't until six people in his village were killed by passing soldiers as they walked back from a betel nut field that Eh Na decided he'd had enough and moved to Thailand.

Eh Soe said, when I asked him for an estimate, that he couldn't possibly count the number of days he'd spent as a child doing grueling labor for the Burma army. His community of a hundred didn't have enough slaves to share the work very liberally, and his parents were so poor that they had no choice but to accept the 5¢ from wealthier families who could pay others' children to do their drudgery for them.

"Weren't you mad?" I asked Eh Soe.

"No." He waved his hand and shook his head briskly. "I didn't think anything about it. It's the culture. They had guns. Whoever has power can order people to do whatever they want. I couldn't hate, because I didn't have any idea about anything different."

"I guess that's a good thing about living in camp; most of the guys here didn't have to do forced labor."

"Yes, but they suffered the war. Their parents were in war. They had to flee. They had to live in the jungle. That is much worse. Me, I just have to work for a day, go home at night."

So that's what he did, until he finished primary school and his aunt paid for him to go away to high school in Moulmein, Burma's third-largest city, in the southeast of the country. After that, he earned his certificate at a Rangoon computer school, and spent two months in leadership-management classes in Pegu, another big city, nearby. But there aren't a lot of jobs in Burma, and Eh Soe was out of money, and *he* certainly wasn't interested in joining the armed resistance, so he moved to a refugee camp, re-enrolling in high school at the age of eighteen so he could work on his English, joining Htan Dah at Huay Kaloke. And then you know what happened there.

After two years of English in two different camps, Eh Soe taught fifth-grade science and sixth-grade math and Burmese to other refugees. He had a brother and sister working legally in Bangkok, but Eh Soe had registered as a refugee with the UN, which made him ineligible for a work permit. Not that he could afford one anyway; they cost more than $100 and require at least five trips to Thai government offices. So now he worked at BA, as a community organizer, attempting to fight apathy one villager at a time. It was difficult for him that most of the people he worked so hard to get to—those border mountains were no joke—just wanted to farm, to be left alone by both soldiers and uppity educated refugees come to tell them that their health and empowerment could affect a war they were tired of talking about.

"Some Karen people don't care about education," he told me.

"That's not just Karen people," I said. "My best friend is a teacher in a remote part of Ohio, and she has the same problem with some of her students."

"Real?"

"Sure. Their parents are farmers, and the students want to be farmers, so they don't see why they should take the time away from farming to get an education."

"That's right, that's right. Some Karen people say to me, 'You have an education, and I don't, but we eat the same rice.' But it is very important for Karen people. If they have low education, they have intolerance. That is why Buddhists say to Christians, 'You're not Karen! You have Western religion!' That is why DKBA has split from KNU. If they do not have knowledge, they cannot solve problems. If you're educated, you can live in a house with different beliefs."

"That's very deep, Eh Soe."

"Real! Here, we have Sgaw Karen, Pwo Karen"—and these two groups shared something of a long and complicated rivalry—"animist, Christian, Buddhist. . . . If you have two people who are uneducated and not alike in a house, they cannot live together."

"Seriously, Eh Soe, you're so wise."

He swatted at me.

"So are you going to keep working for BA?"

He shook his head. "I have no idea for the future. What am I going to do? I have no idea." And then, with understatement: "It's a problem. We have no country. *You* can choose whatever you want. The government provides much for you. You are lucky you were born in America. We have no country."

SITTING AT the table Thursday morning, I was less delighted by my early kitchen duties than usual. Though I'd carried the cutting boards and dragged the stone mortar and pestle into the dining room/garage and talked over the meal plan with Htan Dah, who was bright and lovely and had washed the rice and set it cooking, filling the downstairs with the warm nuttiness of it, and I was turning bags full of onions and garlic and vegetables into neat little friable piles of potential breakfast, I wasn't happy. I'd spent the previous night, ridiculously, warring with my ex-girlfriend, via an online chat program, even more ridiculously. We had a ten-year history of being a bad fit and breaking up and redating, both badly, and it had somehow come to yet another head while I was in every sense a world away, thanks to the magic of instant messaging. So now, I was crabby. I was in need of a thing that I felt stupid and guilty about needing, which was making me crabbier, and that was a thing harder to find in this house than justice, or money.

However much time we spent together and tight our friendship, I knew I could not count on Htan Dah for sympathy. When we were talking once, and I hadn't even been looking for it, he'd said, "You don't have any problem that is as serious as my problem." It stung, his implying that I wasn't self-conscious enough to be conscious of that very obvious reality. So I'd said "Of course," but then pointed out that all problems are relative, and that even he didn't have any problem that was as serious as some people's problems (though, honestly, it was hard for me to imagine who those people were). To which he'd agreed that some person, maybe a person in Africa, was worse off—adding, a little scathingly, that he wouldn't dare complain to them.

What I needed was Eh Na, who, while we'd waited the half-hour for class to begin the day before because someone had probably been arrested, had sat patient and peaceful as stone. Eh Na, whose eyes were so wide and quietly eager, like a doll's, that when he'd once asked me what had happened to my knee, which was covered in giant dark-pink bumps, I'd indulged in self-pity and whined, "I got attacked by mosquitoes. It sucks." Eh Na, who wasn't like Htoo Moo, who, had he been there, would have pulled up his shirt and shown me some thick jagged tissue where a village doctor had sewn up a tiger swipe with razor wire and no antiseptic or something, or would have said something like, "You know what sucks? *Forced labor.*" Eh Na, who, despite his scars and the fact that on his first visit back to Burma, post-fleeing, to see his family, he was abducted by government soldiers and given the choice of building a road by hand, with aching, bleeding fingers, or being beaten to death, and on his second trip back found his village burned to the ground, had looked at me compassionately and said, "Oh, that is very terrible," and shaken his head gravely. But Eh Na wasn't here.

When Eh Soe, after we'd already all eaten and cleaned up and the guys had gone back in the house to work, finally dragged his ass out from under his mosquito net and came downstairs and sat at the table, I almost kissed his round little cheeks. *Eh Soe* had a lot of girl trouble! Most recently, when I'd walked in and started talking to him while he was on the phone with his girlfriend, she started a fight with "Who's that girl in the background? Why are you talking to her?" Eh Soe was clearly my man.

"That girl you think looks like a boy is driving me crazy," I told him.

He started laughing.

"Seriously, Eh Soe, I'm in such a bad mood. We got in this huge fight last night. We're always fighting, and I know it would be better if we didn't talk, but at the same time, it's really hard for me not to have her in my life." Eh Soe gave the matter some consideration. "If you buy a shirt," he said finally, "if you can't exchange it, for some reason the shop won't let you, you will wear it until it wears out and is no good anymore even if it's stupid or too big."

I thought about that for a minute. "What?"

"If you start running, you don't stop until you reach your goal."

I thought about that for a minute, too. "Eh Soe! What the fuck are you talking about?"

He waved his hand dismissively. "Love is very mysterious."

"Great, Eh Soe. Thanks. That's totally helpful."

He shrugged.

It was Htan Dah's second-to-last possible day of class, since he was leaving on Monday. The day before, he'd missed again, and he'd seemed to feel bad. He was concerned, too, that his continued absence meant that I was still getting rides with the unsteady Ta Mla. So today, he freed himself of whatever afternoon work and family obligations he had, came up to me when I was getting my papers together, and said, "I will take you to class today."

When we arrived, Collin was holding his guitar. Ta Eh Thaw was killing time sweeping the classroom tiles, stooping over a short wooden broom with long, feathery bristles. She stopped, suddenly, and held it up and looked at it, and I looked at her, and she looked at me and asked, "Do you have?" Pointing to the implement. "In America?"

Collin strummed a few tentative chords while he talked with Wah Doh. I looked over my lesson plan, until I started to recognize a melody.

"Are you playing 'Country Roads'?" I asked. Veteran aid workers and volunteers know that the folk classic is wildly popular in Burma. Among the Karen, it's basically the national anthem. This was only one of many, many, many times I'd hear a refugee get down with John Denver.

Collin smiled his shiny eyes crinkly. "Do you know it?"

I tsked. Please. "I'm from the Midwest," I said, which didn't mean anything to anybody there. "That song is about a state that borders Ohio." Which it is, if you consider the first line to be "Almost heaven, West Virginia." Collin asked me if I could sing, and I said that I could, but I had to stop for lack of knowing the words, apparently, four syllables in.

"Almost heaven," he sang, "free Karen State . . ."

I laughed, and the guys laughed too.

"Blue Ridge Mountains, Shenandoah River," I started singing, but Collin was singing "Taw Nor Mountain, Salween River."

My participation dissolved into hysterical admonitions about the real words, so Wah Doh picked up my harmony, and on they went.

"Life is old there, older than the trees / Younger than the mountain flowing like the breeze / Country roads, take me home / to the place I belong / to Kaw Thoo Lei / Mountain mama / Take me home, country roads."

They stuck pretty faithfully to the lyrics after that, but I couldn't keep up with the surprises ("misty taste of rice wine"). Eh Na watched them, and me, alternately, wide eyes, silent, as usual. Collin handed me a sheet of paper with the lyrics printed on it the next day, so I

could learn them, as well as the (unaltered) words to the Carpenters'
"Top of the World."

My students wanted to plan a party. It was, they maintained,
appropriate that I throw myself a going-away celebration stocked
with all the Thai goods my American money could buy and invite all
of them to it. And actually, since there were two offices, and it wasn't
safe for these mostly Office Two residents to motorbike the ten minutes to Office One, though they did it all the time, it was only fair
that I throw myself two parties, one at each Mae Sot BA branch. I
wasn't leaving for almost two weeks, but I, too, was always happy to
talk about parties, so I devoted the conversation-practice part of our
class to the subject. We went around the room and everyone had to
tell me, in complete English sentences, what they hoped to consume
at their party. Beer. Several students mentioned that they'd like to
see multiple kinds of meat. Foods from Thai restaurants and stalls.
It was widely insisted that I acquire whatever it was that I drank at
American bars, so I promised to find some vodka.

"Have you heard of that?" I asked.

No one had.

We went over their homework after that, but it wasn't easy to concentrate on verb tenses—I mean, *their* language only had one; were all
these conjugations really necessary for white people to express themselves to each other?—with all the excitement, and the weather.

It was glorious outside, again. The rain had let up, and the sun
shone brilliantly on the driveway outside the open door. When
class was over, I went out while Htan Dah finished talking with
his coworkers. The rays were hot, but the breeze from the thick-
forested hills cooled the spot where I stood. Through the doorway,
in the house, Htan Dah stood with his back to me, speaking soft
tonal monosyllables, his cropped pants cut off at the shin, giving way
to thick calves and wide bare feet. I watched him while I warmed
my face and waited, wondering how he was managing to make capri
pants look good.

Back at Office One, I had another class, an impromptu pronunciation class, with Eh Soe. There was an awning at the front of our house,
on the left side, a tin-shingled archway just before a big wooden door
that opened into the living room. There was a table and some wooden
benches out there, under the porch, where Eh Soe was sitting when
Htan Dah and I pulled up. I didn't realize until I joined him there
that this was actually the front door; it was never open, for the rain or
for the secrecy. Eh Soe was translating an interview he'd conducted
in Burma, and I helped him with the words. That was what we were
doing, in the afternoon breeze, when Abby found me.

"Repeat after me," I was saying. "Rape."

"Rop."

"Try again. Rrraaape."

Abby wanted to know if I wanted to go out to dinner. The Blay's
wife had run away from camp for a visit and brought the better part
of a dead pig. Someone said she bought it at the market; someone
said she had killed it herself; someone said her family was somehow
prosperous in camp and had given it as a gift. Either way, the carcass
was on the dining room/garage table, being skinned and hacked into
pieces. Htan Dah had gone off somewhere, so wouldn't be doing the
cooking, so wouldn't be making any less-gamy pork-intensive dishes
for our delicate American palates. The house smelled like blood.
The Australian administrator had asked Abby if she wanted to join
her later at the Italian restaurant in town, so we went to a bar to kill
time, then went out for pizza.

By the time I got home at ten, the garage door was shut. Even
the door into the kitchen from the dining room/garage was closed.
I'd never realized that my housemates locked us in so thoroughly at
night. Tonight, they were locking in their company, too.

I'd passed the truck parked in the driveway, and when someone
let me in the kitchen door, I found red mud all over the floor. In the
living room, three Karen guys I'd never seen were sitting in front of
the little TV. Another one was messing with the wires in the back.

They were subtly rough-looking. I tried talking to them in English, but only Karen came back at me. Since I didn't know how to say anything in that language but "thank you," "white person," "love you" (because that's what Eh Na's name meant), and "eat!" I just smiled at them and walked upstairs.

Htan Dah was wide-awake, splayed on his stomach on the floor of the big room, reading a newspaper.

"What are you doing up?" I asked.

"I cannot sleep. I had coffee."

I sat down next to him, cross-legged. "Who are those guys downstairs?"

"The dark guys?" he asked, his eyes still on the paper.

"Yeah, I guess."

"Soldiers."

"Why are there KNU soldiers watching TV in the living room?"

"They drop off someone from BA who was inside."

"They don't speak English."

Htan Dah looked up, at me as if I were a very slow child. "They live in the jungle."

"Yes, I get that now."

He looked back at his paper. "I wish I lived in the jungle. It is very simple. You don't have to make decision. Just, farming, and living, and hanging around."

"So why don't you just move to the jungle?"

"Because(!). I don't want to fight like them."

"Fair enough." To my left, a couple of guys were asleep on the floor. I looked around. "Where are your wife and baby?"

"Today, they went back to camp."

"Oh, I didn't know that. Are you sad?"

"We cannot do anything. It is usual. Where have you been?"

"Why, did you miss me?"

Htan Dah hesitated, but still didn't look up. "Yes."

"I went to a bar with Abby—"

"Crocodile Tear?"

"Yes, the Crocodile Tear, and then we went to Casa Mia, you know what I'm talking about? Everybody there was white, the white people who work with refugees, I think. They were all wearing T-shirts from NGOs. It seemed weird that they were all out together but only with their white coworkers."

"Uh-huh."

I reached out and tucked my index fingers into Htan Dah's hair near his part, separating out a thin lock with each hand. I pushed the one in my right hand into my palm and held it there with my other three fingers, using my index finger to grab another piece, and then started on a tight, slim braid. "I wished that you were there. I missed you, and Eh Soe, and Htoo Moo." I didn't have a rubber band, so I just held the braid for a second after I finished, looking at it. The pieces slid apart almost as soon as I let go, and I started on another one.

"Uh-huh."

"Htan Dah," I said, staying my hands and looking at him, though he continued to look at the paper. "You're not listening to me."

"Yes!" he said. "I am listening! It is usual for you to hang out with white people. It is not usual to live with refugees. Usually the white people who come here do not live in the house with us."

"Wait, what? Your volunteers don't live here?"

"No! It is . . . optional. Usually they stay in hotel, or in another house, like Abby."

"Really?"

"Yes!"

"I didn't know that."

I dropped another braid. It disintegrated.

"Htan Dah, I don't want you to leave. I'm not ready to go home."

Eh Soe bounded up the stairs. "Darling, where you have been, I have missed you very much," he said, sitting cross-legged on the other side of Htan Dah.

"Aw, Eh Soe, I missed you too. Didn't you hear me say I was going out to dinner?"

"No! I asked everyone where you were, but they didn't have any idea about that."

"We went to the Crocodile Tear, and Casa Mia."

"Are you very drunk?"

"No. I was maybe a little bit drunk earlier, before dinner, but not now."

"Oh! I thought you would be very drunk."

"Really? Why?"

"Because, you are fighting with your girlfriend."

We talked about girlfriends for a while before Eh Soe went to talk to his and I got up to go to bed. There was light coming from the door to the balcony, so I poked my head out. Htoo Moo had set up camp there, lying on top of a mat of green and yellow woven plastic, a wool blanket about him and mosquito net hanging from two of its corners, ready to be strung up by the opposite two when the time came, the mesh in a pile around his legs for now. Someone else was sleeping in the living room, so he'd moved. I said goodnight to him before closing the door, while he continued to read an English/Burmese dictionary of military terms.

FRIDAY MORNING, the boys were all business again as they crowded into the living room for the weekly staff meeting. They took their places on the floor, Htan Dah Indian-style at the front of the room with a dry-erase board, facing them. Eh Soe sat among the crowd with a notebook and pen ready. The people around him murmured to one another, waiting patiently for the engagement to commence.

The *kaw la wah*—white people, that is, Abby and me—however, had worked ourselves up to total frenzy. One of my erstwhile advanced students had walked in the door with eyes red and sticky looking; he'd just come back from some assignment in camp, where he'd contracted pinkeye. He stuck his finger in one infected eye while explaining this to me, eliciting my desperate plea that he keep his hands away from his face and go wash them immediately. He just laughed at me, and continued to rub his itchy eyeballs while walking around the house touching things, computers, doors. Htan Dah had looked up alarmed when I burst into the computer room before the meeting and shouted "Don't touch your face!" at him. Abby went on a mad search of the house for disinfectant. Some of the guys laughed at us when we warned them of the impending ocular-disease epidemic. Some of them laughed at us while asking if we thought we would die from pinkeye. Abby didn't give a shit. When Ta Mla's slaughtering of two chickens in the kitchen before breakfast coincided unhappily with 1) our running out of dish deter-gent and 2) the *Bangkok Post*'s running a front-page article about a massive resurgence of bird-flu outbreak, she ran to 7-Eleven to buy cleaning products.

The hush and calm of the meeting could have spread to Abby and me, who were present, sitting on the edge of the room in chairs. Htan Dah had written the abbreviations of different departments or projects within the organization at the top of the board and was very orderly calling on their representatives for reports and then very meticulously summing up their lulling Karen speeches in one English sentence on the board. Eh Soe, who was acting as secretary, was keep-ing diligent notes, and saying, anytime he missed something, "Please repeat that." Ta Mla and a guy everyone called The Mechanic, who didn't speak a word of English and therefore never spoke to me, and who sometimes wore black fingerless gloves, had their hands on each other's legs and feet, comfortable. They were both wearing T-shirts they'd gotten in school at camp bearing the enumerated tenets of the KNU revolution. So many of the guys had so many of these shirts that it wasn't uncommon for two to be making the ubiquitous, heavy political statement on the same day.

1. For us surrender is out of the question.
2. Recognition of Karen State must be completed.
3. We shall retain our arms.
4. We shall decide our own political destiny.

Everyone was lounging. Everyone was quietly attentive. But Abby and I were already on edge, and then, soon enough, Htan Dah called on the guy the KNU soldiers had dropped off the night before.

Eh Kaw looked bad. His face seemed gaunter than even his slim frame suggested it should have been, and his dark skin was dull, ashen. He'd been on some type of surveying trip in Burma, checking on the progress of a school, it seemed, as well as carrying in some of BA's rations from the Thailand Burma Border Consortium to distribute them. He looked tired as he said whatever it was that made Htan Dah write on the board, "Both of teachers are afraid of SPDC and DKBA." Eh Kaw talked a little bit more, and all the guys started laughing. Htan Dah wrote, "One of the teachers got shock when she heard the firing." He stopped, considering for a moment before adding, "She is timid." Eh Kaw went on for a few more moments, and everyone nodded.

"He has malaria," Htan Dah translated out loud for Abby and me, looking at us.

"Oh no," I said, because I felt bad for him. The personal implications of his misfortune dawned on me surprisingly slowly: This guy and I slept and socialized an easy mosquito's flight away from each other. Lots of my roommates had had malaria before, but Eh Kaw had it right now. As I wasn't taking any prophylactic medication, this was pretty bad news for me.

Days ago, I'd been at the table when the mosquitoes started pouring in and attacking at dusk, and a visiting BA staffer from Bangkok had said, "You're going to get malaria." Technically, according to the research I'd done before I left, Thai cities had eradicated malaria.

But I knew by now that the disease was raging just over the border, which these guys regularly hopped—them and millions of other refugees and migrants, so that the disease was a risk in this border town where I sat.* I'd told the visitor, a chubby Karen guy with glasses and impeccable English, that I could probably survive a bout of malaria. "Not necessarily," he'd said. "If it goes to your brain, it will kill you." It was true that cerebral malaria required immediate treatment. If I were infected and didn't get medicine, I could wake up feeling fine and be dead by the next morning. And I wouldn't be the first BA volunteer to die this way.†

Htan Dah was sounding similar alarms now. "There is a lot of malaria in that area," he said. "You can die easily." I wasn't positive whether he was being dramatic for my benefit or if he was just being perfectly candid and the content made it seem dramatic. I suspected at least a hint of the former, though what he was saying was, of course, true.

He went on to announce that one of the BA trainers had been arrested on his way to camp and had to pay twenty thousand baht—some six hundred dollars—for his release. Abby and I balked at this

---

* This sort of country-crossing was what kept regional malaria workers on their toes. These days, the hardworking staff of the Shoklo Malaria Research Unit—the ones who determined that transmission happens in the early evening—annually treats thirty to forty *thousand* cases of malaria in the political badlands of the Thai-Burma border, plus NGOs treating half that again inside the camps, those cases mostly due to back-and-forth like Eh Kaw's. On an annual budget of $2 million, SMRU keeps the transmission Burma breeds and does nothing to combat way down, preventing the epidemic from spreading. And it's a good thing, because this malaria is the most drug-resistant malaria in the world. And because this is where malaria comes from: Genetic testing has shown that a resistant strain plaguing Africa was carried there from here, and has gradually spread across the entire continent.

† And I would remember that poignantly, dreadfully, oh yes I would, after I got back to the States and a hard fever brought me shaking and tearing my clothes off and pressing my chest to my bathroom floor, against cold winter tile, intermittently vomiting and hallucinating and hoping it wasn't long-incubated cerebral malaria so that I would wake up alive.

number. The staff seemed concerned, though not surprised. Htan
Dah continued, in English, that they were all at increased security
risk, as Thai work permits expired soon and there would be more
cops and more eagerness to check IDs and arrest people. As a final
announcement, he said he had been selected, along with eleven others, to attend the upcoming fall semester at the journalism school in
Chiang Mai.

"Oh!" I said involuntarily, and clapped once, but no one else said
anything, and Htan Dah never broke his impassive meeting face.
Only Abby and I were stirring, I squirming in my seat, she asking me
if I had known that. I hadn't.

"When did you find out you got in(!)?" I asked, accosting Htan
Dah in the computer room after the meeting.

"They sent me email . . . maybe . . . couple days ago."

"A couple days(!)? I can't believe you didn't tell me! That's so
exciting! Why didn't you tell me?"

Htan Dah shrugged. "I forgot."

One of the other staff guys came up to me and handed me a mail-
ing envelope. "For you?" he asked. He'd just picked it up from the
office PO box downtown.

It was indeed addressed to me, from Columbus, Ohio, and had the
size and heft of a hardcover Che Guevara biography. I started jumping up and down.

"Do you know what's in here?" I asked, tearing it open.

"No," Htan Dah said, watching me.

I pulled out the cream-colored tome. The jacket had been lost
somewhere, or maybe I'd never had it, since I'd borrowed the book
from a New Orleans library before Katrina. "What's in it?" Htan Dah
asked. "Money?"

That irritated me a little, though I knew it wasn't an unreasonable
question; these guys sent money, if any money was ever to be had to
be sent, in books. The Blay's brother had decided to leave Burma
to study in India a couple of years ago, getting there, and back, the

only way he could afford—walking—and while he was gone, The Blay had sent him money in books. But "This is that Che biography I was telling you about!" I said. "What do you mean, 'What's in it?' There's nothing in it. There's a book in it. It's a book. It's for you." I handed it over.

"Wow," Htan Dah said, taking it. "Thank you very much." He stuck out his free hand.

I took it, and shook it, but while doing so said, "We're not shaking hands!" and then grabbed him into his second hug ever. He put his arms up, like the Canadian had shown him, but though they were on my back, they didn't give in to the gesture, and neither did his perfectly rigid body, because it hadn't been taught to like mine had.

"Here, let me have this for one second," I said, releasing him and taking the book back. In my mother's house, it was a sin to gift anything with a cover without writing something on the inside of it. I gave it back to him a little while later, inscribed.

For one stylish and attractive revolutionary, the story about another.
May you find it as rousing as I find you.

I went to class. When I got back, I sat down in the living room next to Htoo Moo and watched music videos with him. Before long, he stood up and started doing squats. He put his arms out in front of him and clasped his hands together, standing next to my chair, tilted his ass up and then dropped it nearly to the floor, bending at the knees, his eyes on Eminem on the screen. The sets came closer together and became interspersed with an occasional crack of the neck or shoulder roll as it got later. It was time to play football. Or soccer, as I was keen on calling it. No one seemed to know how it had started, but everyone knew that the hour-long game started at five on weekdays.

"I want to come watch today," I told Htoo Moo. "Is that okay?"

"Yes," he said, smiling. "Very yes."

"Htan Dah, you should come," I said when we walked past him in the kitchen, on our way out.

"I don't think so(!)," he said. "Maybe some other time. Right now I am too fat."

Htoo Moo nodded. I knew he thought Htan Dah was fat; he'd told me so several times.

"Why do you guys keep saying that? You're not fat."

"Yes!" Htan Dah said. He pulled up his shirt, exposing his belly. He pinched the skin and thin layer of fat covering his abs. "I never exercise in the rainy season because I get very lazy. Maybe in the summer I will play."

Htoo Moo and Ta Mla usually took bicycles to the field because they didn't have the money to waste on gas, and it was a short enough ride—and more exercise. But since there were only two bikes, Htoo Moo drove me on the back of a motorbike. Ta Mla pedaled along ahead of us as we went, slowly, out of the neighborhood, off a main street, onto a narrower one lined with rough Thai houses and shops. Before long, we turned onto a dirt road.

We made our way to the back of some sort of farm. The season had turned the path to a sloppy mire, the mud gummy and choppy where it emerged from streams and puddles of rain and farm runoff. Some of the standing water was thick with shit and unrecognizable surface growths. I kept my flip-flopped feet up and hoped not to get any parasites while Htoo Moo did some scary off-roading and maneuvering. The cattle trail wound far into grazing pastures, opening up near the end at one with metal goalposts on its edges, the grass between them trampled away. The field was empty when we arrived at twenty till, but within fifteen minutes, a dozen motorbikes rumbled up to the playing ground.

The guys divided up arbitrarily, an ethnic mix spanning across the field, Karen making up a slight majority among the Thais and Burmans. It was just shirts or skins here. Nearly everyone wore polyester shorts and canvas sneakers. A few had proper cleats. The overcast sky was seven shades of gray, deep and rich against the screaming green grass and trees, as the game started out slowly.

The center midfielder kicked the ball to his teammate, who kicked it to another teammate, and the pack had just started moving when someone kicked it out of bounds. The athletes waited, chatting, looking at the ground, stretching their arms and legs while someone retrieved the ball. The game picked up pace as the shots became well aimed and the players better prepared. The boys broke out their moves. They splashed through the puddles and slipped on slick, bright soil, laughing when they went down, playing vigorously and fast but laughing always, when they kicked the ball, when they missed the ball, when they narrowly avoided stepping into the pair of enormous cow pies in the middle of the field. There was one stone-faced guy, one inevitable guy with a pectoral dragon tattoo, a fashion mullet, and an earring. He had managed to muster a soul patch in this sea of smooth Asian faces. When he fell, landing his white shorts in mud, he did not think it was funny.

Htoo Moo and Ta Mla were on the shirts team, the team that lost the first twenty-minute round. The second started without delay, and the guys were warm and revved up. A Burman boy, maybe eighteen, who worked on the land had sat down out of bounds, having put the cows away for the day. Now he was on his feet, watching the action, dancing around the sideline trying to get a better look, trying to contain himself from bursting into the play. He was too shy to ask if he could cut in, and there were enough alternates already. Four of them lined up next to the field as a fifth counted one, two, three, go and they took off in a race while they waited their turn.

The sun broke the clouds above a nearby fifty-foot pond. Golden light sliced the grounds as the BA boys, who were still in the game, played out the match. However docile he was in life, Ta Mla was not fucking around on this field. He attacked with painfully earnest concentration and determination, dodging the cattle dung, never taking his eye off the ball until he'd passed it or it'd been stolen from him. He switched from offense to goalie midmatch and blocked the ball with his hands, his chest, his knees. No one scored on him. The shirts won.

At the end of the second round, the older guys and guys with wives or cooking duties or lack of stamina left, and the farm kid finally got his chance. He played barefoot, the loose white shirt that had earlier been exposing his washboard torso buttoned up so he could join Htoo Moo and Ta Mla's team. He was fresher than everyone else, and grateful, too, and he charged around the field. But within minutes of the start, the opposing team's ball rolled through the goalposts while the goalie was sauntering around one of them; he'd lost interest, he indicated by laughing, shrugging, and walking away, so the kid got relegated to the more sedentary position. He looked a bit dejected but guarded the goal hard, springing to action whenever the ball came anywhere near him, playing well out of his area and running it all the way to center sometimes. No one cared. Htoo Moo suffered from the same hotdogging, bringing the ball through the offensive lines even when he was playing defense, or booting the ball too hard, to places containing no people.

Three laborers sat near the farmhouse in the distance and watched for a bit. A woman, her face thick with *thanaka*, the cosmetic wood paste in swirls on her cheeks, glanced at the players as she walked past on her way back from the market holding a bottle of whiskey or oil in a paper bag. The skins scored. Soul Patch intercepted the ball with his head, then moaned and rubbed it, actually fixing his hair before carrying on. Htoo Moo took a hard ball to the gut and laughed hysterically. The sun sank, the time ran out, and it started to rain. The skins had won again. The players started toward their bikes. Ta Mla and Htoo Moo walked off the field, tired, panting, filthy, leaving nothing in their wake but two remarkably intact piles of shit.

"DO YOU want to go to a bar?" I asked Htan Dah when we got home. I'd bounded up the stairs to my room as Htoo Moo and Ta Mla made their way to the bathroom to splash the sweat and mud off. Shortly, Htan Dah had walked in. "Come on. We should go celebrate. Let me buy you a drink."

"I would like to," he said. "But I am afraid I will get arrested."

"Okay. Will you drink beer with me if I go buy it?"

Abby and I went and picked up four big bottles of Chang and a bottle of the more expensive and better-tasting Singha for the occasion. We'd barely begun the toasting when in walked a blond, leggy French broad with a fantastic accent, two white guys, and a small bar's worth of booze, more beer plus whiskey and soda water and ice. She'd been a volunteer for BA, then moved on to work for another NGO in Thailand, and was in town for a very drunken visit. We packed the dining room/garage with cigarette smoke and body heat. Eh Soe squeezed in next to me on one of the benches, and we shared the long cheroot he was smoking.

"Stay close to me," he said. "I do not want to talk to these people."

I laughed. "These white people?"

He said yes, and I started laughing harder.

"Why not? Did you know that I'm a white person?"

"I know, but you are different. Usually I do not talk to our volunteers because they don't care about me."

I clucked my tongue. "Eh Soe, I'm sure you're wrong about that."

"It means very much to us that volunteers come and spend their time and money on being with refugees. We appreciate it a lot. But usually they do not live with us and talk with us."

"Has it ever occurred to you that they don't talk to you so much because you're avoiding them? I probably would have avoided you if I could have."

"I am serious." He squealed that last word a bit, and his face was full blush. He was plastered. "I do not want you to leave."

"Aw, Eh Soe, are you going to cry?" I asked.

A lot of the conversation around us had happened to die down, and it was quiet in the instant when Eh Soe said, "Yes, I will cry." Then: "I cannot talk about this."

"Aww," everyone said, sincerely touched because it was sweet, so sweet that an awkward silence followed.

Lah Lah Htoo brought out a stringed Karen instrument, plucking out a twanging melody with a sad lilt. The French girl closed her eyes and stretched her arms out and dipped her fingers then her wrists in hippie-dippie waves as he sang. Htoo Moo grabbed a guitar and sang songs he'd written about revolution, unhurried numbers with the slow earnestness of a pop Chinese love ballad. John Denver was revisited. Someone went upstairs and dragged Eh Kaw up from where he was sleeping on the floor.

"You guys, leave him alone!" Abby said as the peaked, groggy roommate was pulled into the dining room/garage. "He has malaria!"

"He always gets malaria," someone said, and everyone laughed. Eh Kaw smiled, and stuck around for a song or two. The ice melted. The slim and generally silent Gaw Say put his hand on my arm, suddenly brave about touching me and speaking English, and told me he just went poo. Htoo Moo fell asleep at the table. The French girl lost her keys. Htan Dah caught my eye as I exhaled a lungful of cheroot and asked me if I smoked.

"No, but I'm drunk." I held the cigar I'd stolen from Eh Soe out to him. "Do you smoke?"

"No," he said, "but I am living," and took it from me and put it in his mouth.

It was past two in the morning by the time most of the guys had gone to bed. Anyone who was still awake was getting ready to do the same. Htoo Moo was standing on the balcony off my bedroom, looking at the mosquito net he slept under there, yelling, "Who is that?" at the passed-out body in his bed. Htan Dah and I were going opposite ways on the stairwell, and I caught his upper arm as I passed him. "I have a present for you," I said. "Do you want it now?" He nodded.

I went upstairs and grabbed the thick brown envelope out of my bag, along with another little parcel. Before I'd left the States, my mother had given me a small, black, blank hardcover notebook that was, she'd read somewhere, like the ones Hemingway used. I hadn't written in it yet, and decided to repurpose it as a gift to my journalism-school friend. I'd wrapped it in brown paper and spent half an hour practicing drawing the bow I sketched on the front of it with a black rollerball pen, concentrating so hard on the task that it didn't occur to me that my rendition wouldn't look perfect regardless, not to someone who'd never seen a bow in his life.

I met him in the darkness of the living room. People we couldn't see slept on the floor. We walked outside to the small porch at the front of the house, and sat down on perpendicular benches. I gave him the book, which he opened, then turned over and over in his hands, thanking me, saying I'd already given him one book that day. I said it was no big deal, really, since I could get plenty of books in the United States and really wanted him to have these two. I made a short speech in as clear English as I could muster about how he'd been an invaluable friend to me, and had taught me, and fed me, and kept me so much company, and about how I was inspired by his devotion and strength and really believed he could make a difference in his cause, and then I handed him the envelope.

He opened it, and looked inside it, and said nothing. He pulled the cash out a bit, leafing through the edges of the stack, and said, after a moment, "Wow. That's a lot." He was just holding it, and looking at it, and seemed totally at a loss, so I told him it was eighty 1,000-baht bills, about $2,200 then, enough to buy his ID papers. He still didn't say anything, so I grabbed hold of his hand and told him his well-being was important to me, that I was so proud of the opportunities he'd won in Chiang Mai and wanted to help him make it easier, and more possible, in any way I could. He just watched me, even when I'd finished speaking, so we sat there looking at each other.

"Are you excited?" I asked.

When he finally started talking, he formed his sentences slowly, and couldn't catch his breath. "I can't believe it." He pulled the air into his lungs hard. "To me, it seems unbelievable. It is like . . . in a dream. It is a dream." He gasped again. He seemed to be swallowing too thickly, too often, like someone who's about to throw up. "This is the best thing. This is the best moment of my life. I always say to my wife I will get ID, but I never knew how. I cannot express how I appreciate it." One fast, deep breath, short exhale. Another. Then suddenly, panic. "I cannot give you anything," he said. "I would like to give you something. My wife, she can weave."

"Htan Dah, please."

"I can make her weave a traditional shirt. It won't be done in time, because you will leave, but I can post it, I can post it to you for a present after you leave. I wish there was something I could give you. I want to give you something important, but I cannot."

"Htan Dah, please accept this as a gift. You've given me lots of gifts. Do you remember the first thing you said to me?"

He was taken aback; his head drew back a couple of inches. "No."

"You said, 'Can I help you?'"

"I don't remember. I cannot believe you remember."

"You've always helped me here. And if you had money, and I needed it, you would give it to me. You don't understand how little money this is in the course of the money I'll have in my entire life-time. It's nothing. It's really no problem. Also, I told other people in the United States about you and will get some money from them. It's money. It's not important. There's nothing I could do with it in the United States that would be as important as your safety."

I thought he was calming down, but he started panting harder, sucking in tight breaths. He seemed like he was going to cry, though I knew he didn't cry. "I understand," he said. "You want to help me because you love me. And I love you too. So much." We hugged, ultimately, and this time, after a moment, he pressed in with the arms he'd wrapped around me, and no matter how tightly I squeezed him, I couldn't stop him from shaking.

I WOKE up Saturday morning to a tight grip around my ankles. And giggling.

"Htoo Moo!" I yelled as he hoicked me half out from under my sheet. "Stop!"

He pulled again, laughing as I flew out from under my mosquito net and hit the floor. My head throbbed hard. I shut my eyes against the sunlight blaring in through the windows and hollered again. "I'm tired!"

"Ohhh," he cooed. "Why?"

"I drank too much last night! Go away!"

"Ohhh. Was that hard?"

"Fuck off!" I yelled, laughing but trying not to.

I accomplished very little that day. Abby and I made pancakes in a wok, from a Bisquick box she found at the Hong Long Mini-mart. ("How did you make them round?" Htan Dah asked us. When we replied "What?" he clarified, "What bowl did you use to shape them?") I accompanied Htan Dah to the market. Abby and I sliced okra and dipped it in a rice-flour-and-water batter and fried it. I was pretty excited about going back to bed before nightfall until Collin called from Office Two and invited me to what he kept calling his "dog-meat party."

Dog meat, all the refugees assured me, was warm meat; eating it would heat you from your insides. The Blay was at Office Two already when Htan Dah and I arrived. He'd been simmering the dog pieces all day with a special combination of spices in a big pot over the gas range. Htan Dah and I joined the Office Two staff in a circle on their floor as we waited for them to make the final preparations to the meal.

"Thank you for coming to my dog-meat party," Collin said to me.

"Thank you for inviting me. Where did you guys get this dog? Can you buy it at the market?"

At this, everyone looked at each other. Collin just smiled.

"Who killed this dog?" I asked.

Silence.

"Please take this drink," Collin said. One of the other guys handed me a tall, thin glass with Thai whiskey mixed with dark herbal tonic. Everyone was taking a turn with the concoction.

I shook my head. "I'm like Saw Kaw today," I said, pointing at him, because he didn't drink, because he had hepatitis.

"Please," Collin said, and so I took the glass.

"Okay. I'm going to drink this, even though I'm extremely hungover, because it's my duty to the Karen people." A round of cheers went up, and I took the mixture down.

The Blay put a big bowl of dog curry in front of me, dark, dark chunks of seasoned meat in a pile. It was a little tougher to chew than I might have liked, but the flavor was rich and layered. As we picked up the pieces with our fingers, The Blay brought out what everyone insisted was the best part. The dog's face had been skinned and then boiled and long stewed. It sat on the white plate, its skull visible through the seasoned muscles and sinews, its teeth becoming increasingly exposed as the guys peeled meat from it. It was warming, indeed, whether the meat itself or the spices it was cooked in, and I washed away my sweat and hot cheeks with more whiskey.

Which was how I came to be hungover, again, on Htan Dah's last day in town. We two got up early to get food from the market, where we passed a guy he said hi to—who, he told me when I asked, was his brother. We squeezed through the crowd and crowded piles of fish and vegetables on tables and mats on the ground while I said things like "I didn't know you had a brother!" and "Where does he live(!)?" and "How often do you see him(!)?" and Htan Dah explained how

his brother lived in Mae Sot, worked just over at Dr. Cynthia's,*
and everyone in the house who had family spread around in camp
and in Burma and even hiding in nearby villages tried to see them
when they could, but it wasn't so easy to travel. On the way back, we
passed a Honda Civic on the road, and I pointed it out to Htan Dah,
exclaiming that that was exactly what my car at home looked like.
When he asked me how much it cost, I told him, then added, for
context, that that was ten times the amount of money I'd given him,
the amount I'd given him being, therefore, not a lot of money at all,
especially considering how much more important he was than a car,
obviously. This last bit seemed to genuinely surprise and move him,
and he said thank you for saying that, for comparing him favorably
to the importance of a car, which I found upsetting. After breakfast,
we lay spread out all over my big bedroom floor, in the sunshine,
talking and doing nothing in hungover inertia, like undergrads. Eh
Soe joined us for a while. Abby and Ta Mla and Htoo Moo came and
went as well. I came clean about my despair on the first night of the
collapsing air mattress, and told Htan Dah, when he asked me, that I
hadn't asked for help because I hadn't wanted to impose. He told me
how he'd worried that night that I was going to cry, like their previous

---

* Dr. Cynthia Maung, a rumored 2005 Nobel Peace Prize nominee, fled to Thailand after
the '88 demonstrations, carrying a stethoscope, traveling at night to avoid capture, setting
up a wood-scrap safe house for student activists in Mae Sot. Karen leaders soon started
sending their sick there. Now, twenty years later, she and her clinic treat more than ninety
thousand cases a year, half migrants and refugees, half people who've just come all the
way over from Burma to go to the doctor because the health care there sucks so bad. The
clinic is a somewhat haphazard collection of buildings and hospital beds operating illegally
and at the beneficence of the Thai government, swarming with gunshot victims and the
malaria-stricken and women recovering from $4 Burmese back-alley abortions. I visited
there once. There was a girl hobbling around on two prosthetic legs; she'd stepped on a
land mine on her flight out of Burma with her boyfriend and had been hanging around the
clinic for years. There were Western doctors come to assist for a while during their vaca-
tions. Also, there were cartoony public-service posters depicting AIDS as a menacing-
looking purple monster and a strapping, personified condom with arms and eyes punching
it in the face.

volunteer, but that they'd all tried not to impose on me, also, because they knew that white people valued privacy. Eh Soe said that as far as he was concerned, I was a man. Both guys expressed how terrified they were of Mae Sot's stray dogs, Htan Dah maintaining that he was more scared of them than of cops, which shocked Abby and me. (He had "a good relationship," though, with the one on the corner of our street, so would consent to walk, rather than drive, to get ice cream at 7-Eleven with us that night.) Htoo Moo said that if he ever caught an SPDC soldier, he'd torture him, which got me pontificating about hypocrisy and perpetuating violence and so forth. Eh Soe and Htan Dah told me I'd be too busy to email them when I got home because I'd be working, and Americans work a lot. They asked me if I'd call. I insisted that I would. Then, somehow, the day had passed, and the light coming in the windows was turning richer than its pale daytime hue. We went downstairs and threw some dinner together, and Htan Dah said he wanted to take me to Huay Kaloke.

We hopped on his motorbike and drove away from the house, out of town, in the twilight. The roads became narrower and the air cooler as we got farther along pavement cut through forest. I sat behind Htan Dah, who leaned easily into the bends, watching and breathing in the trees. We stopped when they gave way to a grassy clearing, and Htan Dah took the keys out of the ignition.

"What is this?" I asked.

"This is it."

It was just a big field. "Really?" We started onto it, slowly. "What is this now?"

"Part of a farm." His voice was low, quiet, like it always was when we were in public, though there was no one here to notice his accent now. I hated to see him doing this, nearly whispering out of habitual fear. I stuck close to him so I could hear his tour.

He pointed to which way Burma was, just over there, beyond those trees, and where he had lived with his mother—and his father when he wasn't at war—over that way. There was a school, here, he said.

This, this was all houses, all of this. That is about it, he said, hushed. We hadn't been there for five minutes. There wasn't a lot to see. There wasn't a single sign that thousands of refugees had lived there not ten years earlier. Htan Dah stood in the meadow, saying nothing, and didn't make a move to leave, his black hair sharp against the glaucous, staticky light of the darkening sky. I looked away from his quiescent profile. All was long grass, beset by a wall of woods. It was hard to imagine him younger and running for his life here, how people had died here, in all this soft, empty green. Any trace of that had burned thoroughly and easily enough, and the field growth had fully reasserted itself. We turned and walked back through it, thick under our feet, when he was ready to go.

As we neared the motorbike, we passed an old man. He said something to Htan Dah, and Htan Dah smiled and nodded politely back, and we continued toward the road.

"Who's that?" I asked.

"He is Karen. A laborer."

"Do you know him?"

"No."

"What did he say?"

"He said to come back often."

XIV.

There are many people have day dreaming to take resettlement in the third countries. Everywhere I go, I hear talk about a third country, people who live in one of the camp in the north of Thailand name Umphium Mae are excited about to resettlement in the third country which is arrange by the UNHCR. It becomes the hip pop popular in the camp. So that people are crazy on going to the third country and have a dream for their future.

One of my aunts who work in the hospital said "I don't want to attend work because soon I have to go to the foreign country." when they meet each other with friends, they talk about the same issue. Some people are also confused about this issue. It is better to go to the third country or to go back to their homeland? Even though they want to go back they wonder to themselves Where is my land? Where is my house? How do I start my life? Everything is vague for them. As for me I worry about another thing. What should we do if the refugee people go to the third country? Who will struggle for independence? This question comes up from my mind and it makes me upset and worried and hurts my heart. I don't know. So if I visit the house in the camp I ask them "Will you go to the third country? Most people reply "yes". So it makes me tired.

—MU NA, THURSDAY, JULY 6, 2006,
WORKSHOP, MAE SOT, THAILAND

IT WAS possible that my presence reminded my housemates/students/ coworkers of all the freedoms that one could have in a life and that, as my departure grew nearer, their desire to get help acquiring them intensified. It was also possible that the firestorm of questions about and applications for resettlement that were suddenly pushed in my face was ignited by Htan Dah's having left for Mae La. Everyone knew that he, like my student Mu Na, didn't approve of the masses of Karen attempting to expatriate to a third—as in non-Thailand or -Burma—country. He loudly and conspicuously said, whenever I asked him about applying for resettlement, that he wouldn't leave Southeast Asia and the struggle that was his duty to the Karen people. Once, when I was sitting in the living room surrounded by guys, Htan Dah walked in, heard that they were asking me how they could get to America and what life there would be like, then turned around and walked right back out.

Whatever the impetus, resettlement was the prevailing theme when I asked my students, the day after Htan Dah left, to make sentences for me in present perfect tense. "I have been to the US over a hundred times . . . in my imagine," Wah Doh said. Saw Kaw, with the handsome shaved head and strong shoulders and hepatitis, smiled at me sweetly and said, "I have been to Australia . . . in my dream."

Later that night, Ta Mla came into my room to talk, sitting down next to me on the reading bench. I'd come down with a little bit of something ("Of course you're not feeling well," Abby said. "You aren't sleeping. You live in a frat house.") and wasn't my usual energetic self. I'd been told three times in as many days and by as many Karen men that I shouldn't be too thoughtful, because I should be happy, because then I wouldn't get sick, because being unhappy led to disease. Ta Mla had his own advice for me now: "When I get upset," he offered, "nobody can make me feel as happy as playing guitar and sing a song." But he wasn't here to talk about me.

Three weeks ago, he said, a classmate of his who had moved to England had called. Living in England, the friend had told him, was awesome. When I asked Ta Mla if the guy wasn't totally broke, he said, "He said he can move about freely." When I pressed him, asking about the culture shock and the language barrier and the distance between him and his family, Ta Mla said, "Yes, but anywhere he wants to go, he can." This phone call had further convinced Ta Mla that the best place for him might be overseas. "The situation in my country is difficult . . . so that if I go back there, we might not be able . . . to . . . feed ourselves," he said. "There is instability. So if I get opportunity to resettle . . . I would like to go there. The problem is, how do I resettle?"

This was no rhetorical question. Eh Soe had long ago filled out an application for asylum in some country or other and was having a hell of a time figuring out the status of his bid. The only thing he'd gotten so far was an email from the UN in response to his many queries, and it was so brief and cryptic and noncommittal that even I couldn't decipher it with all my native English skills and college degrees.

Even getting that far in the process wasn't so easy. In Ta Mla's opinion, the UN workers in camp didn't adequately assist uneducated families with their applications, and it was unfair,[*] and it made him terribly "unhappy." One time when he was in camp, he'd actually asked the UN workers why this was so, why they didn't give priority to the illiterate, the poorest and most destitute, who needed the most help, since the current system was just rewarding the most educated and best off, the same types who had TVs and the generators to run them and already knew how to help themselves. The workers had responded that that was a difficult question to answer.

The process of getting Ta Mla from that reading bench in Mae Sot to the United States of America would have started with, well,

---

[*] The greater likelihood of the educated and English-proficient to successfully complete the application process also causes serious brain drain in the Karen's Asia-based population. Keeping camp schools staffed with qualified teachers is difficult, since 11 percent had already left by 2008, and an additional 65 percent said they were considering following them.

a preparedness to lie about ever having enlisted or met anyone in the KNU, and then his informing the UNHCR office in the refugee camp where he was registered (and pretended to live, since it was illegal for him to live where he did) of his interest. The UNHCR would refer his case to the US Embassy. That would prompt the Overseas Processing Entity, which is an organization contracted by the United States State Department, and which in this case was run by the International Rescue Committee, to preprocess Ta Mla's application, which would involve filling out a family tree, a short bio, and requisite US government forms, before turning it over to the Department of Homeland Security.

The next step would be an interview by a DHS agent. If Ta Mla lived in Mae La or one of the camps that's relatively easily accessible from big cities, he'd be interviewed there. If he lived in Umpiem, like Htan Dah used to, which is a couple hours' drive from Mae Sot, he and any relevant spouses and/or children would have to be sent to Mae Sot,* where an intergovernmental organization built DHS a little compound in its processing center because DHS had refused to go to Umpiem.† There, Ta Mla and his family would sleep in the compound for four or five days while awaiting DHS interviews. The International Organization for Migration, which is contracted by the US government to prepare the refugees for resettlement and actually move them, would use some of Ta Mla's downtime to sneak in English classes, which the US government does not fund. He would also go through the medical screening process, in which he'd be checked, per the Centers for Disease Control, for TB (but not malaria). If he did have TB, as did up to 15 percent of the camp dwellers, he'd have to start a six-month drug regimen. If he had multiple-drug-resistant TB, however, that, as IOM's cultural orientation officer puts it, "is a problem."

---

* For a while, DHS agents were flying back and forth between Bangkok and Mae Sot to avoid the eight-hour, $8 bus—a matter of no small derision in Mae Sot's rough-and-tumble and cash-strapped NGO community.

† This, also, was a matter of no small derision among NGO workers.

Ta Mla's DHS agent would, by the principles of the Asylum Officer Basic Training course of the Immigration Officer Academy, on which refugee-officer training is based, begin the interview by "attempt[ing] to establish rapport" and "help the applicant feel at ease" in whatever manner the agent saw fit. The agent would then explain the interview process, that all information is confidential, taking time to elaborate, if necessary, on how some governments keep citizen information confidential. Ta Mla would be sworn in, the DHS agent making modifications to the oath if Ta Mla objected to saying "swear" or "so help me God." The agent would then verify Ta Mla's paperwork before pursuing, "in a nonadversarial manner," a line of questioning that would prompt Ta Mla to explain in his own words why he was applying for asylum. He would be allowed to make a closing statement, and then be informed that he'd be notified of the decision by letter.

If Ta Mla's application were approved, then it'd be time to learn to become an American! He would have five days to do this in twenty-five hours' worth of cultural orientation classes run by IOM. The twenty or so students in the room brainstorm about what life in the United States will be like, have their attention brought to some laws that resettled Karen have run afoul of (you cannot just pee anywhere outside, like you can in a village), and are told over and over that it is important to get a job—Any. Job. They role-play important elements of this process, like handshaking. They are given a brochure that says please help me I'm a refugee and I don't speak English that they can point to by way of seeking assistance in finding their connecting flights in US airports. They are given a book in Karen about United States culture. The information is practical, if occasionally brutal:

> The American life-style is not necessarily a good one. It is fast-paced and highly stressful. After work or school, many Americans return home and sit on the couch all evening and watch TV. In addition, many eat a poor diet, full of meat, fats, and sugars, and lacking in

fiber and healthy grains, fruits and vegetables. Cigarette smoking and excessive drinking of alcohol add to the dangers. In addition, the environment is filled with car fumes, chemicals and other harmful substances. As a result, the 'modern' diseases of a rich society—heart disease and cancer—are common. Many Americans are grossly obese and their health is at great danger.

That description, helpfully, is complete with a photograph of a big fat white lady in an unflattering tank top and khaki shorts.

You should know: Crossing the street can be dangerous!

You should know: Your success in America is dependent on your own hard work and efforts.

[When in a job interview,] Don't tell about your hard life or how much you need a job; talk about what an excellent worker you are!

Common Mistakes [in a job interview]: Talking about your problems—the boss does not want a complainer, he wants someone who is positive.

You may notice that in the United States some people have more than one sexual partner. It is ALWAYS a good idea to use a condom in order to protect yourself and your partner from serious diseases.

It is illegal to be married to more than one person at a time in the U.S.

It is illegal to have sex with a minor, even if that person agrees to it.

It is illegal to bribe police officers or other public officials.

Passengers [on an airplane] should use paper, not water, after using the toilet.

Just because you have left your old problems behind in your home country does not mean you have no problems left! In fact, you have traded your old problems for a new set of problems in the United States.

Many of these sentiments are echoed in a DVD developed by the Center for Applied Linguistics in Washington, DC, that opens with a waving American flag and some nice plucky folk guitar. First there are some refugee talking heads, people who've resettled from all sorts of countries providing some realistic expectations for arrival (you'll feel lost, and scared, and sad and alone because you're away from every thing and person you know, but you just have to work really hard). Then there's some basic info (if you work hard and are resilient, you can make a contribution to this great nation like some immigrants before you have; try to learn English; when your plane lands in America, follow the other people on it to find your way out of the airport; "Americans value self-reliance, so you will be expected to work and to take responsibility for your own life as soon as possible"; you can apply for food stamps, and try not to be over-whelmed by the number of cereal brands in an American grocery store; you can apply for cash assistance, but it's very limited, because "most Americans believe adults should work to support themselves and their families rather than rely on cash assistance from the gov-ernment"; be aware that said assistance takes a long time and a lot of paperwork to get). There are some helpful tips about interacting with people who try to help you (just because a church gives you assistance doesn't mean you're legally obligated to participate in that religion with those people, and if any resettlement-agency staff pres-sures you to go to church, tell on them; policemen are your friends, not your harassers, and they're not going to hurt you, they're never going to hurt you—"unless you fight them") and how to live in an apartment (your resettlement agency will provide you with a week's worth of food and enough dishes for cooking and eating; figure out which utilities you have to pay and how to pay them). It covers some of the differences you may experience in the culture of work (if you were a doctor or an engineer, you're not anymore, and have to start the certification process over; in America, women can work outside of the house and in the same jobs and offices as men—"in fact, your supervisor may *be* a woman!"; in America, both parents often have to work; "the United States is a land of opportunity for those who are willing to work hard") and education (there's no shame in going to school as an adult; enroll your kids in school immediately; "discipline in most schools does not include beating"). If you feel so sad or anxious about the changes and challenges in your new American life that you feel like you can't go on living anymore, the video explains, you should seek help if that feeling lasts for more than a couple of weeks (particularly vulnerable are the elderly, "who may find that in the United States they no longer hold positions of respect"). Then there's a list of rules that may not apply in your old country but do in ours (you can't smoke wherever you want; you can't use drugs; hitting your spouse to ensure that your spouse respects you is "not what we do in this country"; don't hit your kid; don't drive drunk or high; don't say sexually offensive things to your coworkers; again, seriously, no sex with minors).

Some of the advice is actually a lot more realistic and honest than what Americans are taught. The Karen learn that credit cards are best avoided, and so is food from boxes and cans, and buying a car is such a money suck that you should try to use public transportation if you can, and American commercialism is ruinous—you really don't need the stuff advertising tries to sell you, so resist its suggestions— and competition in the job market is so strong that most people have to work for low pay, like in kitchens and hotels. The tutorial about surviving in American culture basically counsels refugees to do everything in their power to not become a part of it.

But overall, the message is clearly about hope and hard work. Consider your life in America like starting your entire life over, one of the talking heads advises. Consider yourself a child—don't be afraid, but be open-minded and inquisitive, says another. It'll be worth one or two really hard years, the fact that you will have freedom and can go wherever you want to go, says one more. Concludes a long-resettled Vietnamese man, "The beginning is tough, but the tough get going, and will be all right."

That, Ta Mla, is how you resettle.

The time between DHS approval and Ta Mla's leaving for the United States would probably be four to six months. He could take anything he liked with him, so long as it all fit inside one bag and weighed less than twenty kilos. It's not unlikely that he'd be given just a few days' notice of his departure and assigned American city. This, combined with having to move to and sleep in the processing center for five days; plus the (true) stories circulating that on a couple of occasions Karen refugees have arrived in a United States airport to find no one from the way-overwhelmed and -underfunded stateside resettlement agencies waiting for them, prompting an ungodly panic; plus the fact that though their housing has been pre-arranged, they must start paying rent and utilities within ninety days, and they arrive already in the hole, having to start paying back the cost of their thousand-dollar plane tickets within six months has, some say, knocked the United States out of No. 1 most desirable place to resettle.

Theoretically, Ta Mla didn't really want to leave at all, not for the United States or anywhere. He'd been at BA for only a year, but he'd been on two different HRD trips, for a total of four and a half months working inside. In addition to documenting human rights violations, he conducted training sessions to help villagers document them on their own. Most of the time, no NGO workers like himself were there to write all the crucial information down, after all, so he taught people to do it and help others do it themselves in ten-day, six-hour-a-day training sessions. He loved going back to his country and meeting people who still lived there and feeling like he was doing something important for them.

But the visits haunted him, too. In one village, the SPDC had just come and gone, and Ta Mla took down the story of Ler Moo, who had one child and a pregnant wife and owned literally just the clothes on his back. Ler Moo explained to Ta Mla that the SPDC had burned down his rice storage and house and everything in it. His wife needed medicine. "Nephew," he said, as a matter of brotherhood, not bloodlines, "could you help me?"

But Ta Mla couldn't. He didn't have any medicine, and where would he get it? He didn't have any money. He had to move on to the next village. Before he left, he gave Ler Moo two of his three sets of clothes, though it meant Ta Mla wouldn't be able to change for two months.

Not that his laundry was near the top of his concerns. Two of the villages he visited that time came under attack, and he had to grab his shit and start running with everyone else. One of the villages was burned down; the other wasn't, but its inhabitants were too afraid to move back into it, so the populations of both were absorbed into a jungle that already held hundreds of thousands of hapless IDPs. Ta Mla built two tents out of bamboo, as many as his hunger-depleted strength would allow, though he knew they wouldn't be much use to three hundred stranded villagers. Some of the next villages he went to were already deserted. All he could do then was take pictures of the house-shaped piles of ash, charcoal shadows of what used to be there, big barren squares among the trees. Back in Thailand, he kept the pictures in a small plastic album, and he looked at them all the time, and he wondered, he said, what happened to the man who called him nephew, the man with the sick pregnant wife who was one of a number he couldn't even count anymore that he had been powerless to help.

"I love my country, and I love . . . my neighbor," he told me. "I don't want to separate from my country, but if I stay there, I can be . . . unhappy, because we have no opportunity. I would like to go to US . . . so I can get . . . education. Practical . . . experience, and real education. Then I can organize with Karen people in US to . . . become activist. So they will pressure . . . international community about Burma. It's not fair what they do to my people." He was holding his stomach without seeming to realize it as he talked, the way he did when he got upset. "It makes me . . . very . . . unhappy."

So he wanted me to help him fill out an application for resettlement.

Eh Soe did, too, and the next day, he brought me his paperwork for the Commonwealth of Australia. He was not waffling on the issue, and made no attempt to hide from anyone that he was fully ready to get the fuck out of Dodge. Together we debated how he should handle the FIRST NAME and LAST NAME lines, since Karen don't have the latter. He marked down his birthday and his supposed address in camp and that no, he didn't have any relatives in Australia.

"What about your girlfriend?" I asked. "Is she applying too?"

"I think she will apply. Maybe we will get married so we can go together. I don't know what to do about this problem."

"Am I ever going to meet this girl? How often do you see her?"

"Once a week."

I smiled and deepened my voice. "You guys make out?"

Eh Soe blushed and smiled and looked at the floor. I'd taught them this phrase. He knew what I meant. "Yes."

"Where?"

"At her house. Or in the garden, you know the garden?"

I did. The garden was better known to Abby and me as the park, between our house and downtown. It had a temple in it, the steps of which were lined with dozens of shin-high rooster statues. We called it the rooster park. "Really? There?"

"Sure. A lot of Thai people go there to make out."

This, I did not know.

Eh Soe studied his paper for a minute before handing it over. "I don't understand this one," he said. He pointed to the section in question.

"It says that people in Australia enjoy some of the best health standards in the world, and they want to know if you have ever had any serious illnesses or have any now."

"No," Eh Soe said. He did have wicked splashes of scars on his arms. They'd been caused by some sort of incredibly painful skin disease, but he didn't know what it was, and that had been a long time ago anyway. "I am okay. I am just a little bit fat."*

When we finished, he picked up the papers and straightened them out, holding loosely to the stacked edges and tapping the bottoms against the reading bench. "I will be in Australia or US maybe 2010," he said easily. It was 2006.

I shook my head. "I wish I had a tenth of your guys' patience."

Eh Soe stood up to leave. "What are you doing now?" he asked.

"I think I need to lie down. I don't feel totally great." I'd earlier been talking to a guy who was glum because he'd heard that the village his parents lived in had had to flee from attack, and he wasn't sure if they were okay, although the good news was that he didn't think the

---

* Eh Soe's potbelly was getting to him that day. He'd told me at breakfast that he was on a diet. "I'd like to reduce my weight," he'd said. "I eat only few. And I will not drink any more beer." He'd mistaken the disbelief on my face for disappointment. "Except for your party." As an additional part of his new weight-loss regimen, and because, he told me, he was afraid that being inactive would cause him to get diseases, he also went and played soccer that night with Htoo Moo. I was sitting at the table on the front porch when they returned. "How was it?" I asked, and Eh Soe shook his head brusquely. He had mud on his shoes, whereas Htoo Moo was covered in it from waist to toe, his legs coated like an elephant's. "That is a very terrible place," Eh Soe said while Htoo Moo, disgusted, shook his head at what a pussy he was.

village was burned down. It made me feel tired. Over at Office Two, before class, Wah Doh had told me that he was sad because he missed his family and couldn't figure out how to enact his plan of becoming famous so that he could tell the world about his people so that he could save them. That had made me feel tired. That, and the fact that Htoo Moo and That Khaing had got wasted the night before and found it hilarious to run into my room, where I was trying to sleep, and turn the lights on, which would make me yell and eventually get up and turn them off myself, which would then be followed by them popping in and turning them on again and laughing hysterically.

"You shouldn't think too much," Eh Soe told me as he walked out of the room. "It will make you unhappy."

XV.

ON THE Friday morning after Htan Dah left, as a thick rain poured fast onto Mae Sot in hard, fat drops, Abby and I followed Htoo Moo out of the house and into the cold and gray street. She and I were wrapped in plastic raincoats and high-top Gore-Tex and leather hiking boots. He stepped gingerly through deep puddles in flip-flops, denim capri pants, which, for some reason, he did not pull off so well as Htan Dah did, and a jean shirt with an embroidered breast pocket that I was almost positive was made for a woman. He held an umbrella as he rounded the side-street corners, stopping when we arrived at an intersection with the main road that led into town. We stood quietly, waiting, until a *songthaew* pulled up. Htoo Moo talked to the driver through the window in Thai, gesturing, then gestured at Abby and me to climb into the back of the truck, which had benches lining the opposite lengths, under the metal arch that covered it.

The road to Mae La, thirty-five miles north and a bit west, is winding and potholed. Abby and I sat on the wet, left bench, staying at the back of the empty truck rather than taking fuller shelter near its front; the more air that rushed over my face, the better my chances of not throwing up. I kept my eyes fixed on one corner of one leaky plastic sheet that had been drawn down over the usually open sides of the vehicle while we drove, my head lolling reluctantly with the

motion as we stopped, picked up passengers, let them off, all carrying
their cargo in the omnipresent woven plastic bags with multicolored
stripes, the unofficial suitcase of the Third World. However damp
the wind and cool the rain that whipped through the spaces in the
plastic paneling and slapped our cheeks and foreheads, my insides
felt too warm and dull. I swallowed hard in my increasingly tight
throat when the driver hit the brakes, my insides lurching into the
inside of my skin, my stomach up into my lungs, my head throbbing, bobbing with the lilt of the twisting hills. When, after an hour,
we finally stepped off the truck next to Htan Dah, waiting with his
hands in the pockets of a black track jacket, I made him stand still
with me on the side of the road for a minute to keep from collapsing
to my knees in a pool of vomit.

From a distance, Mae La is a little bit gorgeous. The earth of the
settlement slopes high up from the road, the neat thatched roofs of
dwellings poking out of a vibrantly green forest, the border mountains a few miles to the west. You had to get right inside it to realize
that there were fifty thousand people packed into those one and a
half square miles. Though *you* probably couldn't get right in it; Htan
Dah had called me at Office One the night before to say that he'd
confirmed a camp leader's approval of our visit, who had in turn told
the Thai soldiers guarding the camp to be on the lookout for two
white girls who were coming to conduct business and to let them go
about it.

Abby and I followed our friend and host, learning within seconds
that the terrain was as difficult as it was lush. Narrow, uneven paths
ran around huts crammed helter-skelter on the hill. The rain had let
up for the moment, but for the duration of the monsoon season, the
steep trails are more like swamps, slick with rivers of mud and washing water and rainwater and pig and chicken shit streaming down
toward the concrete road that skirts the settlement. The shelters
were on stilts, little ladders connecting their doorless entryways to
the oozing ground. Htan Dah was wearing mesh shorts, like a runner.

He stepped careful and steady, his flip-flops sinking past their beds in muck before he lifted a bare calf and planted a foot farther up the slope. He gestured around him at things we could or couldn't see from here—"There is school"; "Over there so-and-so used to live"—but we were concentrating too hard on not slipping to pay much attention. Though he kept his hands in his pockets, Abby and I grabbed on to trees, people's houses, to keep our balance. Stuck flip-flops had been abandoned everywhere; Abby and I counted them until we lost track. We averted our eyes when we passed someone bathing clumsily, her clothes half off, at one of the communal pumps set among the huts, and we moved out of the way of others carrying water buckets back to their kitchens to cook or shower. Htan Dah turned around occasionally, checking on our progress, stopping so we had a chance to catch up. The treads of our boots had been overwhelmed by caked mud, rendered useless in seconds. I looked up at him while he waited for us a short ways up the hill without a trace of a smile on his face.

"This sucks," he said.

"Yeah!" Abby, in front of me, panted. "You know how much it sucks, Htan Dah? A lot!" She stepped down in a place her balance didn't like, and her leg skidded out from under her. Already in a wide stance, I put my hands out, helping to steady her by her ass.

"We can go to the office, or we can visit *there*," Htan Dah said. He pointed up the hill at a nondescript building, like every building, another bamboo-and-thatch number.

"What is it?" I asked.

"A clinic. For TB."

They were never going to let us back through United States Customs. "That's okay," I said. I was still carsick, and exhausted. I looked at Abby. "I think we've had enough of a tour."

"Seriously," she said.

The Mae La BA office was also small and bamboo and stilted. The ladder to the front doorway led into the cooking area, where a charcoal fire glowed in a bucket on a concrete slab on the floor. The doorway at the back of the kitchen led to another room, a shallow one, with just enough space for a dining table with some benches, and at the back of that room was another doorway, to the rest of the house—an open, empty living room. It was compact and immaculately tidy. It was cold, having no windproofing or windows or doors. The split bamboo slatting the floor gave a little to my footstep. I wondered, walking across it with my feet unencumbered of my defiled socks and boots, glimpsing flickers of chickens wandering below through the spaces in the wood, whether my coworkers missed this spring under their steps when they walked the Mae Sot house's tile.

Htan Dah cooked for us, as usual, though he did it on his haunches, on the floor, over coals rather than standing at our gas range. Abby and I hovered in the doorway, chatting with him as he worked with the help of a couple of guys, the little kitchen filled to capacity with squatting men. They were making pork, but also stir-fried greens and omelets with onions, which Htan Dah often prepared for us in Mae Sot. Ta Eh Thaw, the only Karen girl in Office One, had been making similar meatless fare in Htan Dah's absence, and we'd eventually realized that the detailed and extensive instructions he'd left her while he was gone included feeding us.

After breakfast, we all retired to the cool semidarkness of the main room, cloud-filtered daylight seeping in through the hole for the door in the back wall. Htan Dah changed into a *longyi* of green, white, and black plaid. We sat cross-legged with the small group of calmly eager new staff members. They looked like teenagers. Some of them were.

We went around in a circle. Abby and I introduced ourselves, and then the guys tried their best English to tell us their names and where they were from. Htan Dah drew a little map of Burma on a dry-erase board propped up on the floor, against the wall. He indicated with his marker where in the country the boys' homes had been. Most of them were from the lowlands, further inland than the eastern hills of Karen State.

Htan Dah had some training to do yet, so Abby and I sat quietly for a while as he sat on the floor and spoke, dry-erase marker in hand. I studied a large poster of cartoon depictions of the things you couldn't do to a child per the UN Convention on the Rights of the Child, then went to the other room to lie on the floor. Abby pulled out a book.

When Htan Dah was done, the three of us retired onto the little back porch, he sitting on one side, leaning against the house, I sitting on the other, she leaning against one of the poles that supported the awning protecting us from the rain falling all around.

"Are you done with your training?" I asked.

"Yes."

"So you can come home with us?"

"Yes(!)."

"What were you guys talking about in there?"

"I was telling them why they have to fight. In training, we do history, Burmese history, Karen history, because many people don't know about the war." Htan Dah had told me about this before. When he traveled to camp to give lectures and screen videos, there were always audience members, young ones, who didn't realize there was a war on; they were so used to living in camp that some didn't even know they were refugees.

"Aren't these guys Karen?"

"Yes(!). But even Karen people, many Karen people do not understand what is the political situation in their country because they have no way to get information. You know, these guys are from the city. They do not even speak Karen."

"Really?" Abby and I asked.

"Yes! The government does not allow them to teach Karen in the school, so they speak only Burmese."

"So how do you talk to them?"

"In Burmese." He thought about this for a second and frowned. "I do not like to write on the board in Burmese. I fear that I will . . . spelling . . . incorrectly."

We listened to the rain. The sound came in layers, the pitch lower and denser, a wall of precipitation falling in the distance, the drops that slapped the leaves of the nearby flora higher and more distinctive. The chickens clucked lightly below us. I realized what had been giving the camp an eerie sense of emptiness.

"It's so quiet here," I said. The silence was thoroughly penetrating. The most-reported number of people living in a Karen refugee camp household is six. Most Karen refugee camps in Thailand don't meet the UNHCR's minimum space standards. Fifty thousand refugees packed in here, and not a fucking sound.

Htan Dah shrugged. "Yes," he said. "Nothing to do." He was looking out past the porch. Beyond it, bright trees on the close succession of hills shocked the gray of the sky. He was right that there was nothing to do in Mae La. But keeping up Mae La, which was more populous than some small countries, took a lot of doing. It had twenty-four primary and secondary schools. Aide Medicale Internationale had 250 workers there, and in addition to the aforementioned vast feeding and education infrastructure, nine international NGOs handled health and sanitation in the camps. Everything from eye care to prosthesis supply was provided on a budget of $6 million a year, to take 2007's expenditures. Running the whole camp show required no fewer than twenty NGOs and added up to an annual price tag of $66 million, with the United States providing the biggest piece of the funding pie, 27 percent. But no amount of money was going to give the inhabitants something to do in them.

"I prefer camp," Htan Dah said quietly, apparently to no one. I looked at him, but he still looked off from the porch, into the distance.

"Really?" I asked. "But you just said when we were walking up here that it sucks. Weren't you so bored in camp that you just did drugs all the time?" This was a rhetorical question. He'd already told me that he'd freebased meth for years. He would sneak out of camp with a friend and go to a nearby Mon village and buy some pills. In Huay Kaloke, they cost more than a dollar each. In Umpiem, they were half as much, because they were actually made in the village that sold them, Htan Dah thought. He and his friend would wait in the front room of the dealer's place while someone went to get the goods—in the back of the house, outside, at another house, they couldn't see where. Htan Dah used the money his mom earned illegally doing labor, which she gave him to buy food, so he would have more variety than his rations afforded him in his diet. Twice a week he and his friends would close themselves in one of the communal bamboo bathroom stalls with a lighter and a crushed pill and a piece of foil. A lot of refugees liked it because it gave them energy against all the odds, Htan Dah said. Personally, he didn't really like the way it made him feel, unable to sleep or eat, but oh, my god, was he bored,* and he did like the ceremony, the way it made him seem to belong to something, part of a community, and the smell of it, and the fact that it was one interesting thing in his life. He also found it helpful for prolonging drinking binges. But then he "lost control" and sold his watch, the only valuable object he ever owned, an addiction cliché

---

* The UNHCR and Committee for Coordination of Services to Displaced Persons in Thailand report that the refugees' endless boredom and confinement breed drug and alcohol addiction, as well as violent crime. DARE has some eighty employees trying to handle the drug problem in the camps, but unfortunately, no real legal body is responsible for the stateless camp dwellers, so KNU members can serve as de facto law. Sexual and gender-based violence generally go unpunished. The leaders are allegedly unfair to the very small minority of other minorities—Shan, Mon, for example—and Burmans in the camps. The UNHCR charges that in extreme cases the rebels have punished individuals by dragging them back into Burma and executing them. For the most part, Thai authorities don't get involved, but when they do, it can be just more bad news: Thirty percent of assaults on refugees in camp are perpetrated by Thai security guards.

that apparently knows no international borders. Eventually, he quit, cold turkey, because he was afraid he'd get arrested, or sick. Eh Soe had shown me a picture of Htan Dah from that time, and he was so gaunt I couldn't recognize him. ("Who's this?" "It's Htan Dah!" "What's the matter with his face?" "That's when he was doing drugs.")

Htan Dah shrugged. "Yes, but here we can play guitar, and laugh, without . . . police, and worrying."

We watched a little girl, who looked like she was about five, walk down the path below the elevated porch. She navigated the steep, choppy mud in pink gum boots and a purple dress, miraculously retaining her balance with a giant bucket of water in her arms and no traction on her feet.

"Okay," I said. "So why don't you move back to camp?"

"Because. In camp, I cannot work. I cannot work for my people. Just, sitting, and talking, and eating, and sleeping—it accomplishes nothing."

We debated staying for dinner, and staying the night, but Abby wasn't wild about the prospect. "Also," Htan Dah said, "we have this pork." Someone had slaughtered a pig and cleaved off a giant hunk as a gift to Htan Dah. He'd finished the training he'd come for, and he was anxious to get the pork back to BA, where there was electricity and a refrigerator. Currently, it was sitting on the porch in a garbage bag, as it had been for some time.

So we three and the pork bag hopped a *songthaew* toward Mae Sot. Abby went down hard in the mud as we climbed aboard with a full load of passengers. The driver got into the front seat, then got out again, and came around to rescue Abby or me from the Asian riffraff packing the back. I took him up on the shotgun offer in the name of my nausea. Htan Dah stood on the back bumper and held on to the arch rail for the whole wretchedly winding road back.

At Office One, Htan Dah's pork in the fridge and his email checked, in the still twilight, after work and before whiskey, I sat in my room writing things down. The house was as quiet as a refugee camp.

"What are you doing?" Htan Dah asked. He walked through my doorway slowly, long seconds between his steps, always so tentative in interrupting.

"Nothing," I said. I put my pen down. "What are you doing?"

"Nothing."

"Okay," I said, laughing. "Let's go to a bar."

"Okay."

My eyes widened. "Really? Wait, seriously?"

Htan Dah nodded, one hard chin dip. "Sure. Why not?"

Debilitating fear of police? Irrational terror of stray dogs? Deportment for everyone? "No reason!" I said. "Can we walk?"

So it was that we walked out of the driveway and down the street and toward downtown. We cut through the temple grounds, with the Buddhas long- and slim-faced, strung white lights twinkling in the air around the stupa. Though I'd been in Mae Sot five weeks, I'd never walked all the way into town after dusk. In the darkness, the streets were still warm and wet. Tuk-tuks and cars and motorbikes crowded them as usual, and the storefronts were still cramped. "Have you never been to a bar before, ever?" I asked Htan Dah.

"No! Never! I—"

"Yes, I know, you're a refugee. I was just asking."

The Crocodile Tear sat in a row of guesthouses and restaurants for tourists. The bar itself evidently pandered to both NGO workers and wealthy Thai businessmen interested in simulating the experience of getting hammered in Middle America. Our menu boasted cocktails with names like Billabong, featuring ingredients that didn't exist in Thailand at large, triple sec and curaçao of multiple colors. A band onstage was covering "Paint It Black" in very questionable English.

"I used to get drunk and dance around like a jackass to this song in college," I said, watching the bloated, flushed Thai men singing along at the table next to us.

"I think they are very happy," Htan Dah said. He took in our surroundings without turning his head much, as discreetly as possible.

Wood walls, wood tables. Bottles of booze lined up behind a short wood bar in the back corner, where the girls in tight T-shirts filled drink orders. Fat guys singing Rolling Stones. Oh, nope. Now they were moving on to "Brown-Eyed Girl."

"What do you want to drink?" I asked Htan Dah.

"I don't know!" In ascending notes. "I don't know what to drink! I don't know what I'm doing. What do you think?"

"Well, generally, I drink a lot of vodka. Have you ever had vodka?"

"No. But I would like to try."

"Okay. We should celebrate. Have you ever done a shot?"

"No!" he exclaimed, enthusiastically even for him. He smiled broadly, like he was the luckiest son of a bitch living. "I have never been shot!"

I laughed hard, though that probably wasn't funny. I ordered two shots of vodka and a pack of Marlboros and explained that we were going to throw back the little glasses the girl in the little shirt brought us. Htan Dah watched me grip my shot glass lightly, my thumb and two forefingers on either side of its middle. He did the same, and followed me as well when I picked it up and held it out toward him.

"Congratulations," I said. "Here's to getting into J-school." Htan Dah nodded another hard nod.

I clinked the lip of my glass into his and looked at him square. "Down in one. Ready?"

We ordered a round of tequila shots, since he'd never had tequila before. He liked that better than vodka, so we had another round of those. He'd never ordered and been served food out before, despite his living so close to all these sit-down establishments for so long, so we got plates of hot red curry and steaming rice. We shot more booze and played Who Would You Rather? using the big table of tourist girls behind us. I picked the prettier one every time. Invariably, he chose as his theoretical lover whichever of the choices looked more "flexible"—as in adaptable or easygoing, not as in doing the splits.

We hollered at each other over the band, whose set Htan Dah knew as well as I did. We smoked cigarettes and sang along with a sweet mix of oldies and classic and soft rock. As Long as You Love Me. House of the Rising Sun. Take Me to Your Heart—product of Danish boy band Michael Learns to Rock, which, an escaped Chinese-immigrant porter swore to Htoo Moo, didn't write it but just translated it into English after stealing it from Cantopop star Jacky "God of Songs" Cheung.* Feel Like Makin' Love. Love Will Keep Us Alive. People Are Strange. The Boxer. More Than Words. Lola. Horse With No Name. Sundown.

"Gordon Lightfoot!?" someone screamed.

Okay; it was me.

Hours later, a door or two or three down from the Crocodile Tear, the Thai proprietor of a very dark bar looked at me like I had lost my mind when I leaned into the counter and asked him for a room. Though I had no doubt that this craphole was patronized nearly exclusively by people of significantly lower character than myself, and he did ultimately consent, he hesitated long to sell me a vacancy. He seemed suspicious of my slurring, or of the Karen refugee standing behind me, hair long and thick with camp's cook smoke. Possibly both.

Htan Dah and I walked down a narrow sidewalk out the back, following it to our room, where I slid the key into the door. An awful neon light flickered on when I flipped the switch. It was an airless, windowless cell with hardly the room for the queen-size bed. We left our flip-flops at the door and narrowly skirted the mattress, Htan Dah following me into the bathroom. "Here," I said, pointing. I set the dial to max on the small, electric on-demand water heater attached to the showerhead. I turned the water on and held my hand in the stream. After a moment, it warmed up. "See?"

"Ah, okay," he said, touching it. "I see I see I see."

I dropped down on the rock-hard mattress and heard the bathroom

---

* This, for the record, is true.

door close, then the slight, rustling sounds of disrobing as my brain spun around where I lay still on a pillow. Then there was the splash of water dropping weakly to the floor, echoing around the bathroom tile, the tinkling puncturing the throbbing static building in my eardrums, the music from the bar pumping a hard bass that vibrated in my chest but I barely heard as my head swam away from sentience.

DAWN IN downtown Mae Sot was hollow.

Htan Dah and I opened our room door onto gray, lonely streets. We wound our way back home through the slight chill, past muted steel-pot clangings of preparing street vendors who moved quick but not hurriedly, the smell of the beginnings of humidity and char. My forehead pounded something fierce, and I squinted against even the ashen light.

"I kind of feel like I'm doing a walk of shame," I said.

Htan Dah looked at me with expectant confusion, waiting for me to explain.

"It's when you walk home by yourself after partying too hard and sleeping somewhere you shouldn't have. Like, you smell bad, and you're hungover, and tired, and look like shit, and it's too early to be on the street."

Htan Dah nodded thoughtfully. "So," he said solemnly, after a moment. "This is my first walk of shame."

I tipped my aching head back, opening my mouth and throat up to laughter. "Well, no. I'm pretty sure you have to have sex to have a walk of shame. And you're supposed to be, like, carrying your underwear in your pocket."

It was Saturday, the Saturday before the Tuesday I was leaving, which meant that that night was the night of the long-awaited and emphatically promised party I was to throw at Office Two. The sky was warmer and oranger by the time Htan Dah and I somewhat staggered back into our house, and my exhaustion and nausea had advanced to the point where I was daunted by even what little I had to do before the sun set again: prepare for more drinking, mainly. Also, procure enough food and booze to satisfy a houseful of twenty-year-old men expecting to party their faces off. Also, as I'd invited Htan Dah as my ride and escort, help fulfill his dinner duties for Office One before we left. Which was what we were doing, later, when Ta Mla burst into the dining room/garage, angrier than I'd ever seen him, gesturing agitatedly and spewing a storm of pissed-off Karen.

"I hate them!" he exploded after an extended tirade in his first language. He looked at me and explained in shaking and broken English that a cop standing by the side of the road had waved him over as Ta Mla rode past on his bicycle. He'd just been going out for some exercise, and he'd even bought one of the yellow fabric "We Love the King" wristbands after the last time he'd been arrested, in an effort to better blend in with the Thais. No dice.

"That policeman," Ta Mla seethed, grasping his stomach, "he knows me very well." Indeed he did; it was the same guy who'd arrested him two weeks before. This time, Ta Mla had been cashless and alone, and the officer had, whether out of cruelty, or boredom, or both, made him sit handcuffed on the curb when Ta Mla couldn't produce the papers the cop knew he didn't have. He let Ta Mla sweat it out there for an hour or so before allowing him to call a coworker who could bring the $5 bribe that would set him free. And Ta Mla, sweet, subtle, terrorist-boot-camp-dropout Ta Mla, swore now, in the dining room/garage, "If I had a hand grenade, I would explode him."

Htan Dah had paused his chili-paste pounding to watch Ta Mla, the marble pestle impotent in his hand while he listened to him. When Ta Mla finally stalked off into the house, Htan Dah went back to gently slamming the tool into the mortar, his head bent low over his task, his hair hanging toward the table.

After a minute, he started chuckling.

"What's up?" I asked.

He looked up, smiling. "Ta Mla is so mad," he said, chuckling some more.

I shook my head. Just the hollering had made my heart beat faster and my stomach clench. "Did he say who brought him the money?"

"Yes, it was Walt. You know, Walt was arrested today, too. Earlier than Ta Mla. He had to pay Thai police twice today."

Walt had briefly been a student in my advanced class, but his duties in the organization and at Office Two had soon necessitated his attrition. I liked Walt, and not just because he went by an easy-to-pronounce nickname and had issued a hearty "Hello!" that brought me nearly to relieved tears on one of my first days, when most everyone else was ignoring me and their own English abilities. He had a lanky, self-conscious shuffle. He loved math and listened to English self-study CDs. When he'd read aloud his writing exercise in class one day, it had been about how he worried that he'd never find a girlfriend because he was ugly.

"Hey, pal," I said when I encountered his big, shy smile at Office Two later that night. "I heard you had an exciting day." Htan Dah and I had come bearing heavy plastic bags on our fingers, the favors we'd hustled around town accumulating after Office One had been fed. Walt stood chatting with me, with his head tipped and shoulders stooped, in the way of a person who isn't comfortable in his height, while Htan Dah and I opened our bags and unleashed a mighty party spread on the floor.

"Yes," Walt said. He laughed. "Very busy today."

"How come you got away so easily, when Ta Mla needed you to rescue him?"

"Ta Mla doesn't speak Thai. Me, I speak some Thai, so I just talked to the policeman, very calm."

"What did you say?"

"I said, 'Hey, friend, why don't you go buy yourself some whiskey?' I just hand him five hundred baht. And he just"—Walt waved the back of his hand, as if he were swatting a fly away from his face—"let me go."

"Wow, Walt. You offered him money before he even asked you for it?"

Htan Dah laughed. "Walt is very smooth talker."

Walt laughed again, too, his giant teeth gleaming at us. You'd never guess, looking at him, talking to him, that he used to be a dedicated warmonger.

WALT WAS born a soldier, of a soldier. He'd lived in a KNU base camp until it was attacked, when he was five, and his mother took him to Huay Kaloke. They moved to another camp, Maw Ker, before Huay Kaloke was burned down, though ultimately that camp was burned down, too. When he was ten, his father was killed in battle. When he was sixteen, he enlisted.* By then, Walt had seen a lot of fighting and fleeing, and he wanted revenge.

By the time Walt was out of boot camp and stalking the jungle with an AK-47, Manerplaw had fallen, Four Cuts had ravaged thousands of villages, the DKBA had robbed the KNU of much of its land and border-tax income, and the rebel fighters were tired, their numbers and munitions depleted. They sometimes supplemented their ammunition with homemade gunpowder: bat shit plus mangowood charcoal plus sulfur. But Walt didn't need ample supplies and backup to love being at war; he had plenty of anger to fuel him through two years of long, jungle-tramping days, little food, and little assurance that shooting at his enemies through the trees was making any difference.

When he was eighteen, his brigade fell. When his commander

---

* The KNU claims, and Walt corroborated, that it doesn't recruit child soldiers—anymore. But back then, at least, if a kid wanted to take up arms and fight after he'd, say, seen his mom raped, he certainly wasn't turned away, and there have additionally been rare reports in the past of children pressed into KNU service. (The Burma army, by contrast, was estimated to have *seventy thousand* child soldiers in 2002. Many of them, like the one Htoo Moo interviewed who'd been picked up at a bus stop, are conscripted.)

bailed and the rations ran out, he moved to Bangkok with seven other soldiers. They worked as housepainters on a six-month contract, living in a tin shed they'd built out of scrap. The illegal immigrants were supposed to be paid when the contract was up. They weren't. "It's better to die than become a slave," Walt told his comrades, and with that, he rejoined the Karen guerrillas, the fourth brigade, which eventually became better known to the world as God's Army.*

For two months in the late '90s, Walt continued fighting in the jungle, alongside Jesus-loving kids with assault weapons. When he went to visit family in a refugee camp at age nineteen, his uncle was a little concerned for Walt's future. Learn first, he told him. Then decide if you still want to fight after that. So Walt moved into camp, finished high school, and quit his military career for good.†

He'd joined BA as a village organizer, he said, so he could fight for freedom, justice, and peace—the same nonviolent ideals for which he'd previously been fighting, only violently. Unlike his coworkers, who hadn't actually been to war, Walt's hero wasn't Che, but Gandhi. He'd said to me in all earnestness once that an eye for an eye leaves the whole world blind. And he aspired to his icon's stamina. "Wars are between armies," he'd told me when I asked him if he

---

* "Wait a minute," Abby, who was sitting nearby when Walt told me this story on the front porch one day, had interrupted. "You know those crazy brothers?" "Yes, I know them," Walt had said. "I stayed with them. I worshipped with them morning and night." The crazy brothers were Luther and Johnny Htoo, tough, barefoot, lice-ridden, illiterate nine-year-old Karen twins who smoked a lot and were rumored to be magical and bulletproof. The pair, fundamentalist Christians, started commanding the Soldiers of the Holy Mountain—"God's Army" was a media construct—in 1997, when they led a victorious battle against the Burma army, supposedly at the behest of the Lord's coming to them in a vision. They made huge news in 2000 when a group of their soldiers reportedly stormed a hospital in Thailand and took several hundred hostages before being slain by Thai commandos. Except that that was a media misstatement, also, as the attack was actually led by a (Burman) fringe group of the All Burma Students Democratic Front. But that was all later, anyway, after Walt left them.

† Luther and Johnny Htoo ultimately gave up their arms as well and settled in Thailand, where they enjoyed playing guitar.

was thinking of resettling. "What about all the people in between? People can change the situation on the ground. Don't forget the people. Get them involved in the resistance. I think I can do many things here. If I resettle, I will start my life again. I'll think about myself there, not my people, which is what I need to do. If you have a family, they come first. But I want to get married, and my children can take on responsibility to fight. I'll still fight, too. When I get old, I'll be teacher or trainer or writer. Even if I get married, I won't give up."

Walt sat next to me when everyone settled in a circle around the party goods in the middle of the Office Two floor. Htan Dah and I presided over the display proudly, our backs straight as we sat Indian-style while the guests surveyed what we had brought. Roti from the joint across from the mosque, stuffed with meat and vegetables. Bags of potato chips, which my coworkers for some reason considered an estimable treat. Thai noodles and curries in street vendors' plastic bags. Enough Chang beer to kill a man. Ice. Two bottles of hard-found, "charcoal filtered," "imported from Kentucky" vodka that cost nearly as much as everything else combined. Orange juice—also a rare and expensive commodity—because the boys wanted to try a screwdriver like a white person might order out, and because only a fool, or an addict, would drink this low-quality vodka straight.

We broke into the food with our fingers and a few communal spoons. We cracked open the Chang and the vodka. I mixed drinks and handed them around, though not to Saw Kaw, with the hepatitis, and raised my glass and made everyone raise their glasses and said "Cheers," and everyone repeated after me and after much clinking of cups, we started drinking.

HTAN DAH was flushed and through his screwdriver first.

"You really sucked that down," I said.

He nodded at me once, pink and smiling and glassy.

"Are you ready for another?"

He nodded again, still smiling.

I held out my hand. "Okay. Give me your motorbike keys. You know we're not driving home if you're getting wasted."

Htan Dah just kept looking at me and smiling.

This issue had been something of an upset between us, and between me and everyone else at BA, in the aftermath of the dog-meat party, from which Abby and I had taken the long walk home together because of Htan Dah's liberal imbibing of whiskey and herbal tonic. He was sitting on the floor of the upstairs landing when I finally got back to the house that night, and asked me how my walk had been, with some attitude. Ultimately, I asked him what the hell his problem was, and he hollered at me that I was afraid that he'd topple the motorbike, that I didn't go with him because I thought he was unreliable. When I heard the hurt quake in his voice, I explained my thoroughly impersonal aversion to drinking and driving, that I thought he was an excellent driver but never let anyone who'd been drinking drive me anywhere, ever. But I'd made no such progress with anyone else in my White Girls Against Drunk Driving campaign. Htan Dah always said that in a Karen family, women were in charge,* but I was outnumbered, and even in this woman-respecting culture, my questioning Htan Dah's ability to operate a motorbike under the influence of alcohol was out of line.† We two held each other's gaze in the moment of shocked silence after I'd

---

* Although the British colonialists mocked the Burmans for also being submissive to women, they were, on paper, at least, not so much so. According to the *Attasankhepa Vannaná Dammathát*, or Institutes of Burmese Law, of 1882, "Of the three kinds of wives that may be put away"—wife like a murderess (?), wife like a thief, and wife like a master—"and the four kinds of wives that may be cherished"—wife like a sister, wife like a mother, wife like a slave, and wife like a friend—"the one that is like a slave is the most excellent." Further, wives who were not good wives "may be corrected by beating or abusing them within the hearing of the public."

† I was, according to the above Burmese laws, exhibiting *two* of the kinds of blemishes of a woman: "taking intoxicating drinks" and "finding fault or quarrelling" with a man. (The other four are "failure to take an interest in household affairs and in her duties towards her husband, and idleness"; "frequenting the houses of others"; "intimacy with another man"; and "habitually sitting in the doorway of the house and looking at other men.")

demanded the keys, before the inevitable eruption of protest came fierce and flurrying around the room.

"What?!" several of his comrades started yelling at once.

"We are excellent drivers!"

"Whether he is drunk or not, it does not affect his driving!"

"You cannot say to him that he cannot drive a motorbike!"

I parted the verbal melee with hard shaking of my head. "No. No. Drunk drivers are more likely to get in accidents. Period. This is not up for discussion. It's completely idiotic."

"We know what we're doing."

"Maybe for you, you cannot drive a motorbike when you are drunk. But for us, it is no problem."

"It is stupid to walk."

"You're stupid!"* I yelled. "And if you think a bunch of drunk guys are going to pressure me into riding around on a motorbike at night in Thailand with another drunk guy, you've got the wrong fucking girl."

Htan Dah stayed out of it, never pitching in a word as the boys and I fought on, until I lost interest in arguing something so ridiculous and turned my attention back to him. "Htan Dah," I said, reaching out my upturned palm again. "Give me your keys."

The shouting died down as he locked me with eyes friendly but unwavering. After a moment, he reached into his pocket, pulled his keys out, and handed them over, and a cry went up all around us.

---

* "The eight kinds of husbands whom the wife has the right to abuse are—
one who is excessively lascivious;
one who is ill for a length of time;
one who is very poor;
one who is very stupid;
one who is infirm;
one who is very old and sluggish;
one who is very lazy;
one who is physically incapable.
If the wife loses patience and abuses or reviles any of the said kinds of husbands, let her have the right of doing so."

"ENGLISH, YOU guys," I said. There were snatches of Karen conversation here and there, always, particularly among the guys who didn't speak much English, like That Khaing, but everyone was getting lazier as they got drunker, and it was becoming the dominant mode of discourse. "While I'm still here. If I'm going to get you all drunk, you're at least going to practice your English."

"Yes!" Walt backed me up, his voice just a little louder under the influence, but as smooth and soothing as ever. "English. So, we will make a rule."

"Yes," Saw Kaw echoed. "You must speak only English. Or else . . ." He considered for a moment. "You must . . . take off your pants."

It was so agreed.

LAH LAH Htoo sat with a guitar in his lap. At the last party, he'd played a hard-twanging, pentatonic melody on the Karen instrument while he sang flowing minor notes, a traditional song, apparently about a river, that was so haunting that the drunk French girl and I had nearly wept. But that instrument was back at Office One, and the one Lah Lah Htoo held now was idle, as well, as he tipped his head back and looked at me through half-closed eyes.

"Do you think that we will see each other again?" he asked, one arm dangling over the body of the guitar.

This had been a popular question lately. Three days prior, I had answered in the affirmative to Saw Kaw, who thought about my "yes" for a moment before nodding, concurring, "I believe before you die, we will meet again." In the meantime, I'd told him, we could write, and drew stars and squiggly lines around my email address on the back of his notebook. "Don't forget," I'd written. Underneath, he'd added, "I never forget it."

"Of course we'll see each other again," I told Lah Lah Htoo. I looked at Htan Dah. "I'll come back to Thailand soon."

"When?" several voices asked.

"Probably next summer. I have to figure it out with work, and money."

"So," Walt said, "we will see each other again maybe next year."

"I hope," I said. "Hopefully next year."

"When we see each other again," Lah Lah Htoo said, "it will be in Burma." The other guys cheered. "When we see each other again, you will come to Burma. And you will not need a visa to enter. And I will pick you up at the airport." His face was barely wide enough for his smile, and he was hollering a bit, over the approving shouts of the other guys. "In a car. In *my* car!" Lah Lah Htoo had left his village when he was a teenager, when SPDC troops had come to capture people for portering, when he'd run away with the rest of his family and neighbors, and hadn't been back since. A silence settled over his coworkers in the wake of his fantastic predictions, and they all smiled softly and looked off or at the floor or at the wall as they considered cars and airports, and I thought about doomed POWs in movies who know their fate is sealed but talk anyway about how they're going to eat a big cheeseburger when they get back to America, and I kept quiet as long as the guys were quiet, bowing my head as if in reverence of something that had died.

OUR TWENTY-four 22-ouncers of Chang were poured out one sloshing glassful at a time. Sticking to screwdrivers, I watched as the bottles were continuously picked up and dumped artlessly over ice. That Khaing frowned at a particularly foamy pour, setting the glass in front of him to wait for the head to subside.

"Look," I said, "do you guys ever do this?" I rubbed my index finger against the right side of my nose, into the crease where my nostril met my cheek. Then I stuck my finger in That Khaing's beer.

He and Saw Kaw looked from the violated beer to my face.

"No," Saw Kaw said. "We don't ever do that."

"Yeah, I actually never do it either," I said. "I just remember these guys I went to college with doing it. I don't really know why I'm doing it now. But look!" I pointed to the glass with my free index finger. "Grease makes the bubbles go away."

"Oah? I see I see I see."

That Khaing seemed not to be following us. Scowling, he asked
Saw Kaw for clarification. In Karen.

"English, That Khaing!" I shouted, startling him. He laughed,
embarrassed, when he registered what I'd said.

"I am sorry," he said.

"I'm sorry, too." I was. His English was barely beginner-level. "I
know it's hard, and it's late, but you're never going to get better if
you don't try."

Walt, sitting next to me against the wall, took the cheroot out of
his mouth. "So," he said. "You must take off your fucking pants."

"*THERAMU,*" COLLIN said, meaning "teacher," his eyes twinkling ferociously.

"What?"

He hesitated. He seemed nervous.

"What, Collin?"

"Will you show us . . . Ohio . . . kiss?"

I narrowed my eyes. "What's this?" Everyone else laughed, also
nervously. "What do you mean, 'Ohio kiss'?"

"A kiss for greeting," Collin said, "in Ohio. How you do a greeting
kiss in Ohio."

"You guys never kiss as a greeting, you're saying. You've never
kissed your mothers." A couple of the guys shook their heads, though
these were statements more than questions; it stood to reason that
they didn't kiss hello or goodbye if they didn't hug. "Uh, okay." I
turned to Saw Kaw, who was sitting to my left. "Pucker your lips."
I puckered my lips and leaned toward him, possible hepatitis transmission be damned, I guess, and he attempted to imitate what I was
doing and failed somehow.

I leaned back. "No. Pucker your lips. Like this." I showed him
again what I meant, and he again tried to purse his lips, but they
wouldn't come out and together at the same time, and the rest of the
men in the room were trying as well, and also failing. "I don't . . ."
I shook my head. It seemed like it should be funny, but I was just

confused. "I don't understand how it could be hard to do what I'm doing. Saw Kaw. Look at me." I puckered up again. He leaned toward me and failed to push his lips away from his face, like I was doing, but he at least pushed them together, and this time not so tight that they disappeared into each other like a frustrated Muppet's.

Close enough. I pressed my mouth to his, then quickly away, backing up with the light smack of breaking my lips a little apart. Which Saw Kaw didn't reciprocate, of course, just keeping his mouth as close to the way I'd shown him as he could, immobile, so that the sound and smooch fell dully against his unresponsive face.

WAH DOH had disappeared. One of my beginner students, an older, handsome soft-talker, slipped through a wooden door I'd never been behind before and found him. "Wah Doh," he said, returning, "would like . . . to talk to you."

The room on the other side of the door was cozy, not too much bigger than my Columbus apartment bathroom. The air felt like it hadn't been moved around in days. Wah Doh was supine on the floor amid shallow layers of blankets and longyis. By the count of mosquito nets rolled up against the walls, at least four guys slept in here.

"What's goin' on?" I asked, lying down next to him.

"I have this question," he said. His voice was light and raspy. His eyes were closed. Though his words were coming fast as usual, he wasn't shoving them out of his body with all his tiny might. They escaped, instead, with the quiet urgency of a deathbed whisper. "How to sacrifice myself for my people."

I said nothing, which was what I usually did when Wah Doh started relieving himself of a stream of consciousness.

"I am excited to be . . . village organizer. I want to help my people. It is important to work for change, for . . . freeing oppression without violence. I want to fight. I don't want to fight with violence. I don't want to resettle because I will want . . . to come back . . . to Thailand. Only I can resettle if I know I have way back to Thailand, only to resettle long enough to get . . . education, then come back to Thailand, because I can help my people here. If I resettle I will stay away too long, maybe four years, five years, at least, before I can get back. But how to get education in Thailand or in my country?"

This question was meant as a rhetorical rephrasing of a statement: I cannot get an education in Thailand or Burma. It was hardly the least of the things he couldn't do in either country, of course; it wasn't safe for him to walk into his front yard in this one, and when he'd visited his parents in Burma two months prior, authorities were arresting any nonresident Karen who came through, on suspicion of their being rebels or sympathizers. They were even detaining merchants who'd just come to sell rice, and Wah Doh couldn't afford to pay off the officers. Though he'd planned to stay with his family for two months, he'd had to leave after hiding for four days.

"If I get arrested, I cannot work for my people, so I don't want to get arrested. Aung San Suu Kyi is arrested because she is too well known in Burma. I must be unknown in Burma . . . but well known . . . everywhere else. If I am famous, I will give speeches in Burma and everyone else will hear about Burma in the news. This is my plan. I think I can make my plan by the time I am sixty."

He laid his hand in my upturned palm, grabbed loose hold of my fingers as the guys sometimes did to each other at meetings or parties, we both on our backs, he looking at the inside of his eyelids. With my thumb and pinkie, I encircled his wrist, where an elder had hammered small blue dots into his skin with an inked needle. They freckled his temples, too, for protection, like the legendary tattoos of the followers of an anticolonialist monk, Saya San, whose marks had failed to keep British bullets from killing them.

"I am writing proverbs." Wah Doh was fading. He picked up his wrist, and mine with it, and landed the back of my hand onto his perfectly inert mouth before dropping our arms back down. "To stand, you need not only gravity and pressure, but also your energy."

I couldn't help but make a face at that.

"I need more education. If we have strong education, no one can kill us, because they dare not to." He picked up my hand and pressed it lightly against his stationary lips again. "When I was born, I brought nothing, but before I die, I will leave something for my people."

OUTSIDE, A breeze was trying to slog through the humidity. Htan Dah and I started back across the suburbs of Mae Sot, late, my having promised to protect him—from feral dogs—out of the way. All was silent but for the occasional barking we stirred up as we passed in the dark.

"I think Wah Doh was asking me for money," I said.

"Really?" Htan Dah's face was pained. He hated his peers' asking me for money like he hated taking it, even when it had been for his personal safety, or food. "What did he say?"

"He was talking about how he needed to get more education, but didn't want to resettle. I think he wanted me to tell him I could somehow get the UN to accept him for resettlement and then pay for him to go to America and then pay for him to go to school and live in America and then pay for him to come back to Thailand." These requests were motivated as much by a gross overestimation of my personal wealth as by desperation. Two days earlier Eh Na, too, had asked me for money, however much I thought necessary to bring a load of Karen children out of the jungle, build them a shelter in camp, and indefinitely keep them in school supplies and supplemental rations once they were installed in it. It was hard to explain to him that I couldn't afford it—even if I hadn't just transferred a vast amount of savings to Htan Dah—because he'd asked me just a day before how much money I made, and I'd said eighty thousand baht, or some two grand, a month, to which he'd replied, after letting that sink in for a minute, "I don't think in my life I will have that much." He'd shown me all the money he had in his life currently, the only kind of money a lot of Karen had, passed down from grandmothers, from times that were more prosperous, from times when they were on the winning team: two ancient rupees folded in a cloth.

I'd told Htan Dah how bad I'd felt about turning Eh Na down. I'd also told him, several times, laughing, about how anytime Eh Soe saw me pull out my wallet, he said, "Can I have some money?" Now Htan Dah was frowning.

"I'm sorry," he said.

"Don't be sorry. I mean, I get it. If I had no options, I'd ask anyone I met for money."

"What did you tell him?"

"I didn't tell him anything. He didn't really ask. Just kept talking, hoping I would offer, I think." We'd turned out of the subdivision and onto the highway toward downtown, toward Office One. "He was doing this totally weird thing to my hand while we were talking, though. He kept putting it on his mouth. But he didn't like, do anything with his lips, just touched us together. Like this." I took Htan Dah's hand and connected the back of it with the lower half of my face.

"Yes," he laughed. "I think he was very drunk. He was kissing you."

"He was kissing me? What do you mean? Why was he doing it like that?"

"Because! That is . . . how we do it(!)."

"Do what? Kiss? What do you mean, that's how you do it?"

I clucked my tongue. That's how we do it, he says. But then puckering up was mission impossible.

"Hold on!" I stopped him and put my hands up—*wait a minute*—

and raised my voice. "That's how you guys kiss, with your faces totally straight and relaxed like that?"

"Yes!"

"*Reeealllly?*"

Htan Dah stood on the side of the road, on the other side of my exclamation, speechless, tense. I was, suddenly, screeching at him.

"You really don't pucker your lips like this(!)?"

"No! Didn't you notice that we didn't know what we were doing?"

"Yes! But it never occurred to me that that was why!"

"Why not?"

Because I just couldn't have imagined that. Because for all the distance between our worlds, with the land-mine-dodging and child-soldiering and starving on rice soup and midnight-burning refugee camps and murdered fathers—this, *this* was crazy. "I just can't believe that! Do you ever open your mouths?"

"No."

"*Ever? REALLY?*"

"No!"

"You don't use your tongues!?"

"I have seen," Htan Dah offered, "in movies."

"In *movies!*" I exploded.

"Yes!"

"Are you seriously telling me that you guys don't kiss with your mouths open or use your tongues!?" Clearly, he was seriously telling me that, but I couldn't help the screaming.

He laughed self-consciously, and at me. "No! We don't do it!" he shouted back. "I didn't know . . . that people really do that."

"EH SOE!" I tore into the house yelling for my roommate when we got back. I found him lying on his bench. When I flipped on the lights, he looked out at me from behind his mosquito net, groggily alarmed in his underwear.

"When you kiss your girlfriend, do you ever open your mouth?"

Eh Soe relaxed his head back down and tsked. "That's just Hollywood," he said.

"That's not just Hollywood!" I shrieked. "People really do that! All the time!"*

"Real?" he asked with mild interest, then rolled back over.

"GIVE ME Karen kisses," I requested the next day, when Eh Soe was awake. I'd sat down next to him on the reading bench in our room after breakfast.

"Real?"

"Yes!" Though Eh Soe had a girlfriend, Eh Soe was also kind of a racist, so I knew his kissing me would be strictly perfunctory and not a violation of his relationship commitments. Once, he'd come to take a nap on the bench, and I'd already been lying on it. When I'd told him I wasn't moving but he could lie down with me, he'd jumped down at my side. "Isn't your girlfriend going to be mad you're in bed with another woman?" I'd asked. He'd tsked. "You're a white person. You're not a *real* woman."

Eh Soe leaned toward me now and made his mouth closed and lax before placing it and his nose lightly against mine and inhaling. He withdrew a very little, then did it again, and then again to the sides of my mouth, my cheek, breathing in through his nose every time our slack faces made soft contact.†

---

* When Yale researchers released a sexual-behavior study of 190 societies in 1951, it reported that 4 percent didn't kiss. The Balinese, for example, instead brought their faces close enough to breathe in each other's warmth and smell. Some South African Thongans who caught sight of Europeans kissing a few decades earlier had exclaimed, "Look at these people! They suck each other! They eat each other's saliva and dirt!" So though tonguing is older than Vatsyayana, it's not universal, and my acting like everybody had always been doing it all the time wasn't exactly justified. Even Kinsey, in his 1953 *Sexual Behavior in the Human Female*, found that as few as 80 percent of American women who'd had premarital sex had Frenched—which is to say that as many as 20 percent of them had had premarital sex without ever Frenching.

† The Yale researchers had observed a similar foreplay among the Filipino Tinguian. FYI.

"Like that," he said, pulling away and shrugging.

"Wow." I shook my head. "So when you said you and your girl-friend make out in the park, that's what you meant?"

"Yeah, sure."

"Karen people don't French," I announced to Abby next door, after folding my legs beneath me across from where she sat on her chalky concrete floor.

She looked up from her laptop and said "What?" like she hadn't heard me.

"The guys. They don't French."

"What do you mean?"

"I mean, they think it's movie make-believe, like the dinosaurs in *Jurassic Park*."

"*Really?*" she asked, her eyes going wide. "Wait." She considered for a moment. "What do you mean? So what do they do?"

"Relax your face," I said. "Don't—don't do anything. Just leave your face like that." I leaned over and mashed my face gently into hers, inhaling every time our features met.

"Wow," she said when I'd sat back on my haunches. "That's . . . thoroughly unerotic."*

"Apparently they don't open their mouths for anything, not for kissing, no licking." I paused dramatically. "No. Oral."

Abby's mouth dropped open. "Seriously?"

"Seriously. Although . . ." I started laughing. "When I was ask-ing Eh Soe and Htan Dah about it, and described it to them, they were like, 'Oh, yeah, we've seen that in special Internet movies,' and couldn't *believe* that it ever happened in real life."

Abby moved her head in a slow, disbelieving shake.

"Yeah. And no noise!" I suddenly remembered them saying. "They have completely spitless, soundless sex. Which, I guess that makes

---

* Tongue kissing, say behavioral scientists, is a modification of "a ritualized feeding gesture handed down to us by our primate ancestors." Which doesn't sound that erotic, either.

sense in a culture where you get married and possibly move into a hut with your mom. But I was totally trying to talk Eh Soe into Frenching his girlfriend, and he just kept laughing and shuddering."

Like the day before it, that day was simultaneous party recovery and party preparation. It was Office One's turn for me to throw myself a going-away party for them, and Abby had decided to throw her going-away simultaneously, though she wasn't leaving for a couple of weeks, and since she wasn't throwing a separate party for Office One and Office Two, Office Two was also invited, though I'd thrown them a party just several hours before. Abby and I had a lot of work to do before dark. And with the combined purchasing powers of two white girls in Thailand, nothing could stop this party from attaining total awesomeness.

I had to apologize for dragging ass and needing a nap ("I'm sorry, Abby. I haven't changed my clothes or slept or been sober for more than a few hours at a time since Friday, and I've mostly just been eating bags of peanuts from 7-Eleven." "What are you, nineteen?"), but by the time our guests arrived we'd brought a torrent of provisions to bear on the dining room/garage table. *Three* bottles of shitty "Kentucky" vodka. Three more cartons of orange juice, because we had little choice, because there was no cranberry juice for sale in Mae Sot. Eight heaping orders of pad thai. Three chicken-and-potato roti. Six limes. Lemons and sugar—I wasn't really the kind of girl to do or peddle lemon-drop shooters, but there was ceremony in it! A big bottle of Coke. Ice. Another twenty-four oversize bottles of Chang. Sixteen sweet waffles with corn, from Abby's favorite street griddle, which Abby wanted to withhold until some of the savory foods had been worked through. A chocolate fucking cake, in a country where you could hardly find a loaf of bread, inscribed with love and our names in red frosting. We managed to spend about eighty bucks, no small feat considering that that was what our big old house cost in monthly rent. There was curry that someone had made for dinner, too, and I tossed a slightly smoked pack of Marlboro Reds into the

midst of the callipygian crew crowding around the table listening to
Poe K'Ler Htoo tell a story about Htoo Moo's sending an inappropriate interoffice email.

Lemon drops with a Chang back for everyone. Eh Soe raced
to get wasted, per his preference, per his disregard for the terrible
headache he'd complain about the whole next day if he drank on
an empty stomach because he wanted to get very drunk very fast. ("I
like this feeling.") "When you get back to the United States," he was
soon asking me, "can you send me some pills to lose weight? I don't
understand why some other people drink beer and don't exercise and
they don't get fatty. Why isn't Htan Dah fat?" He jumped to his feet
and thrust his hands out and started dancing about in place crazily,
excited by the heated debate, when I threw my fist into the table
and hollered at several guys for again mocking my insistence against
drunk driving.

"This is a democracy," Walt said, breaking in to settle the fight.
"Democracy is essential for human rights. If there is an issue, we
will vote." I lost the right to take away everyone's keys, but won the
English-only initiative. So when Collin asked Poe K'Ler Htoo for
a lighter in Karen, Walt informed him that he had to take off his
fucking pants, which was a sure sign that Walt had had enough. In
response to said request for the lighter, Poe K'Ler Htoo said gravely
that he was happy to hand it over, because we should all love each
other, very much, which was a sure sign that he'd had enough, too.
Collin as well, insistent on more Ohio kisses and telling me I was
like the rain, coming to cool things and make things pleasant and
then leaving and everything was sweltering again. And Abby *must*
have been drunk, because she made eye contact with me across
the table, raised her brows, and asked, "Should we break out the
W-A-F-F—"

"Dude," I said. "They're not dogs. Or retarded." I started laughing.
"Or even illiterate. I think they know how to spell 'waffles.'"

Ta Mla had been pretty quiet all night. But I wasn't worried about him. He'd had a dark day that day before, when he'd come raging into the dining room/garage after his arrest, but today, despite his ever-renewing trauma, he was triumphant again. He'd left the house early to go to church,★ and had returned beaming like the very sunshine. There'd been white people at mass, Irishmen. They'd told Ta Mla they were interested in what was happening to Burma, to him, and that had made him feel "strong." Now he finally spoke up, having left and then reentered the room with a box wrapped in shiny pink paper.

"We want to thank you," he said, handing me the box. For my time and skills. It meant a lot to them. In this box was a gesture and though the gesture was small they hoped I would accept it and remember them by it. Everybody smiling and clapping and blushing with booze and heat, and me pretending that this speech and box hadn't been given a hundred times before. Inside was a Karen shirt, like the guys sometimes wore around the house. I picked up the coarse woven cotton and held it up for everyone to see, mauve with white stitching rimming the short sleeves and V-neck, yellow and violet diamond-shaped detailing across the middle, bottom enringed by thread fringe.

Throughout the night, Htan Dah and I played host, getting up and getting more food, more ice, opening beer bottles from and doing dishes in the kitchen, intermittently sitting down at the table to crash shallow glasses of vodka, take them down, and suck sugared lemon slices, until everyone left or passed out, and suddenly it was quiet and Htan Dah leaned hard against the kitchen wall and said,

---

★ Ta Mla was an animist, not a Christian. But in his own religion, if, say, an ancestor spirit or nature spirit is angered, even by accident, the defendant has to figure out what he did, which may require chicken bones and/or a shaman, and then fix it, which may require sacrificing an animal, and/or a shaman's calling Ta Mla's soul back to his body and quickly securing it there with bracelets made of string. That sort of spirituality required a lot more work, and resources he didn't really have anymore. So sometimes, Ta Mla went to church.

"I'm going to throw up." The only remaining light was the neon overhead in the kitchen and the sliver beneath the bathroom door Htan Dah had closed behind him. I walked further into the house and wandered the living room, on the cool tiles, pacing, carefully, around shadows of bodies strewn on the floor.

THE SUN was barely up when the laborers resumed their construction across the street for the day. I slept fitfully through the dawn hammering, refusing to move until the light was strong enough to blind me straight through my eyelids. I got up to watch through the window. They were building a hotel, someone had told me. They had erected a long, shallow frame, a tight maze of wood, on top of which twenty men were standing in a line on a narrow support beam. They kept their balance in bare feet as they moved buckets full of something between them along the length of the structure, yelling to each other as they swung the handles from one man to the next. I scowled at them.

Downstairs, Htoo Moo and Htan Dah and Poe K'Ler Htoo occupied the same seats at the picnic table that they had the night before, in the same clothes. The latter two had coffee cups of ice and Chang in front of them.

"Good morning!" Htan Dah said, at the same time that I asked, "Are you fucking kidding me?"

"Do you want some beer?" he asked cheerfully.

"Uh, no." I sat down on a bench, next to Htoo Moo, who smiled at me. "Hey pal," I said.

He just smiled some more, and nodded.

"How are you?"

"I am still drunk."

"Okay." I turned back to Htan Dah. "When do you want to go to the bus station?"

"Bus station?" Htoo Moo asked.

"Yeah, bus station. I have to go get my ticket to Bangkok. I leave tomorrow." I turned to Htan Dah again.

"Whenever," he said, shrugging.

"So, you will leave tomorrow," Htoo Moo said, looking at no one.

"That's right."

He frowned.

I put my arm around him. "Aw, Htoo Moo, are you gonna be sad?"

"Yes," he said. "Very yes."

"Do you think you might cry?"

"Yes." Htan Dah and Poe K'Ler Htoo laughed at him.

"Do you ever cry when volunteers leave?"

"Sometimes." More laughing from the other drunk guys.

"Really?"

"Yes." Nod. Smile. "But I go where no one can see me."

After spending the afternoon with Htan Dah, after getting bus tickets, after dinner was bought, and made, and eaten, and the sun had reset, I was back in the same spot and the same conversation, only with Abby in place of Poe K'Ler Htoo and instead of Htoo Moo, Eh Soe.

"I will be very sad when you leave tomorrow," my roommate told me.

"Me too," I said. "I don't want to go. I'm not ready to go."

"So you can stay," Htan Dah said. I looked at him. Earlier, when we'd been alone, I'd asked him what he was thinking about because he was being so quiet. "Nothing," he'd said, but when I'd pressed him, he'd said, "Tomorrow."

"That's right," Eh Soe said. "You can call Ohio and tell them you will stay here in Thailand."

"She has to go back to work, you guys." Abby was being reasonable. Like everyone else in my life was being reasonable. I had, indeed, emailed some of my best friends and my mother and threatened to not leave. Was that really the best use of my time and resources, they wanted to know? Shouldn't I come back to the States as planned, and then decide if I wanted to—make a *plan* to—go back later? Was

I taking into account that working with refugees and in war zones was emotional crack?

"It's true. I do have to go back to work. They're counting on me to teach a bunch of classes this fall." I sighed. "Let's go out for ice cream."

Abby and I jumped on the back of Eh Soe and Htan Dah's motorbikes, respectively, and headed north, away from town. Our destination: Khao Mao Khao Fang, the fancy open-air restaurant set back from the highway, which was for some reason designed to create the experience of eating in the middle of a very clean jungle. The tables were arranged around a sprawling lake overflowing with plants and trees and waterfalls, and tributaries winding their way under walkways, and real ferns and flora so perfect that it all, frankly, looked fake.

As we walked under the canopy of displaced rainforest, Htan Dah was nervous, I could tell. It was his first restaurant, right on the heels of his first bar, and he was sober, now. We were conspicuous enough, we two leggy white broads out with refugees in public, and I was a storm of fast English and enthusiasm, my excitement raising my voice, which was drawing extra attention to us as we sat down, and when Htan Dah and I had to get back up and walk back through the restaurant to go to the bathroom, he became overwhelmed.

"Wait!" he choked as I turned my back to him, toward the ladies' room. I turned back around, and could almost see his heart beating too fast. "I don't know what to do," he said.

"It's okay." I reached out and ran my hand down his forearm, from his elbow to his wrist. "I'm gonna go in here." I nodded at the door on the right. "You go in there." I nodded at the door on the left. "Then we'll meet back either right here, or if you don't see me when you come out, I'll meet you back at the table."

Reseated, we two decided to split an extravagantly expensive banana split. We all would also share a couple of coconuts with the tops sliced open and straws sticking out of them. "Do you guys want to order for us?" I asked.

Htan Dah said, "You can," while Eh Soe shook his head.

"But you guys speak Thai."

"They don't speak English?" Htan Dah asked.

"Yeah, I mean, a little." Curiosity had driven Abby and me to Khao Mao Khao Fang once before. I'd had a red cocktail that came in a glass shaped like a headless naked lady. "But they definitely speak Thai better. Because they're Thai. And you guys speak Thai."

Here Htan Dah and Eh Soe denigrated their ability to speak Thai, as always, and Abby and I chastised them for being overmodest, as we'd both seen them do it plenty well at markets.

"Normally, you would order in English," Eh Soe said.

"That's just because we don't speak Thai! But you do!"

"Not here," Htan Dah said. "You're not."

Abby and I ordered for the table, in English, with plenty of pointing at the items on the menu. The quality of the banana split was middling. The gigantism of the coconuts was daunting. When we'd all had enough, Eh Soe started twisting and turning and looking around the restaurant in his seat.

"Now what?" he asked.

"Now we wait for a bill," Abby said.

"When is it coming?"

"We have to ask for it," I said. "They never bring you the bill in Thai restaurants. Whereas in American restaurants, generally you can't keep a waiter from slapping a bill on your table."

"Because," Htan Dah ventured, "time is money?"

I laughed. "That's right."

I wanted to go to the lake by Office Two, to go for a ride, to stay out and with my housemates, but Eh Soe complained that it was dark, it was late, he wanted to go home so he could lie down. So we called Eh Soe a princess, called it a night, went back.

And lie down we did. Eh Soe went straight upstairs and took his place on his bench. Htan Dah sprawled prone on the floor next to it. I got on the floor, too, on my back, propping my feet up on Eh Soe's legs on the bench and my head on Htan Dah's butt.

"I was terribly disappointed by the conversation last night," Eh Soe said, sitting up a little against the wall I'd posted the "No Smoking" sign on to light a cheroot.

"Really?" I asked. "You seemed like you were having a good time."

"I don't understand why we have to be talking about democracyyy, human riiights. . . ."

"That was like, fifteen minutes' worth of conversation."

He shook his head. "I don't want to talk about this. People are too drunk and talk about it for too long."

Abby joined us, having checked her email downstairs, sitting down on the edge of Eh Soe's bench. "What are you guys doing?" she asked.

"This," I said.

She wiped her forehead. "God. It's hot in here."

"Yeah, it's pretty muggy," I agreed. It was late for it to be so sticky. "It's got to still be, what do you think . . ." I stopped and turned my face toward Htan Dah, my cheek against his butt cheek. "Do you guys use Fahrenheit or Celsius?"

Silence.

"Do you know what I'm talking about?"

No.

"They're temperature scales, broken up into degrees. So I could say how hot or cold something is with a number of degrees on the scale."

"Oh, yes. When we have malaria," Eh Soe volunteered, "the doctor says, 'You have one hundred and two fever.'"

"Yeah, right. So that's your temperature on the Fahrenheit scale. That's the scale we use in the States. So guess how many degrees it is in here right now."

Htan Dah shrugged. "Six?"

I rotated my head on his posterior and turned to Abby. "How many degrees is it in here right now?"

"Eighty."

"Yeah, see, I was going to say seventy-eight. So obviously that's about what the temperature is." Abby and I were smiling at each other. "We know that scale well enough to be able to tell the temperatures of things." We were really impressive.

"Why?" Eh Soe asked.

"Because, if you know what the temperature is, you know, like, what to wear if you're going outside," Abby said.

"We have temperatures," Htan Dah said. "Hot . . . not so hot . . . cold. . . ."

"Yeah, but we live in a place with seasons, and we need to know exactly what the temperature is so we know if we need to take a sweater, or a coat."

Htan Dah and Eh Soe said nothing, because they were polite, but their faces clearly weren't buying our assertion that they'd never survive with just an adjectival scale in the West, where total accurate internalization of an established scientific unit of temperature measurement was essential. I couldn't say, now that I was actually thinking about it, that I was convinced, either. I would have traded that superpower for the one Htan Dah had that told him when an egg was done boiling, or the one that'd enabled him to wake me up in a windowless hotel and say, his voice low and soft and even in the boozy dark, "Dawn is coming," and be right.

We tacitly agreed to drop it, quiet for a moment. Abby passed the lull by looking over my lounging configuration as though registering it for the first time. "Are you comfortable?" she asked me.

"On this ass?" I tapped the back of my head against its shapely rest. "Absolutely."

Eh Soe laughed. "If Htan Dah's wife catches him on the floor like this with a Karen girl," he said, "she will cut off his . . . rations." He laughed harder. "His skin rations." And harder. "The rations at night."

"We get it, Eh Soe," I said. "But I'm not an actual girl, right, because I'm *kaw la wah*."

Eh Soe nodded while he wiped his eyes. "That's right, that's right."

Abby went to bed, and Eh Soe went to go get ready for bed, and just like that, it was time for bed on my last night in the Mae Sot house of BA.

Htan Dah and I sat up, across from each other, cross-legged on the floor.

"Thanks for keeping me fed, and keeping me company," I said. "Even on the first morning, you kept me company when I had breakfast."

"Yes. I worried that you will be lonely, or homesick. I didn't want you to cry."

"Isn't it weird that people come to help you and just cry all the time?"

He shrugged. "It is normal."

"Well, seriously, I'm very grateful to you. Thank you."

"Thank you!" He smiled. "And, you are welcome!"

We counted the hours back from my morning bus departure to determine what time we'd have to wake up to go to the market. The answer was, really, really early.

"I'll cook for you," Htan Dah said. "I can go to the market and cook. You can sleep."

I shook my head. "I can sleep anytime. I can't spend time with you anytime."

"That's true."

I climbed under my mosquito net onto my mattress, and he crawled to the foot of it, lay on his back on the floorboards, and went to sleep.

MY ALARM went off before dawn.

I reached for the dull, subdued beeping and slapped it quiet, pushing myself onto my side. The objects around me began to take shape—wide mosquito net, tilted window slats, lifeless figure a few feet away. I slid underneath the netting.

"It's time to get up," I said, sidling up to where Htan Dah lay with his body rigid against hard wood, exactly as he'd lain down. I pressed the length of my body against his arm. I was still for a moment. "Htan Dah," I said. I shook him gently. "It's time to get up." These refugees were used to packed rooms. They slept like the dead.

Htan Dah breathed in hard when I said his name and shook him again. "You can sleep," he said, just above a whisper. "I can go to the market alone."

"Stop it."

We pulled onto our side street on his motorbike. Mae Sot was silent in the darkness. Out on the main thoroughfare, even the roosters were tranquil. Passengers in Asia may not generally hold on to their drivers, but I wrapped my arms tight around Htan Dah's waist. We were alone on the road. He drove slowly. I watched stray dogs pass and the stately white municipal building approach from my usual place behind him, his hair catching on the wind we were making. He leaned back and turned his head toward me a little so I could hear him.

"Time is so fast," he said.

We pulled through the only intersection on the route big enough to have a light, toward the shortcut through the temple grounds strung with lights, and I dug my fingers into him, pressed my face between his shoulder blades, and cried.

We had two hours before we had to leave for the bus station. Though the time was disappearing fast, consumed by a rash of banal errands, the moments moved weirdly, exquisitely slowly: turning my hips to miss a table corner in a narrow walkway in the market. Palming a head of cauliflower, hard florets against my fingers like braille. Laying a knife on a garlic clove, parallel to the cutting board, and pressing until the skin cracked. Laying my weight on my mattress to push the air out. Considering, as I repacked my bag, how stupid it was to bring these shoes that I hadn't worn since the plane, as though I'd have needed an alternative to flip-flops, while Htan Dah watched and speculated that we'd see each other again in 2008—in two years—and I insisted sooner than that. Explaining to Eh Soe that I'd left that shampoo in the bathroom on purpose, so they could use it. Instructing Htoo Moo that these blue bullet-like pills were calcium, good for his bones, he would absorb more of the nutrients if he took them with food. Standing in the driveway in a circle of Eh Soe and Htan Dah and Htan Dah's friend who'd happened to show up, the three of them debating how to best divide up our bodies and my luggage on motorbikes to get to the bus station, Ta Mla and Htoo Moo ambling around waiting for them to decide so it'd be time for them to officially say goodbye to me and go back in the house and get back to work. Next to the idling bus, I leaned my back against Htan Dah's chest, and Eh Soe and I stared alternately at each other and the ground. In my bus seat, I watched the two of them watching me through the window and then they were gone. They went home and changed into red and white Karen shirts, respectively, and took Abby, soon on her own way out of Mae Sot, to an annual Karen cere-mony on the day of that August full moon, swarming with thousands of migrants and refugees who ate fried yellow beans and banana stem soup together and then rubbed strings on each other's forearms to call their spirits back to their bodies before binding them together at the wrist with the string. Several days later, the guys slipped into Burma to attend the 56th annual commemoration of martyrs of the KNU's war.

BACK IN the States, I rolled out of bed late to pull together school clothes and syllabi, passing hot, jet-lagged nights in front of hours of syndicated sitcoms. When I slept, I dreamed that my grade-school best friend and I walked into a small town somewhere in America with our arms slung around each other's shoulders. She became con-cerned that this group of guys, buff and in tank tops and following us a little too closely, was going to start trouble. Maybe they for some reason thought we were transvestites, she speculated, and this wasn't the type of town that took kindly to that. When they confronted us, forming a half circle in our path that we couldn't escape, we explained that we weren't doing anything wrong, that is, that we were biological women, but it didn't matter. They were there, I knew, to fight us for the ease and the fun. My friend punched one in the face and we ran, and thought we'd lost them, but ultimately their shadows crept over us as we squatted in a lonely patch of grass with the sun at our backs. They chased us into a souvenir shop and cornered us, and I screamed at the two employees who stood watching to call the police, call the police, I was impossibly alert and alarmed, and the employees didn't move and I knew that there were no police who would help, and the men closed in around us, calmly smiling, and as my hope for getting away died I felt the blood under my electric skin give up and give in, the cells bursting at the realization of predictable and unpreventable horror. When I woke up, I tried to calm myself with gratitude that it wasn't happening, it's not happening, look, see, you're in a bed. Safe girl. Lucky girl. But my brain couldn't make my body move, paralyzed, still, by my heart's hard-pounding panic, whatever I told it. It's not happening, shhhh, safe girl, lucky girl . . .

IN MAE Sot, Htoo Moo woke up around seven. He opened his eyes to the mosquito net surrounding him, and beyond that, the underside of the overhanging roof. He got up, peed, washed his face, and walked back out onto the balcony, wrapping himself in his gray wool blanket to write in his journal while the early chill pricked his cheeks.

Eh Soe rolled on his bench, groaning, reluctant. In the big room next door, Ta Mla and Gaw Say weren't sleeping, but they lay still on the hardwood floor. Downstairs, Htan Dah was standing at the sink rinsing six cups of rice. He could hear over the water running into the big metal pot that it was raining, hard; the drops met the tin roof in steady sheets. He looked straight ahead, not looking, as he scooped up handfuls of the grain and rubbed the granules between his palms.

Soon, Eh Soe plodded downstairs, turned on a computer, and brought the jumpy, metallic notes of the BBC Burmese news stream theme into the room as other staff members came in, still rubbing their eyes, to immediately take their places at the desks. Ta Mla did the dishes from last night, dropped the stone mortar gently on the table, and pestled herbs and peppers into curry paste. The morning had started. Htan Dah pulled himself away from the sink and the soothing swoosh of rice through his fingers and put it on to simmer, grabbed his keys, straddled his motorbike, and got to work, pushing himself out into the driving rain.

It was indeed 2008 the next time I saw Htan Dah.

He was standing on a sidewalk, squinting against the sun at my approach, power lines overhead. We were in the San Francisco Bay Area, where we both lived.

The year I volunteered for BA, 2006, nearly five thousand people from Burma resettled to other countries through Thailand. That's just 3 percent of the number of Burmese refugees at that time, but it was double the number that had done so the year before. Then in 2007, the 2006 number tripled.

The difference was made by Condoleezza Rice. In May 2006, two months before I arrived in Mae Sot, the US secretary of state granted a waiver of material support for Burmese refugees who lived in Thailand's Tham Hin camp, which was disgustingly overcrowded and increasingly crime-infested. It didn't get those who actually *were* terrorists—former or current soldiers or card-carrying members of the KNU—off the hook, but it opened the door for those refugees in Tham Hin who'd been ineligible to become Americans for having given rice or a glass of water to a rebel.* A few months later, three

---

* "Supporters" and even victims of plenty of other terrorist groups are still liable for contributing to them, voluntarily or otherwise. As of late 2009, the Sri Lankan fisherman who gave the Tamil Tigers money for his own ransom had yet to be granted asylum.

weeks after I left, Rice extended the waiver to more Karen refugees in Thailand. In January 2007, the US extended eligibility to all refugees who'd provided material support to the Karen National Union. In 2008, the Karen National Union had its designation as a terrorist organization under the Immigration and Nationality Act removed altogether.

In 2009, the fifty-thousandth Burmese refugee processed for resettlement in Thailand was shipped out of Asia, in the largest UN resettlement program in the world. Most of them go to the United States, which accepted nearly fifteen thousand in 2008 alone. That year, Htan Dah and his wife and son arrived in Northern California.

I started jumping up and down when I saw him, and he smiled a little and I ran and threw my arms around his neck. He put his arms up in reciprocation because he was supposed to, but neither they nor any other part of his body gave in to the hug, and I apologized for violating his customs, but I couldn't help it.

"It's so good to see you! Oh my god how are you(!)? Are you so excited to be in the United States?"

He wasn't.

"When I moved here, our neighbors," he told me, speaking of the Karen family that lived next door, that had been in the United States for years, "they said, 'Now that you are in America, you have to be afraid of everyone.' So now I'm a scaredy-cat."

"You don't have to be afraid of everyone. Who are you afraid of?"

"I don't know! Maybe . . . hooligans."

"Hooligans! Htan Dah, that's absurd. I walk around all the time, all over the place, all by myself."

"For you it is different! You were born here. You're an American."

At some point, I asked him if he had gone to any bars in his neighborhood.

"I'm too scared to go to white-people bars," he said.

"There's not really any such thing as white-people bars. You can go wherever you want. You live in California. There are tons of Asians here. People will just think you're Chinese."

"But I do not want to go outside! My neighbors also. Like me, they just stay inside, and eat, and sleep, and watch TV."* The only time he left was for his ESL instruction, twenty hours a week worth of class with other immigrants, Mexicans and Vietnamese. He went to that only because he had to in order to keep getting his $680 welfare check. For his family of three. He said he wasn't well enough to walk around America. He said he and his family were all still airsick. They'd been here for a month.

The next time I spoke to him, on the phone, I tried to talk him into letting me pick him up and drive him and his son to the state fair. When he refused vehemently, I told him that he had to go outside at some point, especially if his wife, who spoke no English, wouldn't, since he'd told me their kid was tired of being in their apartment all the time and begged to be let out. I swore to him that there would be lots of people of different races together, so we would blend in with everyone else, and no one would pay him any attention.

"People will look at me!" he shouted. "I have no idea what I am doing, what to do!" His voice caught, panicked. He was getting increasingly agitated, and I'd never heard him so worked up. "People will think I am some kind of . . . monkey!" He sounded like he was panting, or choking, even. "I do not know how to act! I am refugee, from the jungle. My son wants to go outside all the time, but I don't want to take him. He has only been in refugee camp, so he is curious about everything, and he cries when I won't take him outside. I wish I was IDP."†

"Shut up. You do not." He laughed guiltily, imagining, I imagine,

---

* Here both families were exhibiting one of the classic symptoms of culture shock laid out in the Comic Sans text of the English-translation cultural orientation book: "Withdrawal and avoidance of contact with people from the new culture."

† That's another symptom: "Glorifying the native culture and emphasizing the negative in the new culture."

hundreds of thousands of IDPs rolling over in their living jungle graves. He did calm down, eventually—and agree to go to the Sacramento fairgrounds.

After more than a year, he was still "a little bit" sad to be here. Like I'd inwardly threatened to call Delta and book the next flight back home my first night in Mae Sot, Htan Dah still threatened to return to Thailand every time I talked to him. "I want to go back to the place where I was born, where it is familiar, with my people," he said. "I miss my friends. I miss working at BA. I feel like I have a big load to carry." He was not, understandably, all that pumped about becoming part of the American underclass. He still wasn't working, because he was working to get his GED, and was eager to get a job, though he knew that finding one was hardly the end of his problems. "People have to have many jobs. They work long hours and then come home and go to bed and just start over. That is American life. I have no idea how I will pay my rent, and electricity, and food. Here, I have no time to work for my people. I have to work for my family, for survival, for food. If possible I would like to go back." Worrying that he was overworrying me, he added, "But it's no problem. I will cope with my situation, in maybe five or six years. I'm good. I learn from everything. There's no time to be sad. It's time to learn."

Part of Htan Dah's reluctance to give his all to the massive readjustment was his absolute reluctance to leave Southeast Asia in the first place. He'd always been, together with Walt, the strongest BA proponent of staying and (peacefully) fighting, and his new American inaction—however arguably ineffective his old Thai action—plagues him. He and his wife fought bitterly over the issue of resettlement; she turned in their family's application behind his back, and he ultimately conceded that it was the best thing for their son, which was hard to contest. Even Htan Dah, after he'd trekked deep into the Thai hills to pay off villagers and headmen and civil workers and had his picture taken, and papers were forged and the identity of a dead Thai Karen had been assumed—even after he'd stopped getting arrested, thanks to his several-thousand-dollar ID—he still hadn't been able to shake the panic, out of doors, the fear that he'd be found out for being what he really was. He'd still mostly avoided traveling. He was born in a refugee camp, and his kid was born in a refugee camp, and if he'd stayed in Thailand his kid's kid probably would have been born in a refugee camp, too.

Maintaining that status quo is certainly the junta's plan. In 2009, the two sides of the China-EU summit failed to reach an agreement about whether the world should stay out of Burma's business. Media in the West were fretting about a North Korean ship breaking Korea's arms-exporting sanctions to deliver weapons to Burma, while media in the East were broadcasting photographs confirming years-old suspicions that North Korea helped the junta build a top-secret underground tunnel system near the new capital; outlets in both hemispheres have turned out such headlines as BURMA, NORTH KOREA IN AN UNHOLY MILITARY ALLIANCE and IS BURMA THE NEXT IRAN? and IS MYANMAR GOING NUCLEAR WITH KOREA'S HELP? and IS THERE A BURMA-NORTH KOREA-IRAN NUCLEAR CONSPIRACY? Even US Secretary of State Hillary Clinton acknowledged "growing concerns about military cooperation between North Korea and Burma, which we take very seriously." Some Southeast Asian politicians suggested that Burma be suspended from ASEAN, but not enough of them. Nicolas Sarkozy and Gordon Brown and Barack Obama and Julia Roberts called for the release* of Aung San Suu Kyi, who was tried and had her house arrest again extended after she hosted a misguided middle-aged American fan who stole into her compound uninvited. The Obama/Biden campaign had promised that the two "will press China to end its support for regimes in Sudan, Burma, Iran and Zimbabwe." But the president's unwillingness to press that Most Favored

---

* Burma's response, per usual, was to trash-talk: Other countries, the government said, "should refrain from interfering in internal affairs that will affect peace and security of the region" or else "possibly affect mutual understanding and friendly relations."

Nation and major US stakeholder to do anything was always pretty clear, even before Hillary Clinton said China and the US would just have to "agree to disagree" on things like human rights when there were problems such as the economy to be dealt with. The administration unveiled its new Burma policy, which involves a combination of the sanctions that have never worked and "engagement," which ASEAN has been using with Burma totally unsuccessfully for years. The Genocide Prevention Task Force, led by Obama adviser and former secretary of state Madeleine Albright, put Burma on the genocide watch list, not that watching has ever been a particularly effective form of assistance to people on the business end of a genocide. The International Criminal Court issued an arrest warrant for the Sudanese president, and so the president of East Timor, José Ramos-Horta, a Nobel Peace Prize laureate, swore he was going to talk the court into similarly charging Than Shwe. And while a few people made some noise about trying to make Burma do something, the junta continued construction on an elaborate new airport that will accommodate its commerce further exploding.

One August day, Roger P. Winter, director of the US Committee for Refugees, surveyed the Karen refugee situation on the Thai border. "The spirit in the camps," he said, "is a strange mixture of hopefulness with vibrations of a fading dream." I could write that same description now. Only Roger P. Winter said that in 1986. Htan Dah and his wife recently had another baby, their "American baby"; as far as that kid's welfare is concerned, they left just in time. No shit, Htan Dah's wife didn't want to wait around Southeast Asia for a sea change. Her new baby could be in college by then. *Or* freebasing meth in a Thai containment camp.

IN THAILAND, Mae Sot Office One still has cool tile floors and the warm earthy smell of constant rice. It still teems with young Karen men.

Most of my former comrades in Chang aren't there, swept up in the tide of Burmese resettlers currently leaving Thailand at a rate of three hundred a week. Htan Dah lives in the type of American place described by a word I recently taught him: suburbs. Htoo Moo joined his brother in England. Eh Soe moved to Sydney, but not before impregnating his girlfriend, and is working three jobs and trying to get her and the baby to Australia. Ta Mla lives in Milwaukee, where he can go outside whenever he wants. Kaw Ku, who returned to Mae Sot from inside shortly before I left, so didn't spend much time with me, started calling me after he was relocated to Lakewood, Ohio. I offered him a lot of useless apologies, for his crushing poverty and loneliness and the weather. "It's okay," he replied. "You can never find a good place to live in the world. Only in heaven."

But some of the faces still at BA are familiar. Saw Kaw has been transferred to another city but remains in the organization. He sends me emails with the subject line "Don't forget." (To which I reply in the subject line, "I never forget.") Walt has been promoted to a more intensive role at BA and says he'll stay in Thailand no matter what. He has not filled out any resettlement applications. Lah Lah Htoo has moved on to an organization that handles the refugees' education. He's considering resettlement. There are lots of new faces, too, guys rushing or milling about in jeans or longyis, pressing back a little, however thorough the spirit breaking and insurmountable the pile of obstacles.

These new recruits seem to have chosen wisely from among their other options in Southeast Asia—forced laborer, IDP, KNU soldier, camp dweller—even though they're in hiding. Despite the dangers of being on the run in Mae Sot, they're in better shape than their people and families in camp. The effects of the world financial meltdown have managed to smack into the packed UN settlements. Since donations are down and commodity prices and the Thai baht are up, the Thailand Burma Border Consortium has been forced to reduce food rations. "Luxuries," such as soap, have been cut entirely. The Burma Forces Welfare Association of the Royal Commonwealth Ex-Services League no longer has enough money to distribute small stipends to the hundred surviving Karen in camp who fought for the British.

Even being in the KNU wouldn't afford them the protection it once had in Thai border towns. The guerrilla organization—having lost more territory and trade routes and money and men—is of increasingly limited use to its neighbor. Its old enemy is now one of Thailand's major trading partners, and its new enemy, the DKBA, now runs a bulk of the cross-border trade and is therefore a much more valuable ally to the Thai police. After decades of complicity, cooperation, and sanctuary, Thailand has told the KNU, which has long been largely based there, to get out, and go back where it came from.

IN BURMA, the junta is conducting evil business as usual, even in the face of some unusual business: In 2008, it announced it would hold elections in 2010. These would be the first Burmese elections in twenty years, which is a slight improvement in the thirty-year gap between the previous two. But obviously no one in the world believed they were going to be free or fair or legitimate. Under the junta-drafted constitution, which took thirteen years to write, and which the populace supposedly overwhelming supported—it passed with 92 percent yeas! And in a vote held in the middle of Cyclone Nargis's chaos!—the military is basically its own sovereign entity with total immunity.* Anyway, we know what happened after the 1990 election. We know, too, what happened during 2007's massive uprising in Burma, when thousands of maroon- and saffron-robe-clad monks and dissenters marched through the streets peacefully, until the military started shooting at people and killed a Japanese journalist and at least one monk and a couple dozen other Burmese. The

---

* Adopting that constitution through a national referendum was step four of the junta's "Seven-Step Roadmap" to democracy, which it unveiled in 2003 to calm people down after its thugs seemingly tried to assassinate Aung San Suu Kyi. The fifth step is the upcoming election. The final destination, of course, is the bliss of "a modern, developed and democratic nation."

Internet was shut down. Some citizens braved videotaping it and blogging about it, which kept the death toll down, many believe, and a lot of citizens were arrested. Whether the people of Burma overcome the obstacles to rising up—cell phone prices kept at more than four times the per-capita gross national income; government surveillance of all text messaging; oppression and censorship so thorough that Burmans and minorities throughout the country don't know that, just like in '88, they're all on the same side; having no unified opposition group, since the members of Aung San Suu Kyi's National League for Democracy have been mostly jailed or exiled or buried, and even within the NLD there are warring factions, too; the plain fact that, as Dr. Cynthia has pointed out, it's really hard to muster the time and strength to get involved in politics when your family is starving—Burma's leaders are no doubt counting on the same old outcome. Dissent will be crushed by the monster military machine. Cronies will be installed. And the brief international media blitz won't cover the aftermath—like it didn't cover the doubling of the political-prisoner population or the locked-away monks or the 104-year prison sentences for peaceful dissenters last time. Or the junta's exporting all its rice on the cheap even though its country is in a state of food emergency post–Cyclone Nargis. Or the imprisoning of Burmese aid volunteers who tried to distribute relief to Nargis's victims.

Part of the Election Day preparations involve the military's trying to reinforce control over those always troublesome minority militias. Most major insurgent groups have been in cease-fires on the fringe for decades, and the government is trying to bring them into its fold, to achieve complete, cohesive national militarization, ordering that they turn their armies into border guards under the command of the Tatmadaw. The DKBA has happily agreed to report for Burma-army-assisting duty. They've even started conscripting villagers to serve in that capacity. Plenty of other troops had already been forced into the militia of six thousand, of course, whether physically or circumstantially. "If I didn't go to the DKBA, my family would have starved," one wounded soldier told an interviewer.

The chairman of the DKBA says the army's decision to sign a cease-fire and join forces with the government has been "beneficial." Seriously! Their alliance has granted them freedom from Tatmadaw attack and a cut of the border trade. Teak, gold, antimony, zinc, tin— the business interests that bankroll the junta continue to drive the war between the DKBA and KNU, as the former aims to capture all possible logging and mining territory. They've got education, and commerce, and don't live in free-fire zones. And all they have to do to maintain the upper hand is continue to attack other Karen, some of whom are insurgents, and many of whom probably philosophically or physically support the insurgents, anyway.

Those KNU insurgents have never signed a cease-fire—not now that they're down to four thousand troops, not in all this war's sixty years. Maybe it doesn't matter anyway. It's not like life for the general nonwarring Burmese population is free from forced labor and portering and torture and oppression and starvation. And cease-fires haven't stopped the Burma army from confiscating land and displacing villagers and continually expanding military presence in some other minorities' areas. Cease-fire or no, war could still rage for the resources and territory in Karen State, whether between Burman and Karen, or Karen and Karen, or Karen and someone else.

The KNU and SPDC have talked about calling the war off a couple of times, but it just never works out. Once, while they were in the midst of peace negotiations, a KNU brigade stormed a Burma army weapons depot. Once, KNU leadership rejected the proposed terms—like surrendering their arms—as, and I quote, "out of the question." When the junta courted cease-fire talks with the KNU in 2009, the Burma army, together with the DKBA, launched a massive attack on the Karen insurgents about ten days later. So as I write this, the Tatmadaw and DKBA have captured several of the few remaining KNU bases and are shelling unprotected IDP camps,

and thousands of refugees, having run out of places to run, are making their way over mountains and land mines with babies and diarrhea and no provisions, through soldiers, snake bites, and brumes
of malarial mosquitoes, another refugee flood into Thailand. And
after the assassination of the DKBA commander who was rumored
to have orchestrated the assassination of the KNU general-secretary,
the DKBA says it's going to destroy Mae La, Thailand's most populous Karen refugee camp, next.

Several groups have broken away from the KNU since the '90s
and agreed with the junta, in the face of interminable conflict with
it, to stop fighting—or in the case of the DKBA, just start fighting
other Karen. But Burma's dystopia breeds new Walts and Ta Mlas
and other troops who are looking for revenge or purpose every day.
And not just in the hills; small bombs planted by unknown groups
have started going off in Rangoon. Everyone in the world knows
what some people will inevitably choose given the choice between
battling for liberty and rolling over and dying. In the face of the
demand to make their inactive militia part of the murderous Burma
army's border force, the Mon have said no, and that, further, if they
are asked to disarm, they "will do something." The Kachin who've
been in a cease-fire since 1994 also said no, and are now actively
recruiting. The still terrifying and now druglording Wa's twenty-
thousand-strong army is refusing to submit to anyone's authority.
To prove it, just in case someone wants to make them try, they are
preparing for war. And the Kokang broke a two-decade truce with
a firefight that sent thousands fleeing across the border into China.
As a porter Htoo Moo interviewed put it, in a poem he wrote after
he escaped:

> We have wounds on our shoulders and heads
> We have to climb mountains and are beaten like cattle
> We have to suffer from this powerlessness
> They tortured us cruelly. . . .

We, the escaped porters, have hearts filled with hatred. . . .
When we escape we feel grief for the porters who cannot escape
When we think of this we want to fight back to the military
government. . . .
Together we will struggle from now on!

"To stop the war is to surrender," General Mu Tu See, the KNU's current commander in chief, once said. "The atrocities will go on because these people are not for democracy."

Did he consider the war a success, given the staggering casualties?

"It's a draw. Nobody is winning, and nobody will win."

SOURCING

THE FIRST rule of fact-checking is that everything you read and hear is wrong.

Were you to be hired as a fact-checker, as I was in 2007, at *Mother Jones*—or the other remaining bastions of fact-check, like *The Atlantic*, or *The New Yorker*, or *Harper's*—you would be taught that information cannot be trusted. It is, rather, presumed fallacious until proved otherwise. Statistics and news clips must be subjected to intense tests of verification. Don't even think the word "Wikipedia." In my first meeting, among new coworkers of startling cynicism and genius, the announcement that the source of some fact was a *book* set off a mighty wave of scoffing and eye rolling around the conference table.

In true fact-checking, literally every word of every factual statement must be traced to a primary source, whether a document or the corroborated accounts of independent experts or witnesses. "Primary source" means that if the story you're fact-checking says some soldier was the forty-fourth Canadian soldier to die in Afghanistan since 2002, you're calling the Canadian Army. Once, I heard one of our fact-checkers call a bar in Mexico to ask, in Spanish, whether its floor was metal, per William T. Vollmann's assertion.

For the record, it was. But often, it's not. People just get things wrong. They read them wrong, or remember them wrong or the way they want to, or the information they read right was wrong in the first place. You hear the same fact a thousand times, but if you track down its origins, you find out all the repeaters are using the same source, and source zero was just guessing, or citing a highly question-able source or study. Or *mis*citing a highly questionable source or study. Or confusing the details, so that by now, everybody's under the erroneous impression that a shot of espresso contains more caffeine than a cup of coffee.

So I wasn't a week into my job before I, too, had undergone the com-pletely life-changing installation of an irrevocable—and warranted—skepticism of everything I heard or read. So it's life-ruining, also. Which is why I did something writers rarely do—which is subject their manu-scripts to a *Mother Jones*-style fact-check—and that they rarely do for really good reason—which is that holy fucking shit is it hard.

Enter former *MoJo* research editor Leigh Ferrara, a fact-checking and multitasking wizard, and the hardest-working and most charm-ing person you could hope to be stuck in a studio apartment with for twelve-hour fact-review marathons. The manuscript I gave Leigh had 1,240 footnotes, plus piles of sources noted haphazardly within the text, plus a bunch of sentences with no sourcing at all. So: I'd read and subsequently written that Burma had the fourth-highest child-mortality rate in the world, and Leigh had to figure out whether that was true or not. It's not. Burma is thirty-sixth on that list, actu-ally, which Leigh tracked down in UNICEF's "State of the World's Children 2009." That took care of eleven words, out of more than a hundred thousand, probably at least half of which she was respon-sible for. And that was a pretty easy one.

For historical details, we unearthed and paged through colonial-ists' reports and missionaries' diaries, or cross-checked information with other historical accounts we'd made sure weren't all using the same one original source—as is often the case—and/or vetted the minutiae and main ideas with scholars and specialists. We tracked down witnesses to and experts on subjects way outside the spot-light of popular scrutiny. We then evaluated those sources, trying to determine if they were reliable and where they were getting *their* information. One of Leigh's experts helpfully eliminated a handful of questions from her long list of outstanding facts; then she realized the source of his expertise was a book we'd already determined to be mistake-tastic.

Further complicating the fact-checking process was the inconve-nience that there's often no such thing as "fact." Another figure I'd cited was that trade between China and Burma was up to $2.6 billion in 2008, from $630 million in 2001. That turned out to be "true" (shout-out to *The Wall Street Journal* for its Burma info's being totally solid*), based on data Leigh uncovered in the United Nations Com-modity Trade Statistics Database. Mexicali's 13 Negro bar either does or does not have a metal floor, but the trouble with this trade statistic is perfectly summed up immediately following it in the *WSJ* article where it appeared: "Analysts say the official numbers vastly understate the full extent of China's investments in Myanmar." Mmmm, analysts do say that. Knowing that—however meticulously we sourced our facts, and though every estimate we were working so hard to find and confirm was at least the best possible estimate in existence—"true" is often still kind of a relative concept . . . it's demoralizing.

We both had dark moments while trying to keep a million little pieces needing verification up in the air. I had nightmares about work-ing on the final edits and not being able to write any of the words I wanted because I didn't have sourcing for them and there was no time for further fact-checking. Leigh started inadvertently holding her breath when opening emails from sources, because they might

---

* Ditto *The Washington Post*, which I have additional affection for because they clearly make an effort to cover Burma. And *The Irrawaddy*, the Burmese exile paper, does work that, in addition to filling a critical reporting void, is incredibly reliable.

say that she was out of luck, or an idiot, because the assertion she was asking them to confirm—which I'd pulled from non-fact-checked books or articles—was absurd. We each went through a period of extreme temporomandibular pain, at which point we realized we'd started clenching our teeth furiously. We took turns psyching each other up, holding up opposite sides of motivational conversation:

"Why are we doing this?"

"It's fine. We're doing a great job. People are going to give us trophies when they realize how thorough we've been."

"Yeah, because anyone will ever even notice that we did this, and they totally give trophies for fact-checking."

"You're doing a great job. It'll all be worth it when we get the trophies."

It *was* worth it, actually. I wrote, for example, a long and exciting description of some freaky shit a certain Burmese hill tribe did during a certain world war. I won't go into who the source was or the possible sourcing mistakes made, but the upshot is that if I hadn't omitted and you had repeated this story at a cocktail party, at worst a scholar of any of several disciplines would've recognized it as a complete load of crap. At the very least, you'd have been going around spreading freaky lies. And that's how Leigh and I comforted ourselves during the aforementioned marathon reviews, comparing three hundred pages of single-spaced notes from more than seven hundred paper and electronic and human sources while I made changes on more pages than not.

"I can't believe how much money and how much of our lives this has cost."

"You can't put a price on truth."

"You're right. We're heroes."

In one chapter, I riffed, based on what I'd read, on how the KMT used Dodge and Ford trucks—Dodge and Ford trucks!—and how that was further evidence of how ridiculous the United States's denial of assisting the Chinese rebels in Burma was. But you won't find that in the book, because a foreign-relations scholar pointed out to me that anyone could get mass-produced American vehicles anywhere, there were parades of them on the Ho Chi Minh Trail during Vietnam, did I think the United States was also assisting the Viet Cong? I constructed, and then had to thoroughly de- and recon-struct, a story about ancient Burmese race relations after reading a mountain of history books—books that apparently every archaeolo-gist and Southeast Asian history specialist (we consulted five) knows are based on long-discredited colonial theory riddled with "sheer fantasy" and "Orientalist cliché." I wrote an entire chapter based on a first-rate historical account of some stupid and misguided action on the part of the United States that oh, man, did I want to be true. One expert corroborated that it was. Three others said it wasn't, exactly. A declassified State Department memo settled the dispute in favor of the nays. It's cool; there was plenty of equally stupid and misguided action to take its place. See chapter six.

"No matter how hard we work, we're going to miss something. All this work and we'll still know that there are mistakes we didn't catch. It's so futile."

"No! Trophies!"

We terrorized the United States Department of Homeland Secu-rity, the World Health Organization, the United Nations Office on Drugs and Crime, the United Nations High Commissioner for Refu-gees, the history and epidemiology departments of several universi-ties, the authors of dozens of books, the staffs of countless NGOs, lawyers and doctors and soldiers and refugees and multinational cor-porations and activists. And so on. I'd be swimming in debt without the research support that was provided by the Investigative Fund at The Nation Institute and the Fund for Investigative Journalism. But no matter how much time and money went into reporting this story, and digging up obscure and untold details (see the stats comparing eastern Burma with Darfur, chapter twelve), and then making sure they were right—no matter how many months Leigh worked (ten, if you really want to know, so you can imagine how long it would take to fact-check a book in which half the narrative isn't recounted conversations about socialism and blow jobs*), she still could've misinterpreted information herself, and the information could still have flaws, and though the changes we made were hundreds, the mistakes we caught were certainly not every one, and never could be, even if we had unlimited resources and lived in the Library of Congress.

So. Herewith, the sourcing. This isn't every annotation. For most items, we had several sources and interviews beyond what's listed here that went into corroborating and quadruple-checking, and to keep this relatively clean I didn't include all of them here. The Smithsonian Department of Botany research botanist and curator Leigh contacted to confirm that coconut palms are indeed common in a certain area of Burma, for example, is not listed, nor a hundred other unsung experts. But often, I've provided sourcing even for important stuff that's pretty well documented, as a jumping-off point for anyone who wants to learn more. At this point, I'd feel pretty confident breaking any tidbit in this book out at a cocktail party full of Southeast Asia wonks. But now you can decide for yourself, and if a scholar or skeptic you're drinking with questions your source, you can say, you know, "Report E/CN.4/1995/65 of the United Nations Economic and Social Council, Commission on Human Rights." Or "Knowles' 1829 *Memoir of Mrs. Ann H. Judson, Late Missionary to Burmah; Including a History of the American Baptist Mission in the Burman Empire.* No, no, the second edition."

---

* FYI, those were fact-checked against only my own notes. As for interviews with the BA guys, though there was no reason to disbelieve anything they said, when possible we still checked the details of their stories against other survivors' interviews or published accounts. They always matched up.

I.

Burma spends .3 percent of GDP on health care: Watkins et al., p. 296.

Russia, Pakistan, North Korea have sold weapons to Burma: Russia: Amnesty International 2, pp. 62–70; Pakistan, North Korea: *Lintner.*

Gatherings of more than five people illegal: *Steinberg.*

Torture tactics awful and weird: Testimony of activist and torture victim Ko Aung, quoted in Rogers, pp. 123–124. "My skin was shredded by the pecks of those birds, and covered in blood . . ."

30 percent of Burmese children under five devastatingly malnourished: UNICEF, p. 123; *Hansford.*

10 percent of Burmese children die before age of five: UNICEF, p. 119.

350,000 soldiers actively deployed in Burma army: Selth 2, pp. 11–12. Although this is the best estimate going, it is, Selth acknowledges, rough (interview).

100-pound porter loads: Escaped porters interviewed on tape, video, and paper by Htoo Moo; other human rights documenters regularly estimate the weight of the carry as up to at least fifty kilograms.

Rape of little girls/gang style/involving mutilation/preceding murder: Shan Human Rights Foundation and Shan Women's Action Network (SWAN). In this one survey of sexual violence by Burmese troops, 61 percent of incidences were gang rapes, 25 percent ended in murder, one of the victims was five. Additionally: "In many of the incidents documented, the women were not only raped, but were also physically tortured in other ways, including being beaten, suffocated by having plastic put over their head, and having their breasts cut off." Story of rape victim being shot through her vagina recounted in Rogers, p. 26.

More torture tactics used on Karen: Rogers, pp. 242 and 207; Thornton, p. 66.

China is Burma's ally: See chapter 12.

Sino-Tibetan sounds: *Watkins.* Karen dialects—there are about twenty—fall under the Tibeto-Burman grouping, a subset of Sino-Tibetan languages.

"peacefully, quietly, unobtrusively": Quoted in Tucker, p. 14.

Average annual Thai income: UNICEF, p. 120.

Wet season/dry season weather patterns: US Army Air Forces Tactical Center, Arctic, Desert and Tropic Information Center.

Death by Thai motorbike: Thailand Public Health Ministry statistics, *Chiang Mai Mail.*

Thailand not signatory to 1951 UN refugee convention: UNHCR 8.

Thailand formally accepted assistance from UNHCR: Lang 1, p. 8.

UNHCR has no right to grant refugee status: *McKinsey.*

157,000 refugees in nine camps: Registered plus unregistered, as of July 2009. *Thompson.*

Bangkok classifies refugees as "displaced persons"/illegal immigrants: Lang 1, p. 3.

"running away from soldiers": ZOA Refugee Care Thailand 1, pp. 15, 50.

UNHCR–registered refugees deported: Human Rights Watch 3, part III: Expulsion to Burma.

Prison for bamboo-collecting refugees: US Committee for Refugees and Immigrants 1, p. 86.

II.

Background on the Pyu: *Moore; Lieberman.*

The Pyu's legendary devotion to love and Buddhism: Thant Myint-U, p. 52.

Mranma = Bama = Burman: Lintner 4.

For a brief but excellent slice of old-school ethnopolitical life and strife in Burma, see Lieberman.

Some people who think the Karen got there first: Dun, p. 2; Harvey, p. 3.

The Karen came from the north: Barron et al. speculate that the Karen migrated south from Tibet and Yunnan, p. 29. Lieberman concedes that though it's impossible to know for sure, "linguistic and racial data are at least consistent with a north to south movement of considerable antiquity" (interview).

"on almost inaccessible heights": Mouhot quoted in Falla, p. 18.

Translations of the Karen lunar calendar: *Moffatt*.

"The houses of these strange people": Snodgrass, p. 141.

Shit-poultices can be more problematic than you might think. Thornton, p. 90, describes the calf-size, festering hole in the thigh of a man whose traditional healer applied plants, poop, or both to what started out as a pimple.

Disparaging Burmans: Lieberman, p. 469, and interview.

Magnificence of sixteenth-century Burma and all the goods you could buy ("notwithstanding the constant wars"): Scott 1, pp. 16–17.

20th-century writer quoted on the reports of those who've witnessed it: Clifford, pp. 84–85.

For a dramatic account of the wicked series of wars for Burma's dominance, start reading Thant Myint-U on p. 63.

Alaungpaya made a huge pile of Mon heads and sent it to them: It was on a raft. He "sent it up with the flood tide; the watchers on the city walls saw it float by and read their own doom, while the vultures rose and fell." Harvey, p. 232.

Mon and Burmans enslaved the Karen: *Lieberman*.

Alaungpaya destroyed their villages: Pascal Khoo Thwe, p. 35.

"These people appeared heartily glad to see us": Snodgrass, pp. 141–142.

Description, costs of the first Anglo-Burman fight: Thant Myint-U, pp. 113–125.

British looking for another fight: Former vice-chancellor of the University of Rangoon and chairman of the Burma Historical Commission Maung Htin Aung writes that even the British recognized that "the War of 1852 was an act of unprovoked aggression" in Trager, p. viii; the details of how the excuse was that Rangoon had fined some ships over some customs something-rather, though Rangoon immediately rescinded the fine, can be found in Thant Myint-U, p. 133.

Burmans go on Karen-killing rampage post-Shwedagon capture: Harry Ignatius Marshall, p. 306; Luther, pp. 86–91.

Warring revolutionaries and loyalists: Thant Myint-U, p. 134.

King Thibaw's paramount titles: Scott 1, p. 5.

King Thibaw's bloody ascension: Andrew Marshall, p. 41; Thant Myint-U, p. 158.

English newspapers touting royal massacre drama: Pascal Khoo Thwe, p. 13.

Kengtung's tigers(!) headlines: Andrew Marshall, p. 187.

The ill-fated affair of Pierre and Mattie Calogreedy, and aftermath: Thant Myint-U, beginning p. 10.

III.

Martus human rights violation database: See last note of chapter 9.

Frontline interviewee served seven years in prison: "Burma: State of Fear."

BBC interviewee gets 25 years: Burmese Women's Union.

Burma's rank in Press Freedom Index: Reporters Without Borders.

Third most journalists in jail: Committee to Protect Journalists 2.

The exile newspaper with the misquoted Napoleon tagline is the *New Era Journal*.

International guidelines recommend six feet square (3.5 square meters) of hut floor per refugee: TBBC 10.

IV.

Iraq War of the 1800s: Thant Myint-U, pp. 22–23.

British having a hell of a time with/being brutal during the Burmese occupation: Thant Myint-U, pp. 28–29.

"wiped out the village and shot everyone we saw": Quoted in Andrew Marshall, p. 175.

Any literate Karen would be shot: Falla, p. 142.

Karen were a fifth of the Burma Rifles: Harry Ignatius Marshall, p. 314.

Minorities are majority of Burma army: Thant Myint-U, p. 195.

"oppress them or suffer them in any way to be oppressed": Quoted in Tucker, p. 38.

Quarter of a million incoming Indians: Tucker, p. 31.

Immigration riots, British smackdown: Thant Myint-U, pp. 210–216.

Burma Independence Army wreaking havoc on Karen civilians, eventually demobbed by Japanese: Thant Myint-U, pp. 230–231.

Mighty fighting Kachins wreaking havoc on the Japanese: Webster, pp. 49–52.

Karen WWII heroics and loyalties: Morrison.

"Karen are no fair-weather friends": Quoted in Falla, p. 24.

Japanese pressing Burmese into forced labor: *Seekins*.

British swore Karen independence as their eventual reward: There are many accounts of this, but you can read the corroboration of both one former Karen Allied fighter and one British soldier in Rogers, p. 80; see also Tucker, p. 121.

"staunchest and bravest defenders of British rule": Smeaton, p. 1.

Karen killed 12,500 Japanese at the end of the war there: Morrison, p. 164; *Seekins*.

Japan's casualties in Burma: Allen, p. 640.

Casualties in Hiroshima: Radiation Effects Research Foundation.

Karen delegation to England took a soap-factory tour: Lintner 2, p. 69.

Karen got some money: Morrison, p. 169.

"All loyalties have been discarded": *Hansard* 1.

Aung San's independence agreement was quick/not about minorities' independence: Atlee-Aung San Agreement, quoted in Tucker, p. 120–121.

Aung San preached "autonomous states": Tucker, pp. 151–152.

Aung San signed agreement with minorities: Panglong Agreement of 1947. You can read the whole thing at burmalibrary.org if you Google it. It's pretty short.

Biography, strategy of Ba U Gyi: Keenan.

Karen held their own conference: Martin Smith, p. 83; Lintner 2, p. 70.

KNU boycotted elections: Martin Smith, p. 82.

Aung San's assassination: Thant Myint-U, p. 254.

Misty-eyed British wives: This scene is painted in fantastic detail in Thant Myint-U, p. 257.

New prime minister opposed to autonomous ethnic states: Tucker, p. 152.

Post-independence revolt/meddling British weapons-smugglers: Thant Myint-U, pp. 259–262.

Karen and Burmans started killing each other: Martin Smith, pp. 111-112.

Karen police stopped keeping and started disturbing the peace: Tucker, p. 164; Martin Smith, p. 112.

Christmas and civilian killing of Karen: For varying accounts of these battles, see Martin Smith, p. 117; Tucker, p. 164; Falla, p. 26.

KNU stormed the treasury/Ne Win burned down a school: Martin Smith, p. 117.

Karen settlements attacked with machine guns and mortars: Martin Smith, p. 118.

Siege of Insein: Martin Smith, pp. 117–118, 138–140.

Hundreds killed in first 112 days of fighting: Martin Smith, p. 140, citing an estimate from the *Times* (London) from May 23, 1949.

Could still go to Rangoon movies: Aung Zaw 1.

And shoot at Karen fighters: Thant Myint-U, p. 263.

"Ba U Gyi was no terrorist": Martin Smith, p. 144.

For a pretty accessible breakdown of material support/immigration laws, see UNHCR 6.

For an excellent report on the absurd inclusions and insidious results of the material-support laws—including the fate of the two conspiring Albany Iraqis—see Umansky.

No exceptions from material-support made for those under duress: UNHCR 6, p. 2. "Litigation is pending as to whether the statute contemplates a *de minimis* amount of support for it to be considered 'material' support and whether the statute includes an implied duress exception for those who are forced to provide assistance under threat of harm to themselves or others.

DHS and DOJ take the position that there is no *de minimis* amount of support and that there is no duress exception."

The sad story of the Sri Lankan fisherman: Umansky.

"clear and convincing evidence": *Real ID Act of 2005.*

Laws criminalizing material support: Umansky.

V.

Leo Nichols gets a fax machine/gets sentenced/gets tortured/dies: Amnesty International 1; Moe Aye.

Crazy computer restrictions: *1996 Computer Science Development Law.*

Internet cafés raided like meth labs: Yeni 1.

Café workers also required to capture screenshots, info from customers: Min Lwin 2.

Burma worst place in the world to blog: Committee to Protect Journalists 3.

Blogger sentenced to 20 years in prison: 28-year-old Nay Phone Latt. See Saw Yan Naing 3, or just Google him.

Humanitarian geeks in India and Germany: Crispin and *Blum*, respectively.

VI.

Eisenhower's speech was given to the American Society of Newspaper Editors on April 16, 1953.

Bad-news Burma bandits, etc.: Thant Myint-U, p. 269.

"Communist control of Burma"/"British and American officials generally agree": Quoted in McMahon, pp. 53–54.

KMT loses in China/recruits Shans in Burma: Thant Myint-U, pp. 273–274.

CIA's first secret war: Lintner 1.

United States supporting 15,000 KMT soldiers/trying to aid Korea effort/scare Burma/even *The NYT* knows it: Kahin and Kahin, pp. 10–11. For way more information on the KMT intervention, see Taylor.

"racial and geographic units": From the papers of former secretary of state John Foster Dulles, quoted in Kahin and Kahin, p. 10.

White NYC and DC (or French Foreign Legion?) guys killed: Lintner 2, p. 113.

US ambassador to Rangoon was lied to, resigned: Kahin and Kahin, p. 10.

US admitted role in KMT invasion a decade later: Thant Myint-U, p. 301; US Department of State 2.

US military aid to Burma: McMahon, Appendix 3; US Department of State 1, p. 106.

Thai aid to KMT: Linter 2, p. 115.

Ba U Gyi "lackey of imperialism": Martin Smith, p. 149.

Burma army takes over businesses/takes over as caretaker government, takes on the KMT with the help of the PLA: Thant Myint-U, pp. 276/284–288, respectively.

KMT sold guns to other insurgents: Kahin and Kahin, p. 11.

The KMT's role in opium trafficking has been widely reported. McCoy is one extensive source, pp. 162–178, as well as chapters 7 and 8.

New Shan army: Thant Myint-U, p. 287.

New Kachin army: Thant Myint-U, p. 288.

Karen had been pushed back to the hills: Thant Myint-U, p. 276.

Ba U Gyi gunned down: Keenan, p. 19; Lintner 2, p. 276.

Ne Win:
> workin' at the post office: Lintner 2, p. 36; Thant Myint-U, p. 294.

> childhood dreams, losing the election, staging a coup, starting to ruin everything for everybody except golf buddy LBJ: Thant Myint-U, pp. 281–302.

VII.

Insein biggest prison/built by British: AAPP (Burma) 4.

Burma has 44 prisons: *Bo Kyi.*

For a thorough, if maybe not superbly rendered, Westerner's account of do-ing time in a Burmese prison, see Mawdsley.

Red Cross started visiting Burmese prisons in 1999: ICRC.

Prison authorities bugged a UN interview: *The Irrawaddy* 4.

Red Cross basically kicked out of Burma after 2005: ICRC.

There's more accounting of porters' wounds in Pascal Khoo Thwe, pp. 237–238.

Burma army officers studied British warfare abroad: Aung Zaw 1.

KNU claimed tens of millions in revenue: Martin Smith, p. 283.

Tatmadaw fights through the rainy season: Martin Smith, p. 395, has a de-tailed account of the end of dry-season-only offensives, which started in '84.

10,000 Burmese refugees in Thailand by 1984: CCSDPT 1.

80,000 by 1994: UNHCR 2.

KNU used villagers as porters: Burma Issues 2, p. 19.

KNU leaders saving all the chocolate and cigarettes for themselves: Rogers, p. 145.

DKBA's being buddies with the junta: Thornton, p. 198, recounts that Karen villagers have collected radio transcripts in which the Burma army orders the DKBA to attack the KNLA. See also US House Committee on International Relations.

Karen soldiers' defection to DKBA: Tucker, pp. 231-232; *Fong; Pedersen.*

7,000 refugees at Huay Kaloke in 1997: Karen Refugee Committee 1.

For an account of the second burning of Huay Kaloke more official than— and still in line with—Htan Dah's, see KHRG 1.

"We accept that we were inactive": National Security Council Secretary-General Boonsak Kamheangridirong, quoted in *The Nation* 2.

For one collection of official testimonies on Thailand's forcibly repatriating Burmese refugees, see US House Committee on International Relations in sources. Also Lang 1; Burma Issues 1; *Thompson*.

Thailand signatory to Convention on the Rights of the Child: UNHCHR.

UN, EU, US not happy about repatriation: *Thompson*.

Thailand's commander in chief says refugees want to be thrown out: Burma Issues 1; *Thompson*.

"violations appear to be committed consistently": United Nations 3.

Karen refugees not victims of warfare: Nanuam and Srat-tha.

UNHCR says more than 105,000 Burmese refugees in Thailand in 1997/it's helping 2,100 of them: UNHCR 1, p. 57 (pdf page).

Thai authorities forbidding refugees from cutting bamboo/NGO got refugees shack-building materials: TBBC 10.

Other camps that have burned down: *Thompson*.

Population of Umpiem Mai eventually 20,000: Karen Refugee Committee 2.

Potters for Peace info/Burmese Youth Project: *Bradner/Bradner*.

4,000 kids killed by unsanitary water per day: Prüss-Üstün et al.

Adoniram Judson in first overseas-American-missionary crew: Global Ministries; Judson College.

Judson's first baptism: Judson, p. 132.

The conveniently Christian-y Karen lore: Rogers, pp. 41–43. Though you can also get this same story plenty of other places, including from a Christian Karen.

My particular favorite historian with a doctorate in Oriental studies: *Lieberman*.

Hottest missionary spot on the globe: Catholics and Seventh Day Adventists, for example, also got in on the action. See Jackson and Land, respectively.

"*This field belongs appropriately to the American Baptist churches*": Knowles, p. 317.

"a very marked decline in the cult of the Karen": Ireland, p. 64.

The missionaries' good works: Harry Ignatius Marshall, pp. 300, 309.

Widely published American missionary tracts: Wayland, Judson, Knowles (in sources) are just a few of the volumes. Ann Judson's memoir was in its tenth edition within ten years of its original printing; Trager, p. 114, also discusses their popularity.

"almost to a man dishonest": Wayland, p. 150.

"the tigers do not seem so ferocious"/"go down to the tomb without God and without hope": Quoted in Trager, p. x.

"the best . . . means of eventually introducing the humanizing influences of the Christian religion": Quoted in Trager, p. ix.

Tucker, p. 32, talks about the devastation of undermining the crucial Buddhist Burmese social fabric; Trager, p. 145, too, remarks on the prevalence of boozing, gambling, and opium-doing thirty years into British rule.

Christian Karen being crucified: Rogers, p. 54.

74 churches attended by nearly 8,000 Burmese Christians by Judson's death: World Council of Churches.

Estimates of how Christian the Karen population in Burma is: Falla, p. 46 (20 percent); Barron et al., p. 28 (30 percent); Rogers, p. 32 (40 percent); South, p. 37 (citing the Burma Ethnic Research Group, 25 to 30 percent).

60 percent of Karen in Thai refugee camps Christian: ZOA Refugee Care Thailand 1, p. 46. This survey strikes me as having particularly thorough sampling. Another estimate, from the International Rescue Committee, p. 2, puts the percentage at a nearby 52.

Missionary speculation that the Karen must have met the Nestorians: Smeaton, p. 189.

Or maybe a really early Italian missionary made it to the Karen: Smeaton, p. 188.

British guy mistaken for the messiah: Don Richardson, pp. 65–67.

Muslim guy probably not the messiah: Don Richardson, p. 68.

Burma spends about 1 percent of GDP on education: Watkins et al. p. 267. Some estimates put the number at more like .3 percent.

Burmese government reports adult literacy at more than 90 percent: UNESCO Institute for Statistics.

Burmese government reports 20 percent adult literacy in LDC app: United Nations 2, pp. 18–19; *Cortez*.

Only half of Burmese children enrolled in secondary school: UNICEF, p. 135.

Way more than in Afghanistan: Just 28 percent of Afghan boys/9 percent of girls are enrolled in secondary school. UNICEF, p. 134.

Pascal Khoo Thwe weirded out: Pascal Khoo Thwe, p. 276.

Educational journals shut down: *The Irrawaddy* 5.

There's a thorough discussion of corruption and graft in the teaching system in Fink. Expensive after-hours tutoring is on p. 178.

Unless otherwise noted, the details about the refugee camp education system are from ZOA Refugee Care Thailand 1 and van der Stouwe and Oh, both available online.

60 schools and 1,000 classrooms: ZOA Refugee Care Thailand 2.

Library program: Shanti Volunteer Association, p. 3.

Mine-issues program: Handicap International.

Also involved in camp education are Catholic Office for Emergency Relief and Refugees, the International Rescue Committee, Jesuit Refugee Service, Women's Education for Advancement and Empowerment, and the Taipei Overseas Peace Service. CCSDPT 2.

40,000 students: ZOA Refugee Care Thailand 2.

Bigger than at least 98 percent of United States school districts: US Department of Education.

Highest proportion of temporary classrooms: UNHCR 3, p. 5.

$7 million education budget: CCSDPT 3, p. 18.

12 percent comes from the US: CCSDPT 3, p. 20.

USAID money: *Solomon*.

Budget shortfalls: CCSDPT 3, p. 20.

Australian-university courses, graduates: *Solomon*.

Some graduates trained to be teachers: World Education.

Camp schools offer FSP, LMC, EIP: *Solomon*.

VIII.

Thant Myint-U has colorful descriptions of the Burma-Siam fights, pp. 70–99.

Pascal Khoo Thwe overheard Burmese military officials at an embassy griping that Thais were whining about one of their villages being burned down, p. 266.

"Thai and Burmese troops have clashed twice": *The Nation* 4.

"Four Thai rangers": Bachoe.

A good rundown of KNU history and structure, including communist rifts, can be found at the Transnational and Non-State Armed Groups database online.

Seventh Day Adventist (Bo Mya) presiding over Old Testament-strict KNU: Rogers, p. 105.

You can see a picture of someone modeling the anti-communist Karen Freedom Fighter shirt in Falla, p. 104.

Scary Shan/Chinese/commie alliances . . . Thailand started selling KNU arms and letting them hang out on Thai soil: Thant Myint-U, pp. 298–299. Anyone who's ever been on the ground there could confirm the KNU–Thailand friendship just as well.

Thailand and Burma become trading partners in 1990: McCoy, p. 423; Lintner 3.

KNU colonel arrested, charged, released by Thais: Min Lwin 8.

Thais giving KNU leftover US military-operation ammo: *The Nation* 3.

Frenchman says Karen and Siamese are happy together/King Chulalongkorn grants citizenship, writes poetry about tranquility: Falla, pp. 187–188.

Writes poetry about stinkiness: Falla, p. 37.

IX.

Zero percent of refugees in camp have no religion: ZOA Refugee Care Thailand 1, p. 46. Pascal Khoo Thwe posits, p. 65, that nothing could eradicate the Burmese's extreme spirituality—at least not while their physical lives are so poor.

Thailand Burma Border Consortium history, budget, rations: TBBC 8 and 10; *Thompson.*

Increased rations for pregnant women/severely malnourished children: TBBC 10.

For an account of being a drunk infant, rather than an account of white girls freaking out about one, see Pascal Khoo Thwe, p. 21.

UN definition of *IDP*: UNOCHA, Introduction #2.

Burma one of world's worst displacement situations four years running: IDMC 1–4. It has also appeared on the list of places in which an IDP is least likely to receive support from the government (IDMC 5).

Well more than half a million IDPs in eastern Burma alone: 451,000 just in rural areas there. TBBC 9.

More than twice as many IDPs as in Afghanistan: IDMC 7.

Advocacy-group definition of *IDP*: Nanda Kyaw Thu, p. 4.

The story of the great Japanese-stalking tiger: Webster, pp. 48–49, as told to him by Japanese private Atsumi Oda.

Killer tree: Natives' anecdotes; *Hendricks.* Beware the *Antiaris toxicaria.*

How to survive in the jungle: US Army Air Forces Office of Flying Safety, Safety Education Division.

Pascal Khoo Thwe describes helpful jungle-rice-cooking tips on pp. 216–217.

"in stark contrast to the complete rejection of mine use": International Campaign to Ban Landmines.

Land mines cause 1 in 25 deaths in eastern Burma: *Mullany*, with caveats; this is a good example of one of those facts that tests the meaning of "fact": "The stat . . . may or may not be 'true.' Clearly it depends on where in eastern Burma, when, and in what time period. . . . [W]e report that overall, 4% of deaths were due to landmines, which is equivalent to 1 in 25—Now, I don't have the raw data at my fingertips, but I believe the uncertainty around that estimate must range from 1 in 15 deaths to about 1 in 44 deaths. . . ."

Many of Burma's IDP kids suffer from acute malnutrition: 9.5 percent. UK Department for International Development, p. 19.

IDP children in eastern Burma have one-in-five chance of dying before age five: Back Pack Health Worker Team, p. 32.

Details about the Back Pack Health Worker Team: *Wells*.

Nobody knows how many Karen there are: Barron et al. cite the lack of info on p. 28.

Burma hasn't had a census in decades: *Lintner*; Martin Smith, p. 30.

More than 150,000 refugees in Thailand by 2006: TBBC 1.

Nearly 100,000 Burmese refugees outside Thailand: UNHCR 9.

For descriptions from visitors to Karen State before the fall of Manerplaw, see Mirante (around p. 88) and Falla.

For an account of the fall of Manerplaw, see Rogers, p. 143.

FBR's Dave (Eubank) very rarely gives interviews, but there's an extensive one in Rogers, starting on p. 181. The quotes from Dave and his wife, as well as some of the information about them and FBR, come from there. Other details: *Eubank*; *Fitzgerald*. Data and stats about the FBR teams are available on FBR's website. You can watch their training exercises, along with the footage described, on their YouTube channel.

Galatians quote is from 6:9.

Find the State Department's Country Reports on Human Rights Practices at state.gov/g/drl/rls/hrrpt/.

State Department–report rejection: Permanent Mission of the Union of Myanmar to the United Nations Office and Other International Organizations, Geneva.

Martus is open-source software supported by a nonprofit tech organization, Benetech, in Palo Alto, California. In the BA database, the guys document their names, organization, and region and as much information about the perpetrators as is available—Burma army unit, soldier rank, name. That's followed by a narrative of the testimony they collected:

> In late April 2004, a woman who lived in the suburban area of Murng-Su town was gang-raped and stabbed to death in the neck with a knife by a group of SPDC troops, in a forest near her cucumber garden just outside the town.

> On 25 April 2004, Naang Zum, aged 18, was watering her cucumber garden when a group of about 15 SPDC troops came and forcibly took her into a nearby forest. . . .

X.

You can read *Cruel and Vicious Repression of Myanmar Peoples by Imperialists and Fascists and the True Story about the Plunder of the Royal Jewels* at the Library of Congress. If you're so inclined.

No TV until 1980: Newcomb, p. 2147.

Burma becomes a net rice importer: Pascal Khoo Thwe, pp. 56–57.

"Burma is a country that has never known, and can never know, famine": Scott 1, p. 145.

The displayed royal jewels are rumored to be fake: Andrew Marshall, pp. 70–71.

You can read about Ne Win's demonetization in Lintner 2, pp. 273–274, and Pascal Khoo Thwe, pp. 134-135.

Cities guarded by the gates of the zodiac: Thant Myint-U, p. 45.

"Tuesday and Saturday are bad days to do anything": Scott 1, p. 127.

Up to 80 percent of the country's currency became useless: Lintner 2, p. 273.

There are dozens of published accounts of the tea-shop fight and ensuing riots. A good one can be found in Lintner 2, pp. 274–275. Pascal Khoo Thwe, who was there, talks about the 1988 protests on pp. 155–164.

Burmese students protested Rangoon University Act: Aye Kyaw, p. 86; Tucker, p. 219.

Ne Win's resignation speech: Thant Myint-U, p. 32.

He'd previously banned all opposition parties: Martin Smith, p. 204.

8.8.88: Thant Myint-U dramatically reenacts the scene starting on p. 33. Find a detailed account also in Martin Smith, beginning on p. 4.

"It is hard to describe the thrill": Pascal Khoo Thwe, p. 160.

JWI–hiring company superclose to junta: R. Jeffrey Smith; McAllister; Barnes; Eaves.

Speculation that the PR firms were involved in the name change: *The Washington Post*; Tan.

For a longer list of preapproved party insignia, as well as the other very specific details of the 1990 elections, see Martin Smith, p. 412.

"Don't gamble with the Burmans": US Army Air Forces Tactical Center Arctic, Desert and Tropic Information Center. More good advice: Don't "argue with Hindus about caste" or go fishing in Buddhist temple pools, and know that if you stare at a Muslim woman, "her male relatives may kill you both."

Censorship of publications and porn: *1962 Printers and Publishers Registration Law*; OpenNet Initiative 1, p. 5.; Article 19, pp. 29–33; Freedom House.

BBC and Voice of America broadcasts jammed: In 1995. *Connors*; Article 19, p. 32 (pdf page).

One of the occasions when CNN was blacked out came during the 2008 anti-government protests in neighboring Thailand. See Saw Yan Naing 1.

Universities shut down all the time, for long periods at a time: *Steinberg*.

Students spread out away from main campuses: Min Khet Maung.

200,000 Tatmadaw soldiers in '88: Selth 2, p. 11.

400,000 in '96: Arnott 1, p. 3.

You can read about Pascal Khoo Thwe's personal post-demonstration flight into the jungle beginning on p. 189, some firefights with the Burma army starting on pp. 226 and 237, and the regime's creepy radio entreaties and leaflet-dropping on pp. 189 and 209, respectively.

Thant Myint-U was with the student rebels while they were hoping for US/Western reinforcements, pp. vii and 39.

Pascal Khoo Thwe was at the failed conference of the student/ethnic rebel coalition, pp. 208–209.

The '88 melee barely covered in the United States: *The New York Times, Los Angeles Times*, and Associated Press did run the story, but in no way commensurate with its significance, nothing even remotely comparable to, for example, 2009's protests in Iran. A quick search in ProQuest turns up five times as many article hits for the latter.

"jealousy against establishment of a peaceful and prosperous socialist state": Mirante, p. 309.

XI.

American journalist drugged, stripped, and covered in shit: Jenkins.

Rangoon spy facility: *Sydney Morning Herald*; Chenard; *Bangkok Post* 5; *The Irrawaddy* 2.

Thai army general speculating on Burma's intelligence spending/Thais concerned Burmese spies getting migrant IDs: *Bangkok Phuchatkan*.

Thais recommended making civilians spies that spy on Burmese spies: *The Nation* 4.

Ten armed Burmese nationals in Thailand admitted they were sent by Burma: Min Lwin 4.

Burmese spies in Thailand spy on both Thais and defected Burmese: *Bangkok Post* 7.

"There are Burmese government agents everywhere": Andrews 2.

Tatmadaw intelligence report on KNU, NGOs: Min Lwin 7.

BBC reporter stalked by unsavvy spy: McGeown.

Friendship Bridge's opening ceremony: *The Irrawaddy* 1.

Map of the Asian Highway: United Nations 10.

Royal Thai Government paid for the bridge: *The Nation* 1.

Cost 80 million baht: *The Nation* 1; *Bangkok Post* 6.

Years of delays: *The Nation* 1; *Bangkok Post* 4.

Thailand earning $28 million a month from Myawaddy-Mae Sot trade: According to the Tak Chamber of Commerce, reported in Lawi Weng 4.

1,400 feet of concrete: *The Nation* 1; *The Irrawaddy* 1; Lintner 3.

Burmese movies forbidden from depicting poverty: Kyi Wai 3.

The battle for Myawaddy: *Bangkok Post* 1; Falla, p. 28; Martin Smith, p. 270.

Blown-up oil depot and freaked-out cows: *Bangkok Post* 2.

Pascal Khoo Thwe compares modern Burma to Nazi Germany on p. 187.

Foreigners not allowed to continue past Myawaddy: *Thompson*.

Reproduction of Shwedagon Pagoda in the new capital: *The Irrawaddy* 8; Andrews 1.

Civil servants given days to pack up: BBC News 3; McGirk; Sipress; Pedrosa.

Information minister said in BBC that the junta needed a more strategic location: BBC News 3.

Information minister told Al Jazeera that the junta needed more space and more pastoral scenery: Pedrosa.

In 2002, Aung San Suu Kyi told the BBC, "We have not yet come to the point where we encourage people to come to Burma as tourists": BBC News 1.

Mandalay moat refurbished with slave labor: Burma Campaign UK 4.

Rough Guides is one guidebook without a Burma volume. Said the FAQs on its website, "Rough Guides don't publish a guide for Burma because the democratically elected leader, who is currently held under house arrest, has called for a tourism boycott."

Tourism isn't on the CIA's World Factbook list of Burma's industries.

Burma vs. Thailand:
    12 times the infant mortality rate: UNICEF, pp. 119–120.

    15 times the child mortality rate: UNICEF, pp. 119–120.

    Second-highest child mortality rate in Asia: UNICEF, p. 117.

    Life expectancy nearly a decade lower: UNICEF, pp. 119–120.

    GNI 1/15 of Thailand's: UNICEF, pp. 119–120.

    Spends 40¢, rather than $63, per capita on health care: *Nelwan*.

    Provides 0 percent of child vaccinations rather than 100: *Hansford*.

Burma vs. the world:
    One of only five countries forbidding Boy Scouts: *Amalvy*. (The other four are China, North Korea, Laos, and Cuba.)

    Poorest country on the continent: UNICEF, pp. 142–145.

    One of seven poorest in the world: UNICEF, pp. 142–145.

The exact amount of Burma's weapons expenditures is hard to know. One prominent expert estimated that the country had bought $2 billion worth from just China as of more than a decade ago.

On Doctors Without Borders's shit list: DWB.

Has more child soldiers than any other country: *Becker.*

One of eight worst violators of religious freedom: US Commission on International Religious Freedom.

One of ten worst human rights violators: US Department of State 8, Introduction.

Tied with Iraq for second place in corruption: Transparency International.

Home to fourth-worst dictator: Wallechinsky.

KNU "world's most pleasant and civilised guerrilla group": Falla, p. 107.

Activists' lawyers and families imprisoned: Saw Yan Naing 4; Wai Moe 3 and Min Lwin 9 (respectively).

2 million Burmese migrant workers in Thailand, three quarters of them illegal: TBBC 2.

Particularly vulnerable to abuse are the women migrants, not just from their employers and authorities but from other migrants and street gangs, who say things like "Burmese women are illegal migrants and we can't be arrested if we rape them": Lawi Weng 1.

Lots of women and children from Burma are sex slaves in Thailand: More info can be found at Development and Education Programme for Daughters and Communities' website: depdc.org. The book about them I decidedly didn't enjoy reading was Human Rights Watch 1.

XII.

Susan Rice's comment about Burma comes from her January 2009 confirmation hearing, quoted in Jha 1.

For a picture of Laura Bush at Mae La, see Wiseman. For a jubilant press release about the mosquito-net donation, see United Nations Foundation.

Clinton barred new US investment in Burma in 1997: Code of Federal Regulations.

Freedom and Democracy Act: *Burmese Freedom and Democracy Act of 2003*.

"outpost of tyranny": Rice; BBC News 2.

G.W. Bush called Burma out: In 2006, 2007, and 2008. Text available at gpoaccess.gov.

Block Burmese Jade Act: *Tom Lantos Block Burmese JADE (Junta's Anti-Democratic Efforts) Act of 2008*.

The White House representative and policy coordinator for Burma nominee was Michael Jonathan Green. *Daily Digest*.

Refugees testifying to Congress: Jha 4.

Experts testifying to Congress: Jha 3.

Australian sanctions: Stephen Smith.

EU sanctions/arms embargo: Burma Campaign UK 3.

The Jennifer Aniston/Woody Harrelson video was just one of a slew of celebrity-packed videos released in the US Campaign for Burma's "30 Days for a Million Voices/Burma: It Can't Wait" series. Some of them are funny, and some of them are randomly inappropriate (I'm talking about you, Sarah Silverman). Find spots starring everyone from Judd Apatow to Tila Tequila to Sheryl Crow at the US Campaign for Burma's YouTube channel.

For the Lady, an album dedicated to Aung San Suu Kyi, was released by Rhino in 2004. U2 was involved. Obviously.

Open celebrity letter was released by Not On Our Watch.

Htoo Moo told me about his participation in the malaria epidemiology studies, and Dr. François Nosten confirmed all the details. The latter also did a lot of lamenting about those mosquito nets Laura Bush brought.

Alan Hoffman was a lobbyist for Unocal: OpenSecrets.org 1.

Alan Hoffman was Joe Biden's chief of staff: Columbia Books Inc. data.

Chevron gets sweet tax concessions and should "consider voluntary divestment over time": *Tom Lantos Block Burmese JADE (Junta's Anti-Democratic Efforts) Act of 2008*. The EU is also still into Burma's oil and gas: For an interview in which the CEO of French Big Oil company Total says that critics of his company's involvement there "can go to hell," see McNicoll.

Foreign countries pulled out Burma aid post–'88 uprisings/regime ushered in new era of allowing foreign investment: Thant Myint-U, pp. 328–330.

Remember, from chapter 8, that the Thais started making trade deals with Burma in 1990—pretty soon after all that 1988 dissent-squashing.

Sanctions advocates: Most people. The governments of the US and Australia and Europe, for example, as well as the main Burma-advocacy groups of the US and the UK, the US Campaign for Burma and Burma Campaign UK. Sanctions-haters: For two other writers' takes, check out Kristof and Pedersen.

China's building a pipeline for overland Burma energy transport: CNPC.

80 percent of China's imported crude goes through Strait of Malacca: Energy Information Administration 1; Energy Information Administration 2; Shwe Gas Movement.

Thailand has rights to 1.7 trillion cubic feet of gas in one concession: PTTEP.

Indian firm gets 5 trillion cubic feet of gas: ONGC Videsh.

Russia has several firms drilling: Burma Campaign UK 2.

France, Thailand, and Chevron operate a wildly profitable pipeline: Earth-Rights International 4, p. 77.

Daewoo plans to make more than $10 billion over 25 years in Shwe gas fields: Kim.

US firm Transocean did exploratory drilling for Daewoo: *Cantwell.*

ASEAN's free-trade agreement with India: ASEAN.

India has agreed to invest billions in two hydroelectric dams: Burma Rivers Network 1.

EU discussing ASEAN free-trade agreement/UK doesn't want it to benefit Burma: *Hansard* 2.

England has oil and gas dealings in Burma, too: Burma Campaign UK 2.

165 percent increase in China's mining/oil and gas/hydro investment: EarthRights International 2, p. 1.

Burma-China trade up to $2.6 billion: UN Comtrade Database.

Burma's estimated $2.5 billion trade surplus/$5 billion in currency reserves: *Turnell.*

Burma says greedy-ass Americans would buy elephants on credit if they could: *The Irrawaddy* 6.

Reagan administration spent millions for Agent Orange chemical and spraying planes: US Department of State 3.

Shans complained about deadly poison, not wild about farming for food post-spraying: Mirante, pp. 222 and 225, respectively.

Chemical was under EPA review at the time: Environmental Protection Agency.

Wrobleski went on to work for JWI as lobbyist, then prez: OpenSecrets.org 2.

Burma wins world's-top-opium-producer title/usurped by Afghanistan in 1999, 2003: UNODC 3, p. 34.

Tens of thousands of Burmese textile workers out of jobs/State Department says they're taking up sex work instead: Daley.

Burmese timber coming into US via China: Global Witness.

Burmese gems coming into US via Thailand/$8 billion in jewelry exports from there: US Government Accountability Office/p. 11.

More foreign companies invested in Burma's energy sector in 2008 than ever: Boot 3; Burma Campaign UK 2.

Foreign investment doubled in first nine months of 2008/2007 Foreign investment in oil and gas more than triple that of 2006: Burma Ministry of National Planning and Development surveys cited in Associated Press 3 and 1, respectively.

Chevron said that if it leaves, someone worse will just take its place: (Then-Vice Chairman Peter Robertson: "I know for a fact that they are better off by us being there than by anybody else being there.") Boot 1.

Dam projects causing all sorts of personal and planetary destruction: Burma Rivers Network 2.

Organisation for Economic Co-operation and Development complaint against Daewoo: EarthRights International 3.

The Burmese People v. Unocal: EarthRights International 1; *Redford.*

Norway banned investment in a Chinese firm for providing for Burma's military: Ministry of Finance (Norway).

Germany, Singapore, and Pakistan sold the junta military equipment: *Lintner*. Russia, Ukraine, and Serbia did, too: Amnesty 1, pp. 62–70.

Cargo ships of weapons unloaded in the middle of the night: Min Lwin 12.

North Korean weapons: *Lintner*.

Burmese foreign minister and North Korea agree to be friends after a 25-year fight: Associated Press 2; Mungpi 2.

China gets to buy all Daewoo's Shwe gas: Daewoo International; Shwe Gas Movement, p. 1.

Chinese weapons: See chapter 11 sourcing, under "Burma vs. the world."

BP bought Burmah Castrol for $5 billion in 2000: BP.

Herbert Hoover found fortune in Burma: Nash, pp. 433–439; Liggett, pp. 193–197.

"little inclined to yield to threats": Scott 1, p. 17.

19th-century British envoys to Burma, and their failures: Hall, pp. 97–100; Symes.

Ill-fated Thais, Chinese, Mon: Thant Myint-U, p. 106.

Ill-fated Manchu of 1767: Thant Myint-U, pp. 101–104.

Ill-fated Portuguese of 1613: Hall, p. 50; Thant Myint-U, pp. 78–79.

Throwdown with Kublai Khan: Thant Myint-U, pp. 60–61.

His Excellency King Bagyidaw's most excellent title: Scott 1, p. 87.

King Thibaw declares war, impending elephanterie on England: Scott 1, p. 41.

Burma army soldiers underpaid: Desertions and assassinations, too, are becoming a problem. Min Lwin 3.

UN admits failure to prevent genocide in Rwanda and Bosnia and Herzegovina: United Nations 6; United Nations 5.

2005 World Summit resolution of responsibility to protect: United Nations 11.

Case for genocide built before the 2007 draft resolution on Burma: Horton. For a summary of Horton's paper, which runs more than 600 pages, see Nicholas Thompson.

Systematic rape now recognized as key feature of genocide: Aegis Trust and United Nations Department of Public Information.

"Your blood must be left in the village": Apple, p. 24.

Soldiers force minority women into marriage as enslavement: United Nations 7.

ANU's Strategic and Defence Studies Centre aware of special Karen-killing terror squad of the Tatmadaw: *Ball.*

Terror squad's tactics: Rogers, p. 158.

Academics, journalists, activists say Karen not subject of genocide: Nicholas Thompson.

More than 3,000 ethnic villages destroyed in Burma: TBBC 6.

Comparable to the number destroyed in Darfur: International Human Rights Clinic at Harvard Law School, p. iii.

Nearly 3 million displaced in Darfur: IDMC 6, p. 1.

Again, well more than half a million displaced in eastern Burma alone: TBBC 9.

Millions have fled the country: At least 750,000 Rohingya, Human Rights Watch 5, p. 6; some 2 million migrant workers in Thailand, TBBC 2; a couple of hundred thousand refugees inside Thailand (TBBC 3) and out (UNHCR 9).

Sudan's mortality rate for children under five: UNICEF, p. 120.

Eastern Burma's under-five mortality rate: Back Pack Health Worker Team, p. 32. An earlier survey found a prevalence of 276 to 291 per 1,000 live births. Lee et al.

Darfur death count: GenocideInDarfur.net.

400,000 killed in Burma by 1990: Martin Smith, p. 101.

Body count "would reach as high as millions": General Saw Maung, quoted in Pedersen, p. 121, and Martin Smith, p. 101.

Slow and indirect genocide is still genocide: *The Prosecutor v. Clément Kayishema and Obed Ruzindana*, paragraph 115; *The Prosecutor v. Jean-Paul Akayesu*, paragraph 505.

Intent can be inferred: *The Prosecutor v. Clément Kayishema and Obed Ruzindana*, paragraph 527.

"the result of policy at the highest level, entailing political and legal responsibility": United Nations 4.

Refugee-camp kids' drawings: La Guardia.

"Soon the Karen will no longer exist": You can see one of these messages in the footage of *Give Them a Chance to Read*.

25,000 Karenni in camps in Thailand/more than 50,000 internally displaced: *Thompson*.

Shan race = enemy to be destroyed: Thomson.

Shan women = targets of rape for "admixture of blood": Horton, section 13.8.

No atrocity crimes in the '07 draft resolution: United Nations 8.

China and Russia veto: United Nations 9.

Armenian genocide finally recognized by UNHRC: United Nations 1; *Adalian*.

Jurists say Rwanda and Darfur are precedents for Burma: International Human Rights Clinic at Harvard Law School.

"world cannot wait"/"*prima facie* case of international criminal law violations": International Human Rights Clinic at Harvard Law School, pp. iv and 2–3, respectively.

More than 50 congresspeople sent letter to President Obama: US Campaign for Burma.

Rohingya:
   Report: From the esteemed William Schabas (project manager: Nancie Prud'homme). Available on the Irish Centre for Human Rights website.

   Hundreds of thousands driven out of Burma: Human Rights Watch 5, p. 6; Refugees International.

"Rohingya are . . . ugly as ogres": Human Rights Watch 5, p. 7, quoting a letter Consul General Ye Myint Aung wrote to heads of foreign missions. HRW has a copy of the letter on file.

25 percent suffer acute malnutrition: Young.

Forced labor/wrongful imprisonment/no citizenship/no traveling/no anything without permission: Human Rights Watch 5.

Caught trying to get jobs and sentenced to prison: Saw Yan Naing 2.

A couple hundred thousand in Bangladesh/about 60,000 in camps/settlements: *Prud'homme*.

Making big news: Even Angelina Jolie got involved. Srivalo.

Being towed back out to sea: Lawi Weng 2.

"do something to assist the people of Burma": US Department of State 5.

"engaged in ethnic cleansing against minorities within Burma": *Burmese Freedom and Democracy Act of 2003*.

China, Russia, Japan rejected proposal to talk about Burma in 2006: Lynch.

UN secretary-general advocate of noncoercive measures: Luck, p. 1.

Noncoercive measures not going to work: And the UN knows it. You can see both Secretary-General Ban Ki-moon and his special envoy, Ibrahim Gambari, grumbling about how little progress the diplomatic process has made in Burma in Wai Moe 1 and Jha 2.

Villagers buried to their necks and bludgeoned with a shovel: Nicholas Thompson.

Burma gets less than a tenth of the aid Cambodia does: Watkins et al., p. 292.

People with AIDS on meds waiting list: Kyi Wai.

Relief is less than $3 per person/vs. $50 in Sudan: Watkins et al., p. 292.

US Burma policy ignoring Karen/other ethnicities' crises/massacres: You can see them being pointedly unincluded in the concerns listed by Secretary of State Hillary Clinton ("It's so critical that [Aung San Suu Kyi] be released from this persecution that she has been under. And if she were released, that would open up opportunities, at least for my country, to expand our relationship with Burma, including investments in Burma.") and State Department spokesman Ian Kelly ("We want a government that responds to the needs of its people; a government that frees political prisoners unconditionally, including Aung San Suu Kyi; and the start of a dialogue, of a constructive dialogue, with the political opposition there.") in US Department of State 11 and Jha 5, respectively.

Wa:

> Being headhunters, naked, dirty, scary: Chapter 22 of Scott 3 is all about the Wa. You can even see photographic proof of their propensity for nudity there, if you want.

> Helped communists hold Burmese territory until the late '80s: Thant Myint-U, p. 323; *Kramer*.

> Commander wanted by the US: US Department of State 12.

Burma cultivated 29 percent more opium in 2007: UNODC 2, p. 7.

Plus tons of amphetamine pills: UNODC 3, pp. 120–121.

"Ice Triangle": Wyler, p. 9.

Plus lots of the raw material for ecstasy: UNODC 1. The chemical is called safrole.

"'failed demonstrably' to meet its international counternarcotics obligations": US Department of State 10.

Seven major and a dozen subnationalities: *Smith*.

"so corrupt it turns my stomach": McCoy, p. 412.

"a well-founded fear of being persecuted": From the 1951 UN Convention Relating to the Status of Refugees. UNHCR 7, p. 16.

Thailand one of seven worst countries in which to be a refugee: US Committee for Refugees and Immigrants 3, p. 5.

The story of the creation of the Karen and Europeans is recounted in Hinton, pp. 42–43.

Burmese watching election, waiting for invasion: Wai Moe 2.

President Obama's inauguration speech censored: Min Lwin 5.

Sifting tea leaves for signs of change: Kyaw Zwa Moe.

Burmese not warned that Cyclone Nargis was coming: Mungpi 1; Jagan.

Nargis killed 140,000: UNISDR.

"You're coming to save us, aren't you?": *The New York Times* 2.

XIII.

The story of Toh Meh Pah: Falla, pp. 11–14.

Dave's dog proverb and Mordor metaphor: Rogers, pp. 196 and 181–182, respectively.

Only a few hours of electricity in Rangoon a day: Saw Yan Naing 12.

Some cities buy private, overpriced electricity: Aung Hla Tun 1.

Climate-controlled penguin habitat: *The New York Times* 1 and 2; Beaton.

Burma ratified Forced Labour Convention in '55/ILO told Burma to quit forced labor in '64: International Labour Organization 1.

Extended supplementary agreement in 2009: International Labour Organization 2.

Internal ILO paper reported concerns: International Labour Organization 3.

Details of the ILO's dealings with Burma were also confirmed by Steve Marshall.

Junta says forced labor is voluntary labor: Burma Issues 2, p. 18.

Two people arrested for having videotaped forced labor: Committee to Protect Journalists 1.

Collection of government orders for forced labor: KHRG 3.

Getting work permits costly, complicated: US Committee for Refugees and Immigrants 2.

Details about the Shoklo Malaria Research Unit's work: *Nosten*. A lot of the information can be found also on SMRU's website, shoklo-unit.com.

Details about Dr. Cynthia: *Cynthia Maung*; Mae Tao Clinic; *Wells*. You can read an extensive interview with her in Thornton, beginning on p. 82.

$4 Burmese abortions: Kyi Wai 2.

XIV.

Camp teachers repatriating: UK Department for International Development, p. 12.

Process, details of getting Ta Mla to the United States: *Morrissey*; *Price*.

Up to 15 percent of camp residents have TB: *Morrissey*.

Principles of the Asylum Officer Basic Training Course: Immigration Officer Academy.

Refugee officer training based on Asylum Officer Basic Training course: US Department of State 9, Appendix F.

Book about culture in the United States: International Organization for Migration 1.

Video about culture in the United States: *Welcome to the United States: Refugee Guide to Resettlement, Orientation Video, English Version*.

Time between resettlement approval and departure: UNHCR 4; *Price*.

Stateside assistance to refugees after their arrival: *Wills*.

XV.

50,000 refugees in Mae La in 2006: TBBC 4.

Mae La encompasses one and a half square miles: TBBC 8.

Burmese government doesn't allow minority language instruction in schools: Wai Moe 8.

Six people in most refugee huts: ZOA Refugee Care Thailand 1, p. 48.

Karen refugee camps don't meet UNHCR's minimum space standards: UK Department for International Development, p. 10.

24 primary and secondary schools in Mae La: ZOA Refugee Care Thailand 1, p. 70.

AMI has 250 workers in Mae La: CCSDPT 4, p. iii.

Nine NGOs handle health and sanitation: CCSDPT 5.

Refugee camp health care costs $6 million/refugee camp all care costs $66 million: CCSDPT 3, p. 18.

United States pays 27 percent: CCSDPT 3, p. 19.

Camps breeding drug abuse/mental illness/violence/crime: UK Department for International Development, p. 11.

DARE's camp programs: CCSDPT 4, p. xiv.

KNU and Thai guards dispensing very questionable camp justice: US Committee for Refugees and Immigrants 2.

KNU claims it doesn't recruit children anymore: The organization signed a deed of commitment to quit using kids in 2007. United Nations 12, p. 33.

Report of child forced into KNU soldiering: United Nations 12, p. 16.

Burma army had 70,000 child soldiers in 2002: Human Rights Watch 2, p. 187.

Bat shit, charcoal, and sulfur ammunition: Falla, p. 113.

Luther and Johnny Htoo and God's Army/Soldiers of the Holy Mountain details: *Eubank*; Human Rights Watch 2, p. 157; Rogers, pp. 112–114.

"the three kinds of wives that may be put away"/the six kinds of blemishes of a woman: Nisbet, p. 454.

"may be corrected by beating or abusing them within the hearing of the public": Nisbet, p. 456.

"The eight kinds of husbands whom the wife has the right to abuse": Nisbet, p. 455.

4 percent of societies studied didn't kiss: 8 of the 190 cultures in Clellan and Beach, p. 49.

"Look at these people!": Junod, p. 353.

Frenching habits of Kinsey's premarital-sex-having surveyees: Kinsey, p. 252.

Foreplay of the Tinguian: Clellan and Beach, p. 49.

Frenching a "ritualized feeding gesture": Eibl-Eibesfeldt, p. 135.

Karen animism practices: Falla, beginning p. 91; *Harvey*.

EPILOGUE.

5,000 Burmese resettled through Thailand in 2006: International Organization for Migration 2.

3 percent of the refugees at the time: TBBC 5.

Double the number the year before/tripled in 2007: International Organization for Migration 2.

Condoleezza Rice signed Tham Hin material-support waiver: US Department of State 6.

Update on the Sri Lankan fisherman: *Schulman*.

Rice extended waiver to more Karen camps: US Department of State 7.

Waiver extended to all Karen: US Department of Homeland Security.

KNU no longer terrorist organization: US Department of Homeland Security, US Citizenship and Immigration Services 2.

More than 50,000 Burmese resettled through Thailand/UN's largest resettlement program: UNHCR 10.

Nearly 15,000 went to US in 2008: International Organization for Migration 2.

Quotes from the cultural orientation book: International Organization for Migration 1.

China and EU failed to reach consensus on Burma: Arkar Moe 2.

North Korean ship on supposed weapons-delivering mission to Burma: Sang-hun.

North Korea helped junta build tunnels: Lintner 6.

BURMA, NORTH KOREA IN AN UNHOLY MILITARY ALLIANCE: Aung Zaw 2.

IS BURMA THE NEXT IRAN?: Bremmer.

IS MYANMAR GOING NUCLEAR WITH NORTH KOREA'S HELP?: Gray.

IS THERE A BURMA-NORTH KOREA-IRAN NUCLEAR CONSPIRACY?: Selth 1.

Clinton's "growing concerns": Sullivan.

Politicians want Burma out of ASEAN: *The Irrawaddy* 9.

Burma wants politicians to "refrain from interfering in internal affairs": Joshi.

"Barack Obama and Joe Biden will press China": Obama/Biden.

US and China can "agree to disagree": See Sisk for one of many reports of this comment.

Obama extended sanctions: *Corporate Estimated Tax Shift Act of 2009.*

Burma put on genocide watch list: Albright and Cohen, p. 36.

ICC issued arrest warrant for Sudanese president: International Criminal Court.

East Timor president called for ICC charges against Than Shwe: Arkar Moe 1.

Than Shwe's building a big new airport: Boot 2.

"The spirit in the camps": Falla, p. 195.

300 resettlers leaving Thailand a week: As of January 2009. International Organization for Migration 2.

Rations reduced/no more soap: Andrews 3; *Jhowry.*

No more money for camp ex-Empire soldiers: Andrew 3; *Davis.*

DKBA and cross-border trade: Saw Yan Naing 11.

Thailand told KNU to get out: *The Irrawaddy* 7.

Executive director of Human Rights Watch's Asia Division summed up general expectations for the 2010 election when he said, "There is no reason to believe or even hope that the vote in 2010 will be free and fair. The point of the election is to put a civilian face on a military regime by handpicking the winners." See *The Irrawaddy* 4.

13 years to write the constitution: Thant Myint-U has a good rundown of the history of the constitution, pp. 337–339.

92 percent yeas: Human Rights Watch 4; International Center for Transitional Justice, p. 3.

Military has total immunity: International Center for Transitional Justice.

"Roadmap" to democracy: Arnott 2.

For a great documentary about the Burmese who videotaped the Saffron Revolution, including footage of the Japanese journalist being shot point-blank and the floating dead body of a monk, see *Burma VJ*.

Couple dozen Burmese killed: Human Rights Documentation Unit, NCGUB, pp. 573–590.

Internet shut down: OpenNet Initiative 2.

Cell phone prices more than four times GNI: Min Lwin 1 (cell phone prices); UNICEF, p. 119 (GNI).

Government surveillance of text messaging: Min Lwin 1.

Lots of NLD jailed or exiled or dead: Ludu Sein Win. As of June 2006, according to this former political prisoner's report, of those elected to parliament, "105 have been jailed, 79 have been forced into silence, 73 have died and 54 have gone into exile."

Dr. Cynthia thinks involvement and politics and starving families often don't mix: Thornton, p. 89.

Political-prisoner population doubled: Lawi Weng 8; AAPP (Burma) 3.

Monks sentenced to prison: Macan-Marker 1.

Dissenter sentenced to 104 years: AAPP (Burma) 1.

Junta export of rice amid famine: Min Lwin 6.

Junta imprisonment of aid volunteers: AAPP (Burma) 2.

DKBA's conscripting border guards: Saw Yan Naing 7.

Conscripting militiamen in general: Cho.

DKBA has 6,000 troops: Wai Moe 7.

"If I didn't go to the DKBA": Ellgee.

DKBA cease-fire "beneficial": Saw Yan Naing 5.

DKBA's business interests: Saw Yan Naing 9; *Maung Aung Myoe*.

KNU has 4,000 troops: *Eubank*.

Some minorities in cease-fire areas still screwed: Min Lwin 10; Wai Moe 4.

Cease-fire talks between KNU and SPDC: Discussion of some in Saw Yan Naing 5; Thant Myint-U, p. 331; *Bangkok Post* 3.

KNU storming brigade during cease-fire talks: International Institute for Strategic Studies.

"out of the question": *Bangkok Post* 3.

2009 SPDC talk of KNU cease-fire → massive attack: Saw Yan Naing 6.

Captured KNU bases: *The Irrawaddy* 10; *Maung Aung Myoe*.

Shelled IDPs/another refugee flood: Sai Soe Win Latt.

Assassinations/Mae La is next: Saw Yan Naing 10.

Significant groups broken away from KNU: There's a good, fast breakdown of some of the splits in Saw Yan Naing 5; see another in Wai Moe 6.

Bombs in Rangoon: Aung Hla Tun 2; Embassy of the United States of America, Rangoon, Burma; *The Irrawaddy* 3.

Mon don't want to be in junta border guard: Lawi Weng 6.

Mon "will do something": Lawi Weng 3.

Kachin army recruiting: Min Lwin 11.

20,000 Wa: *Kramer*.

Wa getting ready for war: Saw Yan Naing 8.

Kokangs broke long-standing cease-fire: Wai Moe 9.

"Nobody is winning, and nobody will win": Quoted in Thomson.

SOURCES

AAPP (Assistance Association for Political Prisoners) (Burma).
    1. "ABFSU Member Sentenced to 104 Years in Jail." Press release, January 14, 2009.
    2. "AAPP Cyclone Nargis Anniversary Report." May 2009.
    3. "Chronology of Political Prisoner[s] in Burma for September 2009."
    4. aappb.org.

Adalian, Rouben. Director, Armenian National Institute.

Aegis Trust and United Nations Department of Public Information. "Genocide: Whose Responsibility?" *Lessons from Rwanda* exhibition, 2007.

Albright, Madeleine K. and William S. Cohen. "Preventing Genocide: A Blueprint for US Policymakers." United States Holocaust Memorial Museum, the American Academy of Diplomacy, and the Endowment of the United States Institute of Peace, 2008.

Allen, Louis. *Burma: The Longest War, 1941–45.* New York: St. Martin's Press, 1984.

Amalvy, Richard. Director, External Relations & Marketing, World Organization of the Scout Movement.

Amnesty International.
    1. "Medical Concern: Myanmar: Death in Custody of Leo Nichols." July 16, 1996.
    2. "Blood at the Crossroads: Making the Case for a Global Arms Trade Treaty." 2008.

Andrews, Jim.
    1. "Tyrants to Revel in Colonial Splendour." *The Daily Telegraph,* December 19, 2005.

2. "'Second Chance City' Welcomes Another Leading Burmese Monk." *The Irrawaddy*, January 28, 2009.

3. "Surviving on a Little Hope and 33 US Cents a Day." *The Irrawaddy*, February 6, 2009.

4. "The Karen Old Soldiers That Britain Forgot." *The Irrawaddy*, February 12, 2009.

Apple, Betsy. "School for Rape: The Burmese Military and Sexual Violence." EarthRights International, 1998.

Arkar Moe.

1. "Is It Time to Take Than Shwe to International Criminal Court?" *The Irrawaddy*, May 20, 2009.

2. "EU-China Summit Fails to Agree on Burma Issue." *The Irrawaddy*, May 22, 2009.

Arnott, David.

1. "Once the Ricebowl of Asia: The Military Destruction of Burma's Economy." February 5, 1998, update. Originally published in *Relations Internationales et Strategiques*, Autumn 1997.

2. "Burma/Myanmar: How to Read the Generals' 'Roadmap': A Brief Guide with Links to the Literature." Internet publication, April 18, 2004.

Article 19. "Burma: Beyond the Law." August 1996.

ASEAN (Association of Southeast Asian Nations). "ASEAN and India Sign the Much Awaited Free Trade Area." Press release, August 13, 2009.

Associated Press.

1. "Foreign Investment in Burma Oil and Gas Sectors More Than Tripled." June 30, 2008.

2. "Burma's FM Makes First Visit to North Korea in 25 Years." October 27, 2008.

3. "Foreign Investment in Burma Soars." January 5, 2009.

Aung Hla Tun.

1. "Burma Blackout." Reuters, April 9, 2007.

2. "Yangon Bomb Wounds 4 as Protest Anniversary Looms." Reuters, September 25, 2008.

Aung Zaw.

1. "The Battle of Insein Never Really Ended." *The Irrawaddy*, February 9, 2009.

2. "Burma, North Korea in an Unholy Military Alliance." *Bangkok Post*, June 29, 2009.

Aye Kyaw. *The Voice of Young Burma.* Ithaca: Southeast Asia Program Publications, Cornell University, 1993.

Bachoe, Ralph. "Refugees Moved to New Camp: Intruders Retreat as Thais Hold Firm." *Bangkok Post*, March 5, 1997.

Back Pack Health Worker Team. "Chronic Emergency: Health and Human Rights in Eastern Burma." 2006.

Ball, Desmond. Professor, Asia-Pacific security expert, Strategic and Defence Studies Centre at the Australian National University.

Bangkok Phuchatkan. "Job Program Said Benefiting Burmese Spies." June 10, 1999.

Bangkok Post.
  1. "The Battle for Myawaddy." March 22, 1974. Accessed online at the Center for Ethnic Studies and Development, cesd-thai.info.
  2. "Burmese Jets Set Oil Ablaze." March 25, 1974. Accessed online at the Center for Ethnic Studies and Development, cesd-thai.info.
  3. "KNU Will Continue Talks with SLORC." August 4, 1996.
  4. "Work on Friendship Bridge Starts Again: Aim to Finish Project within 3 Months." March 8, 1997.
  5. "S'pore Helps Burma's Spies." October 17, 1997.
  6. "Bridging the Gap a Second Time." September 17, 1998.
  7. "In Brief: Spy Security Threat." August 7, 2000.

Barnes, William. "Lobbyists Resign as Junta Fails to Pay Up." *South China Morning Post*, March 17, 1999.

Barron, Sandy, John Okell, Saw Myat Yin, Kenneth VanBik, Arthur Swain, Emma Larkin, Anna J. Allott, and Kirsten Ewers. "Refugees from Burma: Their Backgrounds and Refugee Experiences." Edited by Donald A. Ranard and Sandy Barron. Washington, DC: Center for Applied Linguistics, 2007.

BBC News.
  1. "Aung San Suu Kyi Urges Patience." December 10, 2002.
  2. "Rice Names 'Outposts of Tyranny.'" January 19, 2005.
  3. "Burma Confirms Capital to Move." November 7, 2005.

Beaton, Helen. "Penguins and Golf in Burma's Hidden Capital." *The Independent*, September 19, 2008.

Becker, Jo. Advocacy director, Children Rights Division, Human Rights Watch.

Belanger, Francis W. *Drugs, the US, and Khun Sa*. Bangkok: Editions Duang Kamol, 1989.

Blum, Christian. Management, Resolution GmbH, provider of your-freedom .net.

Bo Kyi. Joint Secretary, Assistance Association for Political Prisoners (Burma).

Boot, William.
  1. "Weekly Business Roundup (July 19, 2008)." *The Irrawaddy*.
  2. "Weekly Business Roundup (May 01, 2009)." *The Irrawaddy*.
  3. "Weekly Business Roundup (December 12, 2008)." *The Irrawaddy*.
BP. "BP Amoco Agrees Recommended Cash Offer to Buy Burmah Castrol for £3 ($4.7) Billion." Press release, March 14, 2000.
Bradner, Curt/Bradner, Cathy. Former directors, Burmese Youth Project, now of Thirst-Aid.
Bremmer, Ian. "Is Burma the Next Iran?" *Slate*, February 15, 2006.
Burma Campaign UK.
  1. "European Union Backs Global Arms Embargo on Burma." Press release, April 30, 2008.
  2. "The Dirty List." burmacampaign.org.uk.
  3. "Sanctions." burmacampaign.org.uk.
  4. "Tourism." burmacampaign.org.uk.
Burma Issues.
  1. "To Forcibly Repatriate or Not: Thailand's Dilemma." April 1997.
  2. "From Prison to Frontline: Portering for SPDC Troops during the Offensive in Eastern Karen State, Burma." January 2005.
Burma Rivers Network.
  1. "Dam Projects—Tamanthi Dam." As of October 8, 2009. burmarivers network.org.
  2. burmariversnetwork.org.
"Burma: State of Fear." PBS *Frontline/World*, October 31, 2006.
"Burma: The Forgotten War." BBC *History of World War II*, BBC Warner, 2005.
Burma VJ. Anders Østergaard/Magic Hour Films, 2009.
Burmese Freedom and Democracy Act of 2003. 108th Cong., 1st sess., HR 2330.
Burmese Women's Union (BWU). "Statement of the BWU on the Long-Term Sentence of Daw San San." April 23, 1998.
Cady, John Frank. *A History of Modern Burma*. Ithaca: Cornell University Press, 1958.
Cantwell, Guy. Director of corporate communications, Transocean.
CCSDPT (Committee for Coordination of Services to Displaced Persons in Thailand).
  1. "Monthly Report for December 1984."
  2. "CCSDPT Agency Services to Burmese Border Camps: June 2006."
  3. "CCSDPT/UNHCR Comprehensive Plan 2007/8."
  4. "CCSDPT Directory for 2009."
  5. "Members." ccsdpt.org.

Charney, Michael W. Senior lecturer in the History of South East Asia, School of Oriental and African Studies, University of London.

Chenard, Celeste. "Burma's Cyber War Rages On." Mizzima News, June 29, 2009.

Chiang Mai Mail. "Motorcycle Accidents Kill 27 People a Day." Vol. 6, No. 32. October 2–October 8, 2007.

Cho, Violet. "DKBA Recruited Villagers for Assault on KNLA." The Irrawaddy, September 30, 2008.

Christophe, Francis. Birmanie, la Dictature du Pavot. Arles: Picquier, 1998.

Clifford, Hugh. Further India: Being the Story of Exploration from the Earliest Times in Burma, Malaya, Siam, and Indo-China. New York: Frederick A. Stokes Company, 1904. Clifford also wrote a volume called Studies in Brown Humanity, which I didn't read but really wanted to.

CNPC (China National Petroleum Corporation). "MOU signed of Myanmar-China Oil Pipeline." Press release, June 19, 2009.

Code of Federal Regulations. "Burmese Sanctions Regulations." Title 31, Chapter V, Part 537.

Columbia Books Inc. data. Biographical information on Alan Hoffman. Accessed through OpenSecrets.org.

Committee to Protect Journalists.
1. 2004 IPFA (International Press Freedom Awards): Aung Pwint and Thaung Tun. cpj.org/awards/2004.
2. "2008 Prison Census: 125 Journalists Jailed." As of December 1, 2008.
3. "10 Worst Countries to Be a Blogger." April 30, 2009.

Connors, Peter. Senior press officer, BBC Global News.

Corporate Estimated Tax Shift Act of 2009. Public Law 111-42. 111th Cong., 1st sess., July 28, 2009.

Cortez, Ana Luiza. Chief, Secretariat of the Committee for Development Policy, Development Policy Analysis Division, United Nations Department of Economic and Social Affairs.

Crispin, Shawn W. "Burning Down Myanmar's Internet Firewall." Asia Times, September 21, 2007.

Cullather, Nick. Associate professor, foreign relations specialist, Department of History, Indiana University.

Cynthia Maung, Dr. Founder and director, Mae Tao Clinic.

Daily Digest. United States Congress. November 17, 2008.

Daley, Matthew P. Deputy assistant secretary, Bureau of East Asian and Pacific Affairs, US Department of State. Testimony before the House International Relations Committee and Subcommittees on International

Terrorism, Nonproliferation, and Human Rights and Asia and the Pacific. October 2, 2003.

Davis, Colonel Paul. Secretary general, Royal Commonwealth Ex-Services League.

Doctors without Borders. "'Top Ten' Humanitarian Crises Reveal Growing Insecurity, Neglected Health Needs." Press release, December 22, 2008.

Dolan, Chris. Partners Relief and Development.

Dun, General Smith. Memoirs of the Four-Foot Colonel. Ithaca: Southeast Asia Program Publications, Cornell University, 1980.

EarthRights International.
   1. "Doe v. Unocal Case History." January 30, 2006.
   2. "China in Burma: The Increasing Investment of Chinese Multinational Corporations in Burma's Hydropower, Oil and Natural Gas, and Mining Sectors." September 2008.
   3. "New OECD Guidelines Case against Daewoo and Korea Gas Corporation." Press release, October 29, 2008.
   4. "Total Impact: The Human Rights, Environmental, and Financial Impacts of Total and Chevron's Yadana Gas Project in Military-Ruled Burma (Myanmar)." September 2009.

Eaves, Elisabeth. "Spin Doctors without Borders." Harper's, March 2004.

Eibl-Eibesfeldt, Irenäus. Love and Hate: The Natural History of Behavior Patterns. Translated by Geoffrey Strachan. New York: Holt, Rinehart and Winston, 1972.

Ellgee, Alex. "Pitting Karen against Karen in a Bloody War." The Irrawaddy, July 1, 2009.

Embassy of the United States of America, Rangoon, Burma. "Bomb Explosions." Warden message, January 14, 2008.

Energy Information Administration (EIA).
   1. "Country Analysis Briefs—China." eia.doe.gov.
   2. "World Oil Transit Chokepoints." eia.doe.gov.

Enriquez, C.M. A Burmese Arcady; An Account of a Long & Intimate Sojourn amongst the Mountain Dwellers of the Burmese Hinterland & of Their Engaging Characteristics and Customs, Etc. Philadelphia: J.B. Lippincott Co., 1923.

Environmental Protection Agency (EPA). "Chemical Information Fact Sheet for 2,4-D." July 1986.

Eubank, David. Founder, Free Burma Rangers.

Falla, Jonathan. True Love and Bartholomew: Rebels on the Burmese Border. Cambridge: Cambridge University Press, 1991.

Fear and Hope: Responding to Burma's Internally Displaced. Front Films/Free Burma Rangers, 2004. (Video.)

Fink, Christina. *Living Silence: Burma Under Military Rule.* London: Zed Books, 2001.

Fitzgerald, Isaac. Former Free Burma Ranger.

Fong, Jack. Assistant professor, Karen/Burma specialist, California State Polytechnic University, Pomona.

Ford, Clellan S. and Frank A. Beach. *Patterns of Sexual Behavior.* New York: Harper & Row, 1951.

Freedom House. "Freedom of the Press—2008." April 29, 2008.

Furukawa, Urara. "Resettlement of Myanmar Refugees from Thailand Camps Hits 50,000 Mark." UNHCR news, June 30, 2009.

Fytche, Lieutenant-General Albert. *Burma Past and Present; With Personal Reminiscences of the Country.* 2 vols. London: C.K. Paul & Co., 1878.

GenocideInDarfur.net. A project of the Genocide Intervention Network.

Gill, Daniel P. Environmental specialist.

Give Them a Chance to Read. Partners Relief and Development, 2009. (Video.)

Global IDP Project and Norwegian Refugee Council. *Internally Displaced People: A Global Survey.* London: Earthscan, 2002.

Global Ministries. "The Sailing of the First American Missionaries Overseas." June 9, 2006.

Global Witness. "A Disharmonious Trade: China and the Continued Destruction of Burma's Northern Frontier Forests." October 2009.

Gray, Denis D. "Is Myanmar Going Nuclear with North Korea's Help?" Associated Press, July 21, 2009.

Green, Michael. "Japan Fails the Test on Democracy and Burma." *The Washington Post,* June 8, 2006.

Gupta-Smith, Vismita. Public Information and Advocacy Officer, World Health Organization Regional Office for South-East Asia.

Hall, D.G.E. *Burma.* London: Hutchinson & Co., 1960.

Handicap International. "Assistance to People with Disabilities and Mine-UXOs Risk Education for Refugees along the Thai-Burmese Border." Project description 2005–2008.

Hansard (House of Commons Daily Debates).

    1. November 5, 1947. Vol. 443 cc1836-961.

    2. April 29, 2009. Statement by Gareth Thomas, MP.

Hansford, Brian. Communication specialist, UNICEF.

Harvey, G.E. *History of Burma: From the Earliest Times to 10 March, 1824, the Beginning of the English Conquest.* London: Longmans, Green and Co., 1925.

Harvey, Graham. Department of Religious Studies, The Open University.

Hendricks, Bill. President, Klyn Nurseries.

Hinton, Elizabeth. *Oldest Brother's Story: Tales of the Pwo Karen*. Chiang Mai: Silkworm Books, 1999.

Horton, Guy. "Dying Alive: An Investigation and Legal Assessment of Human Rights Violations Inflicted in Burma, with Particular Reference to the Internally Displaced, Eastern Peoples." April 2005.

Human Rights Documentation Unit, NCGUB (National Coalition Government of the Union of Burma). "Burma Human Rights Yearbook 2007."

Human Rights Watch.

> 1. *A Modern Form of Slavery: Trafficking of Burmese Women and Girls into Brothels in Thailand*. Asia Watch and Women's Rights Project divisions, December 1993.
> 2. "'My Gun Was as Tall as Me': Child Soldiers in Burma." October 2002.
> 3. "Out of Sight, Out of Mind: Thai Policy toward Burmese Refugees." February 25, 2004.
> 4. "Burma: Reject Constitutional Referendum." May 16, 2008.
> 5. "Perilous Plight: Burma's Rohingya Take to the Seas." May 2009.

ICRC (International Committee of the Red Cross). "The ICRC in Myanmar." icrc.org.

IDMC (Internal Displacement Monitoring Centre).

> 1. "Internal Displacement: Global Overview of Trends and Developments in 2003." February 2004.
> 2. "Internal Displacement: Global Overview of Trends and Developments in 2004." March 2005.
> 3. "Internal Displacement: Global Overview of Trends and Developments in 2005." March 2006.
> 4. "Internal Displacement: Global Overview of Trends and Developments in 2006." April 2007.
> 5. "Internal Displacement: Global Overview of Trends and Developments in 2007." April 2008.
> 6. "Sudan: 4.9 Million IDPs Across Sudan Face Ongoing Turmoil." May 27, 2009.
> 7. "Global Statistics." As of September 2009. internal-displacement.org.

Immigration Officer Academy. "Asylum Officer Basic Training Course, Participant Workbook." September 14, 2006.

In Hiding: A Year of Survival under the Burma Army 2004-2005. Front Films/ Free Burma Rangers, 2005. (Video.)

International Campaign to Ban Landmines. "New Mine Victims Reinforce the Need for Treaty." Press release, April 2, 2009.

International Center for Transitional Justice. "Impunity Prolonged: Burma and Its 2008 Constitution." September 2009.

International Criminal Court. "ICC Issues a Warrant of Arrest for Omar Al Bashir, President of Sudan." Press release, March 4, 2009.

International Human Rights Clinic at Harvard Law School. "Crimes in Burma." May 2009.

International Institute for Strategic Studies. "Myanmar: Timeline: February 23, 2004." Armed Conflict Database, acd.iiss.org.

International Labour Organization (ILO).

1. "Forced Labour in Myanmar (Burma): Report of the Commission of Inquiry Appointed under Article 26 of the Constitution of the International Labour Organization to Examine the Observance by Myanmar of the Forced Labour Convention, 1930 (No. 29)." July 2, 1998.

2. "ILO Renews Supplementary Understanding with Myanmar." Press release, March 2, 2009.

3. "Developments Concerning the Question of the Observance by the Government of Myanmar of the Forced Labour Convention, 1930 (No. 29)." March 2009.

International Organization for Migration (IOM).

1. *US Cultural Orientation: South East Asia, Student Notebook.*

2. "IOM Assisted Departures from Thailand (Refugee Resettlement, Family Reunion, Assisted Voluntary Return, and National Migration) as of 31 January 2009." Internal document.

International Rescue Committee (IRC). "Status and Outlook for Burmese Refugee Resettlement." International Rescue Committee San Francisco, March 2007.

Ireland, Alleyne. "The Province of Burma: A Report Prepared on Behalf of the University of Chicago." Vol. 1. Boston: Houghton, Mifflin and Company, 1907.

The Irrawaddy.

1. "Thai-Burmese Bridge Open, Sort Of." Vol. 5, No. 4/5. August 1997.

2. "Burma Making Small Arms." Vol. 6, No. 4. August 1998.

3. "Rangoon Explosion Rocks USDA Office." July 1, 2008.

4. "Training Eyes on the Junta." September 4, 2008.

5. "Five Burmese Educational Journals Shut Down." October 8, 2008.

6. "Regime Shrugs Off Effects on Burma of Global Economic Crisis." December 17, 2008.

7. "Sleepless in Mae Sot." March 6, 2009.

8. "Than Shwe's New Pagoda Hides More Than a Buddha Relic." March 10, 2009.

9. "Movement to Suspend Burma from ASEAN Grows." May 29, 2009.

10. "KNU to Abandon Bases." June 18, 2009.

Jackson, Samuel Macauley, editor in chief. *The New Schaff-Herzog Encyclopedia of Religious Knowledge*. New York: Funk and Wagnalls, 1908.

Jagan, Larry. "Burma: Cyclone Nargis Exposes Junta's Anti-People Attitude." IPS News. May 7, 2008.

Jenkins, Mark. "The Ghost Road." *Outside*, October 2003.

Jha, Lalit K.

1. "Bush Slaps Sanctions on More Junta Cronies." *The Irrawaddy*, January 16, 2009.

2. "No Tangible Result from Visit: Gambari." *The Irrawaddy*, February 21, 2009.

3. "Burma Expert Urges US to Tighten Sanctions." *The Irrawaddy*, April 24, 2009.

4. "Karen Refugee Testifies to Junta Crimes." *The Irrawaddy*, April 24, 2009.

5. "Campbell to Lead US Burma Engagement." *The Irrawaddy*, September 25, 2009.

Jhowry, Mina. Communications officer, Thailand Burma Border Consortium.

Joshi, Vijay. "Myanmar Defends Trial of Opposition Leader Suu Kyi [*sic*]." Associated Press, May 31, 2009.

Judson College. "America's First Female Foreign Missionary: Ann Judson." judson.edu.

Judson, Edward. *The Life of Adoniram Judson*. Philadelphia: American Baptist Publication Society, 1883.

Junod, Henri A. *The Life of a South African Tribe*. Vol. 1. London: Macmillan, 1927.

Kahin, Audrey R. and George McT. Kahin. *Subversion as Foreign Policy: The Secret Eisenhower and Dulles Debacle in Indonesia*. New York: New Press: W. W. Norton, 1995.

Kaplan, Robert D. "Lifting the Bamboo Curtain." *The Atlantic*, September 2008.

Karen Refugee Committee (KRC).

1. "Monthly Report." January 1997.

2. "Newsletter & Monthly Report." February 2009.

Keenan, Paul. "Voices of the Revolution: Saw Ba U Gyi." Karen History and Culture Preservation Society, March 2008.

Keyes, Charles F., ed. *Ethnic Adaptation and Identity: The Karen on the Thai Frontier with Burma*. Philadelphia: Institute for the Study of Human Issues, 1979.

KHRG (Karen Human Rights Group).
    1. "Attacks on Karen Refugee Camps: 1998." May 29, 1998.
    2. *Suffering in Silence: The Human Rights Nightmare of the Karen People of Burma*. Ed. Claudio O. Delang. Parkland, FL: Universal Publishers, 2001.
    3. "Forced Labor Orders Since the Ban: A Compendium of SPDC Order Documents Demanding Forced Labor Since November 2000." February 8, 2002.

Kim, Eun-jung. "Daewoo International Signs Gas Sales MOU." *Maeil Business Newspaper*, June 23, 2008.

Kinsey, Alfred. *Sexual Behavior in the Human Female*. Bloomington: Indiana University Press, 1998.

Knowles, James D. *Memoir of Mrs. Ann H. Judson, Late Missionary to Burmah; Including a History of the American Baptist Mission in the Burman Empire*. 2nd edition. Boston: Lincoln and Edmands, 1829.

Kramer, Tom. Researcher, Drugs and Democracy Programme, Transnational Institute.

Kristof, Nicholas D. "Our Man in Havana." *The New York Times*, November 8, 2003.

Kyaw Zwa Moe. "UN Envoy Visits Bring Less Interest." *The Irrawaddy*, August 20, 2008.

Kyi Wai.
    1. "HIV Patients Have Long Wait for Drugs." *The Irrawaddy*, October 21, 2008.
    2. "Desperate Decisions." *The Irrawaddy*, December 17, 2008.
    3. "Scenes of Poverty Banned from Burmese Films." *The Irrawaddy*, February 23, 2009.

La Guardia, Anton. "Burma's 'Slow Genocide' Is Revealed Through the Eyes of Its Child Victims." *The Daily Telegraph*, June 24, 2005.

Land, Gary. *Historical Dictionary of the Seventh-Day Adventists*. Oxford: Scarecrow Press, 2005.

Lang, Hazel J.
    1. "The Repatriation Predicament of Burmese Refugees in Thailand: A Preliminary Analysis." Australian National University, July 2001. Working paper for United Nations High Commissioner for Refugees.
    2. *Fear and Sanctuary: Burmese Refugees in Thailand*. Ithaca: Southeast Asia Program Publications, Cornell University, 2002.

Larkin, Emma. *Secret Histories: Finding George Orwell in a Burmese Teashop*. London: John Murray, 2004.

Lawi Weng.
1. "Burmese Migrant Women in Thailand Targeted by Rape Gangs." *The Irrawaddy*, October 20, 2008.
2. "Thailand Urged to Stop Pushing Refugees Out to Sea." *The Irrawaddy*, January 15, 2009.
3. "No Election Participation, No Disarmament: Mon Party." *The Irrawaddy*, January 20, 2009.
4. "New Bridge Proposed in Mae Sot." *The Irrawaddy*, March 16, 2009.
5. "Burma Key to Thailand's Drug Problem." *The Irrawaddy*, March 26, 2009.
6. "Did NMSP Reject Border Guard Role?" *The Irrawaddy*, June 1, 2009.
7. "Another Ceasefire Group Rejects Border Guards Proposal." *The Irrawaddy*, June 8, 2009.
8. "Families of Prisoners Don't Believe Talk of Amnesty." *The Irrawaddy*, July 15, 2009.

Lee, Thomas J., Luke C. Mullany, Adam K. Richards, Heather K. Kuiper, Cynthia Maung, and Chris Beyrer. "Mortality Rates in Conflict Zones in Karen, Karenni, and Mon States in Eastern Burma." *Tropical Medicine and International Health*, Vol. 11, No. 7 (July 2006): 1119–1127.

Lieberman, Victor B. Professor, Department of History/Center for Southeast Asian Studies Faculty/Pre-Modern Burma Virtuoso, University of Michigan.

Lieberman, Victor B. "Ethnic Politics in Eighteenth-Century Burma." *Modern Asian Studies*, Vol. 12, No. 3 (1978): 455-482.

Liggett, Walter W. *The Rise of Herbert Hoover*. New York: The H.K. Fly Company, 2007.

Lintner, Bertil. Author, Burma specialist.

Lintner, Bertil.
1. "The CIA's First Secret War: Americans Helped Stage Raids into China from Burma." *Far Eastern Economic Review*, September 16, 1993.
2. *Burma in Revolt: Opium and Insurgency since 1948.* Boulder: Westview Press, 1994.
3. "Recent Developments on the Thai-Burma Border." International Boundaries Research Unit, Durham University, April 1995.
4. "Myanmar, Bama, Oh Heck, Simply Burma." *The Nation* (Thailand), December 19, 1999.
5. "Burma's Nuclear Temptation." *YaleGlobal*. December 3, 2008.
6. "North Korea's Tunnels, Guns and Kimchi." *Asia Sentinel*, June 11, 2009.

Lintner, Bertil and Michael Black. *Merchants of Madness: The Methamphetamine Explosion in the Golden Triangle.* Chiang Mai: Silkworm Books, 2009.

Luck, Edward C. "The United Nations and the Responsibility to Protect." The Stanley Foundation, Policy Analysis Brief, August 2008.

Ludu Sein Win. "The Burmese People Can't Wait Much Longer." *The New Era Journal,* June 2006.

Luther, Calista V. *The Vintons and the Karens: Memorials of Rev. Justus H. Vinton and Calista H. Vinton.* Boston: W.G. Corthell, Mission Rooms, 1880.

Lynch, Colum. "US to Seek Resolution on Rights in Burma." *The Washington Post,* June 1, 2006.

Macan-Marker, Marwaan.

    1. "Burma's Monks Jailed, Disrobed for Challenging Junta." *The Irrawaddy,* September 22, 2008.

    2. "Military Accused of Crimes against Humanity." *The Irrawaddy,* November 11, 2008.

Mae Tao Clinic. "Annual Report 2008."

Marshall, Andrew. *The Trouser People: A Story of Burma in the Shadow of the Empire.* London: Penguin Books, 2003.

Marshall, Reverend Harry Ignatius. *The Karen People of Burma: A Study in Anthropology and Ethnology.* Columbus: The Ohio State University, 1922.

Marshall, Steve. Burma liaison officer, International Labour Organization.

Maung Aung Myoe. Singapore-based Tatmadaw expert and author of *Building the Tatmadaw: Myanmar Armed Forces Since 1948.*

Mawdsley, James. *The Iron Road: A Stand for Truth and Democracy in Burma.* New York: North Point Press, 2002.

McAllister, Bill. "Message for the Medium." *The Washington Post,* March 11, 1999.

McCoy, Alfred W. *The Politics of Heroin: CIA Complicity in the Global Drug Trade.* New York: Lawrence Hill Books, 1991.

McGeown, Kate. "Burma: Orwellian State, with Teashops." BBC News, June 13, 2006.

McGirk, Jan. "Burma's Rulers Take the Road to Mandalay." *The Independent,* November 8, 2005.

McKinsey, Kitty. Senior regional public information officer, United Nations High Commissioner for Refugees Bureau for Asia and the Pacific.

McMahon, Robert J. *The Limits of Empire: The United States and Southeast Asia Since World War II.* New York: Columbia University Press, 1999.

McNicoll, Tracy. "The Critics Can 'Go to Hell.'" *Newsweek,* August 3, 2009.

Ministry of Finance (Norway). "Supplier of Military Materials to Burma Excluded from Government Pension Fund—Global." Press release, March 13, 2009.

Min Khet Maung. "Visiting a Ghost Town." *The Irrawaddy*, November 5, 2008.

Min Lwin.
  1. "International Text Messaging Approved in Burma." *The Irrawaddy*, August 21, 2008.
  2. "Web Sites Back Online, but Fears of Further Attacks Remain." *The Irrawaddy*, September 22, 2008.
  3. "Desertions, Assassinations Plague Burmese Armed Forces." *The Irrawaddy*, October 9, 2008.
  4. "Junta Militants Arrested in Thailand: BBC." *The Irrawaddy*, December 24, 2008.
  5. "Obama Speech Censored in Burma." *The Irrawaddy*, January 26, 2009.
  6. "Burma's Rice Exports Soar, While Millions Remain Malnourished." *The Irrawaddy*, February 13, 2009.
  7. "Junta's Spies Active Among Ethnic, Exiled Groups." *The Irrawaddy*, February 19, 2009.
  8. "KNU Colonel Released by Thai Army." *The Irrawaddy*, February 25, 2009.
  9. "Monk's Family Members Sentenced in Reprisal." *The Irrawaddy*, March 13, 2009.
  10. "Junta Continually Expanding Forces in Ceasefire Areas." *The Irrawaddy*, March 25, 2009.
  11. "Kachin Recruiting Drive Launched as Tension Mounts." *The Irrawaddy*, June 16, 2009.
  12. "Likely Destination of N Korean Ship Often Used for Weapons Deliveries." *The Irrawaddy*, June 25, 2009.

Mirante, Edith T. *Burmese Looking Glass: A Human Rights Adventure and a Jungle Revolution.* New York: Grove Press, 1993.

Moe Aye (former political prisoner at Insein when Nichols was there). "The Last Days of Mr. Leo Nichols." aappb.org.

Moffatt, Tim. Drum Publication Group.

Moore, Elizabeth. Reader in the Art and Archeology of Southeast Asia, School of Oriental and African Studies, University of London.

Morrison, Ian. *Grandfather Longlegs: The Life and Gallant Death of Major H.P. Seagrim.* London: Faber and Faber, 1947.

Morrissey, Daryl. Cultural orientation officer, International Organization for Migration, Mae Sot, Thailand.

Mullany, Luke C. Associate professor, epidemiology hero, Johns Hopkins Bloomberg School of Public Health.

Mungpi.
1. "Burma Knew of Cyclone Nearly a Week Before It Hit." Mizzima News, May 6, 2008.
2. "Burmese FM Visits North Korea for First Time in 25 Years." Mizzima News, October 28, 2008.

Nanda Kyaw Thu. "The Politics of Subsistence: IDP Coping Strategies as Non-Violent Resistance." Burma Issues 16, No. 3 (March 2006): 4–5.

Nanuam, Wasana and Cheewin Srat-tha. "Army Chief Tells UNHCR to Stay Out: Aid Body Not Allowed to Go Near Refugees." Bangkok Post, March 26, 1997.

Nash, George H. The Life of Herbert Hoover: Master of Emergencies, 1917-1918. New York: W.W. Norton & Company, 1996.

The Nation (Thailand).
1. "One Bridge, Two Different Views." August 15, 1997.
2. "Refugees Caught in the Crossfire." April 1998.
3. "FM Invited to Burma in Bid to Defuse Tension." August 1, 2002.
4. "Number of Burmese Spies Rising." January 22, 2003.

Nelwan, Ilsa. Regional adviser for Health System Infrastructure, World Health Organization, South East Regional Office, New Delhi.

Newcomb, Horace. Encyclopedia of Television. Vol. 1. New York: Fitzroy Dearborn, 2004.

The New York Times.
1. "Myanmar's New Capital: Remote, Lavish and Off Limits." June 23, 2008.
2. "Built to Order: Myanmar's New Capital Isolates and Insulates Junta." June 24, 2008.

1996 Computer Science Development Law. Unofficial transcript available online at burmalibrary.org.

1962 Printers and Publishers Registration Law. Unofficial transcript available online at burmalibrary.org.

Nisbet, John. Burma under British Rule—and Before. Vol. 1. Westminster: A. Constable, 1901.

Nosten, Dr. François. Director of the Shoklo Malaria Research Unit, Thailand.

Obama/Biden. "Barack Obama and Joe Biden: Protecting US Interests and Advancing American Values in Our Relationship with China." Obama for America.

ONGC Videsh. "Assets—Myanmar." ongcindia.com.

OpenNet Initiative (ONI).
  1. "Internet Filtering in Burma, 2005."
  2. "Pulling the Plug: A Technical Review of the Internet Shutdown in
     Burma." Bulletin, 2007.
OpenSecrets.org (Center for Responsive Politics).
  1. "Lobbying Spending Database—Unocal Corp, 2003."
  2. "Revolving Door: Ann Wrobleski Employment Summary."
Pascal Khoo Thwe. *From the Land of Green Ghosts: A Burmese Odyssey*. London: Flamingo, 2003.
Pedersen, Daniel. Journalist, Karen specialist.
Pedersen, Morten B. *Promoting Human Rights in Burma: A Critique of West-
  ern Sanctions Policy*. Lanham, MD: Roman & Littlefield, 2007.
Pedrosa, Veronica. "Myanmar's 'Seat of Kings.'" Al Jazeera English, November 20, 2006.
Permanent Mission of the Union of Myanmar to the United Nations Office
  and Other International Organizations, Geneva. "Ministry of Foreign
  Affairs of Myanmar Rejects US State Department's Human Rights Re-
  port (2008)." Press release no. 2/2009, March 4, 2009.
Phayre, Lieutenant-General Sir Arthur P. *History of Burma, Including Burma
  Proper, Pegu, Taungu, Tenasserim, and Arakan: From the Earliest Time to
  the End of the First War with British India*. London: Trübner & Co., 1883.
Pichai, Usa. "Clinton Concerned about North Korea-Burma Ties." Mizzima
  News, July 23, 2009.
Price, Jack. Director, International Rescue Committee Overseas Processing
  Entity, Mae Sot, Thailand.
The Prosecutor v. Clément Kayishema and Obed Ruzindana (Trial Judg-
  ment). ICTR-95-1-T, International Criminal Tribunal for Rwanda, May
  21, 1999.
The Prosecutor v. Jean-Paul Akayesu (Trial Judgment). ICTR-96-4-T, Inter-
  national Criminal Tribunal for Rwanda, September 2, 1998.
Prud'homme, Nancie. Project manager, EU-China Human Rights Network,
  Irish Centre for Human Rights, National University of Ireland.
Prüss-Üstün, Annette, Robert Bos, Fiona Gore, Jamie Bartram. "Safer Water,
  Better Health: Costs, Benefits and Sustainability of Interventions to Pro-
  tect and Promote Health." World Health Organization, Geneva, 2008.
PTTEP (PTT Exploration and Production). Company information on
  Myanmar blocks M9 & M11 at pttep.com/en. Current as of June 2009.
Radiation Effects Research Foundation. "Frequently Asked Questions: How
  many people died as a result of the atomic bombings?" rerf.or.jp.
Real ID Act of 2005. 109th Cong., 13th sess., HR 1268.

Redford, Katharine. Cofounder and US office director, EarthRights International.

Refugees International. "Rohingya: Burma's Forgotten Minority." December 19, 2008.

Reporters Without Borders. "Only Peace Protects Freedoms in Post-9/11 World." October 22, 2008.

Rice, Condoleezza. Opening statement during the 2005 Secretary of State nomination hearing before the Senate Foreign Relations Committee, January 18, 2005. Can be found at foreign.senate.gov.

Richards, Danny. Senior editor/economist, Economist Intelligence Unit.

Richardson, Don. *Eternity in Their Hearts: Startling Evidence of Belief in the One True God in Hundreds of Cultures throughout the World.* Ventura, CA: Regal Books, 2006.

Richardson, Sophie. "Hillary Clinton's Beijing Gaffe." *Foreign Policy*, February 25, 2009.

Rogers, Benedict. *A Land Without Evil: Stopping the Genocide of Burma's Karen People.* Oxford: Monarch Books, 2004.

Sai Soe Win Latt. "Recent Karen Exodus Raises Questions about UNHCR Role." *The Irrawaddy*, June 17, 2009.

Sang-hun, Choe. "Test Looms as US Tracks North Korean Ship." *The New York Times*, June 21, 2009.

Save the Children. "Acute Malnutrition Summary Sheet."

Saw Yan Naing.

1. "Burmese Media Silent on Thai Turmoil." *The Irrawaddy*, September 3, 2008.

2. "Rohingya Group Jailed for Seeking Work in Rangoon." *The Irrawaddy*, September 22, 2008.

3. "Young Burmese Blogger Sentenced to More Than 20 Years in Jail." *The Irrawaddy*, November 10, 2008.

4. "Burmese Defense Lawyer Flees to Thailand, Blasts Regime." *The Irrawaddy*, December 15, 2008.

5. "Forever at the Frontline." *The Irrawaddy*, January 30, 2009.

6. "Burmese Army, DKBA Mount Four-Day Attack on KNU." *The Irrawaddy*, April 20, 2009.

7. "DKBA Starts Border Guard Recruitment." *The Irrawaddy*, June 2, 2009.

8. "Wa Army Asked to Reconsider Border Guard Role." *The Irrawaddy*, June 4, 2009.

9. "KNU Headquarters Overrun: Now What?" *The Irrawaddy*, June 25, 2009.

10. "Mae La Refugees Fear DKBA Attack." *The Irrawaddy*, July 1, 2009.

11. "Looking in a Broken Mirror." *The Irrawaddy News Magazine*, July 2, 2009.

12. "Dim Lights, Big City." *The Irrawaddy*, September 11, 2009.

Schulman, Steven. Lawyer for Sri Lankan fisherman, partner at Akin Gump Strauss Hauer & Feld LLP.

Scott, Sir James George.

1. *Burma: As It Was, as It Is, and as It Will Be*. London: George Redway, 1886.

2. *Burma: A Handbook of Practical Information*. London: A. Moring, 1906.

3. *Burma and Beyond*. London: Grayson & Grayson, 1932.

Seekins, Donald M. Professor, Burma expert, College of International Studies, Meio University.

Selth, Andrew.

1. "Is There a Burma-North Korea-Iran Nuclear Conspiracy?" *The Interpreter*, February 25, 2009.

2. "Burma's Armed Forces: Looking Down the Barrel." Griffith Asia Institute, 2009.

Shan Human Rights Foundation and Shan Women's Action Network (SWAN). "License to Rape: The Burmese Military Regime's Use of Sexual Violence in the Ongoing War in Shan State." May 2002.

Shanti Volunteer Association. "Annual Report 2005/Activity Plan 2006."

Shwe Gas Movement. "Corridor of Power: China's Trans-Burma Oil and Gas Pipelines." September 2009.

Silverstein, Ken. "Their Men in Washington: Undercover with DC's Lobbyists for Hire." *Harper's*, July 2007.

Sipress, Alan. "As Scrutiny Grows, Burma Moves Its Capital." *The Washington Post*, December 28, 2005.

Sisk, Richard. "Secretary of State Hillary Clinton Says China Talks Can't Be Tied to Human Rights Debates." *New York Daily News*, February 20, 2009.

Slim, 1st Viscount William. *Defeat into Victory: Battling Japan in Burma and India, 1942-1945*. New York: David McKay Company, Inc., 1961.

Smeaton, Donald MacKenzie. *The Loyal Karens of Burma*. London: Kegan Paul, Trench & Co., 1887.

Smith, Martin. Specialist on Burmese politics and history.

Smith, Martin. *Burma: Insurgency and the Politics of Ethnicity*. London: Zed Books, 1991.

Smith, R. Jeffrey. "Burma's Image Problem Is a Moneymaker for US Lobbyists." *The Washington Post*, February 24, 1998.

Smith, Hon. Stephen. Ministerial Statement, October 22, 2008. foreign minister.gov.au.

Snodgrass, Major John James. *Narrative of the Burmese War, Detailing the Operations of Major-General Sir Archibald Campbell's Army, from Its Landing at Rangoon in May 1824, to the Conclusion of a Treaty of Peace at Yandaboo, in February 1826.* London: John Murray, Albemarle-Street, 1827.

Solomon, Brian A. Country director, ZOA Refugee Care Thailand.

South, Ashley. *Ethnic Politics of Burma: States of Conflict.* London: Routledge, 2008.

Spencer, Oliver. Programme officer, Article 19.

Srivalo, Piyanart. "Thai Govt Warns Jolie and UNHCR over Comments on Rohingyas." *The Nation* (Thailand), February 11, 2009.

Steinberg, David. Distinguished Professor, Burma specialist, School of Foreign Service, Georgetown University.

Steps to Freedom. Front Films/Free Burma Rangers, 2004. (Video.)

Sullivan, Michael. "Does Myanmar Want Nuclear Weapons?" NPR, August 24, 2009.

Sydney Morning Herald. "Singapore, a Friend Indeed to Burma." October 1, 2007.

Symes, Michael. *An Account of an Embassy to the Kingdom of Ava, Sent by the Governor-General of India, in the Year 1795.* London: W. Bulmer & Co., 1800.

Tan, Patricia. "Brand USA: Tarnished?" brandchannel.com, Feburary 3, 2000.

Taylor, Robert H. *Foreign and Domestic Consequences of the KMT Intervention in Burma.* Ithaca, NY: Southeast Asia Program Publications, Cornell University, 1973.

TBBC (Thailand Burma Border Consortium).
1. "Burmese border refugee sites with population figures: August 2006."
2. "Programme Report." July to December 2008.
3. "Burmese border refugee sites with population figures: August 2009."
4. "Burmese border refugee sites with population figures: July 2006."
5. "Burmese border refugee sites with population figures: December 2006."
6. "A brief history of the Thailand Burma border situation."
7. "About Us." tbbc.org.
8. "Camps: Mae Sot Area." tbbc.org.

9. "IDPs: Overview." tbbc.org.

10. "What We Do." tbbc.org.

Thant Myint-U. *The River of Lost Footsteps: A Personal History of Burma*. New York: Farrar, Straus and Giroux, 2007.

Thompson, Nicholas. "A Crime with a Name." *Legal Affairs*, March/April 2005.

Thompson, Sally. Deputy Executive Director, TBBC (Thailand Burma Border Consortium).

Thomson, Mike. "New Evidence Backs Claims of Genocide in Burma." *The Daily Telegraph*, March 5, 2006.

Thornton, Phil. *Restless Souls: Rebels, Refugees, Medics and Misfits on the Thai-Burma Border*. Bangkok: Asia Books, 2006.

Tom Lantos Block Burmese JADE (Junta's Anti-Democratic Efforts) Act of 2008. 110th Cong., 2nd sess., HR 3890.

Trager, Helen G. *Burma Through Alien Eyes: Missionary Views of the Burmese in the Nineteenth Century*. New York: Praeger, 1966.

Transnational and Non-State Armed Groups. "Karen National Union (KNU)." Database online at armed-groups.org.

Transparency International. "2008 Corruption Perceptions Index." September 22, 2008.

Tucker, Shelby. *Burma: The Curse of Independence*. London: Pluto Press, 2001.

Turnell, Sean. Associate professor, Burma specialist, Department of Economics, Macquarie University.

UK Department for International Development. "Review of Aid to Refugees and Internally Displaced People on the Thailand-Burma Border." July 2008.

Umansky, Eric. "Department of Pre-Crime." *Mother Jones*, March/April 2008.

UN Comtrade (United Nations Commodity Trade Statistics Database). China-Burma trade data accessed October 2009.

UNESCO (United Nations Educational, Scientific and Cultural Organization) Institute for Statistics. "UIS Statistics in Brief: Education in Myanmar." 2007.

UNHCHR (United Nations High Commissioner for Human Rights). States Parties to the Convention on the Rights of the Child. November 20, 1989.

UNHCR (United Nations High Commissioner for Refugees).

1. "Refugees and Others of Concern to UNHCR." 1997 Statistical Overview, July 1998.

2. "2002 UNHCR Statistical Yearbook: Myanmar."
3. "Refugee Education in 2002/03: Indicators and Standards for 66 Camp Locations." September 2003.
4. "Resettlement Handbook: Country Chapter—USA." June 1, 2004.
5. "Myanmar Thailand Border Age Distribution of Refugee Population as at End March 2006." May 2, 2006.
6. "'Material Support' and Related Bars to Refugee Protection: Summary of Key Provisions of the Immigration and Nationality Act (INA)." December 15, 2006.
7. "Convention and Protocol Relating to the Status of Refugees." August 2007.
8. "States Parties to the 1951 Convention relating to the Status of Refugees and the 1967 Protocol." As of October 1, 2008.
9. Refugee Population Originating from Burma. UNHCR Statistical Online Population Database, 2008.
10. "Thailand: Resettlement of Myanmar Refugees Hits 50,000 Mark." Briefing notes, June 30, 2009.

UNICEF (United Nations Children's Fund). "State of the World's Children 2009." December 2008.

UNISDR (United Nations International Strategy for Disaster Reduction). "Deaths and Economic Losses Jump in 2008." UNISDR 2009/01, January 22, 2009.

United Nations.
1. "Revised and updated report on the question of the prevention and punishment of the crime of genocide." United Nations Economic and Social Council, Commission on Human Rights, Sub-Commission on Prevention of Discrimination and Protection of Minorities, E/CN.4/Sub.2/1985/6, July 2, 1985.
2. "Report on the twenty-third session of the Committee for Development Planning." United Nations Economic and Social Council, 1987, E/1987/23, April 1987.
3. "Report on the situation of human rights in Myanmar, prepared by the Special Rapporteur, Mr. Yozo Yokota, in accordance with Commission resolution 1994/85." United Nations Economic and Social Council, Commission on Human Rights, E/CN.4/1995/65, January 12, 1995.
4. "Interim report on the situation of human rights in Myanmar prepared by the Special Rapporteur of the Commission on Human Rights in accordance with Economic and Social Council decision 1998/261 of 30 July 1998." United Nations General Assembly, A/53/364, September 10, 1998.

5. "Report of the Panel on United Nations Peace Operations." United Nations General Assembly Security Council, A/55/305–S/2000/809, August 21, 2000.

6. "Secretary-General Kofi Annan Promises Major Reform of UN Peacekeeping; Calls on Member States to Provide Funds, Improve Decision-Making." Press release, "Report of the Panel on United Nations Peace Operations," August 23, 2000.

7. "Written statement submitted by the International Centre for Human Rights and Democratic Development (Rights & Democracy), a non-governmental organization in special consultative status." United Nations Economic and Social Council, Commission on Human Rights, E/CN.4/2002/NGO/56, January 31, 2001.

8. "United Kingdom of Great Britain and Northern Ireland and United States of America: draft resolution." United Nations Security Council, S/2007/14, January 12, 2007.

9. "Security Council Fails to Adopt Draft Resolution on Myanmar, Owing to Negative Votes by China, Russian Federation." United Nations Security Council, SC/8939, January 12, 2007.

10. Asian Highway Route Map. United Nations Economic and Social Commission for Asia and the Pacific (ESCAP), 2007. unescap.org/ttdw/common/TIS/AH/maps/ah_map_2007.jpg.

11. "Implementing the Responsibility to Protect." United Nations General Assembly, A/63/677, January 12, 2009.

12. "Children and Armed Conflict: Report of the Secretary-General." United Nations General Assembly Security Council, A/63/785–S/2009/158, March 26, 2009.

United Nations Foundation. "First Lady Laura Bush and United Nations Foundation to Announce Nothing but Nets Distribution of Mosquito Nets to Combat Malaria in Burma (Myanmar)." Press release, August 7, 2008.

UNOCHA (United Nations Office for the Coordination of Humanitarian Affairs). "Guiding Principles on Internal Displacement." ochaonline.un.org.

UNODC (United Nations Office on Drugs and Crime).

1. "Safrole-Rich Essential Oils—Risk of Illicit Use." *Eastern Horizons*. Summer-Autumn 2007.

2. "2008 World Drug Report."

3. "World Drug Report 2009."

US Army Air Forces Office of Flying Safety, Safety Education Division. *Survival: Jungle, Desert, Arctic, Ocean.*

US Army Air Forces Tactical Center, Arctic, Desert and Tropic Information Center. *Handbook of Burma and Northeastern India Informational Bulletin No. 16*. Published by Training Aids Division, Office of the Assistant Chief of Air Staff, Training, Headquarters Army Air Forces, August 1944.

US Campaign for Burma. "Ban Ki-Moon Fails to Obtain Aung San Suu Kyi's Release, Focus Shifts Back to UN Security Council, President Obama Urged to Seek Security Council Action on Burma by US Members of Congress." Press release, July 6, 2009.

US Commission on International Religious Freedom. "Annual Report." May 2009.

US Committee for Refugees and Immigrants.
1. "World Refugee Survey 2004."
2. "World Refugee Survey 2007—Thailand."
3. "World Refugee Survey 2009."

US Department of Education. "Characteristics of the 100 Largest Public Elementary and Secondary School Districts in the United States: 2006–07." National Center for Education Statistics, 2009.

US Department of Homeland Security. "Statement by Homeland Security Secretary Michael Chertoff on the Intention to Use Discretionary Authority for Material Support to Terrorism." Office of the Press Secretary, January 19, 2007.

US Department of Homeland Security, US Citizenship and Immigration Services.
1. "Processing of Asylum Division Cases Involving Material Support." Interoffice memorandum, June 1, 2007.
2. "Department of Homeland Security Exercise of Authority to Exempt Persons Associated with 10 Named Groups from Most Terrorist-Related Inadmissibility Grounds of the Immigration Law." November 25, 2008.

US Department of State.
1. "Regionalism and Security in Mainland Southeast Asia." Secret. Bureau of Intelligence and Research. January 28, 1963. Declassified May 31, 1994.
2. "Memorandum from Secretary of State Rusk to President Johnson." *Foreign Relations of the United States, 1964–1968*, Volume 27, Mainland Southeast Asia; Regional Affairs, Document 101. September 3, 1966.
3. Foreign Assistance Appropriation Act—Fiscal Year 1988 Budget for Burma. International Narcotics Control.
4. "Patterns of Global Terrorism." Office of the Coordinator for Counterterrorism. April 30, 2001.

5. "Transcript: Lawmaker Says Burma Must Stop Brutality Against Minorities." February 12, 2003.

6. "Secretary Decides Material Support Bar Inapplicable to Ethnic Karen Refugees in Tham Hin Camp, Thailand." Bureau of Public Affairs, May 5, 2006.

7. "The Department of State Decides Material Support Inapplicable to Second Group of Karen Refugees in Thailand." Bureau of Public Affairs, August 30, 2006.

8. "Country Reports on Human Rights Practices—2007." Bureau of Democracy, Human Rights, and Labor, March 11, 2008.

9. "International Religious Freedom Report 2008." Bureau of Democracy, Human Rights, and Labor.

10. "2009 International Narcotics Control Strategy Report." Country Reports—Afghanistan through Comoros. Bureau of International Narcotics and Law Enforcement Affairs, February 27, 2009.

11. "Remarks by Secretary Clinton in Laguna Phuket, Thailand." Transcript. Office of the Spokesman, July 22, 2009.

12. "Narcotics Rewards Program: Wei Hsueh-Kang." Bureau of International Narcotics and Law Enforcement Affairs. Accessed at state.gov on August 4, 2009.

US Government Accountability Office. "International Trade: US Agencies Have Taken Some Steps, but Serious Impediments Remain to Restricting Trade in Burmese Rubies and Jadeite." GAO-09-987, September 2009.

US House Committee on International Relations. Subcommittee on International Operations and Human Rights. *Burmese Refugees in Thailand.* 105th Cong., 1st sess., April 16, 1997.

van der Stouwe, Marc and Su-Ann Oh. "Educational Change in a Protracted Refugee Context." *Forced Migration Review* 30 (2008): 47-49.

Wai Moe.

1. "No Political Progress in Burma: UN." *The Irrawaddy*, September 12, 2008.

2. "Big Burmese Interest in Result of US Presidential Election." *The Irrawaddy*, November 5, 2008.

3. "Letters Land Prisoners' Relatives, Guards in Jail." *The Irrawaddy*, December 19, 2008.

4. "Hundreds of Thousands Still Displaced in Burma: Watchdog." *The Irrawaddy*, March 6, 2009.

5. "Negotiations Always Possible for Rebels: Junta Secretary 1." *The Irrawaddy*, March 25, 2009.

6. "Another Armed KNU Group Defects to the Junta." *The Irrawaddy*, April 6, 2009.

7. "DKBA: Burma's Second Largest Non-State Armed Group?" *The Irrawaddy*, June 18, 2009.

8. "Junta Trying to Erase Non-Burman Identities, Say Ethnic Groups." *The Irrawaddy*, April 21, 2009.

9. "Border Guard Force Plan Leads to End of Ceasefire." *The Irrawaddy*, August 31, 2009.

Wallechinsky, David. "The World's 10 Worst Dictators." *Parade*, March 22, 2009.

The Washington Post. "A SLORC by Any Other Name." March 6, 1998.

Watkins, Justin. Professor, Burmese language and literature, School of Oriental and African Studies, University of London.

Watkins, Kevin, director and lead author, et al. "Human Development Report 2007/2008." Published for the United Nations Development Programme (UNDP).

Wayland, Reverend Francis. *A Memoir of the Life and Labors of the Rev. Adoniram Judson, D. D.* Vol. 1. Boston: Phillips, Sampson, and Company, 1853.

Webster, Donovan. *The Burma Road: The Epic Story of the China-Burma-India Theater in World War II.* New York: Farrar, Straus and Giroux, 2003.

Welcome to the United States: Refugee Guide to Resettlement, Orientation Video, English Version. Center for Applied Linguistics, 2004.

Wells, Janet. Global Health Access Program.

The White Monkey. Free Burma Rangers. (Video.)

The White Monkey on a Mission. Free Burma Rangers. (Video.)

Wills, Gina. Public affairs specialist, Bureau of Population, Refugees, and Migration, US Department of State.

Wiseman, Paul. "Laura Bush Visits Burmese Refugees." *USA Today*, August 7, 2008.

World Council of Churches. "Myanmar Baptist Convention." oikoumene .org.

World Education. "Thailand: Training Refugee Teachers on the Thai-Burma Border." worlded.org.

Wyler, Liana Sun. "Burma and Transnational Crime." Congressional Research Service Report RL34225, April 27, 2009.

Yeni.
1. "Burma's IT Generation Combats Regime Repression." *The Irrawaddy*, October 7, 2008.

2. "Washington Hopes Webb Can Clarify Its Policy to Junta." *The Irrawaddy*, August 14, 2009.

Young, Johnny. Executive director, Migration and Refugee Services of the
    US Conference of Catholic Bishops. Testimony on the FY 2010 US Ref-
    ugee Program before the Bureau of Population, Refugees and Migration,
    US Department of State, July 9, 2009.
ZOA Refugee Care Thailand.
        1. "Education Survey 2005."
        2. "2006-2007 Academic Students Statistics in 7 Karen Camps."

ABBREVIATIONS

ASEAN	Association of Southeast Asian Nations
BA	Burma Action
CCSDPT	Committee for Coordination of Services to Displaced Persons in Thailand
DKBA	Democratic Karen Buddhist Army
FBR	Free Burma Rangers
HRD	Human rights documenters
IDP	Internally displaced persons
ILO	International Labour Organization
IOM	International Organization for Migration
KMT	Kuomintang
KNLA	Karen National Liberation Army
KNU	Karen National Union

NGO   Nongovernmental Organization

NLD   National League for Democracy

SPDC   State Peace and Development Council

TBBC   Thailand Burma Border Consortium

UNHCR   United Nations High Commissioner for Refugees

UNICEF   United Nations Children's Fund